HarperEntertainment
A Division of HarperCollins*Publishers*

35th Anniversary Celebration

aw

another world ©

julie poll

ALSO BY JULIE POLL

As the World Turns®:
The Complete Family Scrapbook

Guiding Light®:
The Complete Family Album

HarperEntertainment
A Division of HarperCollins*Publishers*

HarperCollins books may be purchased for
educational, business, or sales promotional use.
For information please write:
Special Markets Department,
HarperCollins Publishers Inc., 10 East 53rd Street,
New York, NY 10022-5299.

FIRST EDITION

Library of Congress Cataloging-in-Publication Data is available

ISBN 0-06-019304-2

99 00 01 02 03 10 9 8 7 6 5 4 3 2 1

a c k n o w l e d g m e n t s

The challenge of writing a celebratory book spanning thirty-five years of a daytime drama is both exciting and daunting, and many people contributed their time, knowledge, and expertise to this special anniversary book.

First and foremost, thanks to John Kelly Genovese, whose vast knowledge of the soap opera genre and excellent writing skills were invaluable in forming the all-important chronology. Thank you, John!

WITH MANY THANKS TO:

NBC and Procter & Gamble Productions for making this distinguished program possible for a landmark thirty-five years; with special thanks to Susan Lee, Senior Vice President, Daytime Programs. And Kathy Talbert, NBC Director of Daytime Programming, East Coast, for her valuable insights.

Mary Alice Dwyer-Dobbin, Executive in Charge of Production, Procter & Gamble, and Phil Dixson, Senior Vice President, Managing Director, for their enthusiastic support.

The publicity department of TeleVest; with special thanks to Another World publicist Gillian Strum for her inestimable help with and support of this project from the word go, along with Karen Swanson, Sheryl Fuchs, Ro Southworth, and Barbara Brady.

Susan Savage and Maria Ferrari, who had the daunting task of clearing all the photographs, and Jennifer Maloney for facilitating everything from interviews to office space.

Robert Launey and Deborah Fineout-Launey of LHH&F for their support.

Executive producer Christopher Goutman, who deserves special thanks for his immediate and enthusiastic support of Another World's anniversary book.

The actors, producers, writers, directors, and crew of Another World, who gave so graciously of their time and made me feel so welcome out there in Brooklyn. Special appreciation to producer Scott Collishaw for grounding me in Another World's rich history (there's a reason he's known as show historian!); also for introducing me to Another World's incredible crew, for locating research (even if it was in "the dungeon"), and for his insights, enthusiasm, and help—many thanks.

Michelle DeVito for her always cheerful assistance; videotape editors Matthew Griffin and Karen Thomas DeKime, for keeping me well supplied with tapes; and production coordinators Jennifer Chambers and Dan Griffin; with special thanks to Louisa Cross, for her help in compiling the show credits.

Ed Rider, head of Procter & Gamble archives in Cincinnati, for making his resources readily available; and Lisa Burns at the P&G archives for seeing that I received the all-important research.

Trudy Wilson and Ryan Thompson at the National Academy of Television Arts and Sciences for their important contributions to this book.

My exceptional intern Alissa Mazur, who spent days and weekends, even when she had another job, organizing reams of research materials and setting up a filing system that made it possible to write the book; Fritz Brekeller for his important research also my studio intern, Sari Schneider, for her considerable help.

Brenda Fite at the Popular Culture Library at Bowling Green State University, for summarizing the early scripts.

My researcher, transcriber, and friend, Donna Hornak, for her always expeditious help, whether it be transcribing a tape that was needed yesterday or organizing the large comprehensive cast list—always with a smile.

Eddie Druedling for sharing his expertise and knowledge in the compilation of the cast list and for his Another World home page, an extraordinary research tool that I leaned on heavily; Sarah Cannell, Eric Patton, and Brian Varekula for their help on the cast list as well.

Another World fan club president Mindi Schulman for her help in setting up interviews with actors whose contributions to Another World and to this book were key.

Jonathan Greene at Globe Photos for locating important photographs from Another World's past.

Lynn Leahey, Editor-in-Chief of Soap Opera Digest: special thanks for sharing her insights into the show and for making the magazine's rich research materials available. Special thanks as well to Jody Reines for her valuable assistance, and to Tammy Cain and Randee Dawn for their cooperation and help.

The publishing team at HarperCollins: John Silbersack, Publisher of HarperEntertainment, and Executive Editor Mauro DiPreta, who had the foresight to do a book on this incredible show, for their support of this project; Anja Schmidt, my wonderful editor, for her patience and her keen eye; Jeannette Jacobs, for her work on the design; and Susan Sanguily, Dianne Walber, April Benavides, Kimberly Craskey, and copy editor Brenda Woodward and proofreader Nora Reichard.

My agent, Rickie Olshan of Don Buchwald & Associates, for her valuable guidance.

And last but never least, a special thank-you to my daughters, Amy and Melissa, for their love and support while their mother spent most of her waking hours in a place called Bay City.

contents

*I*n a fast-forwarding world, where scenes longer than 60 seconds are considered boring, glibness is the standard for intelligent dialogue, and action not emotion is cathartic, we celebrate NBC's longest-running daytime serial, *Another World,* a show created by Irna Phillips in 1964 to explore the credo "We do not live in this world alone, but in a thousand other worlds."

When I arrived at *Another World* in 1972, head writer Harding "Pete" Lemay had decided to flesh out the character of Rachel from the barracuda created by Agnes Nixon. Pete wanted to see what would happen if Rachel had some of her wishes come true. He said, "I've always felt that part of *Another World* was the business of people wanting and striving to get into another world—literally—a world of better privilege and advantages."

It was a daunting task assuming a seminal role among a cast heavily laced with strong, experienced, and highly creative actors. My first day on the set was with Constance Ford. I knew it would take time to reinvent an established mother-daughter relationship, but I didn't expect an opening salvo with my first acting choice. She announced, "Rachel wouldn't do that." I looked to the director for support. He sat there. I looked at Connie and met an arched eyebrow and a gaze 10 degrees below zero. I held my ground. "This Rachel would." I guess Connie appreciated the spunk, if not the choice, and we became friends. However, this was my introduction to the powerful and talented cast of *Another World.*

How grateful I have been for the high standards and daring choices Procter & Gamble made back then: entrusting the production to Paul Rauch and the writing to Pete Lemay—two men with consummate taste, well trained in the arts and determined to assemble the best and the brightest from New York theater to direct and act. Twice I was blessed with remarkable leading men, Douglass Watson and Charles Keating, who were and are not only extraordinary actors, but professionally so accomplished that to turn out a top performance, year in and year out, was never an issue but a glorious and welcome opportunity. In the twenty-six years since, it's been a privilege to portray Rachel Davis Cory Hutchins in the company of a remarkable cast and crew!

And it's been humbling! Not only is *Another World* an inherited tradition among most viewers (many started watching on the knees of their grandmothers), but the audience cares deeply about its show. From kudos and jubilation for a story well told or characters perfectly matched, to fury and distress over the loss of a favorite character or a sour ending to a story, viewers tell us how their personal lives resonate to a particular plot, or loneliness is alleviated by the comfort of familiar faces coming into their living rooms day after day. In the words of a longtime fan: "You and *Another World* have been with our family a very long time, three generations. We grew up with you. If we were to lose *Another World,* it would be like losing a family member. Thank you for being there for us through great stories and the not-so-great ones year after year."

Thank *you, Another World,* for a great gig.

When *Another World* premiered on May 4, 1964, it opened with the mantra *"We do not live in this world alone, but in a thousand other worlds."* Although the show eventually dropped the line, it never dropped the spirit behind the words.

When former head writer Irna Phillips created *Another World*, she envisioned a show that would delve into the "other world" of feelings and emotions which coexists with the everyday material world. According to Phillips, "the events of our lives represent only the surface, and in our minds and feelings we live in many other hidden worlds."

"I thought of it as all of us are looking to get into 'another world,'" says former head writer Harding "Pete" Lemay. "We don't want the world we're in and so we're striving. And it can be emotional, it can be economic. It can be psychological. It can cover all levels, but each of the characters to me was somebody dissatisfied with the world he was in and he wanted to get out of it, into another world. It wasn't that we had many worlds, we just wanted to move. And it worked for me. I think every writer has to find his own image for his show."

Christopher Goutman, executive producer, remarks, "I think that's an invitation. It refers to an emotional place that you can go or a spiritual place. It can refer to one's relationships. But most important, it refers to your imagination. And if we take the audience along on a journey of the imagination that's character-driven, we'll be in a great place. It's a very freeing concept in every aspect— intellectually, emotionally, psychologically. Again, grounding everything in terms of the people we have in place and their histories and not compromising them, but allowing them to move forward today. It's a great mantra."

Actress Victoria Wyndham cites Kahlil Gibran: "The

dream dreaming us." "Is it a dream, or is the dream dreaming us? To me that was about imagination. That each of us lives our own film and it's peopled with our own characters that we project onto the people that we meet. We live our own ideas. Certainly with Rachel her dreams changed a great deal over her lifetime. The dreams started very limited and somewhat antisocial, and her projection of what was important in life colored what she saw—her idea of life was so limited that what she projected on other people made them the sinister other. So what she experienced was difficulty and conflict in others, and in herself, because the projection came back to her. But her imagination was great enough so that given a different idea, in this case from Mac, she made it her own and peopled a far more benign universe for herself to live with, including rich relationships and meaningful family and friends, and the idea of more optimism and a less sinister place. We're all a product of all the things we think and imagine and those are all of our other worlds, and when we're in a bad mood, that world becomes sinister again and when we're in a more beneficent mood, then life becomes loving. I think we're all products of all of the many different people that we are, and the many different moods we are, and the many different images that we generate. And the people we meet have to do with what's in our thoughts and experiences that we have. We're all just sort of projecting our own films and when those films are compatible, we seem to be sharing the same movie theater. And when they're not, somebody's playing down the street."

Actor Charles Keating also quotes "there is a dream dreaming us." "I don't know what other kind of line really can follow in answer to Irna's, other than something as equally poetic, because it's

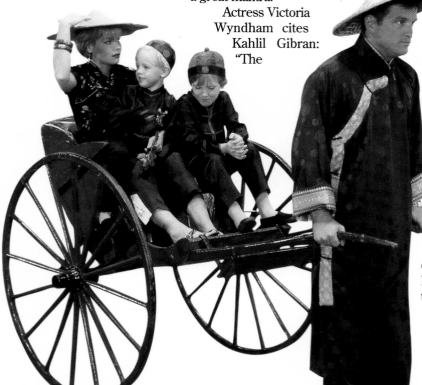

a suggestion of something, isn't it? It's a suggestion that all is not what it seems. And it isn't. And it also is a very clear indication about stylistic choice. It isn't the *Eastenders*. I think it's about a poetic, romantic flight of fancy that can incorporate everything across the board. But it doesn't have to be real and stuck into the limitations."

Mary Alice Dwyer-Dobbin, Executive in Charge of Production, Procter & Gamble, explains, "That's what soaps are all about. In this day and age when I think there are audiences out there who are just looking for more and different and bigger storytelling arenas, it gets redefined yet again for today's audience. And it continues to work perfectly, and wasn't Irna smart even way back then? She knew."

Kathy Talbert, Director of Daytime Programming, East Coast, NBC, agrees, "That's fascinating, because it has a lot to do with how the show is rooted and how it appeals to you. That reality thing. Yes, we have our physical lives, we have our spiritual lives. We have our psyche. How do I interpret this? Well, it's true, we live in lots of different worlds. We live in our fantasy world. We live in our real world. We live in our spiritual world. I think that is very much what this show strives to be about and what soaps are really about. I think that's a very romantic, very fanciful concept. With all the characters, too, they would each have their own world. You are your own universe in some way. They each exist in their own world and that influences your world, influencing someone else's as you cross into their orbit."

Head writer Leah Laiman adds, "The whole Lumina thing is all about living in 'another world.' And it is. In fact, when I thought of that story I did not know that was the mantra. And then when I heard it, I went, 'Well, then I'm doing exactly the right story.' This is a big story. It's not

meant to be a story for one bizarre character. It's meant to go over the whole show, and its aura should fall over the entire canvas. And when I heard that phrase that Irna started with, I just thought, 'This is karma! I was meant to be here to write this story at this time.'"

Jean Passanante, co-head writer, continues, "You are in one universe orbit, but you aspire to move into the orbits of other people that you love and care about. Also, in my own mind, as a writer, I thought, another world—you create a parallel universe when you write a soap opera. And it's a community that's separate and apart from ours, but yet it's one that we enter as audience members."

Producer Scott Collishaw concludes, "I assumed it meant the collision of different worlds within a small community, or even a larger community. I think it meant here you're going to be watching a story about a little town in the Midwest, where everyone's got their little life, when what's really going on is what's happening all around us. In other words, this became representative. This show is a little microcosm of what human existence is. So therefore, you can tackle anything from really emotional current issues, to age-old stories of love and betrayal. Family rivalries. Class rivalries. Class struggle. I think 'we do not live in this world alone, but in a thousand other worlds' means we all try to block out our own little space, our little corner of the world, but we can't help but be intruded upon by the evils that affect every civilization since Man began."

Welcome to our world. . . .

backstory

*P*a and Mother Matthews lived on a farm outside of Bay City, Michigan, with their three children—James (Jim), William (Will), and Janet. The Matthewses were proud to be able to send both of their sons to Bay State University as majors in accounting. After Jim and Will became Certified Public Accountants, they opened their own downtown firm, Matthews & Matthews.

Jim, the eldest, fit the mold of the family accountant. He was subdued but not stuffy, and his supportive wife, Mary, shared his simple pleasures. They lived in a modest colonial house near the university with their three children—rebellious Patricia (Pat), Alice, the practical one, and sensitive Russell (Russ). When Jim's father died, Mother Matthews moved in.

While Jim was the numbers man at the family firm, Will was the salesman. With drink in hand—sometimes a few too many—Will schmoozed his way through Chamber of Commerce functions, projecting his magnetic personality. He had a taste for the finer things, but a phony he wasn't. Unfortunately, the same could not be said for his wife.

Elizabeth Matthews cringed when Jim and Mary's children called her "Aunt Liz." Obsessed with living down her working-class background, this nouveau riche society darling flaunted her full name—only to have it fall on deaf ears. While Jim and his mother tolerated Liz, the opinionated Mary found it excruciating to be in the same room with her sister-in-law. Liz's home was a formal dwelling filled with stiff French Provincial trappings, so it was no wonder that her children, Susan and William, Jr. (Bill), gravitated to Aunt Mary and Uncle Jim's house as their second home. Neither of Liz's children succumbed to her influence, although Susan was more adept than Bill at seeing their mother for the social climber she was.

When Susan was 18, Liz tried to push her into a loveless marriage to someone socially desirable—and deadly boring. To the relief of Will, who understood his headstrong daughter better than anyone, Susan called off the engagement. She went on to become a technician at Memorial Hospital and hoped someday to become a doctor. Yet she dared not voice this dream to her mother, with whom she endured a strained, almost polarized relationship.

Cheerful, uncomplicated Bill Matthews was five years younger than Susan, but he played the role of big brother protector to his cousin Pat, who was his contemporary. Like his father and uncle before him, Bill went to Bay State where he majored in business administration at Bay State. Liz adored Bill, but she was uncompromising in her insistence that he become a CPA in the family tradition.

If anyone in the Matthews family shunned tradition, it was Jim and Will's sister, Janet. The baby of the family, Janet was thirteen years younger than Will. While Jim and Mary wished Janet would find a decent husband and have a houseful of kids, Will understood and accepted Janet for who she was—a vibrant, assertive young woman who lived outside the confines of her upbringing. When Janet showed artistic talent, it was Will who financed her education. And when she needed a hysterectomy for the removal of a tumor, it was Will who paid for the operation. Janet's fiancé, Michael Connors, had already deserted her for a woman who could bear him children.

Devastated, Janet stifled her emotions and determined that she would live a full life independently of any man. She took a downtown apartment and worked as a commercial artist in an advertising agency, where she met a dynamic ad executive named Ken Baxter. Bored with his Junior League wife, Laura, Ken was drawn to Janet's ambition and strong sense of identity. Soon Janet and Ken embarked on an affair.

Since Janet had little to do with her nieces and nephews, she was unaware that Ken's son, Tom, was Bill's fraternity brother—and Pat's first serious boyfriend. Although Pat was falling in love with Tom, he was sour on the prospect of commitment. Tom sensed correctly that his parents had married too young, and was more affected than he let on by their polite but lifeless marriage. Thus he opted to play the field. To the girls at Bay State, Tom Baxter was a real mover.

One girl who was decidedly not moved by Tom was Missy Palmer. Missy was a waitress at the Kopper Kettle, the collegiate hangout, where she served burgers and shakes to the likes of Tom Baxter and Bill Matthews. Missy saw Tom woo a succession of swooning girls, and pegged him for the two-faced amateur Lothario he was.

But Missy had to admit to her social worker and confidante, Ann Fuller, that there was something sweet and simple about Bill Matthews. If only he didn't exist in "another world"—a secure life, alien to her own experience as an orphan passed from one foster home to another. Missy couldn't bear to have Bill get too close to her, for fear he would find out the humiliating truth she kept hidden—that she was illegitimate. She didn't even know who her parents were.

That is why Missy's heart ached for Bill when he lost his father, Will Matthews, to a sudden massive coronary.

✦

1964—1969

"You're not a boy anymore. You're a man now."

That may not be the most appropriate thing for a mother to say to a 20-year-old son, but for Liz Matthews, there was nothing appropriate about losing her 48-year-old husband to a heart attack. Rather than dealing with her grief head-on, Liz set out to mold Bill into the image of his father. He was to take his rightful place at the family accounting firm and be virtually a mate to Liz—that is, until he found someone socially acceptable to marry.

While Bill was the focus of Liz's life, she had no such agenda for Susan. Now 25, Susan avoided her mother and ached to have her own apartment. Liz wouldn't loan her the money for a security deposit, so Susan turned to her Aunt Janet. Remembering how Will had helped her over the years, Janet loaned Susan $2,000 to start to build a life for herself. Liz was livid, for she had nothing but disdain for Janet's free-wheeling lifestyle. The truth was, Liz didn't want her daughter to leave home but had no clue how to reach out to her. Before long, however, Susan left Bay City, leaving Liz to become even more obsessed with Bill.

Once the family came to grips with Will's death, his mother decided to move in with a niece who needed help with her baby. Before Mother Matthews left town, she expressed concern that Janet was a 35-year-old career woman with no plans to marry. Janet told her she wanted no part of "that so-called woman's world. I've chosen 'another world' to live in," she declared.

Ken Baxter shared that world—the city life, with its throbbing nightclubs and cultural offerings. When he went home to Bay City's quiet tree-lined streets, he felt his life pass before him. All his wife, Laura, wanted to do was watch television and talk about her charity activities. And she was starting to drink a little too much—probably from all the boredom. Ken tried to improve their situation; he begged Laura to move back to the city so they could recapture the excitement they had when they were younger. But Laura wouldn't budge, so gradually Ken found himself wanting more than an "arrangement" with Janet. Panicked, Janet as much as told Ken that love was a four-letter word.

Ken's son, Tom, was also of that mind-set, but he dared not reveal that to Pat Matthews. He knew she was a virgin from a loving, protective family, and that titillated him. The only way to get Pat where he wanted her was to make her feel she was the most special girl he had ever met. Bill knew Tom's reputation and warned his Aunt Mary and Uncle Jim that Pat was playing with fire.

✦

Against her family's wishes, Pat went away with Tom and their college friends to the Baxters' lake house for Memorial Day weekend. Shortly after they returned, Tom began breaking dates with Pat. His timing was terrible—for Pat was pregnant with his child.

Eventually Pat summoned the courage to tell Tom that she was pregnant. She hoped against hope that he would sweep her into his arms and ask her to marry him. Instead he responded by a plotting a strategy. How are we going to handle this? Whom do we tell? Perhaps an abortion was the answer. Yes, it was illegal . . . but without a baby to cloud their joy, Tom could be sure Pat was marrying him because she really loved him—or so went Tom's shrewd rationale. The truth was, he planned to ditch Pat and go for his Ph.D. in psychology without the responsibilities of marriage to tie him down. Pat agonized over her decision. She even considered jumping off "Suicide Bridge" on the Bay State campus. Just as she was plunged into this private hell, her sister, Alice, surprised her with a *This Is Your Life* party for her 21st birthday. It was Pat's party, and she could cry if she wanted to—and cry she did.

It was ultimately a conversation with Missy Palmer that struck a chord with Pat. Missy felt sufficiently comfortable with Pat to confide in her about her illegitimacy and her sad life in foster homes. Knowing she could not bear to resign her child to the same fate, Pat agreed to have the abortion. Tom arranged for a Dr. Robert Alberts to do the procedure at his home office while Pat's family was away. En route to the doctor's, Pat asked Tom if he loved her. He flashed his charming smile as he said, "I've told you in so many ways." Pat then walked into the office as Tom waited nonchalantly in his car.

What ensued for Pat was nothing short of a horror. Alberts turned out to be a "butcher." Pat rested at Tom's fraternity house, where she had nightmares about her procedure and soon realized she was gravely ill and in need of help. Her unsuspecting parents were still away, and her sanctimonious Aunt Liz would certainly judge her. So Pat went to Janet and, without naming Tom as the father, told her of her predicament. Janet immediately referred Pat to her longtime friend Dr. Ernest Gregory, who performed a necessary operation, unfortunately making it unlikely that Pat could ever conceive children again.

When Pat's family returned from their vacation, Janet and Ernest told them that Pat had suffered a ruptured ovarian cyst. However, Janet, still unaware that Pat was involved with Tom, confided to Ken about Pat's pregnancy. Ken didn't give Tom up to Janet, but he privately confronted his son about his cruel insensitivity toward Pat. Tom's roommate, Frank Andrews, also told Tom off and began packing to move elsewhere.

Pat told Tom that she was most likely sterile from the abortion he had forced her to endure. Tom replied that while he was sorry, it made no difference to him personally since he never intended to marry her anyway. Pat was thrown into shock and, happening to see Frank's gun, in her trancelike state picked up the gun and shot Tom. Frank walked in to witness Pat mumbling to a dead Tom about being married and happy together. Pat walked home and blocked out the incident, only to have the police arrive at her parents' door. She was booked for first-degree murder. This violent tragedy would ultimately bring the Matthewses' and Baxters' secrets into the open.

Shocked that his daughter would be accused of killing the boy she loved, Jim contacted an old friend and client, Mitchell Dru, about taking Pat's case. Dru, an eminent law professor, was a pussycat to his friends but a tiger in the courtroom. Now in semiretirement, he agreed to act as co-counsel alongside his protégé and surrogate son, a crackerjack criminal lawyer named John Randolph. A widower in his late thirties, John had a teenage daughter, Lee, who affectionately referred to her dad's mentor as "Uncle Dru."

John was quick to rise to the challenge of Pat's case, and Bill Matthews was just as quick to help. Bill preferred the law to accounting, and relished the opportunity to help Pat through her legal difficulties. Of course, Liz disapproved of Bill's involvement with Pat's "mess."

When Bill told John about Tom's reputation with

girls, John went for self-defense against a rape attempt by Tom, but Assistant DA Phil Martin alleged that Tom had impregnated Pat, and Ken corroborated this claim in court. John and Dru had Pat injected with Pentothal, and it was only then that she could finally relive the horror of killing Tom. Thanks to John's brilliant and impassioned summation, the jury found Pat not guilty by reason of temporary insanity.

The events of the trial also forced Ken to reveal his long-standing affair with Janet. Laura denounced both Pat and Janet as tramps, threatening to name Janet as co-respondent in a messy divorce hearing. But Janet had decided that she felt more than friendship for Ernest Gregory, so Ken accepted a transfer to his Los Angeles office. Laura went with him, but the two eventually divorced.

Jim and Mary were hurt that Pat had confided her abortion to Janet rather than coming to them. Nonetheless, they were supportive. Still, they found her increasingly difficult to live with. Rather than dealing with her guilt and torment, Pat became reclusive and began lashing out at her sister, Alice. John Randolph tried to be a friend to Pat and asked her out to dinner a few times, but she steadfastly refused. Finally Jim and Mary insisted that Pat get on with her life and accept John's invitations. They were grateful to him for giving Pat her life back, and looked upon him as a positive influence on their daughter.

But John didn't see himself as merely Pat's lawyer and father confessor. The truth was, he was falling in love with his fragile young client. Once Jim and Dru realized this, they were furious with John for taking advantage of Pat's vulnerability. They knew John was pushing the "dangerous age" of 40, and feared that Pat was getting involved with a confused older man out of sheer gratitude. To further complicate matters, Liz callously offered to send Pat to Europe until the Tom Baxter issue blew over. Liz looked upon her niece as a scarlet woman who blighted the family name, and was willing to pay to sweep her under the rug.

Feeling like dirt, Pat disappeared—only for John to find her. They became engaged, and married soon thereafter. Mary lit into Liz for causing Pat to run away, and was confident that Pat would become more responsible for having married John. Jim gave the newlyweds his blessing, but remained unconvinced that Pat and John were really in love. Dru was also skeptical, for he knew that Lee was extremely possessive of her father.

Like Pat, Janet was also stepping into a dysfunctional fam-

fade in:

AW 87—9/3/64

Pat's bedroom, a short time later. Pat's sleep is deeply troubled. She stirs and moans again. Move in to her sleeping face. Music and sound: a whining, nighmarish effect. We are inside Pat's head, hearing the confused jumble of sounds and voices she hears. Her head twists and turns as if she would escape them.

PAT'S VOICE (VO): How do you tell a man you're going to have a baby—his baby? Did you hear what I said, Tom?

TOM'S VOICE (VO): I told you we'd work this out together, Pat—and we will.

PAT'S VOICE (VO): Tom, you know why I'm agreeing to do this. You said, if there wasn't a baby—then—then we could be married.

TOM'S VOICE (VO): Pat—you're—you're exciting—Pat—oh, Pat—

PAT'S VOICE (VO): It's wrong, Tom. It's wrong. We don't have the right. It's a baby.

TOM'S VOICE (VO): Darling, if there were any other way, we'd do it.

PAT'S VOICE (VO): Oh, Tom, I'm afraid! I'm afraid!

MAN'S VOICE (VO): Miss Matthews? Yes, Mr. Baxter made the appointment. Just come in here. It won't take long. Don't be afraid.

TOM'S VOICE (VO): There's nothing to be afraid of, darling. You have to trust me now—and believe me.

PAT'S VOICE (VO): I do trust you, Tom. That's why I'm here.

MAN'S VOICE (VO): Don't be afraid, Miss Matthews. It won't take long. It'll be all over in a few minutes. It'll be all over soon. Miss Matthews. It'll be all over—all over. Don't be afraid—don't be afraid—

TOM'S VOICE (VO): (Joining the man's voice) Don't be afraid—don't be afraid—(This continues over sound: from a great distance we hear a baby's crying, insistently. It grows slowly, covering Tom's and the man's voices.)

PAT'S VOICE (VO): (In panic) No, Tom! We can't do that to a baby. We don't have the right! It's murder, Tom—murder!!! (The baby's cry has reached its highest pitch. Suddenly Pat wakes up, drenched in perspiration, wide-eyed, in terror. As she opens her eyes, the baby cry cuts off in mid-howl, instantly, as if smothered. Pat lies still a moment, confused, drugged, shocked. Then slowly she pulls herself up and gropes for the phone. It falls onto the bed and, with a great effort, she focuses on it and dials.)

TOM'S VOICE: (Filter) Hello?

PAT: (Barely able to speak) Tom—this is Pat.

*H*e was her lawyer and many years her senior, but not long after John Randolph cleared Pat Matthews of murder charges in the killing of Tom Baxter, the two were married.

ily situation. She sensed that Ernest still loved his ex-fiancée Karen, who had jilted him to marry his more dynamic brother, Dr. Alex Gregory. Janet and Ernest became engaged, but when Alex was killed in a car crash, Janet freed Ernest to reconcile with Karen. Janet then moved to Los Angeles where she took up again with Ken, but the two never married.

❧

Once this family turmoil subsided, Bill finally got up the nerve to bring Missy home for dinner, where she faced a grand inquisition from Liz: What were her plans for the future? Did she make enough money to support her educational goals? What of her family? Missy felt more unworthy of Bill than ever, and proceeded to avoid him. But Bill was determined to bring Missy out of her shell. Without telling Liz, he loaned Missy part of his inheritance so that she could get a better apartment. Missy also won a scholarship to Bay State, where she decided to pursue social work like her friend Ann Fuller. Meanwhile, Bill went to law school and became John's law clerk. He also announced to a horrified Liz that once he passed his bar exams, he intended to marry Missy.

Bill and Missy socialized a great deal with Pat after she married John. One day John came home to find Pat, Bill, and Missy dancing to rock 'n' roll records in his living room. Suddenly the virile 40-year-old felt like an old geezer. To ease his self-consciousness, John had Pat wear her long blond hair in a matronly twist. Soon Pat sank into a depression, as she continued to be haunted by night-mares about Tom and the baby she had destroyed.

Enter her stepdaughter, Lee. Now in Missy's class at Bay State, Lee was at first resentful that John insisted she live at home. But once she saw how ten-uous her father's new marriage appeared to be, Lee seized the opportunity to play with Pat's head. She began playing Tom's frat song, "The Sweetheart of Sigma Chi," on her phonograph whenever she was alone with Pat. She even got to Pat indirectly by flirt-ing with Alice's new boyfriend, football hero Tony Douglas. Tony was pressuring Alice to make their

Newly married Pat Randolph had to deal with jealous stepdaughter Lee. Lee caused a car crash that left her father paralyzed and depressed.

relationship physical, but Alice refused to make the same mistake Pat did. Lee practically laid herself out on a silver platter for the libidi-nous linebacker, but Tony caught on to her "end run" around Alice.

John was also on to Lee, and he let loose with a lac-erating lecture. Furious, Lee sped off in a rainstorm and John followed. Lee lost control of her car, and both skidded into an oncoming truck. While Lee suf-fered minor injuries, John was paralyzed by a blood clot on his spine. Confined to a wheelchair, he began to wallow in self-pity as Pat waited on him hand and foot. He was so humiliated about his condition that he refused to return to work.

To pick up the slack at John's firm, Dru brought in another young protégé, Mike Bauer, whose wife, Julie, had just died of an apparent suicide in a mental hospital. Mike and his little daughter, Hope, moved in with an older widow, Emily Hastings, who cared for Hope after school. Lee found herself bonding with this new family in town, for she felt like an out-cast among the Matthewses. Soon Lee realized she was falling deeply in love with Mike.

John liked Mike and encouraged the relationship, but Mike wasn't ready to settle down again—especially when he came to know Pat. As John became increasingly difficult to live with, a frustrated Pat took a second look at Mike, and the two became attracted to one another. They kissed a few times in secret, but couldn't bring themselves to make love, because of John and Lee. Ultimately, Mike couldn't condone a dead-end relationship with a married woman, so he decided to leave Bay City and return to Springfield. He arranged for Pat to meet him in a park to share a good-bye kiss—unaware that Lee had happened upon them unnoticed!

❧

However, this secret paled in comparison to a new development in town. Liz was obsessed with finding out about Missy's mysterious background. Liz's friend Helen Moore prayed that Liz would not make trouble, because she herself knew about Missy's parentage! Helen's visiting chum from San Francisco, Kathryn Corning, was Missy's biological mother.

The story began with a tumultuous World War II romance. Kathryn lived in San Diego while her much older husband, Navy Commander Corning, served overseas. As the long, lonely months wore on for Kathryn, she met a handsome young navy pilot from Chicago named Rick Summers. The two fell in love, and Kathryn soon found herself pregnant by the dashing newcomer. She was all set to leave her husband and marry Rick—but the day she left the hospital with her infant daughter, Rick was killed in a routine flight. Kathryn was stricken not only with grief, but with panic. Her husband had been gone a year and there was no way she could pass her baby off as his. With no one to turn to, Kathryn registered the child at an orphanage under the name Melissa Palmer, and went on with her marriage after the war was over, as if nothing had happened.

Now Kathryn was in Bay City. Without revealing herself as Missy's mother, she befriended the girl and taught her how to love and accept herself. Armed with the new self-confidence Kathryn gave her, Missy finally agreed to marry Bill. Kathryn was thrilled to be a part of Missy's life and planned to tell her the truth someday. Thus she returned to San Francisco to close up her house, with the intention of moving permanently to Bay City. But it was not to be: while in San Francisco, Kathryn suffered a fatal heart attack.

Bill learned of Kathryn's death and was curious upon discovering that the woman had left Missy a small fortune. Since Missy was excitedly preparing for their wedding, Bill decided not to tell her of Kathryn's death until after the bridal shower. He was yet unaware that Liz had long been suspicious of Kathryn's motherly interest in Missy, and was pawing through Kathryn's personal effects! Liz came up with Rick Summers's picture, as well as a birth certificate for Kathryn's daughter. With the reluctant help of her lawyer friend, Fred Douglas, Liz got the name, rank, and serial number of Rick Summers and matched Missy's fingerprints with those on the birth certificate. Here, at last, was proof that her son was about to bring an illegitimate girl into the Matthews family fold. Liz was not about to let that happen!

On the eve of Bill and Missy's wedding day, Liz privately confronted Missy. She icily informed the girl that Kathryn had died and accused her of keeping the secret that Kathryn was her mother. Missy was shocked and insisted she knew nothing about it, but Liz didn't believe her. She recounted the entire story of Missy's parentage, and as a parting shot threatened to tell all to Bill unless Missy did herself.

Liz wanted to leave Missy feeling like the lowest form of white trash. In fact, Missy felt lower still. Kathryn Corning had thrown her away, come back to tease her with motherly concern, then died on her. The only way she could validate her existence, Missy figured, was to go to Chicago and find her father.

Thus she took a train to the Windy City, where a brassy waitress named Madge Murray recognized her! Apparently Missy was the last to know that she was the "Missing Heiress" for whom TV news programs were offering rewards.

Hoping to rake in some bucks, Madge called the Bay City police to report Missy's whereabouts. Meanwhile, Missy developed a fever and walked the streets of Chicago in delirium, narrowly escaping an oncoming car. Luckily the driver stopped in time and took her to his apartment, where he nursed her back to health. As Missy recovered, the man saw a report about the missing heiress, and realized he was sitting on a gold mine.

The man in question was Danny Fargo, a two-bit lounge lizard and con artist extraordinaire. Danny was in hock up to his eyeballs to his gullible girlfriend, Madge Murray's younger sister, Flo. When Flo saw Missy in Danny's apartment, he told her he intended to bilk Missy and then whisk Flo away with the wad of cash. But Madge had Danny pegged as a fraud and knew he would break her sister's heart. Danny positioned himself as Missy's only friend, getting her to open up to him about her background. Out of gratitude,

Troubled Lee Randolph found herself falling in love with Mike Bauer, a young lawyer from Springfield, brought in to help ease the caseload at her father's firm.

Missy gave him her engagement ring, which he promptly pawned. When Bill came to Chicago looking for Missy, he asked about Missy at The Alley, the club where Danny and the Murray sisters worked. Danny lied and said that Missy had disappeared. He never told Missy Bill was looking for her.

Finally, Danny had Missy where he wanted her. She learned that her grandfather, Rick Summers, had died several months earlier. Lonely and desperate to have a name, she impulsively married Danny in a dreary civil ceremony. She told him that the marriage was in name only, and he agreed . . . for now.

Back in Bay City, Bill gave up all hope that Missy would ever return to him. He was now fair game for Lenore Moore, Helen's aggressive debutante daughter. Lenore had grown up with the Matthews children and had a long-standing unrequited crush on Bill. Helen told Lenore to back off, but Liz considered Lenore prize daughter-in-law material and egged her on to pursue Bill. After Bill passed his bar exams, he became engaged to Lenore.

Missy saw Bill and Lenore's picture in the society pages and swore she would stay away from Bay City for good. Ironically, it was Danny who would bring her back home. He gave her a sob story about his "sick mother" who would die unless they went to Bay City to claim Missy's inheritance. Once again, Missy fell for Danny's line.

When the newlywed Fargos came to town, the Matthewses were shocked that Missy had married such a blatant small-time operator. Danny was shameless in demanding Missy's money from Fred Douglas, who was acting as guardian of her inheritance. Fred replied that the money was in a trust fund and therefore not subject to a lump sum disbursement.

Missy made the mistake of telling Liz that she married Danny only to have a name. Deducing that the marriage had not been consummated, Liz threw this issue in Danny's face. Danny indignantly shot back at her, "I'll show you who's a man!" Liz threw down the gauntlet: "No, don't show me, Danny. Show Melissa." She snickered. "I wish you luck."

The saga of dastardly Danny was now to reach a fever pitch. When Missy told him their marriage was a mistake, he forced himself on her and vowed never to give her a divorce. Danny then hit Liz up for $500,000 under threat of telling Bill that Liz had caused Missy to run away. Madge and Flo arrived to get the goods on Danny, as did an embittered young ex-con from Bay City named Sam Lucas. Five years earlier, Danny and Sam had pulled a heist, only for Danny to abscond with the loot while Sam was thrown in jail. Now Sam wanted his fair share.

It was thanks to Pat that Bill and Missy were able to reconcile amidst all this turmoil. Pat told Missy that Bill had searched for her in Chicago but Danny had thrown him off the track. Missy was now painfully aware that she had married a con man. She went to Bill and admitted that she was Kathryn Corning's illegitimate daughter—leaving out the part about Liz having told her. Bill was completely understanding, and the two admitted their love. Bill and Lenore amicably called off their engagement, but a happy ending was still far out of reach for Missy: She found Danny shot dead in their hotel suite, and when she unthinkingly placed her hands on the gun, the hotel detective arrived and called the police. She was arrested for killing Danny in the heat of passion, which was a charge of Murder Two.

Walter Curtin wanted Murder One. Bay City's complex, charismatic new district attorney had visions of glory as he attacked the Fargo case. Liz wanted to make sure Walter didn't see Bill as a suspect, so she convinced Lenore to lie that she and Bill were still engaged. Walter told Lenore he knew otherwise, but had to admit he admired her strength and spunk. It was through Lenore that Walter developed an almost macabre fascination with Missy's case. Missy reminded him of the woman who had dumped him for someone with a more prestigious background, and he identified with Lenore as a fellow jilted lover. By sending Missy up the river, he felt he could indirectly punish his ex-fiancée.

With such a formidable prosecutor gunning for her, Missy needed strong representation. Elderly Mitchell Dru couldn't act as chief counsel; he was so weak from overwork that Jim and Mary had to convince him to live with them. It was then that John Randolph finally rallied, defending Missy from his wheelchair. But although John was in top form, he couldn't surmount a major setback in the case: Missy discovered she was pregnant with Danny's child! Bill was completely sympathetic, but Liz overheard him mention the pregnancy and ran to Walter with the information. Walter agreed not to reveal that Liz was the source of this bombshell, and used it to claim that Missy killed Danny in order to pass the child off as Bill's. And so Walter got his Murder One conviction—all thanks to Liz.

Of course, Bill wouldn't give up on the woman he loved. He investigated Madge and Flo Murray, who were back in Chicago, as possible suspects. Missy told John she suspected Sam, but she had no last name to go on.

As fate would have it, Sam Lucas and his family would figure in a new chapter of the lives of Pat Randolph and her younger siblings, Alice and Russ. Alice left the art institute to become a nurse, while Russ returned from medical school to start his internship. Russ was soon enraptured by one of his first patients—the sultry, feisty young Rachel Davis.

✦

Rachel was a working-class girl with a million-dollar dream of Hollywood stardom. Her father, a drifter named Gerald Ketcham Davis, had deserted the family when Rachel was an infant. Left alone with no support, Rachel's strong-willed mother, Ada, worked long hours as a manicurist to support her daughter and younger brother—who happened to be Sam Lucas. Sam had turned to a life of crime so he could finance the movie career his niece, Rachel, craved, and had demanded his take from Danny toward that end.

Now Danny was gone, and Sam was living down his criminal past by working for Ernie Downs, a good-hearted mechanic who became a father figure to him. But greed was still driving Rachel, whose lust for the good life ran in her veins. When she took a second look at handsome, trusting Russ Matthews, Rachel abandoned all notions of stardom and fancied herself a rich doctor's wife.

Meanwhile, Bill and Dru discovered that Charlie Rushinberger, Madge's boyfriend, had withheld the fact that she was in Bay City when Danny was killed. Just as the lawyers prepared to close in on Madge, she was startled to hear Flo screaming in her sleep that she had killed Danny! Flo had no memory of the murder or the nightmares, so Madge enlisted Dru to test her recollection of that fateful night. Flo was finally able to remember a physical struggle with Danny, in which she grabbed a gun and killed him in self-defense. Because of her drunken stupor, Flo had blocked the scene out. Walter let Flo off and she moved back to Chicago. Madge stayed in Bay City, however, and became a close friend to Ada.

As Walter shut the books on Missy's case, he pursued Lenore in earnest and they became engaged. Walter apologized sincerely to Missy, but remained neurotically jealous over Lenore's lingering but unrequited feelings for Bill. Lenore, meanwhile, shed her debutante image and became a nurse. Once she convinced Pat and Alice she was no longer after Bill, Lenore became the Matthews sisters' closest and dearest friend. She also took the troubled young Lee Randolph under her wing.

Feeling lonely and alienated, Lee confided to Lenore that she had lost Mike Bauer because of his feelings for her stepmother, Pat. Lee accused Pat of carrying on with Mike behind her back, and was fearful when John underwent a risky operation that ultimately restored the use of his legs. Tired of being powerless, Lee told John she had seen Pat and Mike together. Instead of raging at Pat as Lee hoped he would, John angrily said to Lee, "You shouldn't have told me." John told Pat he felt responsible for driving her into Mike's arms, and they made peace.

Now that Sam Lucas had a new vision for his life, he took an interest in Lee and encouraged her to turn over a new leaf, as well. But Lee was certain she had lost her father for good, and became a hippie in Bay City's seamy Bedfordtown district. There she befriended Lahoma Vane, an earthy southern gal who

Seductive, tempestuous Rachel Davis knew how to get what she wanted. Born on the wrong side of the tracks, she saw marriage to respectable Russ Matthews and being a rich doctor's wife as her ticket out.

9

became her roommate, and Richard ("Lefty") Burns, a sleazy drug trafficker who'd had past dealings with Sam and Danny Fargo. Lahoma had eyes for Sam and tried to convince him that Lee wasn't from their world. But they shared a fear that Lee was embarking on a dangerous friendship with Lefty, who was introducing her to a life of booze and wild rides.

Just as Lenore had Lee convinced they should room together in a better neighborhood, Lefty slipped LSD into Lee's coffee and tried to rape her while she "tripped." But Lee came out of her hallucination and fought Lefty off, stabbing him with a fireplace poker and killing him in the process. Sam came on the scene and took the rap when he realized that Lee had no recollection of killing Lefty. Since Lee was acting normally at that point, Sam had no reason to suspect that she was drugged. Walter had a homicide lieutenant, Dick Nolan, arrest Sam for Lefty's murder. To complicate matters, Dick had feelings for John Randolph's secretary, Peggy Harris.

John agreed to defend Sam, but the case never went to trial. Lee hallucinated—making it obvious that she had been drugged—and recalled killing Lefty to fend off his rape attempt. After Walter absolved her of any guilt, Lee and Sam became engaged and happily made wedding plans as Sam joined John's office as a law clerk. However, Lee discovered that LSD could produce malformed children and couldn't bear to bring Sam any more heartache, so she told him she no longer loved him and broke their engagement.

Missy felt just as unworthy of Bill, especially

Walter Curtin was a complex and charismatic DA with aspirations of running for state attorney general. In keeping with his ambitions, his Bay City Country Club wedding to socialite Lenore Curtin was a lavish affair.

when she gave birth to Danny Fargo's baby boy. She named him Richard ("Ricky") in memory of her deceased father, Rick Summers. John convinced Missy to accept Bill's marriage proposal, and gave Liz such a tongue-lashing that she suffered a minor heart attack! As concerned as Bill was for his mother, he put Missy first and insisted they go through with their marriage plans. Thus, while an unsuspecting Liz recovered in the hospital, Bill and Missy were married in an intimate ceremony at Jim and Mary's home. Alice almost caught the bouquet, but Rachel literally grabbed it from her. This little scene was an eerie indication of things to come.

Although Bill still had no idea that Liz had helped send Missy to prison, he was fed up with his mother's antics. He rented an apartment and told Liz he was letting Missy and Ricky live there. No one had told Liz of Bill and Missy's marriage, but as usual, Liz sniffed it out when she called Missy in a disguised voice, only to hear Missy identify herself as "Mrs. William Matthews, Jr." Once she got over her shock, Liz tried a different approach. She shamed Bill and Missy into moving back to her house, then faked seizures so that Missy could wait on her hand and foot! Between raising Ricky and answering Liz's constant calls of "Melissa, dear," Missy had no time alone with Bill.

Sensing Bill's frustration, Walter irrationally feared that Bill would move back in Lenore's direction, so Walter set out to get Bill and Missy away from Liz's influence. He revealed to a stunned John that Liz had helped him nail Missy for Danny's murder. John passed this along to Missy, but she insisted Bill should never learn the extent of Liz's machinations. Having grown up an orphan, Missy refused to drive a further wedge between her husband and his mother.

Russ Matthews was well aware that his mother, Mary, disapproved of his whirlwind courtship with Rachel. That's why he held off telling his family that he and Rachel had eloped! Rachel told Ada, however, and later shared with her mother that she and Russ were expecting a child. Liz overheard them, and of course the secret was out. Mary bit her tongue, but Jim wished the newlyweds well, and let them live in the family home. The young couple was doomed from the start, however, for Rachel suffered a miscarriage.

On other fronts, Peggy Harris and Dick Nolan were married, but Dick was soon killed in the line of duty. Madge learned that Flo had married a decent man named Max in Chicago, so Madge went back there to marry Charlie. With Madge gone, a lonely Ada bonded with Ernie Downs over their mutual concern for Sam. Despite Rachel's condescending attitude toward Ernie, he and Ada were married.

While the Downses' wedding was modest, the Bay City Country Club provided the backdrop for Lenore and Walter Curtin's lavish nuptials. The grandiosity was Walter's idea because he was running for state attorney general. It was at this wedding that Walter introduced his new friend and campaign supporter, Steven Frame.

Steven was a young, self-made land developer who owned a football team and a house in St. Croix. Steve struck up a conversation with Alice at the wedding, and the two immediately hit it off. He liked her simplicity; she was awed by his worldliness. Alice agreed to date Steve and was thrilled when he hired Jim to do the accounting for his Bay City office. Rachel urged Alice not to let this prize get away, but as Rachel said the words, her stomach was churning. The truth was, Steve was exactly the type of man she wished she had married. He was suave and quietly assertive. And he had money. *Lots* of money.

Rachel found any excuse to double-date with Alice and Steve, each time sporting a fancy new dress from Bryant's department store. Of course, she found just as many excuses to avoid Russ in the bedroom. Russ suggested they have another child, but Rachel nixed it. She had no intention of playing

Lee Randolph was high on drugs when she killed dealer "Lefty" Burns, and her fiancé, Sam Lucas, was arrested for the crime. Throughout the ordeal, John Randolph's secretary, Peggy Harris, remained supportive, even though it was her boyfriend who arrested Sam.

the little mommy now that she was doing charity work to impress Liz. Rachel didn't realize that Russ's aunt was laughing behind her back.

Steve Frame wasn't. He came from a background more impoverished than Rachel's, and for all her awkwardness he understood her need to better herself. But Steve was really falling in love with Alice, and would probably have avoided Rachel's advances had it not been for Alice's immaturity. Alice was simply afraid of loving such a powerful man. She had always identified herself with her practical mother, who kept a comfortable home for a man who made a comfortable salary. Steven Frame was alien to Alice's little world, so she avoided him. Rachel wasted no time telling Steve that Alice was foolish not to appreciate him. He responded, "The way you do."

Sam felt unappreciated by Lee, as well. Lee made the mistake of confiding to Lahoma that she had rejected Sam because of the LSD risks. Instead of telling Sam the truth, Lahoma offered Sam her shoulder to cry on, and he married her on the rebound. As Sam was working toward a law degree, Lahoma began studying so that she could better herself and fit into his new world. But Sam's world came tumbling down: One night while driving, Lee had a hallucinatory vision of Lefty Burns and crashed her car. She was hospitalized, and soon after, she died.

Devastated by the loss of his only child, John could only react by trying to replace her in his life. He tried to become legal guardian to a client, teenage shoplifter Emily Mason, whose hard-driving mother, Anne, literally worked herself to death. Emily stopped shoplifting but became involved with an errant hippie, Mike Thayer. Pat and John took Emily in and helped her straighten herself out, but she decided not to remain with them. She chose instead to follow her late mother's agenda and went to boarding school.

Liz's agenda for Bill was about to explode in her face, when Bill overheard her admit to Fred Douglas that she was responsible for telling Walter that Missy was pregnant by Danny. Bill confronted Liz, stormed out, and had a serious car accident. He underwent an operation and recovered at the hospital, where Lenore—acting as both nurse and friend—sat by his side. Walter fumed with jealousy, to the point where John and Fred feared he needed psychological help. To make matters worse for Walter, he lost his election bid because he had no feeling for working people's problems.

Shaken by Bill's near death, Liz finally apologized to her son and he eventually forgave her. Bill bought a charming new house for himself, Missy, and Ricky—only to land a major account in California. And so Bill and Missy decided to move westward to begin a new life.

Competitive with Bill to the end, Walter became obsessed with buying his imagined rival's house, but he was unable to secure financing because of his profligate spending history. So he left the DA post to make better money as John and Dru's partner. He also made Lenore leave her hospital job so that he could appear the successful breadwinner. Yet he bought Bill and Missy's house in Lenore's name.

As Bill left Bay City, his sister, Susan, returned—as neurotic as ever and full of recriminations against Liz for making her into a failure with men. Ironically, Susan found that she had a rapport with Fred Douglas, with whom Liz shared a close but platonic friendship. The older but still virile Fred was the first man since her father who truly understood Susan.

The two became romantically involved, and Liz reacted with hurt and anger, realizing too late that she had let Fred get away because she was so focused on running her family's lives. With Liz's reluctant blessing, Susan and Fred were married.

As luck would have it, Liz saw Steve and Rachel lunching intimately and told Russ. When Russ confronted Rachel, she taunted him about what a real man Steve was. An embittered Russ ranted that he was the head of the house, and they were getting their own apartment or else. Rachel knuckled under, but rolled her eyes when her in-laws threw her a housewarming shower—the sexiest gift of the day was a toaster. Rachel raged about the party to Russ, and he reacted by spanking her like an errant child!

Then the inevitable happened. Tired of wasting her womanhood, Rachel left Russ and moved back in with Ada. In a heartbeat, she was in Steve's bed.

Rachel was convinced she had Steve in the bag. With smug self-confidence, she told a shocked Ada that she and Steve had made love and that she intended to divorce Russ.

But Rachel had another thing coming—namely, a baby! When Rachel told Steve they were going to have a child, he coldly denied paternity and sent her away. He realized he loved Alice more than ever, and was not about to let Rachel use him as a rung on the social ladder.

Determined not to be left alone as her mother was, Rachel charmed Russ into a reconciliation and told him he was about to become a dad!

Rachel regretted that move, however, when Alice and Steve announced their impending marriage! During the engagement party, Rachel came to Alice's bedroom and told her sister-in-law she was in love with Steve and expecting his child. A shattered Alice broke her engagement.

Rachel gave birth to a baby boy, James Gerald ("Jamie") Matthews. Contemptuous of both Steve and Rachel, Mary ached to tell Russ about Jamie's probable paternity. But Jim didn't want to ruin Russ's happiness, and he set up a trust fund for Jamie.

Ada was disgusted by Rachel's behavior, not to

*I*t was to be a night of celebration for the young engaged couple, but right before the party, Rachel told Alice that she was pregnant with Steve Frame's child. A devastated Alice broke her engagement to Steve and ran away to Europe.

mention fearful for the marriage of her brother, Sam. A guilty Lahoma admitted that Lee had broken her engagement to Sam only because she was afraid of having children. Sam was so livid at Lahoma for her secrecy that he left her. Defeated, Lahoma got a hostess job at the Purple Plum bar and dated a redneck loser named Ron Styles.

Lahoma was used to feeling down and out, but Liz was decidedly uncomfortable in that position. For the first time since Will's death, she was lonely. She had lost her son to the woman he loved, and the man she herself adored to her own daughter! But a newcomer to Bay City brought hope for Liz in the romance department. He was Wayne Addison, an entrepreneur several years younger than she. The dynamic president of Western General Electronics, Wayne was proposing a merger with Steve and promised lucrative business to Walter. He was assisted by an efficient right-hand woman, Bernice Robinson. It was all a sham. Wayne was a con man, Bernice was his ex-wife and accomplice, and Western General Electronics was a phantom.

As 1969 drew to a close, Sam refused to reconcile with Lahoma, who talked of divorce. Fred's career took him away from Susan a great deal, to Liz's glee. Pat and Lenore both hoped to have a baby. Alice warned Rachel to watch her step or she would tell Russ that Jamie was Steve's son. But Rachel still hoped to find "the good life" with Steve, never dreaming that Wayne was using Walter as a means to leave Steve penniless . . . and dead.

❧

1970—1974

The years 1970 to 1974 rocked Bay City down to its roots. Families were torn apart, friends became enemies, and some prominent people acted in ways even their closest associates never believed possible.

First, tragedy struck Liz Matthews. Her beloved son, Bill, was killed in a boating accident in California, leaving a devastated Missy to return home with her toddler son, Ricky. Liz and Missy shared their common grief, but were soon at odds when Missy became friends with the newly reconciled Sam and Lahoma Lucas. Having finally passed the bar exams, Sam looked after Missy out of respect for Bill, who had inspired him to become a lawyer. But Liz couldn't shake the fact that Sam was related to Rachel, and told Missy that the Lucases were not her "kind of people."

What Liz didn't realize was that Sam was going places—fast. John introduced him to Rafe Carter, senior partner at the Carter & Grant law firm fifty miles away in Somerset. With John's blessing, Rafe hired Sam to help with the firm's major account, Delaney Brands, a food corporation that employed nearly half the small town of Somerset. The company's blustering president, Jasper Delaney, bullied his son, Robert, into the family business despite his obvious calling as an architect. Sam knew he was stepping into a difficult situation, but he was happy to start anew with Lahoma in a place that held no memories of Lee Randolph. And Missy, tired of Liz's dominance, joined the Lucases and moved with Ricky to Somerset.

As Sam learned his way in his new surroundings, Robert Delaney introduced him to the garrulous owner of the town's most swank nightclub, The Riverboat. It was none other than Gerald Davis—Sam's former brother-in-law! When Sam relayed this news to Ada, she went to tell Gerald that Rachel had grown to become the female version of himself—a liar and a cheat. Ada wished Rachel would bond with Ernie as a stepfather, but Rachel treated the simple mechanic like a nonentity up until the day he died of a heart attack.

Rachel was elated to know her father's whereabouts and rushed to meet him. Their initial meeting was pleasant enough, but Rachel was pained to realize that her place in Gerald's life would be, at best, minimal. Since moving to Somerset, Gerald had married and divorced a sympathetic woman named Marsha, with whom he had a daughter, Pamela ("Pammy"). Now Pammy was a teenager and the apple of her daddy's eye. Rachel knew where she wasn't wanted, and returned home.

Not that home was paradise. Rachel's "rich doctor's wife" fantasy was shattered when Russ and his doctor pal Dan Shearer opened a downtown clinic to serve Bay City's poor and working class. Rachel groaned when she saw her husband's new surroundings and fantasized about dumping Russ for Steven Frame. For the moment, Rachel was trapped—but not for long. When Russ finally figured out that Jamie couldn't be his child, he coldly told Rachel they were finished. Meanwhile, Alice remained in France, sorting out her feelings for Steve. Racked with guilt, Steve vowed he would wait forever for the one woman he truly loved. So certain was Steve that Alice would return to him that he commissioned Robert Delaney to design a house for himself and Alice to live in as husband and wife. That is, if he lived that long . . .

Meanwhile, slimy Wayne Addison was secretly plotting to merge his phantom corporation with Frame Enterprises, then put out a contract on Steve's life! Wayne's tool in this master plan was none other than Steve's closest friend, Walter Curtin. Knowing that Walter was desperately in debt, Wayne hit his hot button—hard. He paid Walter under the table to swindle Steve and convince him to merge with Wayne. Walter was full of self-loathing, but was driven by his obsession to provide Lenore with the material things he thought she deserved. He dreamed of building not one, but two houses—one for himself and Lenore, and one for his mother-in-law, Helen Moore.

Although Walter was able to perpetuate his pathetic charade, a cloud of suspicion grew around Wayne. Back in Somerset, Sam knew that Wayne had once bilked Robert Delaney, but was duty-bound by an embarrassed Jasper to keep this as privileged information. Wayne told Liz he wanted to marry her, only to drop out of sight for weeks at a time with no explanation. Wayne was only using Liz as an excuse to stay in Bay City until he disposed of Steve. Bernice, Wayne's ex and accomplice, warned him not to add murder to the mix.

Once Susan and Fred saw Liz rushing blindly toward marriage, they realized they had made the same mistake themselves. Susan had married Fred only to punish Liz, and Fred had wanted only to prove that he was still attractive to younger women.

Fred went to Japan indefinitely on business, and they amicably dissolved the marriage.

Unfortunately, *amicable* was not a word in Rachel's vocabulary. She talked Steve into putting her and Jamie up in a swank apartment, then hired suave young attorney Brian Blake to take Russ to the cleaners. Before long, Rachel and Brian were holding their client meetings under satin sheets at a resort in St. Thomas. It was Ada and Russ who summoned them home because Jamie was near death from influenzal meningitis. Russ ultimately saved the life of the boy he once believed to be his son—the boy who was now known as Jamie Frame. Out of gratitude, Steve swayed the judge into sparing Russ the indignity of paying Rachel alimony, and shamed Rachel into returning Jim and Mary's trust fund monies, monies meant for Jamie, when they thought he was their grandson. Soon after, Brian dumped Rachel and moved to New York.

Despite Steve's generosity, a judgmental Mary still refused to forgive his indiscretion with Rachel. Yet when Alice wrote to her family from France, Jim and Russ began to hope that Alice and Steve would reconcile. Steve flew to see Alice in Avignon, where she was working at a children's hospital. Although she wanted more time to find herself, Alice admitted she had never stopped loving him. Steve agreed to give her some space and returned to Bay City, hopeful.

As Russ moved on with his life, he became intrigued by one of his clinic patients who lived in the same building as Wayne Addison. She was Cindy Clark, a frail young woman with a mysterious illness. Cindy was embarrassed by her widowed mother, Belle, a crass and bitter woman who nipped at the bottle. Belle pushed Cindy to go out with Russ because he showed signs of becoming a successful doctor. But Cindy was the antithesis of Rachel—she didn't care about success. In essence, she was the perfect woman for Russ.

New hope also dawned for Pat and John. After years of believing that Pat would probably never conceive another child, the couple celebrated the birth of twins, Michael and Marianne. Dan Shearer referred the Randolphs to efficient baby nurse Caroline Johnson, unaware that Caroline was one twisted lady, who blamed herself unjustifiably for her children's deaths, and sought to replace them with Michael and Marianne. To add to this mess, Caroline also wanted John!

John had no idea of Caroline's intentions—nor did he realize that his partner, Walter Curtin, was now in Wayne Addison's pocket. Wayne warned Walter he would have Steve killed unless Walter convinced him to merge with Wayne. To further torment Walter, Wayne began flirting with Lenore! He had finally grown tired of Liz and dumped her, lying that he was in love with another woman. Although Wayne denied it, Liz was irrationally convinced it was Lenore. When Walter and Lenore learned they were expecting a child, Liz fed Walter's jealousy by sharing her suspicions that Wayne was the father!

The world now closed in on Wayne Addison. Just as Steve was about to go ahead with the merger, Sam and Robert raced in from Somerset to tell him Wayne was a crook. When Steve confronted Wayne, the scoundrel said, "I am but the humble instrument that fate has chosen to demonstrate to you that you are not infallible . . . that's all." Shortly thereafter, Wayne sent a goon to run over Steve. It was Rachel who pulled him back in the nick of time.

Concerned that Walter seemed agitated, Lenore went to Wayne's apartment to ask him what was troubling her husband. Wayne responded by making a pass at her. A flustered Lenore ran out—leaving behind a scarf, which Walter had given her. Moments later, Liz arrived to accuse Wayne of fathering Lenore's child. Wayne cruelly slapped Liz and flaunted Lenore's scarf at her, calling Liz a "vain, stupid woman." Liz nervously fingered a statuette before she left. When Lenore returned to retrieve the scarf, she found Wayne dead—hit over the head with the statuette!

In shock, Lenore ran from the scene but bumped into nosy Belle Clark, who quickly implicated Lenore to the police. Other suspects included Steve, Liz, and Bernice, but Lenore was the prime suspect, so DA Tom Albini had her arrested and imprisoned without bail. (Tom was getting back at Walter for holding him back in the DA's office several years earlier.) Tom's assistant, Frank Chadwick, was dating John's secretary,

Peggy, at the time, but she broke off the relationship because of the case.

Lenore's trial began with John acting as her attorney, but a bout with Ménière's syndrome forced him to step down. Caroline relished the opportunity to nurse him back to health, meanwhile discouraging Pat from nursing her babies so that she could further bond with them herself. Tired of feeling useless, Pat told Caroline she was no longer needed. Caroline responded by poisoning Pat's food so that she could nurse the entire family! When Pat recovered, she caught Caroline snooping in a scrapbook about the deaths of Tom Baxter and Lee Randolph and fired her on the spot. Desperate, Caroline kidnapped the twins, but happily the police caught up with her. Caroline was institutionalized, and Michael and Marianne were returned safe and sound.

During John's convalescence, Dru was ready to step in and defend Lenore. Both lawyers were aghast, however, when Walter insisted on representing his own wife. They were further baffled when Walter refused to pursue Bernice as a suspect. In fact, Walter wanted her off the hook for fear she would expose his dealings with Wayne. Walter tried to cast Liz as the killer, but she had an alibi that held up.

There was another unsettling factor in Wayne's murder: Lenore's scarf was missing from the scene. It was in Walter's safe. Walter let his wife stand trial for a murder he himself had committed!

On the day the verdict was to be read, Walter brought the scarf to court in a sealed envelope. Were Lenore found guilty, he was ready to present the scarf and confess to the crime. As luck would have it, Lenore was found innocent. Soon after, the Curtins celebrated the birth of a son, Walter, Jr. ("Wally"), so named because Walter was a shining hero in Lenore's eyes. But as he wrestled with the question of coming clean, Walter felt like scum.

It was Bernice who forced Walter's hand. Furious that John still suspected her, Bernice investigated Walter and discovered that he was in Bay City the night Wayne was murdered. Bernice then struck up a

*W*alter was full of self-loathing, but was driven by his obsession to provide Lenore with the material things he thought she deserved.

friendship with Lenore in order to infiltrate the Curtin household, where she happened upon the envelope containing Lenore's scarf! Bernice pilfered the scarf and sent it to Lenore anonymously in the mail.

As a thunderstorm raged outside, a yet more gut-wrenching storm rocked the Curtin living room. Lenore showed Walter the scarf and he tearfully told her the horrible truth—he had helped Wayne bilk Steve, a man he considered his best friend. It was all so he could pay the mortgage and shower Lenore with gifts. When Walter told Wayne he wanted out, Wayne wouldn't let him off the hook—so Walter pummeled him with the statuette in a fit of rage. Lenore denounced Walter as a pathetic excuse for a human being, and he left to tell John and Steve what he had done. Before he reached John's office, however, Walter lost control of his car and plummeted down a cliff to his death.

After Walter left the house on that tragic day, Lenore let loose with a fury she'd never before displayed. She ransacked her house screaming, "I want none of it! None of it!" Then she received the news that Walter was dead. For her son's sake, Lenore burned the scarf and vowed no one would ever know Walter was a murderer.

Liz was so overwrought by the Wayne Addison fiasco that Susan decided to move in with her, and Liz was deeply moved by her daughter's new show of compassion. Dan Shearer was not happy, however—he was interested in Susan and tolerated no interference from Liz. Susan and Dan eloped, and after her initial shock, Liz gave them her blessing. The newlyweds soon began getting extended visits from Dan's teenage daughter, Barbara, who was escaping her strict mother Gloria. Liz worried about Susan's new family situation, until Rafe Carter briefly moved to Bay City from Somerset.

Rafe dated Liz and convinced her that she should start living her own life.

At this time there were several departures from Bay City. After Rafe accepted a position in Denver, Liz helped Missy and Ricky settle into their new home in Arizona, and authorized Jim to sell her house. Susan and Dan moved to New York and shipped Barbara back to her mother. And "Uncle Dru" retired to travel around the world, with a touching send-off at Pat and John's. The Matthewses gave him luggage along with a photo album dating back to the time he came to live with them. The tears flowed as everyone sang "For He's a Jolly Good Fellow" to a special lawyer and friend.

Russ wanted to marry Cindy, but she felt inferior because of her dismal family background. Her older brother, luckless restaurateur Ted Clark, was back in town escaping a loan shark named Casey. Belle took out all her frustrations on Ted because she blamed him indirectly for the reversal of their family's fortunes: her late husband had been jailed for embezzling from a bank where he worked to pay for Ted's polio treatments. Russ saw potential in Ted, however, and got him a job in the hospital's nutrition department.

At the same time, Cindy began nurse's training and worked at Russ's clinic. To pay Casey back, Ted lifted Cindy's keys and stole drugs from the clinic, spilling gentian violet on his hasty way out. Russ came in, slipped on the substance, and was knocked out. In his delirium he said to Cindy, "Oh, Rachel, it's so wonderful to have you here." When he recovered, Russ convinced Cindy that Rachel was part of his past, and they became engaged.

Ironically, Rachel was to play an unforeseen role in Russ and Cindy's lives. In Somerset, Gerald Davis introduced Rachel to Ted, who was seeking his help in returning to the restaurant business. To her surprise, Rachel found herself drawn to Ted as a soul mate. They were both from the wrong side of the tracks, trying to live down past mistakes. Clinging to one another for comfort, Rachel and Ted married. Russ told Cindy he loved her so much, he didn't mind having his ex-wife as his future in-law. He closed up his clinic and returned to the hospital as a cardiologist.

But the big news was Alice's return to Bay City. She was breathless as Steve showed her the house he'd built for her. Swearing they would never be apart, Alice and Steve were married on the terrace of their lovely new country home. Soon Alice became pregnant, and was delighted that she could give Steve a child.

Rachel had no hope of getting Steve back, but was pragmatic enough to reap the benefits of his money. She convinced Steve and Gerald to back Ted's purchase of a faded local restaurant called The Fireside Inn. Rachel helped run the inn, acting as Ted's partner in every sense. Ada was grateful to her son-in-law for making Rachel the girl she always wanted her to be, and was thrilled when Ted wanted to adopt Jamie. Yet guilt got the better of Ted, and he confessed to stealing the drugs and causing Russ's injury. Ted helped the police trap Casey, but was still sentenced to a year in prison.

Cindy was so humiliated by Ted's actions, she waffled about marrying Russ. Tired of Cindy's immaturity, Russ dated an attractive colleague, Dr. Paula McCrae. Paula was an obsessive career woman who feared marriage because her mother, thrice married jet-setter Irene Kimball, had set a horrible example. Realizing that Russ and Cindy still had feelings for one another, Paula accepted a job in Stockholm. Russ and Cindy became engaged

Walter was consumed by rumors that Lenore was having an affair with his tormenter Wayne Addison. The rumors were untrue, and Lenore had no idea what was causing her husband's jealous fits and dark moods.

again, but their happiness was brief. When Cindy had increasing bouts of dizziness, Russ's friend Dr. David Rogers diagnosed her as having had mitral stenosis since childhood. She had a few weeks to live at most. Russ married Cindy in the hospital, and she died moments later.

A grieving Belle was left with only one child, so she forgave Ted his trespasses. But Steve felt Ted had risked Jamie's life by foiling Casey, and opposed Ted's plan to adopt his son. Steve had promised not to tell Jamie they were father and son, though he still bought the boy expensive gifts and paid for his nursery school. Alice supported Steve's desire to be part of his son's life, though the boy was still unaware that his buddy "Mr. Frame" was really his father. She even had Steve set up a trust fund for Jamie in order to minimize his contact with Rachel. But Rachel used Jamie as an excuse to keep in touch with Steve, now that Ted was in prison and looking like a loser in her eyes.

One fateful day Rachel invited Steve over to discuss Jamie's support. Not wanting to upset his wife, Steve told Alice he had a business emergency and rushed out. While he was gone, Alice decided to clean out a closet and fell off the ladder. She was rushed to the hospital, where she gave birth to a stillborn child. Torn between Alice and Jamie, a guilty Steve didn't tell Alice he had left her alone in order to placate Rachel. It was just as well, for Alice had enough to deal with: She had a perforated uterus, which would keep her from becoming pregnant for at least a year. To get out of herself, Alice decided to return to nursing.

Up to this time, Steve had shared very little with Alice about his background. A brief visit from his sister Emma Ordway prompted him finally to tell his wife about his impoverished family life. Steve had grown up one of seven children in the rural town of Chadwell, Oklahoma. His parents, Henry and Jenny Frame, lost their farm in a fire and hit on hard times. Henry became an embittered drunk who beat his wife and mistreated his children—Steve, Emma, Jason, Sharlene, Janice, Vince, and Willis. Emma married Burt Ordway and they had two daughters, Mary Frances (known as "Frankie") and Molly. Jenny had been deceased for about twenty years, and Henry disappeared a few years after. Steve felt guilty for having deserted his siblings to better himself. For this reason, Steve was determined his son would have the advantages he and his family could only dream about, regardless of who disapproved or got hurt.

Ada told Steve to get lost. She was angry that he was spoiling Jamie and shutting Ted out of the boy's life. To make matters worse, Gerald arrived to help Rachel run the inn and egged her on to pursue Steve. His flashy Riverboat had turned out to be a financial disaster, so Gerald was looking to Steve as a gold mine for himself and Rachel. When Ted was released from prison, he was enraged to discover that Steve was supporting Jamie and seeing him on a regular basis. Rachel tersely told Ted to take it or leave it. Soon after, Ted divorced Rachel and moved with his mother, Belle, to Chicago. Ted's fatherly parole officer, Gil McGowan, became chummy with Ada over their mutual concern for Ted, and these two lovably earthy people began to date seriously.

Ted was not the only one to feel steamrolled by Steven Frame. Now that Walter had left his business affairs a shambles, Steve trusted only John to act as his corporate counsel. This angered Pat, who complained that John was already overworked and a minimal presence at home. John hired Bernice Robinson and a reserved young lawyer named Mark Venable to assist him. Bernice was grateful that John no longer suspected her of killing Wayne Addison, and began coming on to him. Tired of Pat's nagging, John fell for Bernice's wiles and they began an affair. Eventually Pat suspected that John was involved with another woman and started to drink heavily. John began to hate himself because he felt responsible for Pat's condition.

John also regretted the loss of Peggy Nolan in his office, but was happy that she had become a full-fledged lawyer. She began dating Ray Scott, Ted's ex-con pal who worked in the inn's kitchen. This worried Peggy's widowed mother, Gloria Metcalf, a no-nonsense guidance counselor at Bay City High School. Gloria also feared for her younger daughter, Peggy's half-sister Linda, a nurse dating a drifter named Zack Richards. Zack was secretly working for Jake Barnes, the criminal who had lured Ray into a life of crime.

At this time, Gil left the parole office to become a lieutenant on the Bay City police force and began investigating Jake, whom he rightly suspected of plotting a heist. When Jake and Zack approached Ray to go in on the crime, Ray convinced Zack to help him turn on Jake. During the heist, Jake shot Ray. Ray died, and Zack decided to become a cop under Gil's tutelage.

❧

The triangle of Alice, Steve, and Rachel was now to reach a critical juncture. Jamie was bitten by a snake while at a park with Steve and Rachel. They rushed their son to the hospital—only to find that Alice was on duty. Alice was hurt that Steve had lied to her about not seeing Rachel and told him it was alright to see Rachel and Jamie openly. But Steve was ashamed of violating Alice's trust, and banished Rachel from his future visits with Jamie.

Rachel was not about to meet those terms! At Gerald's urging, she set up a meeting with Steve in his office, where she flirtatiously reminded him that he had been with her when Alice lost her baby. Rachel was unaware that her wily father had left a message at the hospital—impersonating Steve and inviting Alice to meet Steve at that very place and time. Just as Gerald hoped, Alice overheard the ugly truth. Unfortunately, she did not stick around long enough to hear Steve repel Rachel's advances. She stole out of the building, left her parents a note saying she couldn't be in the same town with her husband, and flew to New York.

His schemes notwithstanding, Gerald was saddened to learn that Jessica Buchanan, his Riverboat vocalist, and her infant son were killed in a car accident. Jessica had only recently married Robert Delaney, who had accepted Steve's offer to serve as architect for a new housing project in Bay City. Lenore, now working at Frame Enterprises and on Steve's project, shared an office with Robert. Devastated by the loss of his baby, Robert formed a special friendship with Lenore and her toddler son, Wally.

Soon Lenore and Robert were joined by a third newcomer to Steve's stable—his strong-willed sister Janice, who had been around the block a few times. Janice moved in with Steve and took an immediate liking to Rachel, for both women had to fight tooth and nail for everything they wanted out of life. Janice sensed that Rachel wanted Steve—and decided that she herself would snag the handsome, vulnerable Robert.

As Lenore tried to figure out where Robert fit into her life, she was unaware that Bernice was once again making her a pawn. When John refused to leave a drunken Pat for her, Bernice made it appear that John had been carrying on a long-standing affair with Lenore—Pat's closest friend! This sent Pat off the deep end, and she got into such an alcoholic stupor that she was hit by a car. When she came to in the hospital, she accused John and Lenore of being lovers. Lenore shrewdly called Bernice on starting the rumor, and Bernice threatened to expose Walter as a thief and murderer.

It was now confession time. Lenore told John the entire truth about Walter, and John admitted that Bernice was the other woman in his life. Unaware that John had come clean, Bernice arranged to tell Pat about the affair. Hours later, Mary discovered Bernice dead from head injuries on Pat and John's terrace! Gil investigated and arrested Pat for the crime—but he secretly had another suspect in mind. In a masterful bit of police work, Gil took a gamble that the real killer would not want Pat to be punished for a crime that he himself had committed.

Gil's gamble paid off. Mark Venable came forward and admitted he had shoved Bernice in a confrontation. The judge ruled Bernice's death accidental manslaugh-

ter, and Mark left town a free man. Pat and John reconciled and enjoyed a second honeymoon at Steve's house in St. Croix, from which they returned radiant.

While Pat got her life back, her sister, Alice, was embarking on a new one in New York City. Identifying herself as Alice Talbot, she became the live-in nurse for a pleasantly precocious boy named Dennis Carrington, who had congenital heart disease. Dennis lived with his father, prominent journalist Eliot Carrington, who was legally separated from his spoiled jet-setting wife, Iris.

The Carringtons had a household manager named Louise Goddard, a brittle eccentric who talked to plants. Although Louise worked for Eliot during the separation, she was most loyal to Iris and reported every peccadillo Eliot enjoyed. Dennis hoped his parents would someday reconcile, but he liked Alice so much he didn't mind when they began dating. In time, Alice confided her identity to Eliot. She also wrote to her family that she was doing fine but was not yet ready to be found. In so doing, she sent back her wedding pictures and asked Jim to get her belongings out of the house she had shared with Steve.

Jim and Mary still had no idea why Alice had deserted Steve. Mary didn't care to know the reasons, so long as Steve would soon be out of the family. But Jim was the kind father figure Steve never had, and he insisted Steve should have a chance to explain. Of course, Steve was as ignorant as they were about why his wife had disappeared. In fact, he grew so bitter about Alice that he took up with Rachel on the rebound. Russ tried to get Steve to pursue Alice, but to no avail. "Someday you'll find out what Rachel's really like, Steve," Russ told him. "And then, God help you!"

Since Ada made no secret of her disapproval of Steve, Rachel sought refuge in her father-daughter relationship with Gerald. When she and Steve put the inn up for sale, Rachel hoped Gerald would remain a part of her life in Bay City. But weasel that he was, Gerald decided to grab a lucrative restaurant gig in San Francisco. When he left, Gerald admitted to Rachel that he had orchestrated the phone call that ultimately separated Alice and Steve.

Back in New York, Iris realized that Eliot seemed

*T*hinking Steve was having an affair with Rachel, Alice took off for New York and became the governess for handsome journalist Eliot Carrington's ailing young son. Eliot's estranged wife, Iris, was insanely jealous, but although they were extremely fond of each other, Alice and Eliot were never lovers.

more serious about Alice than about any other woman with whom he had been involved. She traced Alice to Bay City and sent Louise, under the assumed name of Dorothy Shaw, to investigate. Louise showed Gil a picture of "Alice Talbot," which Ada promptly recognized. When Steve told the mysterious woman that Alice had left him, Louise was certain Alice was a threat to Iris. Louise didn't realize that Alice and Eliot were not yet lovers—they were taking it one step at a time.

When Louise returned to New York, she discovered that Alice, Eliot, and Dennis were planning a trip to St. Croix. Subsequently, Iris came to Bay City to reveal Alice's plans to Steve and Rachel. Without telling Steve what she knew, Rachel talked him into taking her to St. Croix. There, the four star-crossed lovers ran into one another. Steve asked Alice why she had left him, but she refused to answer. Later she told Rachel that once she was back in the States she would grant Steve a divorce. It was then that Steve told Jamie they were father and son.

It was thanks to Dennis that Alice finally returned home. When Dennis's condition worsened, Alice convinced Russ to treat the boy at his new cardiology unit. This development brought the Carringtons and Louise to Bay City—along with Iris's influential father, millionaire publishing magnate Mackenzie ("Mac") Cory.

A newspaper publisher known in New York's café society circles, the dashing Mac Cory had lost his wife, Eugenia, when Iris was very young. Since then he'd placed Iris in pricey European schools so he could concentrate on his affairs—business and otherwise—while Iris longed to have more of her daddy's attentions. Mac indulged her whims and made her feel as though she was the only permanent woman in his life. Usually fair-minded, Mac acted on Iris's behalf in ways that went against his grain. When Iris first fell in love with Eliot Carrington—then Mac's new protégé at his newspaper—she convinced Mac to sign him to a long-term contract as tight as Fort Knox.

With five years to go on his contract, Eliot convinced Mac he wanted out. Iris panicked, for this meant the end of her strangling grip on her

estranged husband. Considering Alice the enemy, Iris got chummy with another woman who had no use for Alice: Rachel! Always the social climber, Rachel did her research on the rich Corys and was wowed to find them in *Who's Who*.

Still, Rachel and Iris's alliance was uneasy. Iris knew that if Rachel snagged Steve, Alice would be more available to Eliot. And that is exactly what happened. Alice divorced Steve and revealed that she had found Rachel trying to seduce him. Dismayed that Alice had run away instead of confronting him, Steve decided he'd had enough. He hastily married Rachel on the terrace of the home he had built for Alice.

Rachel thought she was home free, but Iris had other plans for Steve. She was momentarily foiled when Eliot figured out that Louise was "Dorothy Shaw" and fired her for compromising his interest in Alice. Iris quickly hired Louise and let her in on her latest plot—to place Alice under surveillance. The two conspirators paid a slippery operator named Leonard Sykes to bug Eliot's new Bay City suite, as well as to spy on Alice using a variety of disguises. One day he was a bartender; the next, an architectural student. Iris's goal was to catch a conversation that proved Alice still loved Steve.

To Iris's delight, Rachel played right into her hands when Rachel found a baby bunting in Steve's attic and sent it to Alice. When Steve found out, he was outraged by his wife's cruelty. Then Gerald returned, once again jobless, and told Steve about his manipulative phone message to Alice, which was the catalyst that had sent her packing to New York. Gerald hoped Steve would be so grateful he would give him a cushy job. Instead Steve ordered him out and arranged to see Alice at Eliot's suite. As Sykes's trusty tape rolled, Alice and Steve swore their mutual love and made plans to reunite.

While Rachel was unaware that Steve was about to ask her for a divorce, her mother, Ada, celebrated her marriage to Gil McGowan. Gil's elder son, Burt, was unable to attend the wedding, but his younger son, Tim, showed up and decided to settle in Bay

City. Gil and Tim hadn't spoken for several years—Gil was stubborn and Tim was a cocky kid. Tim had since become a fine lawyer and made Gil proud, although Gil was worried about his obsession with success. John was impressed with Tim's talents and hired him to help with Steve's account. But John caught on to Tim's coldly ambitious streak and soon dismissed him.

Tim immediately set his sights on Janice Frame, a fellow street fighter with big dreams. But she was happily seducing Robert Delaney, who was frustrated that Lenore was afraid to commit to him. Lenore and Janice also clashed over Steve's love life—Lenore wanted to see him back with Alice, while Janice favored Rachel.

None of them knew that Iris was pulling the strings. Claiming that the tape of Alice and Steve accidentally fell into her hands, Iris played it for Rachel, who in turn played it for Alice. Rachel also told Janice about the tape. Meanwhile, Eliot discovered his suite was bugged and worked with Gil and Zack to find the culprit. The intrepid cops traced the equipment to Sykes, and trapped him with the help of Rachel and Eliot. The tapes proved Iris's guilt, so Eliot had Gil arrest her.

When Gil arrived at Iris's doorstep, she suffered a mental breakdown and began babbling incoherently. Eliot dropped the charges and placed her under the care of Dr. Kurt Landis, a prominent neurologist at the hospital. Iris recovered and granted Eliot a divorce before he went to Europe as a correspondent.

Iris also humbly forgave Alice, who was amused to find that Russ seemed quite drawn to the Cory heiress! Russ had seen Iris's vulnerability when Dennis was hospitalized, and knew there was more to this spoiled rich woman than readily met the eye. Russ encountered competition for Iris's affections from Kurt, until Mac told Iris that he knew Kurt's family—and his reputation as a slick, unfeeling cad.

Alice and Steve, meanwhile, were ecstatic now that they had acknowledged their love. Their one remaining obstacle was Rachel, who refused to grant Steve a divorce without a fight. She was determined that Jamie grow up with both a mother and a father. She called her uncle, Sam Lucas, back to Bay City to represent her. Sam's marriage to Lahoma had disintegrated in Somerset, and Lahoma had disappeared with their daughter, Susannah. John represented Steve, but assured Sam he bore him no ill will for representing his own niece. Around this time, Sam was quite surprised to welcome a second niece into the world when Ada and Gil had a "change-of-life" daughter, Nancy.

The divorce case heated up when Jamie caught Alice and Steve in an embrace. When he tearfully told Rachel, she slapped Alice with an alienation of affection suit. Janice finally caught on to Rachel's dark side and befriended Alice, to the point where they became roommates.

This development infuriated Mary, as did the return of her outspoken sister-in-law, Liz, to Bay City. Liz supported Alice and Steve's romance and would do anything to see them reunite at Rachel's expense. But to Mary's way of thinking, Steve and Rachel deserved each other and Alice was casting herself as the other woman. Now that Alice was rooming with Janice, Mary wrongly assumed that Janice was setting up an illicit rendezvous for Alice and Steve.

Steve had no time for back-street doings, as he was going full steam ahead with his plan to remarry Alice. He went to see Gerald in San Francisco and told John he had secured Gerald's promise to testify against Rachel in the divorce suit! John was suspicious that Gerald would compromise his own daughter, but brought Gerald in anyway as Steve's surprise witness. Gerald admitted to trapping Steve and maneuvering him away from Alice—but lied by saying that Rachel had been in on his plan from day one! Rachel erupted in the courtroom, screaming at the father who inexplicably turned on her after she thought they'd finally become a family. Gerald remained unmoved as Judge Roberts decided Rachel's fate. The judge killed Rachel's alienation suit against Alice and granted Steve the divorce.

But it wasn't celebration time. A suspicious John forced Gerald to admit that Steve had bought him a restaurant in exchange for his partly fictional testimony. When Steve refused to go before Judge Roberts with the truth, John did it for him. The judge thanked John for his candor, awarded Rachel custody of Jamie, and had Steve and Gerald arrested!

Before he was incarcerated, Steve remarried Alice on their terrace—only for a drunken John to arrive late and denounce Steve as a liar. Alice coldly told John she regretted that he was part of her family. Steve and Gerald were then sent to Berryville minimum security prison, where Gerald taunted Steve mercilessly. Finally Steve could take no more and beat up his slimy ex-father-in-law. As a result, Steve was transferred to a maximum security prison. Gerald recovered from his wounds and was released from prison, swearing off Rachel for good.

A schism was now rupturing the Matthews family. Steve vindictively dropped John as his lawyer and set Tim up in his own practice. This brought John's practice close to ruin, for he had been largely dependent on Steve's business for a long time. Mary admired John for putting his legal principles before his allegiance to Steve, but Pat denounced him as a self-righteous fool and banished him from their bedroom. Soon John moved to a hotel room, where he boozed and wallowed in self-pity.

One piece of good news, however, hit Bay City. Lenore realized she loved Robert Delaney, and the two were married.

Enter Vic Hastings, the handsome, hard-driving acting president of Frame Enterprises. Immediately Vic was engaged in a power struggle with Tim, who as corporate counsel secretly aimed to take over all of Steve's holdings. He found his opportunity when Alice became so withdrawn in Steve's absence that she began to lose her mind. Tim convinced Alice to sign over Steve's power of attorney to him, as well as a dubious stock transfer.

Liz became so alarmed about Alice's mental state that she moved in with her niece. Mary felt threatened by this move, knowing that her disapproval of Steve was already driving her and Alice further apart. One night Alice became so disoriented, she went out in her nightclothes looking for Steve. Having learned that Alice was mentally unbalanced, Rachel plagued her with a lie that Steve wanted her and Jamie to move back into the house. Alice became hysterical and was committed to Clareview Sanitarium in nearby Ogden, where she was put under the care of Clareview's chief psychiatrist, Dr. Richard Gavin, an old friend of the Corys.

Lenore and Vic began to suspect that Tim was robbing Alice and Steve blind. They worked long and hard to keep Steve's company running smoothly without Tim's interference, causing Robert to get increasingly fed up with Lenore for putting in only cameo appearances at home. Either she was working or getting enmeshed in Pat and Alice's marital problems—which had reached a fever pitch by this point.

John went back to Pat when she forgave him for turning Steve in. She even worked in his law office without a salary, for John's practice was suffering since Tim had stolen most of his clients. John's self-confidence reached its lowest point since his paralysis, and as a result he became impotent. Because of John's fragile state, Pat didn't dare tell him Alice was in a sanitarium. She knew he would hate himself for having contributed to Alice's emotional downfall.

It was Liz who told John the truth. She had no sympathy for John now that he was taking Rachel on as a client just to pay the bills. With the diplomacy of a pit bull, Liz accused John of selling Alice and Steve down the river for the sake of his prestigious legal career. John felt betrayed by Pat for keeping this from him, and he went back to the hotel—and the bottle.

While Liz was heartless to John, she saved the day for Steve's company. Liz found Tim's stock transfer papers among Alice's effects and presented them to Richard Gavin. He was then able to get Tim's power of attorney revoked, based on Alice's mental incompetence. Janice was teetering on the brink of marrying Tim, until she caught him embezzling Steve's money and transferring it to a Swiss bank account. Desperate, Tim tried to abscond to South America—but his own father, Gil, arrested him. Gil insisted on a high bail, but he was acting more as a father than a cop. He wanted to keep Tim from running and being killed as a fugitive. But Tim escaped anyway, leaving a brokenhearted Janice to drift away from Bay City.

It was now homecoming time for Alice and Steve—albeit separately. Steve was released from prison and returned to his house, where he let Liz continue to stay for a while. And to Mary's delight, Alice recovered and returned to her family home. But Richard suspected that Alice was harboring a secret fear, which kept her clinging to home and hearth rather than to her husband. That fear was confirmed in an examination by Russ's gynecologist friend Dave Gilchrist: Alice was unable to conceive a child and was avoiding Steve so he could find another woman who could bear him a child.

Jamie was so bewildered by these events that he ran away from home. Not surprisingly, it was Dennis who found him safe and sound. These two boys were form-

ing a bond based on common experience—they were children of divorce.

Ironically, Pat and John might have divorced had it not been for Rachel. She saw her disheveled ex-brother-in-law downtown and felt genuinely sorry for him. Like herself, John had suffered at Steve's hands. So Rachel took John under her wing, bringing him work from his office, where Sam was keeping things running. Pat and Sam were frustrated because Rachel kept her promise to John not to reveal his whereabouts. With Rachel's help, however, John stopped drinking and returned to both his marriage and his law practice.

Rachel wasn't so kind to Lenore and Robert's marriage. Lenore agreed to take Jamie on his visits to Steve so he wouldn't have to see Rachel. Robert was furious with Steve for

*I*ris's father, dashing millionaire publishing magnate Mackenzie ("Mac") Cory, came to Bay City to be with his grandson Dennis, who was being treated for a heart condition, and decided to make Bay City his permanent home.

monopolizing Lenore's time, between her work and Jamie. Rachel was also angry about the situation since Lenore was standing between her and Steve. Rachel began feeding Robert's unfounded suspicion that Steve and Lenore were more than friends. Robert was tired of Steve's prominence in his family and professional life, so he left Lenore and opened his own architectural office. His assistant was Carol Lamonte, the embodiment of blond ambition. Mac knew Carol through her mother, his New York society crony Therese Lamonte.

On Rachel's recommendation, Mac hired Robert to design a corporate complex for him, encompassing a large office building, a printing plant, and a warehouse. This was a major coup for Robert, and he finally got to the core of his issues with Steve. He was irrationally confusing Steve with another powerful man in his life—his late, unlamented father, Jasper Delaney. Robert apologized to Steve and engaged him to build Mac's complex. Lenore gave up her job and returned to Robert

Always the social climber, Rachel initially tried to ingratiate herself with Lenore Curtin, but Rachel wasn't pleased when Lenore acted as go-between on Jamie's visits with Steve.

happily. She was unaware that Vic was falling in love with her—but could not help noticing that Carol had more than architectural designs on Robert. Ironically, Vic dated Carol so he could forget Lenore!

Back at the hospital, Rachel "happened" to see Alice's medical folder in Dave Gilchrist's office and confronted Alice with her knowledge that she was unable to conceive. Rachel made no secret of her intention to pursue Steve once again. Alice thought she had lost Steve for good, but when Rachel told Steve that Alice was barren, he was more determined than ever to get Alice back.

As Bay City prepared to ring in 1975, Steve told Alice he could live without children, but not without her. They reconciled and enjoyed a second honeymoon in St. Croix. Not wanting to lose Alice's love, Mary forgave Steve and welcomed him back to the family. John and Steve made amends and agreed to resume their lawyer-client relationship, while Sam located Lahoma and Susannah in Oklahoma and left Bay City to be with them. Carol kept both Dave Gilchrist and Vic Hastings on the string while nursing more intense feelings for Robert. And Richard Gavin left Clareview to become chief of psychiatry at Bay

Rachel just "happened" to see Alice's medical records in Dr. David Gilchrist's office at Bay City General Hospital and learned that her arch rival Alice was unable to conceive.

City General Hospital. The most surprising turn of events was to involve Mac Cory and his deepening relationships with the people of Bay City. As Russ and Iris became more passionate, they were thrilled when Mac began to squire Liz Matthews around town. Liz had become more sympathetic over the years. She had learned from her mistakes with Bill and Susan and was genuinely sorry for the way she had treated Lenore during the Wayne Addison fiasco. To Liz, Mac was the dynamic, powerful individual Will Matthews might have become . . . and Iris, the worshipful debutante daughter Susan never was. Liz's family took to Mac immediately and hoped that a marriage proposal was in the offing.

But Liz was shocked to find that Mac was drawn to the grasping, greedy guttersnipe who had put a black mark on the Matthews family—Rachel! Now that Alice and Steve were reconciled, Rachel realized she didn't need Steve as a means to get what she wanted out of life. She shed her tacky ways and penetrated the Corys' social circle with a vengeance, becoming conversant about art and classical music. She didn't set out to win Mac as a romantic partner, but to her own surprise that is exactly what happened. Mac knew about Rachel's checkered history, from Liz as well as Rachel herself, but none of it mattered to him. In Rachel, he saw a strong-willed young woman with great potential.

Iris set out to rectify that situation. She had gone head to head with plenty of young babes Mac had toyed with, and won every time. Iris assured Liz that Rachel was just another in a line of Mac's "short-term situations," and that she would take care of Rachel in short order.

Rachel . . . Iris . . . Liz. These three iron-willed women were to be prominent in the life of Mackenzie Cory for the next several years—in ways no one could begin to imagine.

❦

1975

The best-laid plans of Liz and Iris were about to go astray. They were dealing with a new Rachel now—still audacious, but with a conscience she herself had never imagined. And it was all thanks to the love of Mac Cory. Here Rachel had finally snagged the wealthiest man in Bay City, only to finally attain what she truly craved: unconditional love and unquestioning acceptance.

Therefore, to the shock of everyone in town, Rachel and Mac announced their engagement.

The resulting reactions were mixed. Lenore and the Matthews family were convinced that Rachel was only after Mac's money; but to the annoyance of their wives, both Robert and John were perceptive enough to buy the "new" Rachel. Ada was guarded because Mac lived in a world far removed from hers or Rachel's, and she feared that the millionaire would tire of her daughter. But in due time, Ada came to adore this unlikely new son-in-law as much as she had loved Russ.

Of course, Iris was out for blood. When she failed to bribe Rachel out of her daddy's life, Iris hired a disinherited Long Island playboy named Philip Wainwright to seduce Rachel. Iris set up this "gentleman gigolo" in his own equestrian academy so he could give Rachel private riding lessons. But

Rachel violently repelled the first advance Philip made toward her.

Russ became engaged to Iris and was both jealous and puzzled about Philip's presence in her life. He was especially suspicious when Philip's sometime girlfriend, a gum-chewing honey named Clarice Hobson, arrived at Iris's doorstep. Russ knew Clarice wasn't Iris's speed and wondered if a game was afoot. Then Rachel and Mac were married quietly in New York, and Philip assumed the game was over.

It wasn't, as Iris told Philip in no uncertain terms. Under pressure from Iris, Philip continued to give Rachel riding lessons and flirt with her. One day, Philip flaunted his manhood to Rachel by challenging the older Mac to a game of polo. Mac characteristically accepted the challenge—and was thrown from his horse!

As Mac recovered from his injuries, an enraged and jealous Liz pinned Rachel against a wall at the hospital. Richard Gavin treated Liz for her near breakdown and tried to convince her to accept losing Mac to Rachel. But Liz began to feel she had no purpose in life. She became withdrawn and reclusive, much to the concern of Helen Moore, Lenore's mother, with whom she shared an apartment. Jim and Mary also felt sorry for Liz and included her in their trip to St. Croix. It was there that a sudden tragedy hit the Matthews family: Mary dropped dead of a massive coronary.

Alice was shattered by this loss, for she was especially close to her mother. Nonetheless, she and Steve were delighted by the arrival of Willis Frame, the younger brother Steve had long hoped to find. A complicated young man with a chip on his shoulder, Willis had drifted after serving in Vietnam. He formed a close friendship with Alice and became a big brother figure to Jamie, but his relationship with Steve was, at best, ambivalent. The more Willis played on Steve's guilt about leaving the family, the more consolation prizes Steve would shower on his brother—whether they be money, gifts, or credit card privileges.

But the biggest prize was a job at Frame Enterprises. At his brother's corporation, Willis learned the ins and outs of construction and architecture. He also got in touch with a hidden desire at the core of his being: Willis Frame wanted to be *Steven* Frame. When no one was looking, Willis would sit behind Steve's desk, which overlooked the rapidly changing Bay City skyline, and imagine himself master of all he surveyed. This dream he shared with Angie Perrini, a fellow employee whose family lived next door to Ada. Angie was a simple girl with simple wants, and cautioned Willis about being so obsessive in his ambitions. Still, she loved him and was thus headed for years of heartache.

It was when Steve planned an extended business trip to Australia that Willis came one step closer to his dream. Steve decided to cut Willis in as a junior partner. No sooner had Steve's plane left the ground than Willis was throwing his weight around at the company, treating the more experienced Vic Hastings as a subordinate.

On the home front, Alice returned to nursing and bonded with a new patient at the hospital. She was Sally Spencer, a ten-year-old girl injured in a car accident that killed her parents, Peter and Janet. Since the girl had no next of kin to claim her, Alice convinced Steve via long distance calls that they should adopt the girl once he returned to the States.

But for the second time in a year, Alice was to endure an unforeseen tragedy. Steve's plane went down in Australia, and he was presumed dead.

Rachel and Jamie would have been devastated by Steve's loss had it not been for Mac. Jamie and Dennis both idolized Mac, and Rachel was looking forward to living in the exquisite new home Mac had bought for her. It was the Clayton estate, a mansion that Rachel had fantasized about living in from the time she was a girl. Robert designed the extensive renovations to the home, Carol oversaw the project, and Willis was in charge of the construction.

This project afforded Carol an opportunity to put the moves on Robert. In keeping with her diabolical nature, Carol investigated the late Walter Curtin and tormented Lenore with anonymous phone calls about him. Lenore was haunted by nightmares about Walter and became irrational with fear that Wally would soon learn the truth about his late father. Finally Carol was able to seduce Robert, and Lenore saw her rival's nightclothes strewn around Robert's office. Disgusted with her life in Bay City, Lenore moved with Wally to Washington, D.C., and granted Robert a divorce. Soon after, Robert fired Carol and ordered her out of his life.

Rachel happily moved into her new mansion with Mac and Jamie, and on Ada's recommendation hired an efficient and caring housekeeper named Beatrice Gordon. Beatrice enlisted Gil's help in locating her daughter, Jennifer, whose disappearance had driven Beatrice to a nervous breakdown. All Gil could determine was that Jennifer had married a shady bigamist named Peter Sprague.

Meanwhile, Alice adopted Sally and introduced her to Beatrice in a chance encounter. Sally recognized Beatrice from a picture given to her by her mother, Janet Spencer. Gil was then able to determine that the late Peter and Janet Spencer were really Peter Sprague and Jennifer Gordon. Beatrice was Sally's grandmother! When Rachel convinced Beatrice to pursue Sally's custody, Liz and Iris snidely accused Rachel of using Beatrice as an instrument against Alice. To further complicate matters, Beatrice's son, Ray, arrived from San Diego and wanted Sally for himself and his wife, Olive. The stage was set for a three-way fight over Sally.

But to the relief of all concerned, Sally's loved ones reached an agreement. Ray backed off in his quest for his daughter because he and Olive were on the outs. Then Beatrice dropped her suit when Alice assured her she would always be a part of Sally's life. Alice was also happy to see Jim becoming close to Beatrice now that he had accepted Mary's death. But a lonely Liz was now hoping to replace Mary in the lives of Jim and his children, and realized she had strong feelings for the brother-in-law who had watched over her since Will's death. Seeing Beatrice as competition, Liz viciously accused Jim of "playing around with the hired help."

Iris tried to use Clarice Hobson's sometime boyfriend Philip Wainwright to break up Rachel and Mac. The plan failed, and Clarice went on to become close friends with Rachel and Mac.

*I*ris was equally condescending when her longtime maid, Louise, had an "adolescent" romance with the Corys' stable man, Rocky Olsen, and also befriended their chauffeur, Leonard Brooks. Iris wanted nothing to do with Rachel's staff, for she was certain she had finally effected the schism she intended for Rachel and Mac's marriage. Mac was now beginning to suspect that Rachel and Philip were having an affair, and talked of divorcing Rachel.

It was too much for Philip to bear. The "gentleman gigolo" discovered he had scruples after all, and revealed to Mac that Iris had hired him to seduce Rachel. Philip amicably parted with Clarice and moved to Arizona, where he found his true niche—teaching children to ride horses. Mac apologized to Rachel for distrusting her, hired Clarice as his receptionist, and told Iris she was disinherited. Russ bitterly broke off his engagement to Iris when he realized how twisted and destructive she was. Iris tried to kill herself with an overdose, but Dave Gilchrist saved her in time. Russ was then to turn to a woman far more honorable than Iris—but no less complicated.

Attorney Barbara Weaver was a model of crisp professionalism at John Randolph's law firm. It was all to masquerade a personal life that was a shambles. A mother who died when she was very young, a strict, distant father, a married man who dallied with her but refused to leave his wife—such were the painful circumstances in Barbara's life. Since her arrival in Bay City, she'd had glimmers of relationships with Vic, Dave, Robert, and Russ. All were dead ends. John was concerned for his associate, for he respected Barbara as a lawyer and considered her a good friend. Yet Barbara was placed in an awkward position when privy to a secret that John's family was keeping from him.

Now that the Randolph twins were teenagers, John was concerned that Pat was too strict with Marianne. In truth, Pat wanted to protect her daughter from making the mistakes that she herself had made. But the ultimate irony came in the form of Chris Pierson, a Bay State student who worked for Willis and tutored Marianne over the summer. Pat was happy when Marianne dated this responsible young man, but John rightly suspected that Chris was a selfish cad like the late, unlamented Tom Baxter. And just as Pat had done with Tom, Marianne made love to Chris in hopes that he would marry her. Instead he made her pregnant and skipped town.

In a twist of fate, Rachel's housekeeper, Beatrice, turned out to be Alice's adopted daughter's grandmother. When Beatrice's son, Ray, came to town, Sally's custody was at stake.

Marianne tearfully confided this to her mother, who was understanding and confided her own tragedy at Tom Baxter's hands. But they kept the pregnancy from John because he and Marianne had a special closeness that Marianne was afraid to destroy. Marianne told Pat, Michael, and Dave Gilchrist that she was considering abortion, but Pat begged her to give the child up for adoption instead. She didn't want that horrible chapter in her history to repeat itself in Marianne's life.

John suspected Pat was keeping something from him, and was hurt by her obvious secrecy. Thus he began spending more time with Barbara professionally and socially—and Liz was the first to notice. The omnipresent Liz was also on hand to overhear Marianne tell Barbara that she'd had an abortion in New York!

One of the reasons John distrusted Chris was that he worked for Willis. John was chagrined that Willis was positioning himself to take over Frame Enterprises and insinuating himself into Alice's and Sally's lives. To get John out of the picture, Carol urged Willis to dump him for her high-powered lawyer pal Scott Bradley. But Willis shrewdly retained John as counsel to score points with Alice.

*M*arianne Randolph, seen here with Jamie Frame, was a handful for her mother, Pat, who tried to shield her daughter from the mistakes she had made in her youth.

Willis was now torn between three women: He loved Angie, he wanted Alice for the money and power she could give him, and he was romping in the sack with fellow schemer Carol Lamonte! Angie was already disgusted by Willis's "unscrupulous tycoon" act, but when she caught him with Carol, that was the last straw. Carol tried to throw Scott in Angie's direction, but Angie instead dated Willis's sympathetic roommate, architect Neil Johnson.

Carol and Willis's gamesmanship knew no bounds. They sabotaged Robert's work when he became an embittered, hard-drinking wreck. In time Angie discovered that Carol had botched Robert's plans for the Steven Frame Memorial Library, which Alice was having built in Chadwell. Robert took up with Clarice and began living with her, but treated her as a mere convenience. Then Iris set her sights on the handsome architect, and decided to win him away from Clarice—whom she considered to be at the bottom of the barrel.

Not that Iris's New York dilettante friends were any bargain. Nosy Sybil Harak, nympho Loretta Simpson, and indolent Tic de Cosgrove blew in and out of Bay City as Ada looked on in disgust.

While Ada hated to see Iris's phony friends in town, Liz shook her head at the arrival of more Frame family members in Bay City. Though Liz had liked Steve and admired his ambition, she looked upon his siblings as pond scum who had no business mixing with her family. Liz gasped, therefore, when Russ found an unlikely soul mate in Willis's older sister Sharlene. Newly widowed by Floyd Watts, Sharlene made up in sweet simplicity what she lacked in poise and self-esteem.

As the year drew to a close, Mac changed his mind about disinheriting Iris. He warned her, however, that he would do so if she did anything else to hurt Rachel. Iris promised to be a good girl . . . until she found out that Rachel and Mac were expecting a child of their own!

1976

This was a time of tragedy for Rachel, new romance for Alice, gut-wrenching hurt for Russ, and a marital crisis for Pat.

Liz blabbed to John that Marianne had had an abortion, but lied in saying that Barbara was responsible for arranging it. It was Liz's intention to turn John away from Barbara, but the opposite happened. Proud and hurt, John accused Pat of placing the twins' welfare before his, and moved out to take up with Barbara. John even talked marriage to her, but Barbara declined, maintaining that marriage and career didn't mix. She insisted that John work things out with Pat one way or another before going any further in their relationship.

As Barbara predicted, John wanted his family back. He and Marianne were closer than ever once she apologized for keeping her life a secret from him, and she hoped her parents would reconcile. But Michael was angry with his father, and Pat found she had a life of her own for the first time. She allowed John to return to their home, but she moved into her own apartment, where she embarked on a new relationship with Dave. Always the righteous lawyer, John threatened to name Dave in an alienation of affection suit unless Pat returned to him.

Pat also took a job at Cory Publishing, where Mac was quick to promote her. As they began working more closely together, Pat and Mac formed a bond that Rachel and Liz mistook for a simmering attraction. It was, in fact, a deep and abiding male-female friendship, which neither Pat nor Mac had previously known. The two would remain confidants for many years to come.

Mac had plenty to confide, for Iris was at it again. She overheard Clarice tell Dave she was pregnant by Robert, so Iris talked Robert into a hasty marriage before he could discover he was to be a father. Iris knew that he was scarred by the loss of his child, plus he missed his stepson, Wally; a child was certain to sway Robert toward Clarice. Showing a revulsion she reserved for the lowest of the low, Iris told Clarice she would take her child if she ever told Robert the truth.

As if her own life weren't complicated enough, Iris continued to work her black magic on her father's marriage. She tried unsuccessfully to push Tracy DeWitt, Mac's rich young ex-fiancée, back in his direction—even though she herself had broken them up back in New York! Then hope arrived in the form of art professor Ken Palmer, whom Mac hired to teach Rachel sculpting. Iris was quick to pick up on Ken's attraction to Rachel.

Tragically, she could not pick up on Rachel's urgent need for help when she called Iris looking for Mac. Rachel was in the midst of a miscarriage, but Iris rudely cut her off in midsentence. Rachel lost the baby, and Mac told Iris she was no longer his daughter.

This sent Iris off the deep end. She put a reluctant Louise and Rocky up to stealing a bust Rachel had sculpted of Mac. Rocky admitted his misdeed to Rachel, and when she demanded that Iris return the bust, Iris threatened to destroy it. It was her only lingering vestige of Mac, and if she couldn't have it, no one would.

No one did. Rachel and Mac learned that Clarice was expecting Robert's child, and told him the news. Clarice confirmed to Robert that it was true and told him of Iris's machinations. His marriage now a lie, an enraged Robert destroyed the bust as well as Iris's portrait. Iris came home to find her living room looking like Atlanta in the final days of the Civil War. She told Louise with a shudder, "It's almost as if I'd been assaulted myself."

To right the wrongs in his life, Robert divorced Iris and offered to marry Clarice. Yet Clarice had a fortitude that belied her "dumb blond" appearance and gently told Robert she was ready to go it alone. Sometime later, Clarice gave birth to a boy, whom she named Cory in loving tribute to Mac. Ada and Gil McGowan joined Mac and Rachel in giving Clarice abundant support.

❧

Back at Frame Enterprises, Willis was not happy to see Alice take a hands-on interest in the company. He worked on Beatrice to convince Alice to spend more time at home with Sally so he could go about his power plays. Sharlene was on to her brother, but Willis had just the ammunition to shut her up. During his stint as a sailor, Willis and his cohorts had come upon a brothel where he saw Sharlene turning tricks! When Russ and Sharlene married, Willis threatened to tell Russ that his wife was a former prostitute.

Willis played yet another angle. Angry that Alice had hired Ray to oversee the Steven Frame Memorial Library project, Willis swiftly dispatched Ray's estranged wife, Olive, to Bay City. A greedy but pathetic viper

When Iris's son Dennis became infatuated with Willis's conniving niece, Molly Ordway, Iris was outraged. However Molly was only leading young Dennis on; her sights were really set on Michael Randolph.

obsessed with security, Olive had looked upon Ray as a loser when they lived in California, but his lucrative new job made him more attractive in her eyes. With a handsome stipend from Willis, Olive arrived with threats to cut Ray off from their sons unless he returned to her.

When Sharlene discovered that Willis and Olive were in cahoots, Willis sank to new depths in dealing with his sister. He brought his old sailor buddies to Bay City, looking on as they tried to initiate a group pleasure session with Sharlene! Russ walked in on the scene and literally beat Willis into a state of remorse over what he had done. Humiliated beyond measure, Sharlene admitted her past to Russ and downed a bottle of pills. Russ saved her and tried very hard to accept her past.

Willis was to endure another defeat. Alice and Ray caught him bribing Olive, causing Alice to shift much of Willis's corporate power to Ray. But Angie continued to believe in Willis, especially when he saved Dennis and Jamie during a storm in the middle of a lake. When Dennis's heart problem flared as a result, Mac saw how distraught Iris was and began to soften toward her.

Clarice Hobson didn't have much luck with men until she met Burt McGowan, son of Ada's late husband, Gil. Good friend Rachel Cory was in attendance at the nuptials.

Once Dennis recovered, he became infatuated with a teenager a few years older than himself. It was Molly Ordway, Willis and Sharlene's conniving niece. Her parents, Emma and Burt, were unable to "keep her down on the farm." Alice let her stay so she could watch Sally, but Beatrice was angry to discover that Molly was more concerned about meeting boys. While Molly led Dennis on, she set her sights on the older Michael Randolph.

Iris knew what Molly was made of and bribed her to stop seeing Dennis, but Dennis found out and refused to knuckle under to his mother's schemes. As it turned out, Iris could have saved her money. She found Michael and Molly *in flagrante* and told Liz! To no one's surprise, neither society matron wanted Molly in her family. They also agreed that, one way or another, Beatrice must be removed from Jim's life.

At this time, Bay City experienced several comings and goings. Robert Delaney, Helen Moore, Vic Hastings, and Neil Johnson all relocated to Washington, D.C. Barbara Weaver hung her attorney's shingle in another town, leaving John to hire a cunning young associate named Jeff Stone. While Scott Bradley represented John in his messy divorce, Pat hired Iris's New York friend and attorney, Keith Morrison. And at the Cory complex, Mac was surprised by the arrival of Gwen Parrish, daughter of wealthy New York socialite Leueen Parrish. Gwen was a talented, brassy architect who would spice up the lives of many Bay City residents.

❦

1977

Ada McGowan was a rock to her family and friends, but a tragedy forced her to lean on her loved ones. Gil found his younger son, Tim, in Bolivia, where the two were killed in a mine explosion. With the love of Rachel, the support of Jim and Clarice, and the professional help of Richard Gavin, Ada came to accept the death of her third husband.

It was Burt McGowan who delivered the horrible

*R*achel is seen here sculpting a bust of Mac that Iris would later steal. An old-fashioned man at heart, Mac was not happy when his independent wife parlayed her sculpting talents into a career.

Lovers and Friends
For Richer For Poorer

When Rachel spent time in nearby Point Claire, she met fellow artist Amy Gifford Cushing. Amy married Austin Cushing, a fun-loving rich boy, whose mother, Edith, forced him to run the family business after the death of his father, Richard Cushing.

Although it was hard to imagine Alice with anyone but her beloved Steve, she agreed to marry Ray Gordon. Sally was overjoyed, but Alice soon realized that the marriage was a mistake.

news. Gil's elder son was an electrical engineer who, unlike his materialistic brother, had an honest work ethic and simple values. Burt took a job at the Cory complex and immediately gravitated to Clarice, who was living with Ada while Cory was an infant. But Burt had competition in Jeff Stone, who panted at the opportunity to control the generous trust fund Mac set up for his little namesake.

Jeff found a fellow schemer in his new legal assistant, Olive Gordon. Olive won a huge divorce settlement from Ray, thanks to a $50,000 loan from Alice, and set her sights on the successful but vulnerable John! A frantic Olive pressured Jeff to do everything possible to facilitate John's divorce, but when he was unable to do so, she revealed his plot to marry Clarice. John fired Jeff on the spot, and the slimy young barrister moved to New York to make the big time. Burt married Clarice and convinced her to return Mac's trust fund money.

After a long marriage that had withstood many trying circumstances, Pat and John's divorce became final. John fell for Olive's childlike charms and married her, and Dave was quick to pick up on Pat's obvious disappointment. Convinced his relationship with Pat was going nowhere, Dave broke off with her. He then found hope for a new romance when a serious schism occurred in the Cory marriage.

The unthinkable now happened. For all Mac's worldliness and intelligence, he was not accustomed to independent women. He fumed when Rachel parlayed her sculpting lessons into a career under her maiden name, Rachel Davis. Rachel aggravated the situation by spending practically every waking hour in her studio. Thus Mac moved to Bayview Towers, where he had an affair with his new neighbor, Gwen! Ken Palmer stepped up his pursuit of Rachel, but she instead gave up her career and resolved to fight Gwen

for her husband. Ken accepted a post at a college out of town, and a lonely Dave stepped in to try and woo Rachel.

Since she was spending more time at home, Rachel reluctantly dismissed Beatrice to cut down on the household expenses. This proved to be a crisis for Beatrice, who had a history of emotional instability. She impulsively kidnapped Sally, but the girl had the sense to phone Alice with her whereabouts. Ashamed of what she had done, Beatrice bade Jim farewell and moved to California, where she took care of Ray and Olive's two sons.

Olive was not the only conniving woman to enter the Randolph family. When Burt Ordway prepared to strong-arm his errant daughter, Molly, back to Chadwell, Molly and Michael ran away to nearby Ogden where they were married! When the newlyweds returned, Michael took menial jobs to put himself through school. He was incredulous to discover that Olive had hired Evan Webster, a slick architect, to design a fancy new house for herself and John. Soon Olive and Evan were poring over the blueprints in bed.

Suspecting that Olive was blowing John's money, Michael and Molly stole and copied Evan's house plans. Their suspicions were correct—it was a veritable palace. Olive caught Molly returning the blueprints and told John, who was far from grateful for his son and daughter-in-law's concern. John and Michael were bitterly at odds over one another's hasty marriages.

Alice and Ray were relieved to have Olive out of the picture, and to Sally's joy they were married. But Alice couldn't shake the thought that Steve, the one great love of her life, was still alive. She was also caught in the middle of a power struggle between Ray and Willis at Frame Enterprises. While Willis had acquired some business acumen, Ray proved to be a rank amateur who covered his insecurity with a massive ego. He even changed the company name to Gordon Enterprises!

Willis hated to see this "pushy nobody" running his brother's business into the ground. Yet he shrewdly sat back and let Ray hang himself so he could move in and play hero to Alice. Just as Willis hoped, Alice developed feelings for him and admitted her marriage to Ray was a mistake. To clear the way for Alice, Willis terminated his affair with Carol, while Angie waited in the wings and hoped Willis would ultimately follow his heart.

Russ, meanwhile, had followed his heart for the last time in his life. Sharlene admitted to him that while she was a prostitute, she had undergone a botched operation for a sexually transmitted disease that had rendered her sterile. Unable to deal with his wife's tortured past, Russ began to drink heavily and even physically abuse Sharlene. Alice took Sharlene in, while Liz took advantage of Russ's inebriated state to open up her drunken nephew like a clam, extracting the entire story of Sharlene's hooker days.

Liz now showed a side to her persona that had been dormant since the zenith of her treachery toward Missy. She told Sharlene that if she didn't leave Russ, she would expose her for the garbage that she was. Sharlene felt completely alone. Her husband hated her to the point of violence. Desperately in need of male approval, Sharlene confided everything to Jim. He was completely understanding and confronted Liz in a rage, lambasting her for her interference and her cruelty. But Liz won the round—Sharlene divorced Russ and left Bay City. Russ eventually stopped drinking and pulled his life back together.

With another Frame safely out of town, Liz and Iris continued to celebrate the increasing penetration of New York society into Bay City. Therese Lamonte, Carol's mother, visited her old friend Mac. Carol had little use for the quirky woman until it became evident that her days were numbered. As Therese sat alone on the Cory terrace listening to birds singing around her, she quietly sang to herself a chorus of "Bye, Bye Blackbird." It was her swan song. Therese died peacefully amid this bucolic scene, and a humbled Carol left town.

The next arrivals from the Big Apple were an engaged couple. Dave's first cousin Corinne Seton was slated to marry Brian Bancroft, the suave law partner of Iris's attorney, Keith Morrison. Keith had feelings for Iris but went back to New York when he found her too much to handle. Brian, on the other hand, found Iris to be a delicious challenge. He had a preference for naughty women, and decided that Corinne was too sedate for his taste. Brian decided to remain in town and become Mac's corporate counsel. Soon he was joined by his playboy son, Ted.

A romantic rondelay was now to ensue. Gwen had the grace to warn Rachel that Iris was spreading false rumors of an affair between Rachel and Dave. Gwen ended her affair with Mac and dated Dave, but when he couldn't get Rachel out of his system, he left Bay City. Iris and Gwen began having cat fights over Brian, while Liz threw Corinne in Russ's direction. But Molly hated Russ for his treatment of Sharlene, and sabotaged Russ and Corinne's dates until Corinne went back to New York. Molly began flirting with Ted behind Michael's back, but Ted instead turned to Michael's sister, Marianne, and took her on an extended trip to Europe.

❦

*R*achel and Mac reconciled amid all of this chaos, but were headed for a dark new chapter in their lives. Their new Swedish housekeeper, Helga Lindemann, and her innocent daughter, Regine, seemed strangely intimidated by their "cousin," Sven Pedersen. Louise overheard Sven persuade Helga to take kickbacks from suppliers. To protect the Corys' integrity, Louise shared this information with the stable man, Rocky Olsen, who vowed to trap Sven. But Sven taped the conversation and let Rocky know he was on to him. To protect their friend from Sven, Jamie and Dennis shielded Rocky in their treehouse, sneaking him food and drinks.

While Rocky remained at large, Sven turned his attention to playing Mac like a puppet. Iris set Mac up to believe that Rachel was carrying on with Quentin Ames, who operated a gallery financed by Iris's countess friend, Elena de Poulignac. Mac confided to Pat that he was sterile, but he was too humiliated to tell Rachel. Rachel found out and was hurt that Mac

had told Pat first, so the Corys once again separated.

This time it was Mac who remained at the house, leaving himself perfectly positioned for Sven's evil plots. One night Mac became so depressed that he drank himself to sleep. Sven then drugged Regine, threw her shoes off, and placed her in bed beside Mac! When Mac woke up, Sven led him to believe he'd had a wild night with Regine. Sven also manipulated Regine into breaking off with her new boyfriend, Cliff Tanner, who was Willis's assistant.

But all bets were off when Iris stepped in. Noticing that Mac was acting disoriented, she paid Sven to spy on her father and keep him sequestered from Rachel. In so doing, Iris happened upon Rocky in the treehouse.

Baffled by Mac's behavior, Rachel consulted attorney Greg Barnard about a divorce. Greg's sister, Joan, was John's longtime receptionist; therefore she felt comfortable sharing with Pat her distrust of Olive. But it was Molly who believed she had the goods on Olive—she walked in on one of Olive and Evan's trysts!

❦

1978

Dangerous times lay ahead for the Corys and the Randolphs, while Iris's life was about to take a sudden and dramatic turn.

Dennis and Jamie were frightened out of their wits when they found Rocky's remains under the floorboards of their treehouse. Sven, of course, had done him in. Iris felt responsible for having unintentionally revealed Rocky's whereabouts, especially when Regine told her that Sven was threatening both Helga and herself. Frightened for Mac, Iris admitted to Rachel that she had bribed Sven to keep her and Mac apart. To sort out her future, Rachel spent time in nearby Point Claire with Austin and Amy Cushing, a young couple she had met in artistic circles.

Sven was to make a discovery that made him feel more powerful than ever: Regine was pregnant! Cliff was the father, but Sven made Regine withhold this fact so that he could convince Mac he had done the deed. Once again Sven drugged Regine to make it appear that she was attempting suicide, and once again Mac was Pavlov's dog. He planned to divorce Rachel so he could do the responsible thing and marry Regine. Despondent over losing Regine, Cliff let himself be seduced by his new gal Friday—Molly! Michael duly discovered their fling and obtained a divorce from Molly, who blew out of town.

Eventually Rachel came home and got to the truth about Sven. Helga was his former lover, and Regine was their daughter. Things got violent when Rachel confronted the diabolical butler. His treachery now revealed, Sven kidnapped Rachel. Happily Mac was able to rescue her, and Sven was arrested for his crimes. Having lived through this horrific ordeal, Mac and Rachel reconciled. They hosted a beautiful wedding for Cliff and Regine, after which the newlyweds went back to Sweden with Helga.

Ray also beat a hasty retreat after he nearly spent Gordon Enterprises into oblivion. As per his plan, Willis charged in on the proverbial white horse and salvaged Frame Enterprises for Alice. Yet as Alice and Willis tried to get romantic, no sparks flew. Willis sensed he was merely a substitute for his late brother Steve, and Alice knew that Willis was still in love with Angie.

The problem was, Willis was nowhere near as decisive in his love life as he was at a construction site. While he remained in emotional paralysis, his older brother Vince Frame arrived and began keeping company with Angie. Vince was a stable, easygoing, uncomplicated sort—everything Willis was not. This development pleased Ada and her next-door neighbor, Angie's widowed mother, Rose Perrini. Jim was also happy, for he was a father figure to Angie now that she was his office manager. Usually not one to interfere, Jim sternly upbraided Willis for keeping Alice and Angie on a string.

Vince began operating a fix-it shop in Ada's detached garage with a new partner—Charlie Hob-son, Clarice's long-estranged father. Clarice forgave Charlie for having left the family years ago, and Ada liked him enough to put him up at her home. Jim found himself becoming jealous of this newcomer, for he was hoping for more than friendship with Ada now that Beatrice had left town. But Liz still had designs on her brother-in-law, and tried to make him believe that Ada and Charlie were cohabiting in a carnal sense! As in days of old, Ada gave Liz a verbal knockout punch as only Ada could deliver it.

Clarice had just begun to bond with Charlie when Burt learned of a great job opportunity in Japan. Burt was a traditional husband who expected his wife to follow him wherever he went. But once again, Clarice quietly stood firm. As much as she appreciated Burt for raising Cory, she was not about to lose her father again. Burt dejectedly moved to Japan alone, while Clarice and Rachel encouraged Ada and Charlie to get closer. Ironically, Liz was beginning to look beyond Charlie's station in life and saw him for the warm, plainspoken human being he was.

Evan Webster knew nothing of warmth. He jubilantly told Olive that he was hiring seedy private eye Claude Kelly to kill John, then planned to abscond with Olive and the Randolph bucks! Olive was horrified, so Evan assured her he wouldn't harm John. Yet he and Claude continued with their plan behind her back. When Evan tried to maneuver John in front of Claude's speeding car, John grew suspicious. Evan proved to be a novice in the murder department and shakily pulled a gun on John. They struggled over the weapon and Evan was shot dead at close range.

Just at that moment, Olive came on the scene and screamed at John, "You have killed the only man I've ever loved!" The police arrested John, but they placed him under psychiatric observation rather than taking him to prison. The horrific ordeal was so devastating to John, he became catatonic.

Pat had a new sense of self now that she was acting editor-in-chief at Cory Publishing. Although she

SOMERSET

Somerset was the first (and longest) of several spin-offs. It was another soap opera, which ran for six years, interchanging its characters with *Another World*.

Somerset was, in essence, a small town run by a large company. More to the point, it was run by the president of that company.

Jasper Delaney employed a sizeable share of Somerset's population at his nationally known food company, Delaney Brands. Whomever he didn't employ, the blustering, bellicose patriarch tried to control in other ways—with varying degrees of success. Naturally, Jasper's troubled family felt the brunt of his tyranny. His fragile eldest daughter, Laura, had a happy marriage to Rex Cooper, Jasper's calm and steady right-hand man. Rex was aware that Laura had conceived their teenage son, Tony Cooper, through a wild character named Harry Wilson, whom Jasper had bribed out of town years before.

Jasper also had two sons who were markedly different from each other. Peter, his youngest, was a college professor who resisted Jasper's attempts to recruit him at Delaney Brands, while Robert glumly stuck it out at the family salt mines, even though he knew his true calling was architecture. Robert's glamorous, social-climbing wife, the former India Bishop, made sure Robert stayed put at Delaney Brands. To ease his self-loathing, Robert took up with the quietly sensuous Jessica Buchanan, a lounge singer at Gerald Davis's Riverboat restaurant.

While India perpetuated the superficial emptiness of the Delaneys, her unpretentious elder sister, Ellen, had a picture-perfect family life. Ellen was married to Ben Grant, Rex Cooper's closest friend and Rafe Carter's junior law partner. The Grants had fraternal teenage twins, David and Jill, of whom they had every reason to be proud. Jill had a mad crush on Tony Cooper, but had to fight the grasping Pammy Davis for his attentions. Pammy had her eyes on the Delaney money that Tony was certain to inherit. She also liked being the apple of her daddy Gerald's eye, now that he was divorced from his disciplinarian mother, Marsha.

Such were the new surroundings of Missy Matthews, her son, Ricky, and their friends Sam and Lahoma Lucas. Missy tried to adjust, enjoying

the attentions of both Peter Delaney and Stan Kurtz, the affable young doctor who treated the Delaneys. But the ghost of Bill Matthews kept getting in the way of Missy's budding romances, so she moved with Ricky to Arizona.

Sam would also have done well to leave, for another reason. A slick operator named Ike Harding came to Somerset and opened a secret casino at the Riverboat. Not only did he charm Marsha into marrying him—he got Sam hooked on gambling.

These interrelated situations all reached an apex when Jasper Delaney was found murdered in an anteroom next to his office. Robert was arrested and stood trial for the crime, for he and Jasper had almost come to blows over his decision to leave India for Jessica. But there turned out to be not one, but two real killers. Laura had had enough of her father's running her life and shot him in a hysterical confrontation; then an unlikely culprit finished the job by smothering Jasper to death. This was none other than Ike Harding, who was in truth Harry Wilson! After telling a shocked Tony they were father and son, Ike was captured and killed by the police. Then, in a tragic turn of events, a desperate Laura shot herself to death with the same German Luger she had used against her toxic father.

With Jasper and Laura gone, a bereaved Rex threw himself into his expanded duties as the new president of Delaney Brands. The newly married Robert and Jessica left town, as did the Lucases and the Davises. India was wooed into a sham of a marriage by a con artist named Chuck Hillman. Soon India caught on to the *Gaslight* routine Chuck was pulling on her, and left town. Jill realized that she and Tony were meant only to be friends, and married a tormented Vietnam veteran named Mitch Farmer.

Tony, in turn, married earthy Ginger Kurtz, the daughter of Stan's older brother, Leo. Stan was embarrassed that Leo had financed his medical education with monies gained from criminal activities. Despite his claims of going straight, Leo was part of a triumvirate of crooks infiltrating Delaney Brands. His partners were Crystal Ames, a stunning blond who wanted to stop playing gun moll and lead a normal life; and Virgil Paris, an oily sleazeball who would savagely rape Ginger.

At the same time, Stan found himself playing investigator in a bizarre scenario. His latest patient, Andrea Moore, was a beautiful and spunky young woman from a wealthy family in nearby Fort Perry. David Grant immediately became smitten with Andrea—and suspicious of her creepy family.

Julian Cannell owned The Somerset Register, a tough crime-fighting newspaper. With him is ace reporter Carrie Wheeler, who lost her father and her lover to the mob.

Stan and David soon proved that Andrea's twisted stepsister, Zoe Cannell, was poisoning her. Zoe knew that her embittered husband, former piano prodigy Julian Cannell, had feelings for Andrea. Meanwhile David and Andrea broke up because of his chauvinistic attitude. After Zoe was caught, Julian took up with Crystal, but the mob got to her in short order.

Julian ultimately found purpose in his life when he took over *The Somerset Register*, the town's fledgling newspaper, and turned it into a potent force against the frequent crime in Somerset. One woman who quickly took notice of the idealistic new journalist was Eve Lawrence, a widow who was briefly engaged to India and Ellen's much-older father, Judge Brad Bishop. A strong woman of patrician beauty, Eve concealed the fact that her teenage daughter, Heather, had been fathered by an old flame, Mark Mercer. Naturally Eve shuddered as Mark took a position at Delaney Brands—especially when Mark's son, Greg, fell for Heather! Ultimately the truth came out, and Greg briefly turned to a newly widowed Jill.

Eve and Julian tried to make a go of romance, but Julian let himself be seduced into marriage by his pathetically insecure boss, Kate Thornton. Kate had a brief affair with attorney Tom Conway, who ended up murdered by a crime syndicate to which he was in debt. Kate had a breakdown and was institutionalized, and Julian took up with the sexy, aggressive Vicki Paisley. Not so coincidentally, Vicki's brother, department store head Ned Paisley, married Eve and whisked her around the world. Heather found happiness with Dr. Jerry Kane after his deranged ex-wife, Dorothy Conrad, tried to kill him.

The town mourned when beloved attorney Ben Grant died of a heart attack, leaving Ellen briefly vulnerable to the charms of slick Dale Robinson, a man young enough to be her son. David married a Polynesian woman, while Jill took up with an older lawyer named Jack Wheeler. Jack's estranged daughter, Carrie, was a crackerjack journalist at the *Register* alongside Greg. They romanced, but Carrie soon lost both Greg and her father, Jack, to mob bullets. Carrie found comfort sometime after with hard-bitten reporter Steve Slade.

Back at Delaney Brands, Rex Cooper overcame a bout with paralysis and developed feelings for Dr. Terri Martin, but instead, she married his doctor pal Stan Kurtz. Rex was also disappointed that Tony left Delaney Brands for the world of advertising, but eventually he let Tony go his own way after he caught himself taking on Jasper Delaney's authoritarian tone with his son.

Jasper, the Unfriendly Ghost, died hard indeed.

was not interested in going back to John, she stood by him during this difficult time. So did Michael and Marianne, now that Marianne was back from her European jaunt and getting over Ted. Marianne became attracted to Greg Barnard, who became John's law partner and handled his defense. Greg got Olive to admit her knowledge of Evan's scheme with Claude Kelly, and as a result John was exonerated by a grand jury.

❧

*I*t was at this time that Susan Shearer returned to Bay City. Liz was thrilled that Susan had become a successful psychiatrist in Boston, but was sad to learn that she was separated from her husband, Dan. Susan helped John recover his senses and come to grips with what Olive had done to him. But the physician was also trying to heal herself. Susan was finally owning up to having held back with Dan in bed because she was ashamed of her incestuous feelings for her late brother, Bill!

Russ was also able to exorcise his demons and became romantically linked with Gwen. Of course, Liz found Gwen to be exceedingly nervy and tried unsuccessfully to match Russ with the quietly refined Countess Elena de Poulignac. Once Russ and Gwen became engaged, Elena backed off. But to Gwen's horror, her overbearing mother, Leueen, moved in with her and became obsessed with finding out about Russ and Sharlene's marriage. Gwen began to doubt that Russ would be a loving or stable husband, so the two called off their engagement. Russ moved to Texas to pursue new opportunities in cardiac medicine.

Iris found a new opportunity for happiness when she finally married Brian Bancroft. As usual, she blew it—not only with her new husband, but with her longtime servant and mother confessor, Louise.

Iris was appalled when Dennis took up with Eileen Simpson, a sweet Catholic girl who lived near

*A*da's neighbor Rose Perrini disapproved of her daughter Angie's relationship with Willis Frame and was happy when Angie married his brother Vince instead.

the steel mill on Elm Street. Iris ordered Louise to spy on Dennis and his "undesirable" girlfriend, but when Louise tipped Dennis off, Iris fired Louise in a rage! Brooks, who was in love with Louise, quit Iris's employ and the two went to work for Rachel and Mac. Louise loved working for the Corys, but would always feel pangs for the complex, self-destructive young woman she had served for so long. Brian and Dennis were also ambivalent, and both told Iris their relationship with her would never be the same.

Brian soon had a fling with a client who made Iris look like the model spouse—Olive! She wanted Brian to represent her in a divorce from John, and Brian was unable to dissuade her from keeping her grandiose new home. But Brian was attracted to what made Olive much like Iris—the combination of a hardened woman and a sad little girl. Olive's sister, Doris Bennett, explained that their promiscuous mother had left them in the care of a grandmother who worked so hard she barely had time for them. All her life Olive had craved a secure marriage with an income to add to that security.

Joey Perrini was drawn to sweet Eileen Simpson, and Eileen felt the same. The two were briefly married before Eileen succumbed to a malignant tumor.

Iris, meanwhile, sold her house to Elena and moved to a penthouse in Bayview Towers. There she hired a new maid, a scatter-brained farm girl named Vivien Gorrow who made high-test martinis. When Iris discovered Brian's affair with Olive, she was determined to save Brian from himself. She didn't need to—Brian was strong enough to dump Olive on his own. Olive's next victim was Dan Shearer, who was back from Boston in hopes of reconciling withSusan. When Alice warned Olive away from Dan, Susan didn't know how to handle Alice and Dan's budding friendship.

Joan Barnard wanted more than friendship from John, but left Bay City when he told her he would always love Pat. Her brother, Greg, however, was far more persistent. He became involved with Marianne but tried to woo her attractive mother, Pat, behind her back! Pat was repulsed, especially when Greg lied to Marianne that Pat had the hots for *him*!

A twisted man, Greg warned Pat that if she didn't come to him, he would marry Marianne and make her miserable. John liked Greg and pooh-poohed Pat's doubts about him, but Pat was determined to trap Greg at his own game. To Pat's relief, Michael had a better choice of a prospective mate in Eileen Simpson, now that Iris's interference had driven her and Dennis apart.

Rose Perrini didn't have Iris's money, but she was no less enmeshed with her children. She made no secret of her disapproval when Willis finally proposed to Angie—or her relief when Angie married Vince instead. Willis got chummy with Gwen as the two worked on projects together, and before long they too were married. But Angie found she was unable to cope with the idea of Willis marrying someone else, so Vince left her in disgust.

Rose also worried about her down-to-earth

teenage son Joey, whom comely Sally Frame considered to be a prize hunk. When Sally unabashedly went after Joey, both he and Alice told her to back off and grow up. Joey was more drawn to the softness and honesty of Eileen, and the feeling was mutual. A disappointed Michael stepped aside.

But the most controversial young romance in Bay City this year involved Jamie Frame. While working on a ranch in Wyoming over the summer, Jamie became involved with his foreman's aggressive daughter, Blaine Ewing. Rachel met Blaine and realized that if she blocked out the girl's western twang, she was seeing her former self! Rachel and Larry Ewing, Blaine's older brother, desperately tried to warn Jamie of Blaine's feminine wiles.

Still, Rachel had something to celebrate. She and Mac had a healthy baby girl whom they named Amanda, after Mac's late mother. But as Iris tried to share their joy, Mac unthinkingly blurted out, "My first born!" and he was forced to admit that he and his first wife, Eugenia, had adopted Iris when she was three weeks old. Devastated, Iris bitterly swore off the man she had so foolishly called Daddy and threw herself into an investigation of her origins.

Assuming she had blue blood in her veins, Iris was elated when a wealthy dowager named Cornelia Exeter arrived, thinking they were mother and daughter.

Not.

❧

1979

Brian was surprised to receive Iris's natural mother in his office. It was not Cornelia Exeter, but an unlikely character named Sylvie Kosloff. A feisty woman of Russian descent, Sylvie ran a cut-rate fashion house in New York's garment district. So much for blue blood. Iris was nothing less than repulsed and would have nothing to do with the woman.

To add to Iris's horror, her son, Dennis, was working at Elena's gallery and living in her guest house. Before too long, her son and her dear friend were engaged in a love affair! Iris turned against Elena with

a vengeance, branding the sympathetic countess a cheap cradle robber.

The situation in the Cory household set the stage Iris to even the score with Mac for lying to her about her origins. Though Rachel wouldn't dare admit it to herself, she was beginning to show traits that put her in a league with Liz and Iris. When Jamie and Blaine married, Rachel cut Jamie off from all financial support, but Mac stepped in and overruled her, telling the newlyweds they were welcome under his roof. Undaunted, Rachel hired Buzz Winslow, Blaine's redneck ex-boyfriend, to work on the Cory grounds and lure the cowgirl back to Wyoming. Iris was quick to notice the acrimony between Rachel and Blaine, so she egged Blaine on to reveal Rachel's manipulations to Mac.

It was celebration time at Iris's penthouse. Mac expressed horror at Rachel for trying to ruin Jamie's marriage, accusing her of being the person everyone had advised him not to marry. She countered by calling him an "aging playboy" and he yelled back, "You ain't seen nothing yet!" Rachel and Mac separated, and Rachel took Amanda away to an artists' colony to get away for a while.

As Brian sorted out his feelings for Iris, he handed the reins to Scott Bradley at the Cory complex and became John's law partner. Michael passed his bar exams and worked under John and Brian—just in time to help Pat.

❧

*P*at went to confront Greg in his apartment. Clad only in a robe, Greg tried to rape Pat—but she grabbed a letter opener and killed him in self-defense. As her psychotic victim lay on the floor, Pat was transported to an early time in her life and screamed, "Tom, you said you'd marry me!" As with Tom Baxter, Pat blocked out the murder scene but was nonetheless arrested.

Marianne was so brainwashed by Greg that she believed her mother was guilty. But Michael knew better, and helped Brian defend Pat in a trial opposite DA

Tom Albini and his assistant, Karen Campbell. Olive became Albini's star witness, lying that she and Greg were lovers and had aroused Pat's jealousy. Olive told Dan that she would retract the story if he married him.

Willis Frame met architect Gwen Parrish at the Cory complex and the two were married. A one-night stand with Angie soon threatened the union.

Instead Dan saw how sick Olive really was and ended their affair.

Fortunately for Pat, Marianne came through for her. She remembered Pat having confused the events of Greg's murder with Tom Baxter's. Michael then put his mother on the witness stand and proved Pat had done just as Marianne indicated. Pat was once again exonerated for a murder on grounds of temporary insanity. Marianne apologized to Pat for ever having doubted her, and looked forward to the time Pat would remarry John so they could be a family again.

It was not to be. Alice and Dan were becoming so intimate, Susan decided to divorce Dan so he could marry her cousin. But Olive was hell-bent on revenge in the wake of Dan's rejection, and set Alice up to die in a fire. Instead John showed up to save Alice's life, and was himself tragically killed in the inferno. Olive was placed in a home for the criminally insane, while a grief-stricken Alice became reclusive and broke off with Dan. Alice admitted that she was still in love with Steve's memory and was convinced that he was still alive. Susan finally came around to Dan sexually, and they returned to Boston together.

Michael bore no ill will toward Karen Campbell for working with Albini, and the two young lawyers began a promising relationship. But Ted Bancroft returned to Bay City and, instead of taking up with Marianne, fell madly in love with Karen. He became a reporter at the *Sentinel* to prove to Karen that he had a purpose in life, and tried to protect her brother, Ben, from loan sharks who gunned for him. Desperate to get Karen away from Michael, Ted tried to spirit Karen and Ben away on a yacht, but the goons came aboard and shot Ted, sending him overboard.

Ted survived the confrontation but became further unbalanced in his mental state. He held Karen hostage aboard the yacht and wired it with dynamite so no one could save her. In a brilliant maneuver, Brian and Michael arrived and painstakingly defused the explosives. Ted was institutionalized, and Michael and Karen married and moved with Ben to Florida.

Yet another romance was threatened by the surprise return of a former Bay City resident. Larry Ewing followed his sister, Blaine, to Bay City and worked for Charlie and Vince. Clarice and Larry were drawn to one another, so much so that Clarice wanted to divorce Burt and marry Larry. Then Burt returned, wanting his wife and stepson back, even though he admitted to having an affair in Japan. He came close to kidnapping little Cory away from Clarice, but Ada talked him out of it. Burt granted Clarice a divorce and moved to Japan for good. Larry married Clarice and entered the police academy.

In the same neighborhood, Vince divorced Angie and married Mimi Haines, a good-hearted waitress at the Honeybee Diner. They left Bay City, leaving Angie free to pursue Willis. When Leueen had the temerity to buy a house for herself, Willis, and Gwen, Willis felt emasculated and allowed himself one night with Angie. Rose was judgmental toward her daughter for seducing Willis and wrote her off. Gwen was also shocked by Angie's tactics and vowed to save her marriage.

Gwen's opportunity came, ironically, from Sylvie Kosloff. Sylvie was determined to have a mother-daughter relationship with Iris, so she opened a branch office of her clothing business in Bay City. Sylvie hired Gwen to design the building, and Gwen in turn convinced Willis to build it so they could work together.

Willis's work impressed Kirk Laverty, the self-made New York millionaire who owned Sylvie's company. Kirk boldly pursued Rachel, but she knew he was married and had no wish to get embroiled in a sticky situation. Kirk and his wife, June, had an open marriage, but he had no idea she was having an affair with his corporate counsel—who just happened to be Jeff Stone!

Kirk had big plans in Bay City. He convinced Willis to sell Frame Enterprises, then with June's knowledge pursued Iris to get control of Cory Publishing. Sylvie was unhappy to see Iris and Kirk become seriously involved, especially since Iris was still married to Brian, and warned Iris that Kirk would hurt her. But Iris refused to listen to the mother she refused to accept.

Then Willis's sister Janice Frame returned to Bay City and renewed her enmity with Rachel. More calculating than ever, Janice was intrigued to meet Mac and became instantly attracted to him—and his money. Rachel mistakenly believed that Mac and Janice were involved and demanded a divorce. She also vowed she would take Amanda before Mac turned her into another Iris. Furious with Rachel, Mac got involved with Janice for real and moved into her apartment!

To weaken Mac's chances of keeping his stockholders' support, Kirk sought to make Mac's living situation look as tawdry as possible. He began to dig up dirt on Janice. In so doing, Kirk learned that Janice had had an affair with a married millionaire named Howard Battis who died of a heart attack in her arms!

Rachel's family continued to fall apart because of her mishandling of Blaine. Jamie refused to talk to his mother, but split with Blaine anyway because of her selfish nature. Blaine took up once again with Buzz and the two decided to hit Iris up for money. Buzz stole Iris's earrings, only for Iris to see them on Blaine and have her arrested. Not wanting Blaine to pay for his crime, Buzz confessed and was extradited to Wyoming.

❦

Brian stayed with Dennis and Elena while he dealt with his confusion over Iris and his guilt over having neglected Ted. Then Elena took on another houseguest—her ravishing stepdaughter, Cecile de Poulignac. Dennis fell for Cecile, and Elena was completely understanding, agreeing to keep their brief interlude a secret from Cecile. But once Blaine blabbed all about it to Cecile, the young romance was over. With his best friend out of the picture, Jamie turned his attention to Cecile—until Blaine found herself pregnant! Jamie wanted to do the noble thing, but Rachel—who had pulled every trick in the book—smelled a ploy.

Blaine found a partner in crime in Sally. Feeling neglected by the reclusive Alice, Sally traded tips with Blaine on how to handle their men. Sally was intent on snagging Joey from Eileen, who was now living with her aunt and uncle, Rita and Paul Connolly. More zealously Catholic than Rose, Rita made Eileen drop Joey because his sister was openly panting for a married man. Rita's treatment of Joey was the last straw for Paul, an earthy foreman at the nearby steel mill. He sought a church annulment on the grounds that Rita knew she was barren from the time they were married, and their marriage had been sexless throughout.

In so doing, Paul found solace with a surprising new woman: Rose! Seeing her own narrow-minded traits in Rita, Rose ultimately softened toward her children. Angie didn't buy Rose's transformation, however, and called her a hypocrite for her involvement with a married man.

Joey was badly in need of his mother's support at this time, however. Sally drugged him and made it appear to Eileen that they were lovers. Eileen didn't realize that Sally was in cahoots (and sometimes sharing her bed) with the smarmy Phil Higley, who sexually abused runaway teens at his "Serenity House." Phil cozied up to Eileen and raped her! Joey beat up Phil, who promptly had him arrested. Scott Bradley replaced Tom Albini as DA and tried every possible way to cut Joey some slack. Sally realized her plot had backfired and told Alice and Eileen she was truly sorry for her machinations. Relieved that Sally had shown remorse, Alice left Sally in Liz's care and accepted a nursing position in Chicago.

Mac and Jamie were also carrying out machinations that they were soon to regret. When Rachel planned to take Amanda away for good, Jamie helped Mac kidnap Amanda and took her to Mac and Janice's apartment! Jamie was sympathetic to Mac and Janice's relationship, since Janice was his aunt. But Jamie had a change of heart and convinced Mac to return Amanda to Rachel. The Corys realized that while they still loved one another, there was too much hurt between them to continue as husband and wife. Thus with full visitation rights granted to Mac, he and Rachel amicably divorced.

The latest man in Rachel's life was Frank Lansing, a writer who rented the apartment above the Cory riding stable. Frank was tormented by memories of Saigon, where he cared for a baby girl who had since disappeared in a bombing. For this reason, Frank was awkward around little Amanda. Rachel realized that as long as Frank was carrying all of this emotional baggage, he would not be prime husband or father material. Soon thereafter, Frank left town.

Another brief visitor to Bay City was Fred Ewing, Larry and Blaine's father. Fred had been an abusive drunk to his children, but was now cleaning up his act. For Larry and Blaine, however, it was too little, too late. Charlie also disliked Fred for aggressively pursuing Ada. Fred eventually knew where he wasn't wanted and rode off into the sunset to Wyoming.

❧

Kirk Laverty knew he wasn't wanted at Cory Publishing, but made it clear he wasn't going anywhere. He put his hostile takeover plan into motion, charming Iris into casting her vote for him against Mac. Willis also sat on the board and swore his allegiance to Mac—until Kirk sneeringly threatened to reveal Janice's dubious fatal encounter with Howard Battis back in New York.

Now that Steve was gone, it was Mac whose respect Willis craved more than anyone else's. But Willis hated himself for having sold out his sister Sharlene, and was not about to do the same thing to Janice. Swallowing hard, he cast his vote for Kirk. But he told Laverty in no uncertain terms that if Kirk ever tarnished Janice in any way, he would kill him. Sylvie shared that desire, for she knew that Kirk was about to dump Iris after the stockholders' meeting and return to June. Jeff didn't want that to happen, for June was the first true love in his empty life.

The good news was that Rachel swayed the majority of the stockholders toward keeping Mac in power. The bad news was that lots of people wanted Kirk Laverty dead.

1980

This tumultuous year would kick off an entire decade of murder and mayhem in Bay City. In addition, two wealthy families paid extended visits to the town in 1980—the Halloways of Philadelphia and the Bellmans of Houston.

When Kirk Laverty was shot dead in his hotel room, there were several suspects: Iris, who knew he was using her to grab Mac's company; Sylvie, who didn't want Kirk to reveal that she was an alcoholic who had given birth to Iris in prison; June, who realized she wanted to hold on to her beloved husband at all costs; and Willis, who would kill to keep Kirk from slandering Janice. The police were also puzzled to discover that Kirk had been working on something at his typewriter, although the ribbon was strangely missing.

Once Iris became the prime suspect, she and her new maid, Vivien, set out to clear her name and began sleuthing. They finally found the ribbon, on which a bleeding Kirk had typed his killer's name. When the women confronted the killer, he took them hostage until intrepid cop Larry Ewing shot him dead. The culprit: Jeff Stone.

In a parallel situation, former adversaries Sally and Eileen teamed up to expose Phil Higley's kinky Serenity House. In so doing, they cleared the way for Scott Bradley to exonerate Joey. Eileen and Joey were all set to marry, until Russ Matthews returned from Texas and discovered that Eileen had a malignant tumor. Without telling Eileen of her fate, Joey married her quietly. She died within hours.

Russ was accompanied by Dr. Kevin Cook, his new friend and mentor from a Dallas cardiac unit. Kevin was estranged from his wife, Reena, a vampy southern belle spoiled rotten by her oil-rich father, John "Striker" Bellman. Reena and her "Daddy" arrived in Bay City and were not pleased to see Kevin pursuing Pat. Iris was chummy with Reena from having spent some time in Texas years before and filled her in on the goings-on in Bay City. With Iris's encouragement, Reena made it clear to Pat that she intended to get Kevin back.

Iris also had an intention of her own—to have the beautiful and prestigious Cecile de Poulignac as her daughter-in-law. She was happy to see Dennis and Cecile bonding, until Blaine miscarried by accidentally ingesting a punch she had spiked for Jamie. This calamitous event prompted Jamie to divorce Blaine and look in Cecile's direction. Cecile realized she was more attracted to Jamie than to Dennis, who was too noble to steal a woman from his best friend.

Knowing no such scruples, Iris hired a lazy, perennially unemployed writer named Philip Lyons to seduce Cecile just long enough to get her away from Jamie. When Pat hired Cecile as an illustrator for Mac's *Brava* magazine, Philip took a job at Cory Publishing to impress Cecile. The plan worked—Cecile was quite taken with the roguish newcomer and broke off with Jamie.

Then came a shocking turnaround. Philip fell genuinely in love with Cecile and gained new self-respect as a writing professional. Soon they were engaged—only for Cecile to find the contract Philip had signed for services rendered to Iris. Once crossed, Cecile revealed that behind that cherubic, innocent face was a vengeful ice princess. She kept mum till the day of her wedding, then left Philip at the altar and told Brian of Iris and Philip's plot. As an added slap in Iris's face, Cecile seduced Dennis and then icily dropped him. Brian didn't condone Cecile's actions, but the new revelation convinced him that Iris would never change despite her protests to the contrary. With great regret, Brian divorced Iris.

It was through the Bellmans that a new chapter in Iris's life was to unfold. Reena was angry that Striker had reconciled with her estranged mother, Vicky, the owner of a Houston television station. Recognizing Reena's love for him as obsessive, Striker advised Reena to concentrate on getting Kevin back. To Pat's disgust, Striker built Kevin a world-class cardiac clinic in Houston in exchange for Kevin's reconciliation with Reena. As the newly reunited Bellman family returned to Houston, Dennis followed to become an art buyer at Reena's new gallery. Then Iris went to Houston for a visit—and was shaken to see a man from her past.

*I*ris's son,
Dennis,
relocated to
Houston to
run an art
gallery.

Texas

Iris married her oil-rich former lover, Alex Wheeler, and had to admit to Dennis that Alex was his father. Dennis was not happy to hear this, for he had been very attached to his legal father, Eliot Carrington, back in New York and Bay City. Dennis fell for sweet Dawn Marshall, whose family irrationally blamed Alex for the suicide of her bankrupt father, Mike. To Iris's horror, Dawn's promiscuous older sister, Paige, seduced and married Dennis.

Eliot Carrington was presumed dead in Europe, only to return with a serious mental illness. Cruelly held captive in a Third World country, he had become delusional. After holding many people hostage at the Top of the World nightclub, he fortunately got professional help. He and Paige realized they loved each other, but never consummated their relationship out of mutual concern for Dennis. But Dennis caught on and branded his wife a whore. Iris and Dennis eventually left Houston separately.

Mike Marshall's suicide especially affected his intense and embittered son, Justin, who had a long and randy history with Reena Cook. Kevin divorced Reena and left Houston. Reena was close to marrying Justin, but thought she would find more stability with humble Max Dekker—until he turned up dead. Alex Wheeler was also killed, leaving behind an unhappily married brother, Grant. After the death of Grant's scheming wife, Judith, at the hands of her psychotic lover, George St. John, Reena and Grant were happily married.

Janice Frame's brooding ex-lover Mitch Blake moved to Bay City and opened a swank nightclub called the Supper Club. He and Janice devised a deadly plan to do in Mac and seize his millions.

It was Alex Wheeler, a craggy oil man who had worked his way up to millionaire status. Vicky Bellman was also nursing feelings for Alex, for they had been involved for years. But Iris was one up on her. She had given birth to his son—Dennis! Eliot Carrington, who was now presumed dead in a Third World country, had been unaware that Iris's Texan ex-flame was Dennis's biological father. Seizing a chance for happiness after causing herself and others no end of turmoil in Bay City, Iris relocated to Houston to be near her son, her friends, and her former lover.

❧

*B*ack in Bay City, Janice had no sooner married Mac than her brooding ex-lover Mitch Blake caught up with her. Rachel sensed that Mitch was the key to Janice's past, so she began flirting with the newcomer to arouse Janice's jealousy. Rachel's intention was for Janice simply to leave Mac for Mitch.

Liz and Pat held out no such hope. Both worked closely with Mac and were horrified by Janice's power plays as a so-called employee at Cory Publishing. Neither was aware, however, that Janice was studying a manuscript Pat had rejected. It was *Harry Must Die,* a thriller about a woman who slowly poisoned her husband to death. Janice realized that in her heart of hearts, she wanted to be that woman. She wanted Mitch, body and soul—with Mac's millions to support them.

Janice presented her plan to Mitch, and with his full knowledge, poisoned Mac little by little. Soon Mac became haggard and incoherent, to the point where Liz searched for clues to his off-kilter behavior. Then Rachel and Liz discovered the manuscript among Janice's belongings and were chilled to realize that Mac was married to a would-be killer.

After a long history of bad blood, Rachel and Liz finally formed an iron-clad alliance in the interest of saving Mac's life. Had it happened years before, it would have been at a society charity event at the Bay City Country Club. But these formerly shallow, upwardly mobile social butterflies had long since matured into women of grit, substance, and purpose. And at this point, their purpose was to wrestle the man they loved away from the vilest creature they had ever known.

When Rachel discovered that Janice was taking Mac to St. Croix—ostensibly so that he could rest—she flew down to the island and found Mitch there. Mitch was already having second thoughts about his part in Janice's plan, so he let Rachel seduce him into leading her to Mac and Janice. Finding Mac near death, Rachel and Janice struggled over a knife in a swimming pool. In the life-or-death struggle, Janice was instantly killed. Rachel saved Mac, and together they returned to Bay City where they were happily remarried. The Corys also celebrated Ada's long-awaited marriage to Charlie Hobson.

Mitch followed the Corys back to Bay City, where he opened a swank nightspot, the Supper Club, in partnership with sleazy Jason Dunlap. Jason was insinuating himself back into the life of his former lover and star chanteuse "Tracy Merrill," who was really Tracy DeWitt, Mac's former fiancée. Now penniless, Tracy was resuming the singing career she had concealed from her upper-crust friends. A lonely Russ was wowed and they soon married, but the Svengali-like Jason plied Tracy with "uppers" to keep her focused on learning new singing material.

✤

*M*eanwhile, Russ's sister Pat went back to the bottle after Kevin rejected her for the Bellman bucks. Cecile went out of her way to sabotage Pat at work, but Pat had a staunch defender in Philip. Jealous that Philip was developing feelings for Pat, the capricious Cecile became hell-bent on winning Philip back!

Pat's daughter, Marianne, was becoming friendly with a soft-spoken young nurse named Kit Farrell, with whom Joey fell in love once he accepted Eileen's death. Kit represented herself as a plain girl from a simple background—until Russ treated a wealthy cardiac patient named Lloyd Bishop at the hospital. Kit went to great lengths to avoid Bishop and his snooty wife, Miranda.

The truth was, Miranda was Kit's aunt—and Kit's actual last name was Halloway. A scion of Philadelphia society, Kit had been kidnapped by the Red Brigade in Italy and wanted to live down this painful episode in her past. But when Joey married Kit, their wedding photo attracted the notice of the newly widowed Miranda. This brought other members of Kit's family to Bay City: her dynamic millionaire father, Taylor Halloway, who had a long-standing affair with his sister-in-law Miranda; her elder brother Rick, an idealistic physicist from whom Taylor expected nothing short of a Nobel Prize; and her elder sister Amy, newly divorced and radiating upper-crust ennui.

Although Taylor liked Joey, Rose arched her back at his blue-blood in-laws. Paul was ready to marry Rose now that he had his annulment from Rita, but

Beyond Bay City: St Croix

Janice took Mac to St. Croix, ostensibly to rest. Taking her cues from a rejected Cory manuscript Harry Must Die, Janice was slowly poisoning Mac to death.

It was a life-or-death struggle in the pool with Janice brandishing a knife, and Janice became the victim of her own deadly plot.

In the end, Rachel saved Mac and they returned to Bay City where they happily remarried.

When Marianne Randolph discovered she was pregnant with Rick Halloway's child, the two were happily married.

he grew disgusted by Rose's narrow-mindedness and broke off with her. Paul, Rose, and Angie all left Bay City separately. Gwen, Angie's romantic rival, had her own construction business until Willis convinced her to move to Australia with him. Other departing residents included Scott Bradley, who vacated his DA post to join the Justice Department in Washington, D.C., and Sally Frame, who joined her adoptive mother, Alice, in Chicago.

However, two former Bay City residents returned and had a profound effect on the Hobsons and the Ewings. Robert Delaney wanted to have a place in his little son Cory's life now that he was divorcing his latest wife, Olivia, a workaholic doctor who acted relieved when she discovered she could not conceive children. And Buzz Winslow resurfaced as part of a crime syndicate on its way to Bay City.

❦

Blaine happened upon Buzz after discovering that the mob had killed Larry's cop friend, Bud Parker, at the behest of his syndicate-linked mobster wife, Hazel. Secretly turning over a new leaf, Blaine infiltrated the mob in order to protect Larry from Hazel's murderous intentions. Larry killed Hazel in a violent confrontation. Then her cohorts snuffed out Buzz when he proved too dumb to handle his new job.

But the mob's stranglehold on Bay City was just beginning. Blaine became interested in Jerry Grove, an affable cop working on his law degree, whose nightclub-singer mother, Margo Lamarr, was being threatened by the mob. In an impulsive move, Blaine married the innocent and unsuspecting Jerry to get closer to the heartbeat of the syndicate's operation. As fate would have it, she need not have married to achieve that end. Jordan Scott, the suavest of the syndicate's key men, was quite taken with Blaine. Eventually Larry told Clarice of his undercover work, and the two reconciled.

Back at the Cory mansion, servants Louise and Brooks were married and became concerned by Mitch's continual presence in Rachel's life. At the same time, Rachel discovered she was pregnant! Russ treated his friend and former wife, as a courtesy, and deduced that given the timing, Mac was not the father. Rachel then confided to Russ and Ada that Mitch had sired her unborn child.

In time Mitch put two and two together and told Rachel he wanted to claim his child. Desperate to save her marriage, Rachel shot and wounded Mitch and ran from the scene—the stables. Unbeknownst to her, a prowler then stole into the stables and a wounded Mitch shot him. The bullet hit a wire, causing the barn to burn.

Mitch survived, albeit with amnesia, and wandered out of town. He had no clue that Zachary Colton, Bay City's flashy new DA, was booking Rachel for the second-degree murder of one Mitchell Blake.

♦

1981

As Brian Bancroft defended Rachel for Mitch's murder, Mac sought refuge in the imminent birth of the child Rachel was carrying. But his world was shattered when Donald Tanner, author of *Harry Must Die*, took the witness stand. Under Zachary Colton's relentless questioning, Tanner revealed that Damtrex—the substance Janice used to poison Mac—had rendered him sterile.

"Rachel!" Mac leapt to his feet. "Tell him the baby is mine!" Rachel tearfully screamed back in front of the horrified spectators, "It's Mitch's!"

Rachel was convicted, and prepared for Mac to divorce her. But after she gave birth to a son, Matthew—named in honor of the Matthews family—Mac decided to stick by his beloved Rachel and raise the boy as his own. Mac assumed this would be his only chance to have the son he always wanted.

But he was wrong. Jordan Scott and his mob boss, Jess Cooper, opened an entertainment complex encompassing Jason's Supper Club, a gambling casino, and a spa known as The Connection. The latter, run by Ilsa, was in fact an oasis where wealthy, sex-starved women went to be rubbed all over by

Marianne and Rick's Wedding Vows

❦

MINISTER: I am very pleased that God has given us such a beautiful day to celebrate the wonderful occasion of the marriage of Rick Halloway to Marianne Randolph. It is a joyous sign that he smiles on this union. And now Rick and Marianne would like to hare their vows with you — their family and friends.

RICK: Today we start a journey together . . .

MARIANNE: A journey which will take us through the rest of our lives.

RICK: We know our destination — the direction our life should take . . .

MARIANNE: But we will not be afraid to explore the back roads. . . .

RICK: Together we'll seek the beauty of the unexpected . . .

MARIANNE: I'll be there for you for the joyous times . . .

RICK: Let us not forget to celebrate the joy of our lives . . .

MARIANNE: . . . the wonder of our love.

RICK: There'll be times of sorrow, too . . .

MARIANNE: I'll be there to reassure you . . . to ease your doubts . . .

RICK: I'll hold and comfort you in the dark of night when pain surrounds you. . . .

MARIANNE: With God's love, may children share in our lives. . . .

RICK: May we show them the joy and the happiness we now share.

MARIANNE: With mutual respect may our love continue to grow.

RICK: I promise to be there for you always.

MARIANNE: And I'll strive never to stray from the path we've chosen together.

RICK & MARIANNE: I love you. . . .

RICK: Let our marriage begin.

MARIANNE: Let our lives together begin.

MINISTER: Rick, do you take this woman to be your lawfully wedded wife?

RICK: I do.

MINISTER: Marianne, do you take this man to be your lawfully wedded husband?

MARIANNE: I do.

MINISTER: With the power vested in me, I now pronounce you husband and wife.

multitalented "masseurs." One of Ilsa's boys, Sandy Alexander, revealed to his girlfriend Melissa Needham that he was the illegitimate son of Mackenzie Cory!

Sandy had grown up in Las Vegas as Alex Sanderson. His struggling single mother, Miriam, waited until her dying day to tell him that he had a wealthy father. Miriam had never told Mac he had a son, because she and Mac lived worlds apart and she was hesitant to make trouble for him. Sandy resented this, for his family's poverty had caused him to become a Vegas street hustler and now a professional boy toy. He hesitated to reveal himself to Mac because he was ashamed of his lifestyle and was determined to extricate himself from Ilsa.

Mac certainly didn't need any more upheaval at this time. He discovered that the charred remains in his barn did not match those of Mitch Blake! When Rachel learned that her stepfather, Charlie Hobson, had died of a heart attack, she convinced the authorities to let her attend the funeral at Ada's side. After the service, Rachel disappeared in search of a trace of Mitch. She was convinced he was still alive.

Her instincts were correct. Rachel tracked down Mitch in Colorado and brought him back to Bay City, where he eventually regained his memory. Rachel won her freedom, but Mac feared he would lose the baby boy to whom he had become attached. His fears became reality when Mitch made known his intention to be a part of little Matt's life.

❖

*L*arry Ewing was in the same position as Mac, now that Robert Delaney was back in town. But Robert's visit proved short-lived because he chose to bow out of little Cory's life so that Cory could have a stable home life with the Ewings. The stability was shaken, however, when Larry started hanging around the entertainment complex and living the fast life. Clarice was appalled by Larry's shallow new values, and considered divorce.

Clarice was unaware that Larry was playing the "bad cop" in order to get close to Jordan and his mob cronies. When Blaine took up with Jordan and divorced Jerry, Larry caught on to Blaine's undercover scheme and vowed to protect his sister. But he was powerless to do so, as Blaine subjected herself to Jordan's mixed bag of passionate abandon and cruel sadomasochism. Larry also discovered that the eminent DA Zachary Colton was a compulsive gambler at Jordan's casino!

Joey and Kit were also drawn into this scenario. Joey felt he didn't belong in Kit's world and had their marriage annulled. He took a job at the entertainment complex and developed protective feelings for Blaine, while Kit dated a lonely Jerry. To worsen Jerry's lot, his mother, Margo, was killed by the mob because she knew too much. But Joey and Kit realized they loved one another after all, despite their different backgrounds, and reconciled.

All of Kit's other relatives went back to Philadelphia except for her brother Rick, who began a relationship with Marianne Randolph. When Marianne became pregnant by Rick, he happily married her. Tragically, she soon miscarried.

Another troubled marriage was that of Russ and Tracy Matthews. Still obsessed with Tracy, Jason egged on Olivia Delaney to take her professional friendship with Russ to a new level. When Olivia wouldn't bite, Jason sank to his lowest point ever. He rigged Russ's car to blow up with him inside it, only for Tracy to enter the car instead! Tracy died instantly in the ensuing explosion. Ironically, once he had grieved over Tracy's untimely death, Russ took up with Olivia and the two left to work in a hospital out of town.

With Russ gone, Jim and Liz were most concerned with Pat, who was still drinking heavily. A newly promoted Cecile fired Pat, but Mac overruled her and rehired his dear friend because of his belief in her. Philip helped Pat to stop drinking and proposed, but Pat was still leery of romantic commitments and opted to concentrate on her career. A hurt Philip departed from Bay City.

Cecile enjoyed playing the corporate game for awhile, but once her inheritance ran out she decided to ensure her future and talked a vulnerable Jamie into a hasty marriage! Cecile knew Mac was grooming Jamie to be his successor. Her plan backfired when Jamie worked so hard to prove his worth that he became addicted to "uppers." Mac pleaded with Jamie to ease his workload but to no avail.

Ada opened a hair salon at the entertainment complex, where she overheard Sandy talking to Melissa about his true relationship to Mac. Ada told Mac, who excitedly replied, "I always wanted a son."

Jamie felt as though he'd lost a father. He became increasingly paranoid under the influence of drugs, as Mac made a place in his conglomerate for Sandy. Marianne became extremely concerned for Jamie—they were first cousins and had known each other since childhood. Indeed, Marianne's Uncle Russ had initially believed that Jamie was his child. Marianne encouraged a friendship between Jamie and Rick, and the newlyweds ultimately helped Jamie lick his drug habit. But Rick began to realize that Marianne was developing deeper feelings for Jamie than for him.

It didn't take long for Cecile to regret that she'd married a drug-addicted workaholic. Now that Mac's biological son was in town, Cecile aimed to snag the hunky blond stud who stood to inherit as much, if not more, of the Cory fortune than her husband. When Cecile began drugging Jamie's drinks, he discovered her treachery and, in his drugged state, raped her!

The Cory family continued to fall apart. Mac was stubbornly adamant about adopting little Matt, so Rachel succumbed to Mitch's charms and moved in with him, resulting in Mac and Rachel's divorce. Mitch sold his interest in the Supper Club and planned to open an art gallery with Rachel. But when Rachel accepted Jamie's financial support for the gallery, an emasculated Mitch got huffy. Jamie put him in his place: "The only man who could ever hold on to Mom is Mac Cory," Jamie told Mitch flatly. "She's made mistakes before. Maybe you're just another one of those mistakes."

While Jamie felt enmity for Mitch, he found an unlikely ally in Sandy. After the mob tried to muscle in on Mac's business holdings and blasted his complex to smithereens, Mac literally rebuilt his company, and Jamie and Sandy banded together to save him from further mob actions. Unbeknownst to Jamie, Cecile seduced Sandy in one of his weaker moments. Sandy felt guilty for sleeping with his stepbrother's wife, but he couldn't fight his attraction to the sexy Cecile.

Sandy also helped Blaine and Jerry go on the run from Jordan, but the slick mobster caught up with the couple. Jordan became so physically abusive to Blaine that she shot him in self-defense and ran. The authorities found Jordan dead and arrested Blaine. In no time, Zachary Colton had Blaine on trial for murder.

As Blaine's defense lawyer, Brian found the trial an uphill battle—until Rick discovered that Blaine's bullet was not the ultimate cause of Jordan's death. After Blaine had fled, someone had injected Jordan with a fatal overdose of a rare anticoagulant. The only person in Bay City with that prescription was Zachary Colton! It turned out that Zachary had snuffed out the injured Jordan because Jordan had threatened to reveal his gambling sickness. Zachary confessed in the courtroom, then was handcuffed and led out in disgrace.

It didn't matter that Pat had hired Cecile; Cecile was now in charge, and she fired her onetime boss.

The Cory family continued to fall apart as Rachel turned to Mitch and they

The syndicate struck again by holding Mac, Jamie, and Sandy hostage. The henchmen shot Mac before the police arrived to arrest them. Mac convalesced at home, where Alice, back from Chicago, acted as his private nurse. Before long, Mac and Alice—the two people who felt the most wronged by Rachel—were engaged to be married! A bitter Rachel intended to sue Mac for Amanda's custody and then join Mitch in San Francisco, where he'd accepted a lucrative photography job.

As Ada fretted over this latest schism in Rachel and Mac's relationship, she was happy to be united with the two estranged sons of her late husband, Charlie: Denver ("Denny") and Leigh Hobson. An ambitious corporate attorney, Denny warned Leigh that his new romance with Sally Frame was standing in the way of his promising hockey career.

Denny took a position with a new company called Black Hawk Industries, where he reported to two immediate bosses—Curtis Eldon and Quinn Harding. Soon Denny met the big boss—a mysterious recluse named Edward Black. Curtis and Quinn were unusually protective of their employer and warned him not to trust Denny with too much information. But Mr. Black strangely identified with Denny, a driven young man determined to rise above his poor background.

From his sequestered office, Mr. Black read the newspaper item announcing the impending marriage of Mackenzie Cory and Alice Frame. He ordered Denny to compile a dossier on the engaged couple ASAP.

❧

1982

Jamie and Sandy were suspicious when the Black Hawk people seemed unusually interested in Mac. Knowing the syndicate still had a presence in Bay City, the young stepbrothers feared that Black Hawk was a mob front. Jamie infiltrated the company by taking a position there, causing Rachel no end of worry. One day she decided to go to the office and find out what Jamie was really doing. There she was shocked to come face-to-face with Edward Black, for she knew him by his real name.

Edward Black was Steven Frame!

The residents of Bay City were now to learn what Alice had believed at the core of her being—that Steve had survived his plane crash. He had sustained extensive injuries, which had necessitated a long hospital stay. Once having regained consciousness and learned about the rumors of his death, he didn't have the heart to tell his family and friends that the rumors had been exaggerated. Thus he decided not to shake up their world with a dramatic reappearance. He married a woman named Pamela and they settled in England. They had a daughter, Diana, before Pamela's untimely death. Now a vibrant, headstrong 16-year-old, Diana arrived in Bay City and met the Americans from her father's past.

Mac was understanding when Alice broke their engagement and planned to remarry the one true love of her life. Mac briefly took up with a neurotic editor named Anne Whitelaw, while Rachel became Steve's friend and collaborator on a sculpture museum project. Although Rachel and Steve tried to keep their relationship platonic, Alice was quick to pick up on Steve's chemistry with the "new and improved" Rachel.

Jim was delighted to welcome Steve back to the family and resume their old business relationship. Soon Jim became suspicious of Denny and his dealings with suppliers. Before he could prove any wrongdoing on Denny's part, however, tragedy struck. While conducting business for Steve in Helsinki, Finland, Jim died of a massive coronary. Liz moved into the family home, which she associated with Jim and Mary. The cozy old place didn't seem so provincial to her anymore.

Jim's suspicions about Denny had been correct. Steve's right-hand man was on the take from corrupt union members and driving a wedge between Steve and his union leader pal, Harry Shea. When the union thugs killed Harry's wife, Loretta, Harry swore his hatred of Steve. The two adversaries therefore discouraged Diana's budding romance with Harry's son, Pete.

When Leigh left Bay City to tour with his hockey team, Denny moved in on Sally, now that Steve was happily acknowledging her as a daughter. Alice didn't trust Denny and was not pleased when he and Sally wed. Sally was elated to hear that Diana and Pete were also marrying and innocently told Steve. Steve angrily broke up the wedding, provoking a negative reaction from Alice. Steve told Alice he expected her support where Diana's welfare was concerned: "People in my life are either on my side or not. Nobody's neutral in my ballpark!"

*J*amie was happy that his beloved father was back in his life. He divorced Cecile and moved in with Marianne, who planned to divorce Rick. But now that Rachel was once again enamored of Steve, Jamie grew disgusted by the hypocrisy and indecision he saw in the people around him. He channeled that bitterness into a book, which he appropriately titled *A View of the Bay,* featuring thinly disguised characterizations of Bay City residents.

The book changed a lot of lives—and set off an avalanche of angry reactions. Pat was becoming involved with Brian and planned to marry him until she saw her tumultuous life misrepresented by Jamie's dramatic license. She told Brian she'd had it with Bay City and accepted a promotion to head Mac's paperback division in New York. Sickened by the way Jamie had hurt her mother, Marianne broke off with him and made a go of her marriage to Rick away from Bay City.

The reviews continued to pour in. Mac rebuked Jamie for writing "the most ill-tempered, malevolent piece of literature I've ever read." He added sadly, "Your intention was to hurt, torture, and expose anyone who's ever been close to you." But Rachel was the one to cut Jamie to the quick. "I can do without that kind of son," Rachel told him. "You're no longer a part of my life." Only Ada and Steve sympathized with Jamie, recognizing the need he felt to write the book.

Soon remorseful, Jamie apologized to his family and hoped it would be forgotten. But Jason saw an opportunity to turn the surrounding controversy into dollar signs and paid Jamie for an option to make the book into a movie!

With Bay City as a backdrop, *A View of the Bay* went into production under the direction of Milo Simonelli, a swaggering continental charmer. Liz was immediately taken by Milo, even though she didn't approve of the movie's subject matter. She was also concerned when Julia Shearer, Susan and Dan's adopted teenage daughter, came to Bay City and took a role in the movie. The production was soon beset by a baffling series of calamities and accidents. It turned out that Milo was sabotaging his own movie so that he could abscond with the insurance money! The movie ceased production, and a relieved Jamie became a writing professor at Bay State University.

Jamie was also relieved to be rid of Cecile but was unaware that she was pregnant. She was uncertain whether Jamie or Sandy was the father but passed it off as Sandy's. Ambitious and greedy, she married the young Mr. Sandy Alexander Cory. Mac took in the newlyweds, but Louise so hated Cecile that she slipped her poisoned mushrooms from her garden! Brooks was livid that Louise had endangered the life of Cecile's unborn child. Of course, Cecile herself was equally guilty. She risked starvation to her fetus by popping diet pills to keep her girlish figure! Fortunately, Cecile delivered a healthy baby girl named Maggie.

Sharing in Cecile's joy was her Aunt Elena, who returned from an extended stay in Paris. Then a wily art smuggler named Louis St. George arrived in Bay City, forcing Elena to admit to a long-held secret: She was really Cecile's mother and Louis, Cecile's father! Elena found comfort from her old friend Brian, who was now mayor of Bay City.

Sandy angrily discovered Cecile's diet pills. Disgusted, he found true love for the first time in his life—with Blaine! But Cecile was not about to lose her meal ticket, so she allied herself with Buzz Winslow's deranged sister Alma Rudder to "gaslight" Blaine. Arriving in Bay City, Alma used

"**P**eople **i**n **m**y **l**ife
are **e**ither **o**n **m**y **s**ide
or **n**ot. Nobody's **n**eutral
in **m**y **b**allpark!"

images of Blaine's sad childhood to torture her. She dressed as Blaine's old rag doll and held up images of the cat Blaine's father had cruelly killed.

It was all for nothing. Sandy told Cecile he wanted a divorce. Cecile hired Mac's ambitious new lawyer Cass Winthrop to put Sandy through the ringer. Cass's younger sister, Stacey, was also an attorney—but he looked down on her as a mere upstart. Besides, she was much too altruistic.

❦

*Q*uinn Harding had much to learn about altruism, for she let herself be party to Denny's scheme and went on the take. But then Quinn was mugged, and Larry's police partner, Bob Morgan, forced Quinn back to the real world. He chided her for losing touch with her people, as did her brother Ed. Soon Quinn and Bob were having an affair, which was quickly discovered by Bob's wife, Henrietta, and rebellious teenage son, R.J. When Bob was indecisive about the women in his life, Henrietta forced his hand by dating Ed! Henrietta also disapproved when R.J. dated Thomasina Mason, a latchkey teenager that Quinn had taken under her wing.

Finding herself closer to her roots, Quinn regretted having aided and abetted Denny—whose schemes escalated in a grotesque fashion. On the eve of Alice and Steve's planned wedding, Steve's high-rise collapsed and left him and Rachel trapped in a subbasement. Denny's cronies had put the skyscraper together with the equivalent of spit and glue. Harry put aside his dislike for Steve and tried to save him and Rachel—but was killed when a steel beam fell on him. Their lives hanging in the balance, Steve made a startling admission to Rachel: "You are the

only person I have always loved and will always love." After Jamie and Sandy saved them from the wreckage, Alice tearfully told Steve that he was free to marry Rachel. God had given her back her beloved Steve—now Rachel was taking him away.

❦

1983

His major Bay City project in ruins, Steven Frame was left virtually penniless, and his all-consuming pride was hurt when he realized he would never be as wealthy or as prominent as his rival, Mac. Rachel only made matters worse when she sneaked money into his account in an effort to bail him out.

To salvage his self-respect, Steve formed the new Frame-Harding Construction Company, with Quinn as his full partner. He innocently agreed to build a club for Ilsa Fredericks, until Jason tipped him off that Ilsa was a mobster. At the same time, Bob Morgan discovered that his troubled son, R.J., was involved with street pushers linked to Ilsa's operation. The police finally vanquished the mob, but the ensuing series of shoot-outs left Jason, Ilsa, and Bob all dead.

Steve eventually forgave Rachel and they made plans to marry. They were on their way to the airport when they were involved in a brutal car accident. Rachel was left blind. Steve was killed.

This tragedy had an enormous ripple effect on Steve's loved ones. Pete and Diana married and left Bay City. Frame-Harding Construction had done well, and Rachel and Jamie inherited the bulk of Steve's estate, but Sally and Diana were well provided for. Unfortunately, the will left Steve's out-of-town siblings feeling hurt and slighted. Quinn resolved to keep Steve's company going. Also, around this time, she adopted Thomasina. Sally divorced Denny, who was jailed for his corrupt activities. And Alice finally came into her own, earning a full-fledged medical degree as Dr. Alice Matthews.

It was Rachel who was left the most lonely and devastated by Steve's loss. She didn't have Mitch, who was in a California prison for conspiring with a

When Bob Morgan helped businesswoman Quinn Harding through a difficult time, the two began an affair. It didn't take Bob's wife, Henrietta, long to discover what was going on.

fathers' rights group to kidnap Matt. Mac wanted her back, but Rachel didn't want his pity. As she tried to cope with her blindness on her own, Mac donned a comical alias as a proper Britisher named "John Caldwell" and in that guise befriended Rachel. One day she regained her sight and was shocked to find her former husband spouting the King's English. With an amused smile, Rachel told Mac, "You can drop your accent now."

*L*ouis St. George's accent was real, but practically everything else about him was fake. Brian Bancroft hated Louis's presence in Elena's life and worked with Sandy to expose the wily art smuggler. But Sandy had a problem. He had to bed Cecile to get into Louis's inner circle. Blaine reluctantly came around about Sandy's forced infidelity and helped him go head-to-head with Cecile over little Maggie's custody. Cecile was represented by Louis's lawyer, a vainglorious drama king with the fitting name of Reuben Marino.

His performance notwithstanding, Marino was powerless when the French authorities closed in on Louis's art-smuggling operation. Before he was extradited to France, Louis almost redeemed himself by damning Cecile as a fortune hunter and recommending that Sandy be granted Maggie's custody. When Sandy won the case, a desperate Cecile tried to claim that Maggie was Jamie's child! Jamie was ready to do battle with his stepbrother until paternity tests proved that Sandy was Maggie's father after all. Louis made peace with Cecile before he died in a French prison hospital, but Elena returned to Europe, having sworn off Cecile for good.

Louis left behind a fortune, which Cecile was forced to share with his estranged wife, a deliciously flamboyant romance novelist named Felicia Gallant. With her young chauffeur/plaything Gil Fenton in tow, Felicia blew into Bay City and joined Mac's stable of writers. Fresh from her movie experience, starstruck Julia Shearer became Felicia's assistant and soon showed writing talent of her own. Julia attracted the notice of Gil, who decided to end his stud status and get a "real job" at Quinn's construction company. Felicia was gracious and accepted Gil's decision.

Enter Cass, who saw Felicia as an ideal cash cow for his rival enterprise, Winthrop Publishing. They had known each other in Europe, and Felicia reluctantly moved over to Cass's camp. But not only was she vulnerable to his charms, she found him to be her ultimate soul mate. Soon the two got hot and heavy and moved in together. But Felicia was unaware that Cass was two-timing her with Cecile, whose divorce from Sandy had become final.

Of course, it wasn't all fun and games for Cass and Cecile. Alma Rudder discovered their affair and hit them up for blackmail money. A devastated Felicia told Cass and Cecile they deserved each other but later realized she couldn't stay angry at her pal Cass for long. Felicia restored her professional allegiance to Mac, and Cass pursued a succession of businesses and schemes.

Meanwhile, Larry and Blaine's sickly estranged mother, Jeanne, came to Bay City. Larry welcomed her, but Blaine found it difficult to forgive Jeanne for having left her in the hands of her abusive father. Then Alma was found stabbed to death in a Bay City hotel room, and Cecile was arrested for the crime. Larry assumed he had the right suspect in custody until he noticed a slash in the back of Jeanne's blouse. Jeanne admitted that she had

Brian Bancroft was involved romantically with Elena de Poulignac and, after her, Donna Love, because they reminded him of Iris. Problems with his drug-addicted son, Ted, led Brian to leave Bay City at the end of his mayoral term.

struggled over a knife with Alma to protect Blaine from her treachery, accidentally killing Alma. Jeanne's health rapidly declined after this revelation, but she was to make one more confession to Larry on her deathbed: She had given birth to another son after leaving Fred behind in Wyoming!

Larry was also busy helping Henrietta deal with his pal Bob's death. Forgiving Quinn her affair with Bob, Henrietta befriended her former romantic rival and the two did the dating scene together. Quinn was pursued by Rachel's doctor, Dr.

When Peter Love announced his engagement to Sally Frame, his sister Donna did everything to stop him from marrying beneath his social station.

Abel Marsh, but found him a bit pushy. And Henrietta—now a successful caterer—was torn between solid architect Roy Bingham and Abel's lounge-lizard twin, "Leo Mars." Henrietta's son, R.J., straightened himself out and became serious about Thomasina, whose feisty Aunt Lily quit "turning tricks" so Quinn would let her remain a part of Thomasina's life.

Back at the Cory household,

Jamie fell hard for Stacey Winthrop and went to work on a new novel. He modeled the hero after Mark Singleton, a maverick contender for the state senate who dumped his political "handlers." Ironically, Mark was Stacey's former lover! Mark was in the midst of divorcing his ruthless wife, Janet, who was in cahoots with his former manager Zack Hill and political boss Jeremiah "The Fat Man" Denby. When Mark decided to return to his law career, Zack was ready to give Sandy an exposé on the seamy doings behind the Singleton campaign. But Denby beat Sandy to the punch and had Zack killed.

Mark married Stacey to throw his tormentors off the track. But the police got Denby and his men anyway, leaving Stacey to rethink her relationships with both Jamie and Mark. She soon divorced Mark and left Bay City. Jamie and his stepsister, Sally, were now to become embroiled in the doings of a filthy rich, horrendously dysfunctional family with the unlikely surname of Love. Rachel and Mac lived near the Love mansion but knew only the basics about the family that occupied it.

✦

Supposedly, Reginald and the late Elizabeth Love left behind four children: snobbish debutante Donna, acid-tongued preppy lawyer Peter, drug-addicted actress/model Nicole, and young Marley. Donna had briefly been married to Carl Hutchins, a slick business associate of Reginald's, who had a playboy son, Perry, by his first wife, Barbara. While Carl was abroad, Perry lived in the Love mansion, where he played on Donna's motherly instincts—and ached to bed Nicole. But Nicole looked upon Perry as a brat and preferred Jamie's company.

As was his weakness, Brian was drawn to Donna because she reminded him of Iris. Donna was horrified that Peter became interested in Sally, with whom he worked in the Cory legal department. Considering Sally to be of questionable heritage, Donna snooped into her background. She ended up discovering a painful secret, which Sally had not before shared with her loved ones.

While drifting around the country a few years earlier, Sally had become pregnant by a married man named David Thatcher. After she gave birth to a baby boy, David and the unethical obstetrician Dr. Royal Dunning arranged for David and his unsuspecting wife, Jennifer, to adopt the boy, now named Kevin.

Now Sally and Peter were engaged, but on the eve of their wedding, Donna confronted Sally with her knowledge of the Thatcher affair. Sensing that Sally was upset about something, Peter graciously postponed the wedding. Relieved, Donna turned her attention to Nicole, who was being menaced by Brian's son, Ted Bancroft. After his release from a mental institution, Ted had become a photographer in New York, where he hooked Nicole on cocaine.

On a happier note, the Cory family celebrated a double-ring ceremony with the marriage of Sandy and Blaine and the remarriage of Rachel and Mac.

✦

1984

Cecile liked Cass's body, but she yearned for the Love money. Thus at Donna's urging, Cecile made herself available to Peter as a friend to lean on. But when Sally came clean to Peter about her past, Cecile taped Donna offering her a bribe to get out of Peter's life. Cecile enjoyed holding the tape over Donna's head and accepted Peter's marriage proposal.

Cecile was also conspiring with Cass to steal Cory Publishing business for Cass's fledgling enterprise. Joining in the scheme was David Thatcher, Sally's slippery former lover, who decided to remain in Bay City after his wife was killed in a car crash. David invested in Cory Publishing so he could have the inside track on his fellow stockholders. He fantasized about living the high life with Sally and little Kevin—until a tragedy sent Cory stock prices plummeting.

Mac was presumed dead when his private plane went down in Canada during a blizzard. Jamie put his writing career on hold to help Sandy run the company in Mac's absence, but Sandy acted as though he didn't want or need Jamie's help. Soon Jamie and Sandy were squabbling over the most minuscule details. Hope sprang eternal when Rachel found Mac alive and brought him back to Bay City, but his son and stepson remained at odds.

This was the perfect time for Carl Hutchins to arrive. Donna's suave but two-faced ex-husband had a brief fling with Felicia and made David the front man in an environmental land scam called Greenspace. Under secret orders from Carl, David nearly duped Sandy into selling Cory land to the Greenspace project for a pittance. Mac was so upset by Sandy's ill-fated venture that he suffered a stroke!

Fortunately, Sandy backed out of Greenspace at the last minute. Nicole revealed her knowledge that Carl was behind the scam, and Sandy was left with a bruised ego. Sandy and Blaine then prepared to write an exposé on Carl, who turned the tables and generously offered Sandy a job! Sandy jumped at the chance to be his own man away from Mac and Jamie, and he accepted.

Blaine at first sided with Sandy during this prolonged family squabble, and was happy to welcome their son, Alexander Mackenzie Cory, into the world. Blaine had second thoughts, however, when Sandy became a pompous autocrat in Carl's mold. Finally she took baby Alexander and moved in with Rachel and Mac, warning Sandy she would not return until he renounced the notorious Carl Hutchins.

But Sandy was wiser to Carl's ways than he was letting on. He continued to investigate his new boss and discovered that Carl had a long-standing hatred of Mac! Back in New York, Carl had convinced his conservative father to sell their family company to Mac. When the senior Mr. Hutchins later realized he could have asked ten times the price, he committed suicide. Carl could not face up to his own guilt surrounding his father's death, so he projected it all onto Mac—and vowed to ruin him.

Shortly after he returned to Bay City, Carl had the sad duty of telling his son, Perry, that his mother was dead. Perry was bitter that nothing he could do could possibly please his exacting father. Craving Carl's approval, Perry shed his playboy ways and worked at Smiley's Diner with the lovable Maisie Watkins, whose coffee was legend among Larry Ewing's police cronies. What Larry didn't realize was that Smiley's sullen new grill man, Josh Peterson, was really his missing brother, Catlin Ewing!

Catlin initially confided his true name only to Maisie, choosing to remain anonymous to the Ewings until he had studied them from a distance. He later found work at Donna's stables and had a brief fling with that sex-starved debutante, but once he revealed his identity, Catlin found his true love: Sally.

Sally met Catlin when he gave little Kevin riding lessons. In the wake of Jennifer's death, Sally was bonding nicely with the little boy without telling him she was his mother. David banked on the growing relationship between mother and son, for he was flat broke and in dire need of the Frame megabucks that Sally could provide. When his uncle, Kevin Fowler, unseated him as guardian of little Kevin's trust fund, David smothered his uncle to death!

Liz and Alice were understanding when Sally told them of her affair with David. Yet they were clearly not pleased by Sally's decision to marry him for the sake of their child. Nor did they realize that Julia was eavesdropping on Sally's monologue, until Liz saw her granddaughter's manuscript for a seamy potboiler about Sally's life! Liz ordered Julia to stop exploiting their family in print, but Julia was resolute about selling Sally's life to Winthrop Publishing.

As Catlin watched dejectedly, Sally and David were married. Later at the reception, the lights went down and David was shot dead! Catlin confessed to the crime to protect Sally, fearing she was the real culprit, but Alice was convinced that Dr. Royal Dunning was behind the attack. Sally confronted Dunning just as he was about to skip to Mexico, and he committed suicide. Cecile and

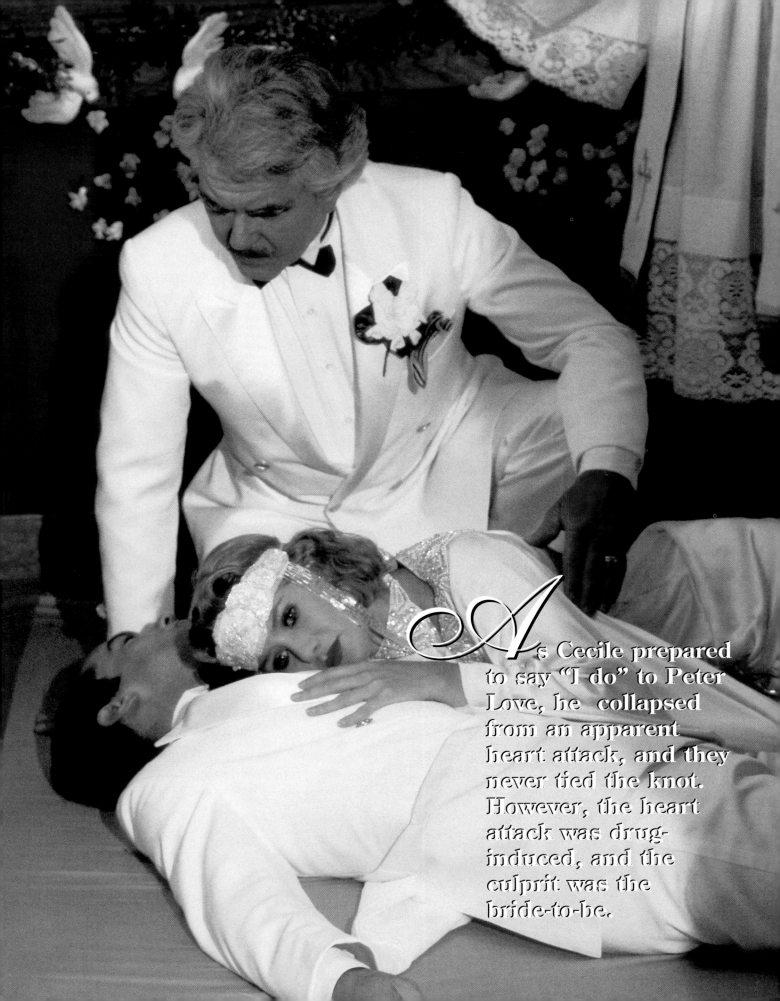

As Cecile prepared to say "I do" to Peter Love, he collapsed from an apparent heart attack, and they never tied the knot. However, the heart attack was drug-induced, and the culprit was the bride-to-be.

Felicia then teamed up to investigate Dunning's black-market baby operation, donning nun's habits as they comforted the unwed mothers who crossed the damnable doctor's path.

Peter was all set to marry Cecile until a heart attack prevented him from saying "I do." Alice discovered he had been drugged, and Donna unearthed evidence of Cecile's double-dealing with David. Peter bitterly told Cecile that their engagement was over and she skipped town. He then turned to Emily Benson, a fragile young nurse who had worked for Royal Dunning. No one realized that Emily was the one who had shot and killed David, and that she had done it for her new boss—Carl Hutchins!

Also in Carl's employ were a hit man named Ross, who trailed Catlin when he escaped police custody, and the quack doctor Herbert Harris. Catlin ended up at the Love estate, where Donna shielded him in a furnished secret room in her wine cellar. Then the evil Dr. Harris hypnotized Sally into finding Catlin and shooting him! Alice treated Catlin for his wounds as he continued to hide from the law.

Mark Singleton now entered the fray. He took up with Alice and helped her investigate the chaos surrounding Sally—only for Emily to attack him. Mark was temporarily paralyzed, but rose from his wheelchair to save Kevin from a minor house fire. Knowing Mark had named her as his assailant, Emily went on the lam and a smitten Peter protected her.

Peter's sister Nicole became further involved with Jamie, but Ted Bancroft was not happy with this development. He planted cocaine on the starry-eyed young couple, resulting in Jamie's arrest for drug possession. To prove to Nicole that he had grown up, Perry pretended to be an addict and entrapped Ted as a dealer. Brian convinced the court to send his son back to an institution rather than to prison and then left Bay City once his mayoral term was over.

Having accepted Nicole as a platonic friend, Perry found an eager romantic interest in Ada's younger daughter, Nancy McGowan. Now a spitfire teenager, Nancy reminded Ada of the young Rachel—vain, sharp-tongued, and obsessed with wealth. She gasped when Ada moved them into the resplendent but tasteful Cory mansion, then drooled at the dripping wealth that surrounded Perry.

It was through Perry that Nancy befriended Donna's youngest sister, Marley Love. Fed up with the snooty European schools that Donna had sent her to, Marley insisted on pursuing a normal existence at Bay City High School. There she met two football stars who were best buddies—Carter Todd, a boy whose widower father, Grant, pushed him to shine in sports, and Ben McKinnon, who also had a widower father, Vince.

Carter took up with Thomasina after R. J. Morgan left town with his newly married mother and stepfather, Henrietta and Roy Bingham. With the Marsh twins also out of town, Quinn and Lily found themselves competing over Grant Todd.

Donna reacted violently when Marley dated Ben, criticizing Marley for crossing class boundaries. In fact, the McKinnons were honest, hardworking people. Vince held a succession of blue-collar jobs to support Ben and his three older sisters—Kathleen, a type-A go-getter with a New York publishing background; tomboy M.J., who became Larry's tough-as-nails police partner; and pretty Cheryl, still away at college.

Larry and M.J. had plenty to keep them busy. Carl's hitman, Ross, murdered Julia Shearer when she helped Cass investigate Carl's doings. To complicate matters, Cass got into hock with a loan shark named Tony "The Tuna" Jones and masqueraded as female floozy "Krystal Lake" to elude him. In an ironic twist, Tony fell hard for Krystal and began squiring "her" around town!

It became clear to those surrounding Cass Winthrop that he was not the cold, calculating schemer he aspired to be. Underneath the affectation was a warm, funny man who couldn't help but charm everyone who crossed his path. Kathleen McKinnon saw a lot of herself in Cass and practically fell over herself to become a part of his life.

Ironically, the most fervent champion of their romance was Felicia!

If only such mirth and mayhem existed in the Cory and Love mansions. Catlin was cleared of all charges and became engaged to Sally, leaving Donna's secret room open for the first time in years. Marley happened upon the room and was dumbfounded. She had no idea that Donna was finally telling Peter the reason for the room's existence.

When she was 17, Donna had become pregnant by a stable hand. Her tyrannical father, Reginald Love, had stashed her away in the room until she gave birth to the child—her "sister," Marley! Donna was fearful of Carl, for he knew that her sister was really her daughter—and would not hesitate to use that fact to further his own ends.

At this point, however, Carl was more preoccupied with the Cory family. He overheard Sandy admit to Jamie that he was playing double agent, and drugged his errant protégé and pawn. Jamie

Despite objections from her socialite sister Donna, Marley dated Ben McKinnon. The teenagers enjoyed an outing in New York with good friends Carter Todd and his girlfriend Thomasina.

rescued Sandy and they buried the hatchet, so Carl turned his attention to Rachel and Mac. He purchased one of Rachel's sculptures, "Perspective of Love," and sent it back to her—in smithereens.

Rachel didn't know it yet, but a shocking new chapter of her life had just begun.

❧

1985

The madness and desperation of Carl Hutchins was now to be fully realized by the people of Bay City. He outbid Mac for the KBAY television station and held Mac hostage in the studio, ordering him to shoot himself as Carl's own father had done. The police arrived in time, however, and Carl gave them the lame story that Mac was losing his mind. The police didn't buy it.

Carl's next move was to catch up with Emily Benson. Pregnant with Peter's child, Emily thought herself unworthy of him and attempted suicide. Carl's hit men finished the job.

Back to the Corys. Carl knew that Larry and M.J. had a warrant out on him for illegal stock dealings,

so he holed up in a mansion owned by his deceased business associate Frederick Chapin. There he managed to lure Rachel and Nancy into a hostage situation. When the feisty Nancy tried to escape, Carl overpowered her and caused her to sustain several injuries. As Rachel watched in disbelief, a different side of Carl suddenly emerged for one brief, shining moment. Instead of tormenting Nancy further, he took her to the hospital and beat a hasty retreat.

The old Carl soon resurfaced. He confronted Mac and shot at him, but Rachel stepped in and caught the bullet. Carl was arrested and said a painful good-bye to Perry, assuring him of his love. He also vowed that he would return.

Carl's bullet left Rachel not only injured but afflicted with amnesia. Mac fumed as his wife innocently flirted with other men! Tired of Mac's jealousy, Rachel moved out of the mansion and rented a room from the couple who had bought Ada's old house. It was Rachel's quirky way of reconstructing her life. Gradually she regained her memory and reconciled with Mac.

❦

There was no such relief at the Love mansion. Jake McKinnon, Vince's brash nephew from Lassiter, Pennsylvania, arrived with his girlfriend Vicky and her doting Irish guardian, Bridget Connell. It was the intention of this triumvirate to bilk Marley out of her trust fund—for Vicky was, in fact, Marley's twin! Donna's father had paid Bridget to spirit Vicky away from his secret room moments after Donna had given birth, and he'd never told Donna of the other girl's existence.

Now that Jake's cousin Ben was at a California prep school, Jake had a clear field to move in on

Marley. Vicky smoldered with jealousy, for Marley was a virginal, uncomplicated girl with a healthy outlook on life. Not like herself, Vicky mused, a screwed-up orphan with heavy makeup and a truck driver's vocabulary. Rather than revealing herself to her family, Vicky impersonated Marley—even to an unsuspecting Jake! She needed to know whether Jake still wanted her or preferred her "good" sister.

Although Vicky managed to fool Donna, Perry suspected that something was amiss with Marley and confronted her at the Love stables. They got into a tussle—and Perry fell off a ladder to his death! Fearful and ashamed, Vicky escaped the scene. Carl was released from prison to tearfully mourn the son he never knew how to love. Nancy was so distraught over Perry's death that she turned to drugs.

Not telling Jake and Bridget she had impersonated Marley, Vicky talked them into drugging Marley so she could live her twin's life for one day. Ironically, she chose the time Donna decided to tell "Marley" that they were not sisters but mother and daughter! Vicky was further shaken to learn that Marley had a rare, potentially fatal blood disease and was in desperate need of a bone-marrow transplant.

After Bob's death, Henrietta Morgan found happiness with architect Roy Bingham.

With her conscience as her guide, Vicky came clean to the Loves and provided the marrow that ultimately saved Marley's life. Donna joyously welcomed her long-lost daughter into the family fold. The question now was, would Vicky rather lose Jake to Marley or fight for her man? It was becoming evident that Jake and Marley were very much in love.

Peter Love was sympathetic to Donna about her unfolding past but was becoming bitter over his own

BEYOND BAY CITY: MAJORCA

When Cecile was abducted to Majorca by the villainous Carl Hutchins, Cass enlisted Kathleen McKinnon's help to find her. Cass was heartbroken when Cecile decided to sail away with a king. However, it didn't take long for Cass to realize that he had found true love when he found Kathleen.

disappointing love life. He couldn't help but gloat when little Kevin refused to accept Sally and Catlin as his parents. Peter tried to work his way back into Sally's life, but she married Catlin. Yet the marriage wasn't legal, thanks to a young lady by the name of Brittany Peterson who arrived in Bay City. Brittany was Catlin's former rodeo partner and wife and now she wanted him back!

Brittany's boyfriend, a diamond-in-the-rough fisherman named Zane Lindquist, accepted her decision and decided to relocate to Bay City himself. He became instantly attracted to a woman much unlike himself—Felicia Gallant—who was now running a French spa, Le Soleil. Felicia was also busy rooting for Cass and Kathleen to get closer, but first Cass had to deal with Tony "The Tuna."

One night on a date with Tony, Krystal Lake's wig fell off and Tony realized who his new lady friend really was! Tony forgave Cass his debt on the condition that Cass play Pygmalion for Tony's punk niece, Dee Jones, and help her enter Bay City society. Cass and Kathleen eventually became involved with Le Soleil, where Sally launched a new modeling career as the "Le Soleil Woman." Catlin, who was now in the police academy, was depressed that Sally had so little time for him and allowed Brittany to seduce him.

Daphne Grimaldi, the woman who called the shots at Le Soleil, was so jealous of Sally's beauty, she actually tried to kill her! Daphne was also interested in nabbing some valuable artifacts and art pieces collected by a consortium known as CLH—which stood for Chapin, Love, and Hutchins.

Frederick Chapin's physician son, Chris, returned to Bay City and helped Nancy kick her drug habit. Nancy fell madly in love with Chris—and it didn't hurt that he was entitled to a treasure trove. In no time the young couple found themselves in Arizona on a madcap adventure, fighting a greedy Carl for the buried CLH treasures. Never ones to sit idle when action was afoot, Cass and Kathleen joined in the three-ring circus—but tragedy struck. Kathleen was paralyzed in a struggle with Carl, and refused Cass's marriage proposal.

Carl Hutchins, the Chapins, and the Loves all felt entitled to the priceless treasures buried in the Arizona desert. Carl was the first to arrive. Chris Chapin, with Nancy McGowen at his side, was hot on Carl's tail. To get information on the hidden treasure, Carl took Marley hostage and left her to die in the desert. Jake McKinnon rescued Marley from the evil Hutchins and it was there that they fell in love. While Carl and the Chapins were fighting over hidden treasure, Sally, now the poster girl for Le Soleil, was in Arizona taping commercials for the spa.

Sally and Catlin's wedded bliss was short-lived because Catlin's former wife, Brittany, arrived in town. Everyone thought she was dead, but she was very much alive and she wanted Catlin back.

On other fronts, Thomasina found herself pregnant by Carter and married him. Alice accepted a position in Washington, D.C., and decided to break off with Mark, who also left Bay City. Nicole went back to New York and entered medical school when Jamie refused to commit to her. Sandy and Blaine also left for a new life with their little boy, Alex.

1986

Mac was not himself. He was forgetful, he was coming up with one harebrained idea after another at Cory Publishing, he even fired Liz, who was now his executive assistant.

The truth was, Mac had breathed in poisoned dust from an amphora that Nancy sent him from Arizona. Nancy had no idea of her gift's inherent toxicity, but naturally a gleeful Carl did. Chris put his professional life on the line and saved Mac with a serum not yet approved by the American Medical Association. And as he had suspected he would, Chris lost his medical license. When Nancy refused Chris's marriage proposal and just wanted to live with him, Chris left Bay City and swore off his "family jewels."

The artifact caper grew more convoluted as Mac's black sheep nephew, Neal Cory, got into the act. Neal tried to get his hands on some of the treasures, as did Vicky and Jake. While Vicky wanted them for herself, however, Jake saw them as the easiest means to give Marley the advantages she deserved. Although Carl was involved, Neal knew that the top man in the jewel operation was a criminal named Fayez. When Vicky got too wise, Fayez tried to kill her—but a strange man saved her life and Fayez escaped. Vicky didn't know it yet, but that man was her father.

❧

Michael Hudson was a poor teenage stable boy when Donna's father horsewhipped him for impregnating her. Now he was a multimillionaire entrepreneur who helped the Feds investigate international espionage. Neal Cory worked for him, but when Neal got too greedy for the jewels, Michael fired him. As Neal disappeared in disgrace, his upstanding younger brother, Adam, arrived and joined the Bay City police force. Soon Adam and M.J. were showing signs of becoming a couple.

Once he was able to bring Carl and Fayez to justice, Michael revealed himself to Donna and their happy daughters. Michael doted on Vicky and Marley, but he openly disapproved of Vicky's growing obsession with separating Marley and Jake. Vicky lied to Marley that she had resumed her sexual relationship with Jake in Arizona. Marley believed her until Jake set her straight and they became engaged.

Donna wanted to marry Michael, but he was not pleased to discover that the fragile, frightened girl from his past was now a superficial snob. Donna was particularly condescending toward Brittany, who became involved with Peter after finalizing her divorce from Catlin. Brittany talked Peter into marrying her by telling him she was pregnant with his

He was a simple fisherman and she was currently the glamorous owner of an international spa. But Zane Lindquist and Felicia Gallant found a common ground and then found love.

child. Soon she gave birth to a son, Peter Jr.

But Peter went over the edge when he figured out that Catlin was little Peter's father and that Brittany had married him for his money. Rather than divorce Brittany and risk becoming a laughingstock in the community, Peter stayed married to her while abusing her both physically and verbally.

Brittany's ordeal made her more determined than ever to get Catlin back. She blurted out to Liz and Sally that she had resumed her affair with Catlin in Bay City. Liz in turn passed this tidbit to Donna, who indeed hoped that Brittany would leave Peter for Catlin. But Catlin instead married Sally, this time for real—only to lose her to a fatal car crash. Before they left town, Clarice and Larry grieved with Catlin.

Felicia married Zane and rejoiced when Kathleen regained her ability to walk. But just as Kathleen was about to walk down the aisle to Cass, he was kidnapped to St. Thomas! There he was shocked to discover that his abductors were taking their orders from Cecile! Cass's former love had married the rich but sterile King of Tanquir, and now Cecile wanted Cass to help her conceive an heir to the throne. Kathleen caught up with them just as the king was assassinated. The king's servants tried to seize power and held Cass, Kathleen, and Cecile hostage. But the king's 13-year-old brother took charge and hauled Cecile back to Tanquir!

Cass and Kathleen returned to Bay City and planned another wedding. Vince reluctantly accepted his daughter's engagement to the peripatetic Cass and went on with his life. With Ada and Maisie, Vince opened a pub called Mary's Place in honor of his late wife.

At this time, Grant Todd died of a massive heart attack, while Carter and Thomasina struggled with money problems. Jamie and Nicole returned separately and considered picking up where they had left off. Jamie, now a doctor, joined Bay City General. Much to Jamie's disappointment, Mitch Blake was sprung from the California prison and

Cass was set to marry Kathleen, but right before the ceremony Cecile abducted him to her island. It seemed that the King of Tanquir was sterile and she wanted Cass to produce an heir.

announced to Rachel that he intended to be a part of Matt's life. Now a teenager, Matt was ambivalent about his father and ran away to New York, but Mitch brought him back to a grateful Rachel and Mac.

❧

But Mitch had another reason for returning to Bay City. He was now working for Reggie "The Vulture" LaSalle, an eccentric international criminal sough by Michael Hudson. When LaSalle, his wife, Marissa, and his adopted son, Scott, arrived in Bay City from Paraguay, all heads turned. The exotic Mr. and Mrs. LaSalle were really Reginald Love and Mary McKinnon!

One more reason for Donna's disapproval of Ben McKinnon was now revealed. Years earlier, Mary had worked at the Love estate and had had an affair with Reginald behind Vince's back. Mary realized it was a brief infatuation and soon told Reginald their affair was finished. But Reginald, drawn to his servant's simplicity, refused to let her go. They struggled aboard a boat and Mary fell overboard. Leading everyone to believe Mary had drowned, Reginald actually saved her life,

only to discover that she had amnesia. So Reginald faked his own death and whisked her away to Paraguay and a new life.

The ripple effect of Reginald and Mary's return was enormous. Zane investigated Reggie's flunkies and was killed in a shoot-out. Scott began romancing Cheryl, Vince's youngest daughter. Marley married Jake and left town to get away from Reginald, and a dejected Vicky began drifting around the country. Michael vowed to protect Donna from Reginald, while a pathetic Peter did everything he could to please his father.

Peter's actions were all in vain. When Peter shot at a mad horse, Brittany—thinking she was Peter's intended victim—shot him! Quinn's attorney friend Zack Edwards defended Brittany, who revealed to the world that Catlin had fathered little Peter. Knowing that his "grandson" was not a Love, Reginald humiliated Peter by handing the baby over to Catlin. He told Catlin flatly, "Get it out of here."

As Mary's memory began to return, Vince eventually forgave her for her past infidelity and accompanied her to Cass and Kathleen's wedding. Thanks to the unfolding of Michael's investigation, Mary realized the full extent of Reginald's treachery and told him they were finished. As the entire Love family looked on, Reginald icily told his arch-enemy, "You will die for this, Michael Hudson."

When Brittany Love shot her husband Peter in self-defense, attorney Zack Edwards took on the case. In a first for daytime drama, real people from different backgrounds and locales were chosen for the jury. With the Honorable Leonard Finz, a former New York State Supreme Court judge presiding, this jury got to determine the outcome of the case. The verdict: guilty as charged.

1987

Brittany was exonerated for shooting Peter and terminated their sham of a marriage. She left Bay City to start a new life with Catlin and little Kevin, as a guilt-ridden Peter poured his heart out to a hooker named Linda. Then, to Reginald's fury, Peter was a prime suspect when Linda ended up murdered! Another possible culprit was Tony Carlisle, Nancy's new boyfriend, a young investigative reporter.

Soon the murders escalated. More prostitutes fell victim to what was obviously a serial killer, then "straight" women such as Nancy were attacked! Adam and M.J. launched an investigation, but M.J. was startled to discover who ran the local prostitution ring. It was the fast-talking Chad Rollo, who had once employed her as a prostitute, in a past life her family knew nothing about.

While M.J. struggled to hide her past, Felicia's psychic niece, Lisa Grady, helped Adam in the investigation. Lisa herself began to receive notes from the killer, stating that he would spare her life as long as she remained "pure." Soon the elusive psycho was referred to at police headquarters as the "Sin Stalker."

On the better side of town, Michael married Donna and barred Reginald from the family mansion. But Donna realized she had blocked out part of her past and consulted a psychiatrist, Dr. Alan Glaser. Alan helped her recall that during her teenage fling with Michael, his older brother, John, came on to her and they had a one-night stand. Although John had been presumed dead in Vietnam, Michael's mother, Clara, was certain he was alive and convinced Michael to search for him.

Clara Hudson believed in her heart that her son John had not died in Vietnam. Michael tracked him down in Singapore, and John returned to the family farm.

True to Clara's intuition, John was alive after all. Michael tracked him to Singapore and brought him back to Bay City, bearded and full of attitude. Clara was overjoyed to be reunited with her son, but warned John to leave Donna alone. Donna was so confused by this development that she confided to Alan Glaser that she felt "like a whore."

Wrong choice of words. Glaser was the infamous "Sin Stalker" who was nabbing the promiscuous women of Bay City! He attacked Donna in the mansion, but John fought him off and was temporarily blinded in the process. Glaser escaped and abducted Lisa to an island, where he engaged her in a macabre "wedding ceremony." The wedding dress belonged to Glaser's late mother, whose threatening voice haunted him and told him what to do.

Adam saved the day, however, and escorted a weeping Glaser to a home for the criminally insane. Lisa got close to Jamie and painfully admitted to him that Glaser had raped her when she was 14. And Peter, cleared of all suspicion, swore off his father and left Bay City a stronger man.

✦

Rachel became a close friend to Felicia and helped her to get over Zane's violent death. But Rachel had mixed feelings when Felicia bonded with Mitch, who agreed to extricate himself from Reginald's employ. Mac finally got over his own jealousy regarding Mitch when Mitch saved his life in a fire. Mac hired Mitch as a photographer for *Brava*, where Rachel was now art editor, and the three agreed to keep Matt's best interests at heart.

Rachel's concept of Amanda's best interests, however, did not mesh with Amanda's own ideas. Rachel tried to turn Amanda into the debutante she never was—but Amanda boldly stood up to her mother, and both Mac and Ada backed Amanda up. When Amanda reluctantly allowed Rachel to throw her a debutante ball at the mansion, the girl passed over the preppies and cozied up to the gruff young man who parked the cars. His name was Sam Fowler, and he was Mitch's younger half-brother!

A comedy of misunderstandings now began. Hell bent on making it on his own, Sam didn't admit his

When Amanda Cory returned from boarding school, she had no interest in the debutante life, but Mac and Rachel wanted to give her a proper welcome and threw her a debutante ball at the mansion.

Dawn Rollo and Scott LaSalle were very much in love when Dawn discovered she had AIDS. She'd contracted the virus through a blood transfusion she'd received years earlier from her mother—a prostitute and drug abuser. A very special love triumphed as these two young people came to terms with the disease.

relationship to Mitch. Rachel noticed his artistic talent and hired him as an illustrator for *Brava,* where he met "Mandy Ashton," a feisty clerical worker. Sam didn't know that Mandy was Amanda—whom he had met only briefly in the dark and who coined the Mandy moniker so that she wouldn't come off as the boss's daughter!

Leave it to Liz to discover Sam's relationship to Mitch in an employment file. The secrets now revealed, Sam bristled at the thought of getting involved with the wealthy Amanda Cory. He had no use for rich people.

Speaking of the rich .... Michael located Vicky in Las Vegas, where she had gambled all her money away. Michael paid her tab on the condition that she come back to Bay City with him and get her life in order. Sensing that Michael and Donna were coming apart at the seams over John, Reginald fed Vicky's fear that Donna would leave Michael for John. Reggie even bribed a geneticist to lie that John had fathered Marley and Vicky, but Jamie ran a test that negated the lie.

Playing right into Reginald's hands, Vicky saw Donna and John talking intimately and sped off in her sports car. She lost control, crashed, and was left in a coma. Jamie treated her at the hospital. Lisa was surprised by the feelings Jamie was showing toward his new patient. Marley returned to offer her sister moral support—but was noncommittal about Jake's whereabouts.

M.J., on the other hand, was open with Adam and her family about her hooker past. Once over their initial shock, M.J.'s loved ones understood. M.J. realized, however, that she still had feelings for Chad, who wasn't such a bad guy after all. Chad took his younger sister Dawn under his wing after their prostitute mother died. Scott took one look at the vulnerable Dawn and began to cool toward Cheryl.

It was Jamie who burst Scott's balloon when he discovered that Dawn had AIDS, thanks to a tainted blood transfusion from her promiscuous mother a few years before. Adding to Scott's confusion was his divided loyalty between Reginald and Mary, as Vince and Mary vacillated about whether or not to remarry.

It was tragedy that would draw Vince and Mary closer together. Cass returned alone from his honeymoon and announced that their plane had crashed on the way back to Bay City and Kathleen had burned with the plane! Just as Vince had finally come to accept Cass, he was horrified when Cass took up with Nicole in a heartbeat.

In actual fact, this was not Cass, but his diabolical lookalike (thanks to extensive plastic surgery) Rex Allingham, who was holding the real Cass prisoner in a series of remote locations. Having already killed Kathleen, Rex was plotting to marry Nicole for her money, then kill her and abscond with the dough while the real Cass rotted in jail! On the day of the wedding Cass escaped and rushed to the scene. Rex's wife had had the hots for Cass and in the ensuing melee she fell from the balcony to her death.

When an armed and dangerous Rex tried to take Nicole hostage in a crowded disco, Cass gallantly came to the rescue by cutting loose a chandelier which fell directly on his evil double's head. It was then that Nicole got to know Cass intimately for the first time.

Amanda bypassed the preppie college boys and chose the darkly handsome artist Sam Fowler, a fellow Cory Publishing employee, as the object of her affections.

*J*osie Watts found romance with Matt Cory, but neither family was happy with the match. Josie and her mother felt inferior to the Corys, and Rachel had grown suspicious of the Frames.

1988

In 1988 a long-lost Frame relative arrived with a dubious connection to the Love family. Jason Frame, Steve's black sheep brother, moved to a Bay City farm that Steve had purchased shortly before his death. Prior to Steve's arrival in Bay City years earlier, Jason had worked at the Love estate and carried on with Reginald's wife, Elizabeth. Mary, still struggling with her memory, recalled that Reginald had shot and killed Elizabeth on the night she was planning to run off with Jason, but made it appear a suicide.

As Michael and Donna awaited the birth of a child, Michael put his investigation of Reginald into high gear and proved that Reginald had murdered Elizabeth. A desperate Reginald held Donna hostage at Nicole's new salon, only for Donna to fall down a flight of stairs and lose her baby. Michael attacked Reginald in a rage and the two fought on the salon's roof. Reginald lost his balance and fell to his death.

Only two people mourned this tragically empty man. One was his adoptive son, Scott, who reconciled with Cheryl and left town after Dawn died of AIDS. The other was Mary, who found happiness again when she remarried Vince. They eventually moved to Minneapolis, where a newly married Adam and M.J. were now top cops.

Quinn Harding had been killed by the Sin Stalker, and in the wake of her death, Jason took over Steve's company and renamed it Frame Construction. He took on John Hudson as a partner and landed a major contract—a new wing at Bay City General Hospital. It was through Jason that John became friendly with Sharlene, who arrived at the farm with her knockout of a teenage daughter, Josie. Sharlene wanted the best for Josie and gave her the last name of Watts, even though her husband, Floyd Watts, had died before Josie was conceived.

Josie's hot new romance with Matt did not sit well with either Rachel or Sharlene, however. Rachel was now of Liz's opinion that the Frames were bad news. Resentful of the Corys' success, Jason told Matt that Rachel had willfully killed his sister Janice and cheated with Mitch behind Mac's back, both lies. Matt, confused, could only react with anger, and soon his attitude had Rachel and Mitch at their wits' end.

Mitch was embarrassed when his and Sam's kleptomaniac mother, Loretta Fowler, came from Seattle to attend Amanda and Sam's wedding. Mitch himself married Felicia, who was now managing a hot spot called Tops owned by the Love family. Felicia and Amanda felt sorry for Loretta and shamed their husbands into accepting their mother.

Amanda was now to become a pawn in a dubious scheme. Jason was secretly reporting to a "chief" who plotted a hostile takeover of Mac's company in the guise of a firm named Bennett Publishing. The chief had a wide sphere of underlings, including Nicole's former flame Drew Marsten, who tried to rape Amanda and then framed Mac for his own murder! Drew was actually still alive, but the chief moved him to Europe and replaced him with the slick Evan Bates. Unlike Drew, Evan's approach was to ingratiate himself with the Corys and become an invaluable asset to the company. Evan's sometime lover was an alluring Australian named Caroline Stafford, a gallery owner in the chief's employ.

Michael had every reason to believe the chief was Carl Hutchins. But it was actually someone from Michael's past in Europe—and many others' in Bay City as well. It was Iris!

Radiating sweetness and light, Iris returned to Bay City swearing to Rachel and Mac that she had buried the hatchet. Though Mac gave her the benefit of the doubt, Rachel was not convinced. Secretly plotting to take over Cory Publishing, Iris immediately became competitive with Amanda and set out to drive a wedge between her and Sam. Iris made Evan pour on the charm to Amanda while Caroline moved in on Sam by sponsoring his artwork. But contrary to Iris's plans, Caroline ultimately set her sights on Cass and competed with Nicole for his affections.

One night, Sam accidentally ran his car into a child who walked into its path. It was a two-year-old boy named Mikey who had been abandoned. The

Lisa Grady and Jamie Frame were very much in love, but Vicky Hudson had the hots for Jamie, and soon this would become the most troubled of triangles.

child survived his injuries and immediately bonded with Michael over their common first name. Michael and Donna tried to adopt Mikey, but a woman named Chris McAlear, who was a construction worker for Frame, also wanted the child and abducted him. John discovered that Chris and her husband had served in Vietnam, where she had seen her husband and little boy blown to bits in a bombing. John retrieved the boy from the deeply troubled Chris and she was institutionalized.

Donna was not happy when Jake followed Marley back to Bay City. While they were living in Los Angeles, Marley had discovered she was infertile and had turned away from Jake. Not one to sit idle, the frustrated Jake had an affair, which Marley soon discovered. Now he wanted her back, but Marley was afraid of being hurt again. Thus Jake found solace in Vicky's bed! But Vicky also had the hots for Jamie and seduced him during a low point in his relationship with Felicia's niece Lisa Grady. Soon Vicky was pregnant! She suspected the child was Jake's, but for Marley's sake she named Jamie as the father.

One night Felicia, Mitch, Cass, and Nicole attended a magic show. The magician, "Oliver Twist," hypnotized Felicia on stage and transported her to a time when she was a scared sixteen-year-old named Fanny Grady. Felicia was about to come to terms with her sad, hidden past.

1989

The truth was out. Donna overheard Iris refer to herself as "the chief" and helped Rachel get the goods on her ice princess stepdaughter once and for all. Mac bitterly wrote his daughter off. This time he meant it.

Rachel and Mac turned their attention to the celebration of Cory Publishing's 25th anniversary. Many former Bay City residents turned out for Mac's classy party in his company's honor—Robert Delaney, the Matthews sisters Pat and Alice, and the brassy Gwen Parrish Frame—everyone except Mac. Mac wrote to Rachel that he was out of town trying to come to terms with his betrayal by his daughter Iris, who was behind the recent takeover attempt by Bennett Publishing.

The Red Swan was Mac's last gift to his beloved Rachel. It would hold the key to a mystery that was about to unfold.

After the party, Gwen expressed to Rachel her resentment that Rachel had inherited the bulk of Steve's estate at Willis's expense. Gwen even physically attacked and injured Rachel—only for Iris to save Rachel's life! Rachel thanked Iris and refused to press charges against Gwen, who was deeply grateful. The Corys and the Frames finally made their peace.

The peace came not a moment too soon. Rachel was devastated to receive word that Mac, while on a business trip to Maine, had died of a heart attack. Hoping for unity within his family, Mac had left equal shares of Cory Publishing to Rachel, Iris, and Amanda. Rachel was then somewhat comforted to receive a package in the mail that Mac had sent her from Maine. It was a striking porcelain figurine called The Red Swan and was accompanied by a tantalizing note from Mac: "Wait until you hear the story behind this baby."

An enigmatic figure named Lucas Castigliano now appeared on the scene. Lucas's connections to the people of Bay City were manifold: He had fathered a child whom teenage Felicia had believed to be stillborn; he was one of Sharlene's "johns" from her prostitute days; he was a reputed art thief whom Michael was shadowing; he was with Mac in Maine the day before he died; and he had an inordinate interest in The Red Swan. So did Griffen Sanders, the new head of the Bay City Ballet, who pilfered the figurine and discussed it cryptically in a conversation with Lucas.

Lucas's arrival immediately threw him into a romantic triangle with Iris and Felicia. Iris hired the dark newcomer for her bold new beauty magazine, *Sophisticate,* and had an affair with him. But fate kept throwing him back to Felicia—whom he had known and loved back in Boston as Fanny Grady. Lucas forced Felicia's Aunt Abigail to admit that Felicia's child had survived after all! Abigail had given the baby girl away at the behest of Felicia's moralistic stepfather, Noah Grady. Now Felicia and Lucas were determined to find the daughter they had lost. A sympathetic Mitch went to Boston to investigate.

Always one to have an angle, Jason lifted a letter Felicia had written to Noah and tantalized her with it. He also blackmailed Iris with his knowledge that she was "the chief" and that she'd had a fling with Michael on the Riviera a few years earlier. The stage was set: Jason was killed and Felicia stood trial for the crime.

❧

Assisting Cass in his investigation was private eye Mary Frances "Frankie" Frame, daughter of Sharlene's older sister Emma Ordway. Frankie had used the Frame surname since the death of Frankie's crass father, Burt Ordway. Nicole

It was an unlikely pairing, but Stacey Winthrop and Derek Dane were clearly drawn to each other.

became wildly jealous of the obvious chemistry between Cass and Frankie.

In addition to the many obvious suspects in the Jason Frame murder case, a hulking but quiet young man named Derek Dane presented himself in town. He began to tail Stacey Winthrop, who was back in Bay City working with Cass and Zack's new law firm, Winthrop & Edwards. Derek was an orphan whom Felicia had read to as a boy, and he admitted having fatally struck Noah Grady with a poker in self-defense.

Under hypnosis, Derek remembered that he had witnessed Jason's murder. The killer was Nicole! On the eve of her wedding to Cass, Nicole admitted to the crime. Still mentally fragile, Nicole hated Jason for the misery he had brought to so many people, including herself. Nicole was institutionalized, and after spending a month in jail, Felicia was freed. This left Cass and Frankie free to investigate Lucas. The craggy Derek and crisply professional Stacey started an offbeat relationship, but Stacey was baffled by Derek's sudden interest in The Red Swan.

After overhearing Iris and Lucas discussing the figurine, Frankie went undercover and got herself hired as Lucas's secretary. Lucas soon caught Frankie spying on him and was livid, but not threatening. "If I was the man you and Cass believe me to be," he told her, "you'd probably be dead by now."

Mitch returned with no leads on Felicia and Lucas's child. He was uncomfortable with the growing bond between Felicia and Lucas, while Felicia felt more threatened than ever by Mitch's friendship with the newly widowed Rachel. However, at this point in her life, Rachel was primarily concerned with keeping Cory Publishing afloat and making Amanda happy.

Rachel went overboard with the latter, however. Stumbling upon proof that Rachel had paid Caroline Stafford to sponsor a show of Sam's art, Iris told Sam. Fiercely independent, Sam used his splashy opening to publicly tell off his mother-in-law. Evan took full advantage of the situation to become closer to Amanda—but he had more substance than anyone realized. He risked his life to save Amanda from a demented kidnapper named Dustin Trent. And he admitted to Rachel who he really was: Earl Battis, the illegitimate son of Janice Frame Cory!

Evan had forgiven Janice for giving him away and wanted to get to know her in his later life. When Janice was killed, Evan, not knowing the facts surrounding his mother's death, blamed Rachel and hooked up with Iris to hit the Cory clan from behind the scenes as a way to avenge her death. But Evan truly loved Amanda and was affected by her family's warmth, so he decided to come clean about his identity.

Amanda's brothers, Jamie and Matt, were also embroiled in triangles. Josie cooled it with Matt because she and her mother, Sharlene, felt inferior to the Corys. At the same time, Lisa broke off with Jamie after a pregnant Vicky fought her tooth and nail. Both on the rebound, Matt and Lisa had a brief affair. Eventually Josie returned to Matt and lost her virginity to him, their relationship stronger than ever.

Jamie married Vicky and they celebrated the birth of a boy, Steven Michael Frame. To right the wrongs of his own confused childhood, Jamie was determined that his son would be not only loved, but legitimized from the first day of his life. But Jake was obsessed with the fact that he and Marley could not have children, and wished and suspected that Steven was his! Jake desperately tried to convince Marley to reconcile with him so they could fight Jamie and Vicky for the boy's custody. However, Marley refused to hurt her sister and went back to Los Angeles alone.

As fate would have it, Jamie found out about Vicky's recent tryst with Jake and told her they were finished. Jamie and Vicky got into a bitter custody battle. Jake testified on Vicky's behalf, hoping to marry Vicky and claim his child. But the judge awarded temporary custody to Jamie.

Jamie celebrated fatherhood in yet another way. With Steve and Mac both deceased, Jamie was delighted when Russ Matthews—the man who originally believed himself to be Jamie's father—became chief of staff at Bay City General Hospital. Russ had married Olivia and had a daughter by the same name shortly before his wife's untimely death. He was a strict, distant father to the spirited young Olivia, who had dreams of becoming a dancer. When Russ and Liz introduced Olivia to the people of Bay City, Olivia immediately set her sights on the artsy Sam.

Sharlene was thrown into a state by Russ's reappearance. She filled John in about Russ's violent reaction to her sordid past, while John came to terms with his own. He had fallen asleep while pulling guard duty in Vietnam, then woke up to find the dead bodies of children who had been killed on his watch! John finally forgave himself by resurrecting an old dream of his—to become a doctor. He resumed studying medicine and worked as an orderly under Russ, who was a hard taskmaster.

One day John noticed that Sharlene had two birth certifi-

It wasn't exactly a match made in heaven when Jamie Frame married Vicky Hudson. Vicky was pregnant and she'd slept with Jake, who was sure the baby was his.

cates for Josie, and made Sharlene admit the truth: Russ was Josie's father! Sharlene had been pregnant during the final stages of her marriage to Russ, but chose to keep her pregnancy a secret so that she and Russ could get on with their separate lives. John convinced Sharlene to tell Russ the truth, and he warmly accepted Josie as his daughter. Shortly thereafter, Russ accepted a prestigious position with L'Academie de Provence in Nice, France—leaving Josie to battle her resentful half-sister, Olivia.

John passed his medical exams and married Sharlene, but his brother, Michael, was not so fortunate. He was seen in public with an exotic beauty named Arianne and told Donna he wanted out of their marriage. In fact, he was only protecting Donna from Lucas,

Paulina came to town as part of the Red Swan mystery. Her intention was to scam the Corys into thinking she was Mac's daughter. As it turned out, she was, but at the time, Rachel was the only one who accepted her.

When Russ Matthews returned to Bay City, John convinced a troubled Sharlene to tell him the truth about Josie's paternity.

whom Michael was investigating on assignment with the Club, an FBI-like organization.

Jake lent spice to Donna's life when he promised to leave Vicky alone in exchange for her financial partnership in his new videotaping business. Donna found herself suddenly attracted to her macho working-class son-in-law, and they had a one-night stand!

But the lion's share of Bay City's spicy intrigue went to Cass. It wasn't enough that Frankie and Caroline were fighting over him—Cecile came back and made it a three-way war! Cass remained closest to Frankie, however, and Caroline and Cecile would both leave town in 1990, leaving the field wide open.

Through Frankie and Cass's investigation into Lucas's possible connection with Mac's death, the intrepid duo discovered that Mac had been about to change his will before he died.

Why would Mac have done such a thing?

When Sharlene began acting strangely, it was revealed that she had another personality—sexy "Sharly"—and Congressman Grant Harrison was very interested.

1990

Rachel decided to undertake her own investigation into her beloved husband's death. She recalled that in his last piece of correspondence to her from Maine, he had written, "Find Ken Jordan." Rachel learned that Jordan owned the Odyssey, the gallery where Mac purchased The Red Swan, and tracked down the handsome art dealer. Aware of their mutual attraction, Ken decided to follow Rachel to Bay City. At the same time, Rachel hired Derek's childhood friend Paulina as little Steven's nanny.

Ken and Paulina were in cahoots. Some twenty-five years earlier, Ken had been Mac's private pilot—as well as his rival for the affections of a Central American woman named Maria. Ken blamed Mac for leaving him for dead after a plane crash, unaware that Mac was trying to find help for him. The two had never found one another until Mac walked into Ken's gallery in Maine, and they argued over the circumstances of the plane crash. Ken also knew—though Mac did not—that Maria had given birth to Mac's baby girl before she died.

After Mac's death, Ken sought a young woman who matched the genetic makeup of a child Mac and Maria could logically have conceived and came up with the poor, orphaned Paulina. Their plan was for Paulina to claim her share of the inheritance, then split it with Ken.

In point of fact, Paulina wanted to be a part of a family more than she wanted the money. When she announced that she was Mac's daughter, Rachel welcomed her—but Iris was instantly suspicious. So was Jake, who hired Paulina as his video assistant. Separately, Iris and Jake discovered Paulina's collusion with Ken and held it over their heads. Paulina didn't want to lose this family that had come to mean so much to her, but Ken wanted to come clean. He now realized that Mac had sought help for him after the plane crash—plus he

They were recovering from broken marriages—he to her sister Vicky, and she to Jake. While on holiday in the south of France, Marley and Jamie tried to heal their broken hearts.

was genuinely falling for Rachel. The two got cozy on an archaeological dig in Arizona and their relationship got sexual.

Between Rachel's attraction to Ken and Felicia's renewed connection with Lucas, Mitch felt squeezed out. He accepted a long-term photography assignment in Africa and amicably divorced Felicia. Lucas eventually made love to Felicia for the first time in years, and Iris coldly ordered him out of her life.

❧

John was bewildered by Sharlene's inconsistent reactions to him. One day she gave him the cold shoulder, the next day she was coming on to him. John discovered that Sharlene actually had multiple personalities! "Sharlene" was the solid farm woman, marketing her preserves and caring for Josie. "Sharly" was the loose woman, the continuation of Sharlene's former persona as a prostitute.

Sharlene had developed this personality disorder at the age of 10, when her brother Jason accepted money from a neighborhood boy for the horrific privilege of raping her. Sharlene's own brother was her first pimp! Sharlene's sister Emma had her institutionalized for a while, but it was now painfully obvious that Sharlene was still in dire need of help.

While Sharlene was faithful to John, "Sharly" aroused the interest of his demanding new patient, Congressman Grant Harrison, chairman of the House Committee on Crime. Released from the hospital after treatment for a rare blood ailment, Grant took Sharly to bed and was determined to have her for keeps! With professional help, Sharlene merged her two personalities and became pregnant with John's child. But Grant couldn't get her out of his system—and he was accustomed to getting what he wanted.

Grant was campaigning for the state Senate on a strong anticrime platform. He knew he could win votes if he found evidence against Lucas—who had no intention of becoming Grant's sacrificial lamb. Josie became one of Lucas's *Sophisticate* models and agreed to spy on Grant for Lucas. She thus discovered Grant's affair with her mother. Although Lucas decided not to use it, Grant lost the Senate race anyway.

Meanwhile, Josie's half-sister, Olivia, competed for the limelight by dancing in Griffen Sanders's ballet troupe. One night as Olivia danced on stage, Lucas shot and killed Griffen from a distance! Michael didn't

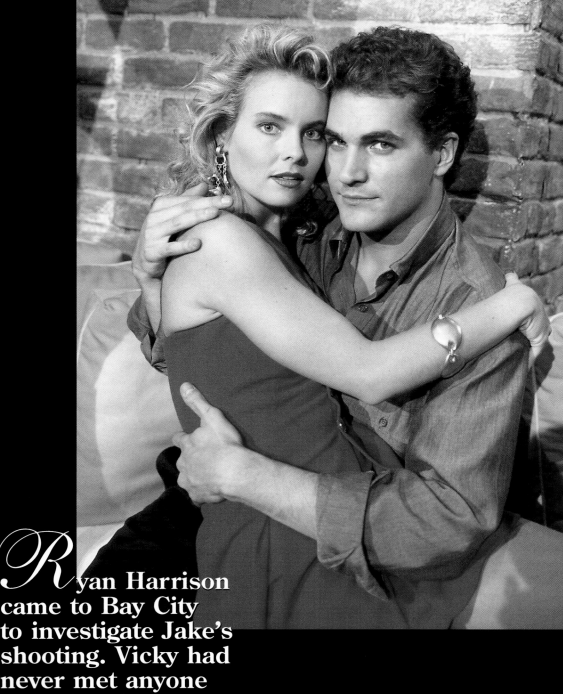

$\mathcal{R}$yan Harrison
came to Bay City
to investigate Jake's
shooting. Vicky had
never met anyone
quite like him.

collar Lucas, because Lucas revealed to Michael that Arianne was a double agent for his unnamed boss, from whom he wanted to free himself. Michael proceeded to have the book thrown at Arianne.

No longer in need of a cover, Michael reconciled with Donna as they tried to adopt little Mikey. But when the boy's parents, Toby and Eve Miller, surfaced, Donna empathized with the couple and let them keep the boy, Michael was disgusted and vowed to divorce Donna after all.

Back at Cory Publishing, Iris bonded with her sister Amanda despite herself. Evan managed to seduce Amanda and made it appear that Sam was "gaslighting" her. Sam caught on and had such a violent fight with Evan that the nefarious Mr. Bates fell down an elevator shaft! Evan survived and, realizing that Amanda would always love Sam, left Bay City in disgrace.

As for other developments, Matt feared for Josie when a deranged fan stalked her. Once he realized the young model was pulling a publicity stunt, Matt dumped her. He became friends with Dean Frame, the funky teenage son of Sharlene's first cousin Henry. Sharlene's twisted new therapist, Dr. Taylor Benson, sabotaged Sharlene's treatment so that she could sink her hooks into John. Stacey moved in with Derek, while Zack moved to Washington, D.C.

Michael and Donna were at least happy to welcome Marley, who returned from Los Angeles. Marley enjoyed a promising new relationship with Jamie after he divorced Vicky. But Jake sensed that Marley still had feelings for him, even though she discovered his one-night stand with Donna. When Marley wouldn't commit to Jake, he raped her. Later that night, Jake was shot by a mystery assailant and fell into a coma, and Marley was accused of the crime.

As Jake lay unconscious, Grant's younger brother, Ryan Harrison, a policeman with connections to the Feds, investigated the shooting. Vicky helped Ryan in his quest for the truth, and realized she had never met a man quite like him. He was as honest and straightforward as Grant was maddeningly not.

Given her track record, Ryan was exactly what Vicky needed.

1991

Cass was knocked for a loop when Kathleen, the beloved wife he had assumed dead, returned to Bay City! Kathleen revealed to an openmouthed Cass that Carl Hutchins had ordered Rex Allingham to sabotage her plane so that she wouldn't write an exposé on Carl.

After a long convalescence, Kathleen had been placed in a witness protection program by the Feds. With Kathleen back in town, Cass was now in the unenviable position of loving two women! Frankie had become pregnant by Cass, but when she miscarried, she feared she would lose Cass to Kathleen.

Kathleen's comatose cousin Jake was the subject of a brouhaha surrounding his shooting. Donna confessed to protect Marley, who was the prime suspect, and revealed her one-night stand with Jake in the process. Then Jake came to and remembered who really shot him: Paulina! Donna's revelation led Michael to file for divorce.

But Jake didn't rush to call the cops. Just as Ken confessed his and Paulina's scam to a horrified Rachel, Paulina turned out to be Mac's daughter after all! Jake blackmailed Paulina into influencing Marley to come back to him. But Marley was engaged to marry Jamie, so Jake had to try another angle—he could marry Paulina for the Cory cash! Paulina was so wowed by Grant, however, that he proposed to her and put Sharlene in the past.

Rachel forgave Paulina and brought her into the Cory Publishing fold. But Iris knew a trickster when she saw one and confronted Paulina: "You're terrified of Jake. I asked myself why. Then it came to me: You were the one who shot him, and he knows it!" Paulina neither confirmed nor denied Iris's accusation and looked forward to a glamorous new life as Mrs. Grant Harrison.

Grant's brother, Ryan, bristled when Carl Hutchins returned to town. Representing the Feds in Bay City while Michael was abroad on assignment, Ryan was hell-bent on proving Carl guilty of a series

Spencer Harrison and Iris Wheeler were an item for awhile, but Spencer seemed more interested in Iris's nemesis, Rachel Cory.

of crimes. Carl tried to make everyone believe he had changed, but he was still up to his old tricks. He had one of his more attractive underlings, Lorna Devon, infiltrate Dean Frame and Matt Cory's new D&M recording studio. Carl's intention was to traffic counterfeit plates with D&M's discs! An unsuspecting Matt took up with Lorna.

It was now revealed that Carl was Lucas's boss and that Lucas wanted out. Carl suspected that Lucas was a masked witness—code-named Signet—who was feeding Kathleen information on Carl. Ryan unmasked the real culprit, and to his shock and surprise, it was his own brother, Grant! Ryan and Vicky investigated further and discovered that thanks to Carl's generous campaign contributions, Grant won the Senate seat he had failed to grab in the previous election. Paulina dropped Grant and married a greedy Jake on the rebound, but Grant continued to lust after her.

Meanwhile, Felicia married Lucas, and they became the guardians of Jenna, the daughter of a deceased friend, Gloria Norris. Curious about why the girl had grown up in a convent, Lucas hoped she might be his and Felicia's long-missing daughter. But Felicia pointed out that Jenna was older than their daughter would have been. Still the newlyweds doted on Jenna and worried about her new romance with Dean Frame.

Olivia was hot for Sam and convinced him to divorce Amanda. Sam moved in with Olivia, but dumped her after catching her faking a dance-related injury to get his sympathy. Amanda was too busy to moon over Sam, for she rightly suspected Carl was behind attempts on many lives in town. Paulina saved Amanda from a suspicious fire at Rachel's studio, while Frankie pushed Kathleen away from an explosion in the nick of time. Grateful beyond words, Kathleen freed Cass to marry Frankie and pursued her writing career in New York.

The iron-willed Amanda had reached her limit with Carl. Not only did she slap him hard across the face—she drugged him into admitting his guilt! Ryan happily arrested Carl.

Spencer Harrison, Grant and Ryan's powerful father, was now to figure into the scenario. Spencer had a fling with Iris but took a stronger liking to Rachel, whose mansion was adjacent to his new digs. To save Grant's reputation, Spencer tried to convince Ryan that he—not Grant—was in Carl's pocket. Ryan didn't know what to believe. Nor did he know how to react when Grant flirted with his lady love, Vicky!

Vicky's sister, Marley, was at loose ends when a jealous Jake broke up her wedding to Jamie. Jake knew his marriage to Paulina was a sham and was still trying to prove that little Steven was his, not Jamie's. Would-be bridegroom Jamie found comfort in his renewed friendship with Dennis Carrington Wheeler, who returned to Bay City.

Meanwhile, Jamie's Aunt Sharlene was cruelly manipulated by her psychiatrist, Taylor Benson, who tried to make her think that "Sharly" was back. When Taylor failed in her attempt to seduce John, he realized that the therapist was sicker than the patient. Investigating the deranged doctor, he discovered she was a imposter named Cindy Woods! Cindy/Taylor then framed John for her own drowning and stashed Sharlene on a boat—which she set afire! The boat exploded and Sharlene was presumed dead.

When Felicia married Lucas, they became the guardians of Jenna Norris, the daughter of Felicia's editor, Gloria Norris, who had passed away. They doted on her as if she were their own.

Kelsey Harrison was struggling to make it in the world of medicine as an intern in BCGH's mentor program, where she was vying for the position of special assistant to Dr. Jamie Frame. Harrison charged Frame with sexual discrimination when he chose Dr. Darryl Beckett over her. Frame publicly admitted that he chose someone other than Dr. Harrison so that his relationship with her wouldn't be put under undue stress. He was suspended from his hospital duties for two weeks.

1992

Marley was sensitive to the fact that Vicky's son, Steven, was proved to be Jamie's—for she herself was sterile. When Vicky innocently offered to carry a surrogate child for Marley and Jamie, Marley reacted angrily. Marley ultimately broke off with Jamie and took up with his pal Dennis, with whom she ran a gallery. Before he and Marley reached the physical stage of their relationship, Dennis had a fling with Olivia. However, Dennis and Marley became quite enamored of one another. Later Marley was insulted to find out that Dennis had bet Jake he could woo her away from Jamie!

Olivia, devastated when Sam remarried Amanda, dropped the bombshell that she was carrying Sam's child! Olivia's surprise was obvious when Amanda not only understood, but wanted to be a part of the child's life! Liz denounced Olivia as selfish, for she suspected that her grandniece had been impregnated by someone other than Sam.

She was right. When Dennis got upset that Marley was edging closer to Jamie, he crashed his sports car and Olivia kept vigil. She then admitted that Dennis was the father of her child! Olivia left Bay City and gave birth to a daughter, Sarah. Dennis followed, determined to be an active father to his little girl. Amanda and Sam had a promising second marriage until Lorna convinced him to dump his Cory job to become a singing star! Amanda refused to accompany Sam on the road, and the marriage fizzled.

Paulina confessed to shooting Jake, who planned to divorce her but did not press charges. This freed Paulina to become engaged to Grant, but Vicky realized she wanted to hold on to Grant for herself! Ironically, Jake realized that his marriage to Paulina wasn't so bad after all.

When Grant whisked Vicky away for a Canadian honeymoon, she tried to get the straitlaced senator to have some fun in the snow. As it happened, it was a very eventful trip.

Vicky later regretted her involvement with the shady Grant and realized her heart belonged with Ryan. Not to be outdone, Grant made sure the tabloids printed rumors of his tryst with Vicky so that Ryan would have second thoughts. He did—and Grant proposed.

Lucas hired a dubious acquaintance, Rick Madison, to investigate Jenna's unknown father. This turned out to be a disastrous decision, for Rick drugged Jenna and made an X-rated video with her! Soon Rick ended up murdered. Lorna got her hands on the tape and showed it on television in an attempt to end Matt's infatuation with Jenna. Ironically, Lorna herself had a porno past, which Carl was holding over her. To Rachel's great relief, Matt dumped Lorna!

Felicia witnessed the confrontation and saw Lorna wearing a ring similar to those she and Lucas had. It clicked—Lorna was the daughter Felicia and Lucas were looking for! The happiness of this reunited family was short-lived, however, when Lucas was fatally shot.

Naturally Ryan suspected Carl, who had been sprung from the big house, and the two struggled on a scaffold. Carl started to fall and Ryan challenged him to come up with one good reason Ryan should let him live. Carl screamed, "Because I'm your father!" Ryan's mother, a writer with the pen name of Justine Kirkland, had conceived him through a long-standing affair with Carl. Ryan was now torn between two fathers.

Spencer ultimately spared Ryan the indignity of arresting him. He admitted reluctantly that Grant had accepted Carl's dirty money for his campaign. However, Carl was cleared of suspicion in the murders of Rick and Lucas. Jake's half-brother, DA Kevin Anderson, collared the real killer of both victims: Rick's unstable sister, Sally. When Jenna moved in with Dean, Felicia was left alone to grieve Lucas's death and turned to drink. Close friends Rachel and Cass bacame increasingly alarmed and staged an intervention.

social issues

Marley found herself torn between two men who were interested in getting more intimately involved with her: Byron Pierce, a wheelchair-bound lawyer working with Cass, whose arrogance and self-assurance masked his insecurities; and Dennis, Marley's partner in the Wheeler Gallery. A cocky womanizer, Dennis tried to prove his manhood by taking chances, like driving racing cars. Dennis and Byron challenged each other to a tennis match to see who would win Marley's love. Marley resented their macho posturing and told them both off, but the competition went ahead as scheduled.

Felicia's buddy Cass was jealous when John, now a grieving widower, had feelings for Frankie. Soon John shifted his attention to Donna, who spent a great deal of time with him and Gregory, his new son by Sharlene. Around this time, Matt discovered that Donna, bilked by her accountant, had to find a job as a party planner. The image-conscious Donna swore Matt to secrecy—and a May-December romance was born!

Iris was another society matron who was gainfully employed these days. She helped Rachel run KBAY-TV, now owned by Cory Publishing, and chaired the hospital board. At the television station, Iris actually agreed with Rachel about one thing: that Felicia made a disastrous mistake in hiring brash, sensationalistic Jake as an interviewer! At Bay City General Hospital, Iris made an unlikely male acquaintance: a blue-collar man named Hank Kent, whose son, Tommy, was terminally ill.

The real intrigue at the hospital involved Kelsey Harrison, Spencer's niece, a hardworking intern who got chummy with Jamie. When Jamie refused to promote her, Kelsey sued the hospital for sex discrimination! Insecure about his own career, Jamie sheepishly admitted that he had withheld the promotion from Kelsey because of their mutual attraction. Jamie moved to Somalia before finally settling in San Francisco, and John began to look seriously in Kelsey's direction.

1993

Felicia's alcoholism cut a wide swath among her circle of relatives and friends. When Rachel named Jenna as Felicia's television replacement, Felicia retaliated by signing with another publishing house! Jenna became pregnant by Dean but couldn't go on with her life until Felicia got her act together. Felicia swore she was off the bottle, but Jenna caught her with a flask and became so upset that she miscarried!

This tragedy was just the shock Felicia needed to

Paulina was torn between two lovers, Ian and Jake. The trio found themselves in the San Cristobal rain forest, in search of three keys. One belonged to Carl's dad, the second to Mac, and the third to Ian's father, Leon. The keys led them to a box containing the secret to a rare drug.

push her into joining Alcoholics Anonymous. There she was surprised to see that Spencer was also in the program! Spencer was winning his battle with booze, but not faring well in his addiction to gambling—or to acquiring companies.

Spencer was making Jake his right-hand man in taking over Cory Publishing, and together they discovered a document alleging that Mac had played a role in destroying the tropical rain forest. To Rachel's shock, Carl disputed the document. Carl told Rachel point-blank that he was buying some Cory stock so he could save the company from Spencer's encroachments! By now, Rachel was baffled as to who or what Carl Hutchins really was.

First and foremost, Carl was acting as a father. Guilty over his mistreatment of his deceased son, Perry, Carl wanted to bypass Spencer and play an active role in Ryan's life. Ryan was hurt when Grant married Vicky and whisked her away to a honeymoon in Banff, Canada. There a mysterious man abducted Vicky and stashed her in a cave! Ryan caught up with Vicky, and their surroundings literal-

ly caved in around them. Vicky and Ryan lived the moment as if it were their last and made love.

Vicky and Ryan survived their ordeal, and when they returned to Bay City, the kidnapper surfaced as the Corys' new groundskeeper! His name was Ian Rain. Visiting Bay City with his daughter, Maggie, Sandy Cory recognized Ian as their former chauffeur. Disgusted by Jake's alliance with Spencer, Paulina became fascinated with Ian.

Together Paulina and Ian went to the San Cristobal rain forest to investigate the involvement of Ian's late father, Leon, with Paulina's mother, Maria, Mac Cory, and the late Andrew Hutchins. Leon had patented a rare drug for a disease that he himself had contracted. Now Ian noticed that Paulina was exhibiting those same symptoms. Back in Bay City, John and Kelsey risked their professional lives by administering the drug to Paulina. The drug saved her life. Furthermore, Ian proved that Hutchins—not Mac—had pillaged the rain forest.

When Vicky wanted to leave Grant for Ryan, Grant drugged her and held her at a clinic. With Carl's help,

Felicia was kidnapped by Walter Trask, a psychotic fan, who was upset that she had abandoned romance novels in favor of writing her memoirs.

Ryan found Vicky and she announced her intention to divorce Grant. The timing was awful: Vicky discovered she was pregnant with Grant's child!

In other developments: John married Kelsey, only to meet a community-center volunteer named Kate Baker who bore a striking resemblance to Sharlene; Cass happily married Frankie; Josie returned to Matt's life just as things were heating up between him and Donna; Jake returned to Cory Publishing and flirted with Amanda; Spencer opened the swank Harbor Club; Cass's intern brother, Morgan Winthrop, was accused of raping Lorna but exonerated when the real culprit was caught; Iris became engaged to Hank; and Carl began an earnest pursuit of Rachel.

It wasn't the Bay City of yesteryear.

1994

Iris and Amanda were appalled by Rachel's engagement to their family's arch-enemy, Carl Hutchins! Grateful to Carl for vindicating Mac in the rain forest fiasco, Rachel fired Jake and named Carl chairman of the Cory board. Just as Carl was about to say "I do" to Rachel, Iris did the unthinkable—she shot him! She thought the gun held blanks.

As Iris was taken to prison, she named an accomplice, Barry Denton, whom Ryan confronted in short order. A shoot-out ensued, leaving Denton fatally injured. Before the hoodlum breathed his last, Ryan demanded to know his boss's identity. Barry mumbled something that sounded like "heaven." Then his soul was presumably transported to the flip side of that word.

Heaven rhymed with *Evan*. The mastermind behind Carl's shooting and Spencer's machinations was Evan Bates Frame! Evan had amassed a conglomerate and a half by now, and decided his life wouldn't be complete without seizing Cory Publishing once and for all. Grant had been courting Amanda, and wasn't pleased when Evan once again tried to charm her. Grant tried everything possible to throw suspicion on Carl, but Carl had gathered evidence against Evan and mentioned to his manservant, Ito, that he wanted Evan taken care of.

With his limited command of the English language, Ito took Carl literally. He tampered with the brakes on Evan's car! Evan and Amanda then climbed aboard the death machine and had a serious accident, which left Amanda paralyzed. It was a marriage made in political heaven when Grant married his paralyzed fiancée. Obsessively jealous over her friendship with Evan, Grant made Amanda's life miserable.

Felicia returned to the Cory Publishing stable, where she was driven hard by her new editor, Marshall Kramer. He was perceptive enough to notice that Felicia had dried up as a romance novelist and was ready to write something more profound: her memoirs. Felicia titled the book *Into the Fire*. Her abandonment of the romance genre so upset one of her biggest fans, Walter Trask, a psychotic who worked in the Cory mail room, that he vowed he would force her to pump out one last romance novel. He kidnapped Felicia, locked her away, and plied the recovering alcoholic with liquor. He even went so far as to try to kill Marshall Kramer. Felicia was eventually saved by Marshall, Cass, and Frankie. Felicia and Marshall shared a few kisses, but nothing came of the relationship and he left Bay City.

Sharlene, on the other hand, was back! She had survived the explosion, and "Kate" was just another one of her personalities. His marriage to Kelsey now invalid, John made another go of his relationship with Sharlene and gave her the support she needed to get well. Both worried about Josie, who had turned a few tricks since her last appearance in Bay City and was now the most nubile waitress at Spencer Harrison's Harbor Club. Josie found romance with Ian when Jake and Paulina realized they couldn't live without each other and remarried.

On the day of their wedding, Jake and Paulina

found an infant with an accompanying note that identified the bundle of joy as Mark. They didn't realize that it was really Kirkland Harrison, Vicky and Grant's baby boy! Vicky didn't want Grant to steal the child from her, so she orchestrated this temporary switch in exchange for staking Jake in his new publishing company!

Cass and Frankie had their own baby girl, Charlie, born in an elevator and delivered by Cass's brother, Morgan, now a doctor at Bay City General. Charlie was named for Frankie's maternal grandmother, Charlotte. When Charlie was diagnosed with a heart defect, Cass discovered that it was caused by a gene in his family. Cass blamed himself for his daughter's illness and sank into a state of manic depression. Frankie was deeply worried that he was losing his grip on reality. Eventually, with help and medication Cass, was cured.

Donna and Matt set up house, but Donna was uncomfortable with their age gap—and Rachel

Desperate to keep Grant from getting custody of Kirkland, Vicky pulled a baby switch, leaving Kirkland with an unsuspecting Paulina, and giving Grant a child he thought was his.

was just plain shocked. Maggie stayed in Bay City and became smitten with a young Hispanic named Tomas, whose estranged wife, Angela, wanted their daughter, Luisa, just to claim an inheritance.

As Rachel split from Carl over his role in Amanda's paralysis, she was devastated by the death of her beloved mother, Ada. With this passing, Bay City lost a rare and genuine human being who spoke the truth as nobody else has spoken it since.

1995

After learning of Vicky's baby-swapping scam, Paulina returned Mark to his real parents. Determined to retain custody of Kirkland, Grant shot himself and framed Vicky. Ryan's investigation uncovered the sordid truth and Grant was forced to confess on the witness stand. Vicky was cleared of all charges.

No sooner was Vicky's baby plot revealed than Jake disappeared. In debt to loan shark Bunny Eberhardt, Jake appeared to die in a car crash. Suffering from amnesia, and thinking his name was indeed Bunny, Jake took a sojourn in Japan and eventually found his way to San Francisco where he romanced a woman named Alison. While Jake was at large, Paulina found more stable companionship with Joe Carlino, a former New York City cop turned private detective.

Meanwhile, Frankie enlisted Joe's help to find the man who had raped Sharlene when she was a girl, hoping this would be the ultimate breakthrough for her schizophrenic aunt.

Joe need not have searched far. It was Bailey Thompson, a member on the hospital board and the prime mover in appointing John the new chief of staff! Bailey was arrested and ended up in a mental institution. Later Sharlene sold her farm when a patient's family sued John for malpractice—and he had virtually no insurance. Cass represented John.

Jake returned to Bay City, but Paulina doubted he would be a faithful husband and instead became engaged to Joe. Together they opened Carlino's restaurant.

It was at this time that Tony "The Tuna" forced Cass and Felicia to help a woman called Apple Annie, whom he believed to be his good luck charm. Instead of telling her daughter, who was studying abroad, that she was poor and sold apples, Annie pretended to be rich. Cass and Felicia agreed to help Annie masquerade as a rich

When it was discovered that Cass and Frankie's little girl, Charlie, had a heart defect, Cass blamed himself and sank into a state of manic depression.

The night Grant was shot, his house caught fire. A paralyzed Amanda and Alli were trapped inside until Evan came to their rescue.

woman when her daughter came for a visit and threw a lavish party. The charade went smoothly until Annie fainted. When she came to, she explained that she had fainted because Rachel Cory resembled her evil sister, Justine Kirkland! It was revealed that Justine had never died—Spencer banished her after she gave birth to Ryan.

Spencer suffered a stroke when the wife he had paid to stay dead to their sons resurfaced in Bay City! Justine had plastic surgery to look like Rachel, whom she tried to kill in hopes of winning Carl back. She drugged Rachel and sent her to a Swiss loony bin, while she assumed Rachel's identity and slept with Carl. Eventually seeing through the hoax, Carl teamed up with Ryan to locate Rachel, but Justine was just getting started. She poisoned Lorna to get her away from Grant and imprisoned Vicky in a dungeon so that she could kidnap Kirkland.

Grant knew that Justine was impersonating Rachel but kept quiet. When the kidnapping went down, Rachel followed Justine to the train trestle and told her nemesis, "It ends here." However, there was more at stake. Grant

and Ryan rushed to the scene and in the struggle that ensued, while Ryan was trying to protect her so that he could find out where she had taken Kirkland, Grant fired his gun and accidentally killed his brother, who was in the line of fire! From that moment on, Carl swore revenge on Grant for killing his son. Justine would

Hit woman Bunny Eberhardt hastened Jake's departure from Bay City. Thought dead, amnesiac Jake stood outside the funeral parlor while wife Paulina and friends and family mourned.

Josie arrived at Apple Annie's party on the arm of current beau Ian Rain. Her dress caused quite a stir. It was given to Josie by a client in LA, who happened to be Annie's ex-husband, and the beads on the neckline were valuable jewels!

resurface in the guise of a nun, Sister Mary, and in a later confrontation, Rachel would stab her murderous look-alike to death in self-defense.

Lorna was involved with the complex Grant despite the disapproval of her mother, Felicia. However, when Lorna became director of public relations at the hospital, she met Grant's more honorable childhood pal Gabe McNamara, the new police captain. Gabe was tender with Lorna but drove his cops hard—especially the unorthodox Sergeant Gary Sinclair, who taught at the police academy. After a confrontation on the docks, where she posed as a prostitute to solve a crime, Josie decided to join the academy. Gary was her instructor and the two were immediately attracted to each other. Gary also found a platonic pal in Felicia—his AA sponsor. However, the troubled sergeant kept falling off the wagon because he blamed himself for the death of a former partner.

Amanda Cory was on the road to recovery when she divorced Grant and went back to work. Maggie romanced Tomas, who won Luisa's custody, but Maggie's gold-digging mama, Cecile, came charging back into town and tried to throw Maggie at a succession of princes and preppies. Maggie then met Nick Terry, a swaggering young newcomer whose long-lost father was another returning Bay City resident: Michael Hudson!

It was Justine's turn to don a disguise when she came back as Sister Mary, intent on killing Rachel. It was the end for the deranged Justine— Rachel killed her in self-defense.

Scarred from her relationship with the manipulative Grant, Lorna found love with Police Captain Gabe McNamara.

1996

Cecile de Poulignac was on a rampage. First she tried to pass Maggie off as Cass's, then she hired Nick Terry's childhood friend Rafael to kidnap her own daughter so that she could collect the ransom! When her lies were exposed, Cecile returned to Europe.

Donna married Matt but grieved alongside Michael when Bridget Connell became seriously ill and died at the hospital. To add to their sorrow, Bridget's life-support system had been unplugged by a euthanasia killer. When Morgan Winthrop's patients, including Bridget, started dying, Morgan was accused of unplugging their life-support systems. The real culprit was Dr. Courtney Evans's abusive ex-boyfriend, Andrew. On a rampage, Andrew raped Courtney, then fell to his death during a fight with Morgan on the hospital roof.

Josie arrested Grant for shooting Ryan and threw him in jail. Carl called one of his convict pals, Blair Baker, a bad female cop known as "the Cobra," to finish Grant off in the slammer. But then Carl instead chose to confront Grant directly at the jailhouse, and the two scuffled. A riot broke out, and when Carl was seriously injured, Grant saved his life! Carl called off the dogs for the time being, and Grant received a pardon from the governor for saving his daughter during the uprising.

John couldn't deal with Sharlene's multiple personalities and had a serious relationship with lonely Felicia. Once John and Sharlene were divorced, Sharlene kept company with both Grant and Michael, who vied for the position of hospital administrator. Thanks to Vicky's pleas to the board, Michael won the post.

A stalker was terrorizing Bay City! Blair and Courtney were dead. Gabe suspected an emotionally fragile Donna, but during the time Donna was in jail, the stalker strangled Frankie to death! Her beloved cousin Josie ascertained that the killer was a doctor nicknamed "Fax," who turned out to be a murderous quack named Newton Fairchild. Before he was killed by Gary, Fax pushed Josie into a manhole, where she was further terrorized by convict Cody Murcer. Grant gave Cody a million dollars so that Grant could play hero and rescue Josie. What Grant didn't expect was that Cody would shoot and kill his good friend Gabe. Cody escaped and harassed Josie, who quit the force. During her attempted wedding to Gary, Cody returned, double-crossed Grant, and tried to kill Josie.

Dr. Courtney Evans was the victim of her abusive boyfriend, Andrew, and she hid it well. Finally she was able to open up to friend and fellow doctor Morgan. Courtney survived Andrew only to be done in by the Bay City stalker.

Carl had every intention of finishing Grant off in prison, but in an ironic twist of fate, Grant rescued Carl in a prison uprising. Grant received a pardon for saving the governor's daughter in the uprising.

Grant shot and killed Cody, but before he died, Cody fired a bullet that paralyzed Sharlene.

Joe and Paulina were thrilled when their son, Dante Mackenzie Carlino, was born. Joe was overprotective of his younger sister, Sofia, who competed with Maggie for Nick's affections. Jake and Matt took over a tabloid newspaper, *The Herald,* where cub reporter Nick modeled his no-holds-barred style after Jake's.

It was around this time that Matt and Donna annulled their marriage.

Vicky moved into a cozy little cottage that had been left to her by Bridget. She was shocked to meet the man Michael had hired to do the renovations, Bobby Reno, who as fate would have it had received Ryan's corneas—for Ryan had consented to donate his organs after his death. But Bobby had yet more in common with Ryan: he was guided by his spirit. It was Ryan who, from beyond, helped Bobby save Steven from an oncoming train. And Kirk conversed with Ryan's ghost up in the attic!

After Jake and Bobby prevented Grant from attacking Vicky, Grant struck in a big way. He hired a masked flunky named Hal Cox to pose as a fake Jake! Grant discovered that Cindy was responsible for the deaths of Gabe's wife and son when she didn't save them from a fire. Cindy had loved her brother-in-law

to the extent that she was willing to lose her sister and nephew to be with him. Grant and Cindy would prove to be a most lethal combination.

❧

1997

Kirk was the only person on earth whom Grant truly loved, now that he was divorced from both Vicky and Amanda. Determined to be Kirk's sole father figure, Grant had Cindy arrange for someone to impersonate Jake to plant a bomb under Bobby Reno's truck. Vicky was injured in the explosion and had a near-death experience in heaven, where Ryan convinced her to go back to the world of the living. To save Lorna from a jealous Cindy, Gabe moved her out of town to be with Jenna. But Cindy loved Gabe and admitted her wrongdoings to him. As Gabe tried to protect Cindy, he was shot and killed by an unseen assailant.

Rachel was tired of Carl's obsession with nailing Grant, but took him back nonetheless. Carl howled with glee as Jake and his imposter confronted Grant together, causing Grant to completely flip out. Grant was remanded to an institution, where he was briefly reunited with fellow nut case nurse Cindy! But this time, Carl and Grant formed a temporary alliance to nail his corrupt boss, Commissioner Raines, who was in cahoots with Cody Murcer. Raines held Paulina hostage, but Joe shot and killed the crooked top cop. Grant then ran against Donna for mayor and won!

When Josie Watts was pursued by Fax, she fell victim to ex-con Cody Murcer.

Felicia broke off with John after she was wooed by Alexander Nikos, a bellicose billionaire from Greece. Alexander looked a lot like her beloved Lucas, but his purpose in Bay City was somewhat different. He was secretly in cahoots with a distrustful Matt to discredit his stepfather, Carl! Both of Rachel's children loathed and feared her new husband and were willing to make a pact with this new devil in town.

Alexander and Carl had blamed each other for a shipping deal gone sour. Alexander ratted Carl out to avenge the death of his wife, Diana, with whom Carl had had a dalliance—and who was killed in a crossfire with cops. It was Alexander's grand plan to woo writers away from Cory Publishing to his own company, Artemis Books, and Felicia was part of the plan. Amanda joined in the plot against Carl by making it appear that he was having an affair with an alluring yuppie named Hadley Prescott.

It didn't work. Carl and Nikos got into a fierce fight and, trying to stop them, Felicia fell through Nikos's skylight, after which she needed reconstructive surgery on her face. Nikos blamed Carl, and in retribution he trapped Rachel in a crypt. Felicia broke the engagement, and Nikos left town, but not before he formed an alliance with Grant to get revenge on Carl.

Rachel discovered Matt's part in the scheme and nearly wrote him off. She empathized with Carl's struggle to prove to the people of Bay City that he had turned over a new leaf.

Rachel was stunned to learn that she was expecting. To complicate matters, she had a life-threatening tumor. Despite family opposition, Rachel was clear that she wanted to have the child. She was in Key West when she went into premature labor, and it was a Dr. Shane Roberts who delivered twins, Cory and Elizabeth.

Depressed over her post-pregnancy weight gain, Paulina got hooked on diet pills, supplied by her "friend" Cindy, under orders from Grant. Grant got the ultimate punishment, however, when Paulina mixed the tablets with alcohol and hit Kirk with her car! Paulina went to rehab to cure the pill habit, but continued drinking. And Grant wasn't finished with her yet. She was clean and sober when, to destroy her credibility in his quest for custody of Kirkland, he sneaked into her house, slipped a drug into her tea, and started a little fire, which he thought he then put out. The house burned down, and Paulina and Dante were lucky to get out alive. The repercussions of that fire continued to haunt Grant.

In a ruse to make Rachel think Carl was having an affair, Amanda disguised herself as Hadley Prescott and planted incriminating evidence.

When Felicia fled the hospital after her devastating accident, Rachel tried to help her injured friend. She would become a victim herself when Nikos locked her in the basement of a deserted church.

To discredit Paulina, Grant drugged her tea and set a fire he thought he put out. Nobody believed Paulina when she said she wasn't responsible for the loss of the Carlino family home.

Paulina, high on pills, didn't see Kirkland coming toward her on his bike. It was to be Jake and Vicky's wedding day. Instead, Vicky kept a bedside vigil.

It became Lila's mission to destroy Vicky's marriage to Jake and make her see what it felt like to lose a loved one.

Kirk was saved by an unlikely person—Bobby. It was gradually becoming common knowledge that Bobby was really Dr. Shane Roberts, a surgeon from Crockett, Texas, who had been wrongly accused of killing his married lover. Shane was returned to death row, but at the eleventh hour, Vicky and Jake were able to prove his innocence—the lover's husband was guilty of the crime. Once he was freed, Shane joined the Bay City General staff. When his southern-belle wife, Lila, arrived, she didn't like her estranged hubby's involvement with Vicky Hudson one bit! Lila's scheming made Vicky see clearly what was right before her eyes—she might be attracted to Shane but she loved Jake. She proposed to him at their special place—the swings in Lassiter.

Gary and Josie married and wanted to adopt Rain, the neglected little daughter of a street pusher known as Popper. But Rain's grandmother, Queenie Wolfe, claimed her.

Nick was wrongly accused of raping Toni Burrell, a policewoman who had an interest in Cass's partner, Tyrone Montgomery—until they thought they were brother and sister! Josie helped her partner nab the real rapist, a bad cop named Chip Rayburn.

Tomas and Maggie left Bay City separately, as did Sharlene.

When Toni Burrell was brutally raped, a drunk Nick Hudson was wrongly accused of the crime.

106

1998

Only Lila knew that Shane was suffering from a terminal illness and that he was working on a cure for his disease that promised to make him wealthy. After Lila slept with Matt, for the purpose of getting pregnant so that she could pass the baby off as Shane's, she told Matt about Shane's work. Seeing dollar signs, Matt sold Carl his Cory Publishing stock so he could market the drug. But Matt continued to be suspicious of Carl, especially when he learned that Carl was in Arizona during the apparent suicide of his longtime nemesis, Chris Chapin. In a phone conversation, Rachel's half-sister Nancy revealed that her former lover's death might have been foul play.

Even though Vicky and Jake were happily married, Lila remained obsessively jealous. Unbeknownst to Matt, Lila manipulated Shane's research to make it seem that the drug wasn't working (when in truth it was), so that he would depend on her to take care of him. Vicky had given a discouraged Shane the family cabin to work in. When she found the evidence that Lila was trying to hide, knowing that Shane was about to give up on his work, she raced to the cabin in a snowstorm and stopped him from burning his valuable notes. Although she was still attracted to him and tempted to make love, Vicky loved Jake more and she resisted the temptation.

When Michael heard where Vicky was headed, he mistook her intentions and went out on the icy roads to stop her. He knew that Jake would never forgive her if she slept with Shane and that there would be an irrevocable rift in the family. As Michael drove toward the lodge, Vicky, who had asked Shane to take her home to Jake, was coming in the opposite direction. Michael's car swerved on the ice and hit Shane's head on. Shane pushed Vicky out of the car and she escaped unhurt, but Michael and Shane were killed. As a result, Lila became irrationally obsessed with destroying Vicky's marriage to Jake, so that she would feel the pain Lila felt in losing a loved one.

No longer the mirror image of her twin, Marley was scarred inside as well as out.

Covered in her husband's blood, Rachel could not be comforted by the children who had tried so hard to destroy this marriage. Later that night, Carl disappeared from the hospital. Rachel would not see him again.

elicia had written a semiautobiographical novel, *Embers in the Snow,* about her long and fascinating history with Cass! In the book she named him Crass instead of Cass, and in a case of life imitating art, the pages began to come to life.

By forging Shane's journal, Grant and Lila made it appear that Vicky had carried on with Shane for a long time. Lila gave the journal to Donna, and although Donna despised Lila, she believed what she read. Donna saw Grant visiting Michael's grave with someone she assumed to be Vicky. Enraged at what she thought her daughter had done, and now seeing her conspiring with Grant, Donna impulsively stepped on the gas. She injured Grant and also hit the woman she thought was Vicky. But it wasn't Vicky—it was Marley, who had come back from China for Michael's funeral. Marley was taken to the hospital, and while she was there, a fire broke out in the ICU. Marley was badly burned and would need extensive plastic surgery. No longer the image of her twin sister, and unable to adjust to her new identity, Marley

was pushed over the edge by this devastating blow.

Cindy told Donna of Grant and Lila's collusion, but Grant silenced her with his knowledge that she had run him over! Grant married Cindy and had her committed, only to get a quickie divorce when she was released. Marley caught on to Cindy's schemes, and revealed that she was now as disturbed as Cindy was! Michael's death, as well as Jake's marriage to Vicky, caused Marley to doubt that she had a place in the world, and she began to obsess about getting Jake away from Vicky. Threatening to name Cindy as her hit-and-run attacker, Marley forced Cindy to help her kidnap and terrorize Vicky!

Joe used the tough love approach on Paulina, threatening to divorce her and sue her for Dante's custody if she didn't get off pills and booze. It worked. Soon after, Paulina and Nick became fascinated by a girl named Remy, who had a foster home background similar to hers. Josie, back from FBI Special Training, formed a nebulous connection with Gary's ex-con brother, Cameron Sinclair, an FBI mole who became Carl's new driver—and Amanda's lover.

On New Year's Eve, 1998, Amanda Cory announced her engagement to Cameron Sinclair.

Lila told Matt what he suspected all along, that the child she was expecting was his, not Shane's. She later gave birth to their daughter, Jasmine Rachel Cassandra Cory, during the Lumina Ball. While Matt was getting Lila medical help, the baby disappeared! Then, under mysterious circumstances, the baby reappeared shortly thereafter, and at the christening Matt proposed and Lila said yes.

Strange things were now beginning to happen. Carl, enraged to discover his stepchildrens' machinations against him, became increasingly paranoid and suffered blinding headaches. Like the Carl Hutchins of old, he secretly conspired with his long-missing half-brother, Scott Guthrie, to engineer what appeared to be a hit on Rachel! Instead, Carl was shot and landed in the hospital. It was Scott who arranged Carl's escape by starting the fire that so severely burned Marley as she lay in the adjacent room. Carl disappeared to Key West and was on the phone with Scott when his plane exploded. Soon after, Scott introduced himself to Rachel, who believed he was a friend of the husband she mourned and hired him to work for Cory Publishing. Around this time the Cory bankroll disappeared.

At the same time, the people of Bay City were barraged by the image of a logo belonging to the Lumina Foundation, a paranormal organization under the directorship of the mysterious Jordan Stark. Rachel sculpted a bust of Jordan in hopes of unearthing his purpose in Bay City. They would discover that he was there in search of his heart.

*L*umina came to town at the end of 1998 and strange things began to happen. At the Lumina Ball, Lila gave birth in a mysteriously stuck elevator, and when the doors opened the baby was gone.

The man behind Lumina is two hundred years old. His name is Jordan Stark, and he will have a major impact on the people of Bay City.

*R*uss Matthews with his daughters: Olivia, who came to town briefly, and Josie, the only member of the Matthews family still living in Bay City.

Members of the Matthews family loved to spend time at Jim and Mary's home. Pictured here are Grandma Matthews, with her granddaughters Alice and Pat and their Aunt Janet (on Granny's right).

f a m i l y   a l b u m s

elcome to the living rooms and backyards of Bay City—a community of multifaceted families. When *Another World* debuted in 1964, the middle-class Matthews and their friends the Randolphs were the focus of the story. In the 1970s, Emmy award–winning writer Harding "Pete" Lemay, searching for "different values," added the Frames from rural Oklahoma and the jet-setting Carringtons and Corys of international society circles. According to producer and show historian Scott Collishaw, "In the late seventies and early eighties, *Another World* was very much like Upstairs, Downstairs—you had the people that lived in the mansion, the people that worked in the mansion, and the people that wanted to get into the mansion." In the eighties, Bay City welcomed the wealthy, dysfunctional Loves, the Hudson brothers, and the blue-collar McKinnons and Perrinis, while

the nineties saw the arrival of the Italian Carlinos and the African-American Burrells. Here's a peek inside some of their family albums.

t h e   m a t t h e w s   f a m i l y

In the 1960s, Bay City's main families were actually two branches of the same family, headed respectively by brothers Bill and Jim Matthews, who were partners in an accounting firm. Bill and Liz and their children, Bill Jr. and Susan, were quite wealthy, while Jim and Mary and their children, Russ, Pat, and Alice, were decidedly middle-class. According to head writer Pete Lemay, the Matthewses were the embodiment of "genteel propriety." Beverly Penbarthy, who played Pat, describes them as "strong, middle-class, high values, middle of the road, politically neutral. They always wanted to do the right thing. And they got mixed up with a lot of problems and usually with people from the wrong side of the tracks." Jim and Mary Matthews were warm, comfortable people with a good solid marriage. However, every one of their children was headed for marital problems of one kind or another. Pat shot and killed her boyfriend, Tom Baxter, after he persuaded her to have an abortion. She later married lawyer John Randolph, who defended her in the trial, and later still gave birth to twins Marianne and Michael. Pat might sometimes have drunk too much, but she managed to raise her children and forge a successful career at *Brava* magazine. Russ's first marriage was to gold digger Rachel Davis and it did not end happily. As for Alice, her tortured romance and marriage to Steven Frame ended when he was presumed dead in a helicopter crash.

Aunt Liz, Bill Matthews's widow, was a social-climbing busybody who constantly interfered in the lives of her children, Susan and Bill Jr.— and it didn't stop there.

The show was not a day old when Bill Matthews died of a heart attack, leaving the widowed Liz to dote on her only son, Bill Jr. Nancy Wickwire, who played Liz, described her as "bitchy, and she speaks her mind." Adds Beverly Penbarthy, "She wasn't a very good person. She was bad. . . . I would call her on it and say, 'How can you do these terrible things?'" Bill fell in love with the poor sweet orphan Missy Palmer, and Liz did everything she could to keep the young lovers apart. Bill and Missy finally married and moved to California, but soon after, Bill was tragically killed in a boating accident.

Liz had always had a troublesome relationship with her daughter, Susan, and it didn't help that Susan married Liz's friend and contemporary, Fred Douglas. Liz did everything in her power to ruin that marriage as well, and eventually Susan and Fred divorced. Susan married Dr. Dan Shearer and moved to Denver.

Ever snobbish and interfering, Liz mellowed in later years, but always remained meddlesome in other people's affairs. As far as Rachel was concerned, Liz managed, grudgingly, to accept her for her good qualities, but there was tension in the air whenever the two crossed paths. After all, she first knew Rachel as a gold digger, and there was a time when Liz had romantic designs on Mac. For a time, Liz took in Susan's troubled adopted daughter, Julia, and then provided a home for Alice's adopted daughter, Sally Frame. Sally was a favorite who could do no wrong in Liz's eyes, and the two formed a special bond. Aunt Liz, as she had come to be known, was a woman alone, who had to depend on herself, but she was of a generation of women who were not prepared to do so. She had lost of lot of people she cherished and so remained overprotective of the family that was left. In later years she went to work as a secretary for Mac Cory.

Russ's daughter Olivia came to town for awhile, but at present the only remaining member of the Matthews family residing in Bay City is Josie Watts Sinclair, daughter of Sharlene Frame and Liz's nephew, Russ.

the cory family

The Corys are, by and large, Bay City's most preeminent family. The first Cory to arrive in Bay City was selfish troublemaker Iris Carrington, ex-wife of Elliot Carrington, a wealthy journalist for whom Alice Frame had worked in New York. Iris was soon followed by her father, publishing tycoon Mackenzie Cory. Rich and powerful, the Corys had a reputation for being nice. The only bad apple, Iris, is now languishing in jail. Each member of this prominent family cherishes their independence, has strong drives when it comes to business, and has some well-placed blind spots when it comes to love. Immune to outside threats, it's the internal conflicts that render them vulnerable.

Cory Publishing, Inc., was founded on May 4, 1964, and has offices in Bay City, New York, Los Angeles, Paris, London, Australia, and Buenos Aires. At one time or another, most of Bay City's residents have worked in their offices, fondly known as "the Complex." Mac Cory was one of a rare breed—a powerful, wealthy man who used his empire for positive growth. He remained ethical to the core in his business dealings, tough and fiercely loyal when anyone in his family was wronged. A self-made man who had built a publishing empire from nothing by the time he arrived in Bay City, Mackenzie Cory was the consummate elder statesman with a touch of flair, and it didn't take long for him to become one of Bay City's leading citizens. Handsome and distinguished, Mac charmed the women, while wielding his share of power in the business world. He was a gentlemen in every sense of the word—fair and honest. Mac Cory believed in the power of the written word and was the mastermind behind such highly regarded periodicals as *Brava* and *Sophisticate*. Almost all of Felicia Gallant's fifty-plus novels were published and distributed by Cory. Cory Publishing is the driving force behind *The Herald*, Bay City's daily newspaper, and at one time owned Bay City's TV Station, KBAY.

Mac wanted to spread his wealth equally among his family, but that wasn't enough for greedy, spoiled Iris. She offered to bail Mac out when his company almost fell victim to a corporate takeover, but Mac realized that she was the one behind the hostile acquisition attempt. Her scheme revealed, Iris pleaded with Mac, "I just wanted you to know how much I loved you!" A man of honor, who had been irrevocably and deeply disappointed, Mac responded, "You're dead to me, Iris. You're not my daughter anymore." After he fired her, he gave her office space to Amanda.

Mac passed away suddenly of a heart attack, right before the company's twenty-fifth anniversary. A fair and generous man, he left Cory Publishing to Amanda, Rachel, and, it was thought, Iris. Iris stepped into

the presidency and Rachel became the chairman of the board. However, the will was rendered invalid. The revised version did not provide for Iris.

Although Rachel knew she'd never find a love like Mac's, she married Carl Hutchins after he reformed. They became the proud parents of Cory and Elizabeth, but only after Rachel survived a dangerous pregnancy and birth. When Rachel was told that she had to abort her children to save her own life, Wyndham recalls, "It was like after everyone else has tried [over the years] to take my children away. … Now, nobody's going to tell me that they can take them

Ever needy of her father's love, Iris plotted to take over Cory Publishing and then bail him out. The plan misfired, and Mac, tired of her schemes, disinherited his spoiled daughter.

away. And I don't care about my own life." It's safe to say that Rachel has come full circle and earned her rightful place as the Cory family matriarch.

the cory family tree

Rachel

Although Iris did everything in her power to stop him, Mac fell in love and married young, rebellious Rachel Davis. Rachel grew up a fighter. She hated her lower-class life and saw herself as having to struggle and scheme just to get what others got naturally. She spent years going after men and money, and then she married Mac, a man who appreciated her independence and her drive. Former head writer Harding "Pete" Lemay wrote in his book *Eight Years*

The Corys are Bay City's most prominent and influential family.

in Another World, "It was . . . inevitable that Iris, insatiable for attention from the father who had banished her to boarding schools, before she had really known him, would use every means at her disposal to prevent him from marrying a woman younger than herself." But marry they did—three times, until Mac's untimely death in 1989, when Rachel became head of the family.

Actress Victoria Wyndham has this to say about being the Cory matriarch:

"The baton has been passed to her through attrition and she takes it extraordinarily seriously for two reasons. It's the heritage that she inherited from Mac, and it's what she learned from her mother about family. I admire Rachel's ability to see family in a greater, more generous way than most of us do, like assimilating Paulina, who was a bastard child of her adored Mac. It fed into her ecumenical sense of family. If she respects someone, they become somebody she'll defend. She doesn't have to necessarily agree with them or even appreciate all of their qualities, but they become somebody who is a part of her community, and community seems to be a family for her. I guess that's from her sense of always feeling like an outsider, so that she is able to embrace a diverse sense of family a lot easier than the rest of us would. What Mac taught her about the redeeming qualities of love seems to be the rule of thumb she applies. Since she was redeemed by his unconditional love and her mother's unconditional love of her no matter how bad she was, if someone allows themselves to be redeemed, then she will go to the ends of the earth for them. She believes in tough love, but it's love, and it's constant."

Rachel and Mac

Rachel and Ada

Matthew

Matthew was named after the Matthews family because, while Rachel was in prison for presumably killing Mitch, the child was supposed to be raised by Russ. But he actually grew up in the Cory household. Wyndham explains, "Matthew was basically raised with Mac's values and wanted to emulate Mac. . . . Mac was the big influence in that boy's life." When Matt found out that Mac was not his biological father, he was devastated. Says actor Matt Crane, who originated and recently returned to the role of Matt, about the discovery: "There is strife when someone finds out . . . because it changes their identity. It totally changes a certain perspective about where you came from and who you are."

Ada

Rachel had a good example in her mother, Ada, whom Pete Lemay called "the mother earth" of the family. Ada was a sharp-tongued truth sayer, who always told it as it was. Actress Sandra Ferguson, who plays Amanda, says of her on-screen grandmother, "Ada could be brutally honest, but then she'd make up for it in affection." Ada was the perfect example of maternal common sense, who could always see the good in the bad, especially when it came to Rachel, whose wild ways caused her much anxiety. Ada and Mac became friends and allies, especially when it came to coping with her daughter's stubbornness and temper.

Jamie

"Rachel and Jamie were two against the world for years and years and years," says Wyndham of Rachel and the son she had with Steven Frame. "Jamie sort of brought his mother up and vice versa; it was a very close relationship." Both Jamie and Matthew, Rachel's son with Mitch Blake, were raised by Mac and became honorary Corys. The two brothers have always been close and never had any kind of falling-out. Jamie, now a doctor, is practicing medicine in San Francisco.

Although they were not Mac's biological sons, Jamie and Matt were raised as Corys.

Matt did forge a good relationship with Mitch when Mitch was in Bay City. And aside from a slight awkwardness when he first found out that Mac was not his biological father, the two remained close until Mac's death. About being a Cory, Crane says, "I think it really grounds him into security and his identity. Family is very important. Everyone needs a certain amount of security and support in their life and Matt Cory gets that from his family. There's a lot that Matt is because Rachel is there for him and the Cory name is what it is and he has the history that he does. . . . That's what Matt Cory is—he's a product

Rachel and Amanda

Mac and Matt

Matt and Amanda

119

of all that." However, Matthew always felt the need to prove his identity outside the Cory family and has never worked at Cory Publishing. Actor Jeff Phillips, who played Matt from March to December of 1998, says, "Proving himself outside of Cory Publishing became his way of distancing himself and creating a name for himself." His loyalty to his family was evident when, in the current Cory crises, Matt took all of his own money and put it into the company.

Of his relationship with his mother, Crane says, "It's almost like a typical mother and son relationship—not in a bad way, but kind of in a good way, where they really are concerned about each other and look out for each other and depend on each other. In the end it's about them and their family and she as head of the household. It's almost like we carry the Cory name and legacy on our shoulders, and I think we feel that together."

Phillips had this to say, "We are her children and you could never take that away. That's one of the things that Amanda and I have in our favor, that she's our mother. She's not going to banish me for anything, or it would have to be a pretty heinous crime. . . . When I told her that I got Lila pregnant, . . . she was very disappointed in me and let me know it . . ." but she still loved him.

Matt and Lila's baby, Jasmine, is the latest addition to the clan. Matthew proposed to and married Lila on Jasmine's christening day. Crane describes the marriage: "Matt's in a situation now, where he knows it's not the best situation, but he doesn't want to admit that to himself. He's in this marriage with Lila and has a child, but it's more about convincing himself that this is what he wants. What he really feels may be something else, but that's taking a backseat to what he feels is important, which is family now, and putting that above actually loving Lila or loving [his ex-girlfriend] Sofia. There's always going to be a bond because of the child. I think as the character stands now, she's the mother of his child, and he'll always love her in a way for that because he loves this child, and it's part of his life and part of him."

Phillips explains Matt's relationship with Amanda:

"That's the thing about family. I could scream at Amanda . . . because I know she won't go anywhere . . . and you really depend on that." Wyndham says Matthew "became Rachel's champion and the one that would interface between her and Amanda."

❧

Amanda

Amanda is Mac and Rachel's only biological child. Actress Sandra Ferguson originated the part of Amanda and recently returned to it. She explains, "My first impression was that she was very rebellious—rebelling against her rich heritage and not wanting to be seen as just a brat of a wealthy family." On being a part of the Cory family, Ferguson says, "It's the center of her existence. Her father was probably the most influential, with her mother following very closely behind." Ferguson expands on her relationship with Mac: "Yes, I think she was doted on, spoiled in an affectionate sort of way. But there was still some strictness. He could be very stern . . . she didn't get away with everything." How does she feel about her brother, Matt? "Kind of like most sisters feel about their brother. Love 'em. Hate 'em. Love 'em. Hate 'em." They are actually very close and protective of each other.

Even though Matt, like Paulina, is a half-sibling, says Ferguson, "I think to Amanda, Matt was an equal. There would never be a line drawn between the siblings. At least not by her."

Perhaps her relationship with her mother is the most complicated. Wyndham says, "Amanda was her daddy's daughter . . . spoiled, doted on by Mac. There's a bit more of a tug-of-war between Rachel and Amanda. Amanda's been headstrong, made a lot of mistakes—the same kind of mistakes that Rachel would have made. It didn't mean she wasn't strong. It just meant she was misguided." Ferguson expands on that relationship: "Love her. Fear her. Hate her. Love her." When Rachel married Mac's arch-enemy, Carl Hutchins, Amanda along with Matt did everything in their power to break up the marriage. Says Ferguson, "Amanda was tormented by the stuff that she did because it ended up hurting her mother, which was not at all her intention. I think her intention was just the opposite, to save her mother, and she ended up realizing that she was doing just the opposite. Throughout all of that, she respected her immensely. And never had any ill will, but certainly had many differences of opinion and doesn't necessarily want to lead her life the way Rachel has led hers. But that also, I think, is very true to form for most women and their mothers."

Amanda started off rebellious, as a lot of teenagers do, yet remained very close with her family. In keeping with family tradition, Amanda's daughter, Alexandra (Alli) Fowler, was named for Mac's mother, Alexandra Cory.

❧

Sandy

Sandy was Mac's illegitimate son from an affair he had with a woman named Miriam Sanderson, who ran off when she discovered she was pregnant. As a young man, Sandy ran away from home and was taken in by Las Vegas crime queen Ilsa Fredericks, who drafted him into her service as a male escort. Sandy used the money to pay for his mother's medical expenses, and when she died he wanted out. Before she passed away, Miriam wrote Sandy's natural father's name in a letter to be opened after her death. He was astonished to discover that his father was the head of Bay City's most prominent family. Because of his underworld ties, Sandy kept his identity a secret and got a job as a construction worker, where he made friends with Ada and Jamie Frame. He went on to work for Cory Publishing as an assistant to Pat Randolph and Cecile. It was Ada who put the pieces together and told Mac that Sandy was his son. Open, generous, and true to character, Mac accepted Sandy and took him into the family fold. What ensued was intense sibling rivalry between Jamie and Sandy for their father's love. It didn't help that Cecile, estranged from Jamie and scheming to get pregnant with a Cory heir, played both men against each other. She and Sandy subsequently married, and Maggie Cory was the product of that union. Sandy eventually divorced Cecile and married Blaine Ewing in a double ceremony with Mac and Rachel (it would be Mac and Rachel's third and final marriage). Mr. and Mrs. Sandy Cory now reside in San Francisco.

❧

Paulina

Mac had already passed away when Paulina came to town claiming to be his daughter. She never knew her father. Says actress Judi Evans Luciano, who plays Paulina, "She was trying to scam the money.

I don't think she really thought she was a Cory, but she wanted to be and then it turned out she was. Then she really had to convince people." Although Rachel accepts her as Mac's and loves her like a daughter, to this day, says Luciano, "There's always that 'I'm just not good enough' in the back of her mind. She's the bastard Cory and she's always trying to prove herself even though Rachel never asks her to." She's always trying to prove that "she's only the half-kid, but she's the best kid. In the beginning she had to prove herself to Rachel because Rachel was like 'Who are you?' And Paulina did lie a few times . . . but now they're very, very close." Does Paulina see Rachel as a surrogate mother? Says Luciano, "Definitely. In fact there have been a couple of times, few and far between, when she's actually called her 'Mom.' After Jake died, Rachel came over before the funeral, and Paulina was feeling very alone and very lost, and she said 'I miss him, Mom . . . I really miss him,' and it was like Rachel was really her mom. And I think she called her 'Mom' when she was in the hospital before she went into rehab. . . . It comes out every now and then, but I know the feeling is always there. It's not even surrogate. That's her mother." Adds Luciano, "She's also the mother Paulina would like to be. Rachel and Paulina come from similar backgrounds. I think Paulina senses that Rachel really understands her because they both came from the wrong side of the tracks and had to scratch and claw their way up. Nothing was ever given to them. They had to fight for everything and they both would kill for their family. They're like two tigresses who get along."

As for Paulina's relationship with her half-siblings, Amanda and Matt, says Luciano, "Good and bad. She expects a lot of herself, so she expects a lot of people. Even though she's got a big heart, she expects the best out of everyone, and especially because Matt and Amanda had it, maybe not easy in their lives, but had a cushy childhood and adolescence, she expects a lot more of them. When they act spoiled or selfish or self-centered or put their needs in front of their mother's, it drives her up the wall. She loves them very much, but she expects them to be their best, and when they're not, it's disappointing. It just baffles and angers her: 'You've had it so good, can't you give a little?' They give in their own way, but it's not the same way, so Paulina doesn't understand it. With other people, she's very accepting, but she draws a straighter line for

The Cory family christens their first grandchild, Alli, named for Mac's grandmother, Alexandra Cory.

them, and expects more out of them because she knows their heart and knows how sensitive and caring they really are. It makes her mad: 'You guys are better than that.'" When Amanda and Matt tried to break up Rachel and Carl, Luciano had this to say, "I think Rachel would forgive sooner, or has. Paulina still hasn't forgiven either one of them for that. It's like, 'How could you do that to your mother?'"

As for Rachel, her trust in Paulina is so great that when things were going down with Carl, it was to Paulina that she entrusted the care of her newborns, Cory and Elizabeth. Says Wyndham, "I think Rachel felt that there would be too much push and pull if anything happened to her and that Paulina would be a good mother and also fair-minded, and make sure that Carl's wishes were taken into consideration. Whereas she didn't feel she could be sure of that with Amanda and Matthew."

Cory cousins Neal and Adam came to live in Bay City in the mid-eighties. Mac's nephew Neal arrived in 1985, the apparent ringleader of a gang of Third World–like revolutionary jewel thieves,

involved in a plot to steal the Pharaoh's treasure with his evil partner, Fayez. To protect his cover with Fayez, Neal followed Fayez's instructions by leading Mac and Rachel to the treasure, thus exposing them to imminent danger. It was actually all a front, because Neal was a government official, working as a double agent, but Mac was furious that his nephew had endangered the family. Frustrated that he couldn't please his uncle, Neal became a stablehand for the Love family. His brother, Adam, arrived in 1986, having been summoned to chastise Neal for his behavior. Fed up with his family's judgments, Neal left town almost immediately. A policeman, Adam had moved through the ranks swiftly, from patrol officer to detective, while working for a law degree at night. Tough to the core one minute, deeply touched the next, he quickly worked his way up to sergeant at the Bay City Police Department, where he met and fell in love with fellow officer M. J. McKinnon. They became engaged. In 1989, in pursuit of M.J., Adam left Bay City.

---

the   frame   family

*S*elf-made millionaire Steve Frame was an only child, or so everyone in Bay City, including his wife, Alice, thought. Pete Lemay, who introduced the Frame family to Bay City, says, "He was so ashamed of his family, he pretended he was an only child." But he had six brothers and sisters who, along with him, grew up knowing deprivation and hardship on a dirt farm in Chadwell, Oklahoma. The first to arrive was proud and reserved Emma Ordway, the eldest. Lemay explains, "Emma came in a great family emergency when she needed money. She came to her rich brother. And Alice says, 'I thought you didn't have any brothers and sisters.' And he confessed the whole thing." Emma needed a thousand dollars to buy the youngest Frame brother, Willis, out of a scrape. And that was only the beginning. According to

scene:
Matthew's room

Matthew has been grounded by Rachel and Mac for using their car without permission. He's confined to his room for the night. Matthew takes an open beer can out from under the bed, takes a swig, and nearly freaks as Amanda enters. Matthew brushes the beer off his wet shirt, hides the beer can, wipes his mouth.

MATTHEW: Don't you ever knock?

AMANDA: Why is your shirt wet?

MATTHEW: Got caught in a storm. Didn't you hear?

AMANDA: All the way down the hall. Who was the maddest?

MATTHEW: Mom, I guess. No, Dad. Oh, hell, I don't know.

AMANDA: Can I ask you something, Matthew?

MATTHEW: Who sent you? Mom or Dad?

AMANDA: Neither one. Actually it was Sam.

MATTHEW: He mad at me too?

AMANDA: Depends. Did you take a couple of his beers out of that old fridge in the garage?

MATTHEW: Does he say I did?

AMANDA: Matthew, he's only trying to help you, so stop playing games. This place smells like a brewery, and it isn't the first time—

MATTHEW: Hey, here it comes. Listen to your sister now, Matthew. She's only doing this for your own good—

AMANDA: That happens to be the truth.

MATTHEW: (charming her) Sis, didn't you ever sneak a glass of wine from Mom? Didn't you ever taste the old man's brandy? You did. You know you did.

AMANDA: OK, but what you're doing is different. Where is it? I can still smell it. I'm going to pour it out.

MATTHEW: (as she starts looking) This is my room—my stuff.

AMANDA: Under the bed. That's where I'd put it. And here it is. There is a struggle for the beer can.

MATTHEW: What's with you, anyway? Always telling me what to do, how to wipe my nose, how to wipe my—

AMANDA: Maybe you need telling, damn it.

(Matthew wins the struggle for the beer can, smiles.)

MATTHEW: Tell Sam he buys lousy beer. (Matthew swigs)

AMANDA: (tries once more to take the beer can) You give that to me, Matthew!

AMANDA: You give that to me, Matthew!

MATTHEW: (having had enough) Do I tell you to stay out of guys' beds so you won't get pregnant—

AMANDA: Why you little bastard!

MATTHEW: That's me, the little bastard. And everybody know it.

AMANDA: Matthew, I'm sorry. Oh, God, Matthew, I shouldn't have said that. Matthew—

MATTHEW: (covering sting) Hey, no sweat. Matthew Cory ain't a Cory. I don't care about that. It's how I got to *be* a bastard. You see, Mom and Dad think that whatever they did when they were young is just fine, terrific. Hey, go for it. Dad played around plenty, and well—we know about Mom, don't we? But me! I'm not even allowed to express an opinion. Which is worse, Amanda? Mom playing around with Mitch Blake, or me having a beer?

AMANDA: (hurting for him) When you put it that way, it makes sense, I guess. But you still have to take care of yourself.

MATTHEW: Don't worry. (he raises the beer can in a toast) Bastards of the world, unite.

He gulps the beer.

End Scene.

Sharlene, the youngest of the Frame siblings, was a young widow when she came to Bay City and married Russ Matthews. She left town when her past as a prostitute was revealed and returned years later with their daughter, Josie.

him and her brother, whom Tim was plotting against. Family loyalty won out and she protected Steve. Janice left town in 1974 and returned four years later, a master manipulator, accompanied by her lover, Mitch Blake. This time she was anything but on Rachel's side. In a plot that mirrored Cory Publishing's rejected murder mystery *Harry Must Die,* Janice and Mitch plotted to break up Rachel's marriage to Mac. The opportunity for a life of luxury knocked when Rachel and Mac divorced, and Janice went after the Cory patriarch, convincing him to marry her. But being Mrs. Cory wasn't enough for Janice. She lured Mac to St. Croix and, following the plot of the novel to a T, began slowly to poison him in hopes of inheriting the Cory fortune. But Rachel was on to her, and in a gripping swimming pool battle, Rachel stabbed her nemesis in self-defense and Janice was out of their lives for good.

The fifth and youngest Frame, Sharlene, arrived in Bay City in 1975, seeking emotional peace. Sharlene was only ten when she was orphaned and she was brought up by her older sister Emma. She married her childhood sweetheart, Floyd Watts, and was widowed a few months later when he was killed in Vietnam. Sharlene went into an emotional tailspin and for several years lived a promiscuous life that she would dearly pay for. When she came to Bay City, she pulled herself together with the help of her older brother Steve and his wife Alice. Sharlene married Alice's older brother, Russ, and successfully concealed her past until her brother Willis, in revenge for Sharlene's alerting Steve that Willis intended to swindle him, revealed to Russ that Sharlene had been a hooker. Unable to face the aftermath of that revelation, Sharlene divorced Russ and left Bay City. She was pregnant with his daughter, Josephine (Josie) Watts, but he would not know that for many years to come. Sharlene returned in 1988 and went to work for Frame Construction. It was there that she met another casualty of the Vietnam War, John Hudson, and the two were married. Their son, Gregory, was born in 1991.

Lemay, they came "one by one. One of us has got money—let's go get him! Willis used him, Vince used him." Theirs was a struggle for social acceptance and financial security—but often not by honest means.

A former merchant marine, petty, ruthless Willis Frame came out of the woodwork in 1975 to take over Frame Enterprises when his brother Steve was presumed dead. He was a man full of macho pride, who exuded sexuality, and Alice began to fall in love with him. But Willis was resentful of his brother's widow's interference in the business. He eventually went to work for Cory Publishing, married fellow employee Gwen Parrish, and having had enough of Bay City, accepted an assignment in Australia.

Janice Frame came to Bay City in 1972 and was the staunchest (and only) supporter of Rachel in her obsessive pursuit of Steve. An unfortunate love affair with Tim McGowan forced Janice to choose between

Everyone thought that self-made millionaire Steven Frame was an only child, when in reality he was one of seven children who grew up poor on a dirt farm in Oklahoma.

Vince Frame came to Bay City in 1978. A furniture maker, he became a partner in Hobson-Frame Furniture and married Angie Perrini. The union was short-lived, and Vince then married Mimi Haines and left Bay City in July of 1979. Steve's younger brother Jason arrived in town in December of 1987. Bold and unpredictable, like all the Frames, Jason, a retired naval officer, was a charmer and an affable opportunist—a woman-in-every-port kind of a guy. Rachel knew right away that Jason spelled trouble. Jason's various schemes and machinations led to his untimely death in a carnival hall of mirrors at the hands of Nicole Love.

The crime brought to town Frankie Frame, daughter of Emma Frame Ordway—whom she often referred to as an overbearing mother—to solve the mystery of her Uncle Jason's death, and that she did. Her sister, Molly, came to Bay City in the mid-seventies, and there's a brother, Wade, as well. Says actress Alice Barrett, who played Frankie, on being a Frame, "Jason was bad. . . . Janice was stabbing people in pools. I don't remember what Willis was all about. Sharlene is nuts." Does she think they're all crazy? "Insane."

After discovering that Cass Winthrop's fiancée killed her Uncle Jason, Frankie fell in love with him and they married. Together they had a daughter, Charlie. Frankie died a violent death at the hands of Bay City stalker, Fax Newman. Her last words were "I beg of you. I have a child."

Other second-generation Frames include Jamie Frame, love child of Rachel and Steven, who was raised by Rachel and Mac. A sensitive and troubled youth, Jamie took a while to find himself. In the early eighties he developed a cocaine problem that he later licked. Always a dreamer, he turned his talents to writing, but his only published novel, *A View from the Bay,* was a Peyton Place exposé of family and friends that sent shock waves through Bay City. He went on to become a respected doctor. A romantic at heart, Jamie was involved with several of Bay City's eligible woman. He did the honorable thing when Vicky Hudson told him she was pregnant with his child and married her. They had a son, Steven. Eventually Vicky and Jamie divorced and he was briefly involved with Marley, Vicky's twin. Jamie went to San Francisco to practice medicine, where he now resides, leaving Vicky to raise Steven. For the sake of their son, they remain friends.

Emma Ordway was the first of the Frame siblings to arrive in Bay City to borrow money from her rich brother.

Willis Frame was calculating and shrewd and jealous of his brother's success. Willis wanted everything his brother Steven had, and that included Steven's wife.

Steve and Alice's adopted daughter, Sally, was a comfort to Alice in the dark days after Steve was presumed dead in a helicopter crash while on a business trip in Australia. A spirited young woman, Sally was tragically killed in a car crash in 1986, as her birth parents had been years before.

Janice Frame, at first a staunch supporter of Rachel's relationship with her brother Steve, went on to marry Rachel's Mac and then tried to kill him for his fortune.

Like all the Frames, Jason was an opportunist—but his schemes went bad, and for that he would pay with his life.

Steve's daughter, from his brief marriage to a woman named Pamela in Australia, came to Bay City in 1981. Affectionately known as Lady Di, Diana Frame became romantically involved with Peter Shea. Pete's father, Harry Shea, was a union boss at his old friend Steven Frame's construction site. Rather than follow in his father's footsteps, Peter wanted to be a veterinarian and was hired to care for Diana's champion thoroughbred, Captain. Although they clashed at first, the teenagers soon became romantically involved and eventually married.

Evan Frame, son of the deranged Janice and her lover Howard Battis, came to Bay City in 1988 seeking revenge against Rachel Cory for killing his mother. If his mother was the wife of a wealthy man when she died, then why was Evan living barely above poverty level? And why didn't he inherit anything when his mother died? Janice had shipped Evan off to be raised by his grandmother and then her brother Willis because she couldn't have a kid around while she went after Mac. Evan never knew his mother and grew up hating the blue-collar life—money and power were his gods, and he groomed himself, like other Frames before him, for the

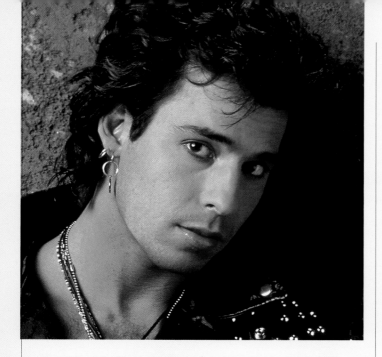

Bad-boy musician Dean Frame, a nephew of Steven Frame, came to Bay City to live with his cousin Frankie. Dean formed a record company with Matt Cory and fell in love with Jenna Norris.

good life. It was actually the scheming Iris who brought Evan to town, to help her take over *Brava*. Once in Bay City Evan fell madly in love with Amanda. They were lovers for a while, but Amanda returned to her husband, Sam, and Evan left town, vowing never to forget the humiliation he had suffered at the hands of the Corys. "I'll be seeing you, Amanda. At night in your dreams. I'll be there for the rest of your life," he said as he left. It was then that he dropped his father's name and took his mother's maiden name of Frame. One day he would make the Corys stand up and take notice of him! He returned in the summer of 1994, infuriated at the sight of Rachel with the devious Carl Hutchins. Once more he vowed revenge, and once more he made a play for Amanda, now married unhappily to Bay City's notorious mayor, Grant Harrison. But Evan's stay was short-lived. He left town when Justine and Grant strongly influenced him to search for employment outside of Bay City.

Dean Frame, son of Henry Frame and nephew to Steve, spent several years in Bay City beginning in 1990. Henry was a gambler who lived a vagabond life in pursuit of the fast buck, but he never found the pot of gold and the hotel rooms just got seedier.

Dean had been on the road with Henry since his mother died years before, and although Henry was close to his son, the transient life they led was unsuitable for a kid. The welfare authorities intervened and separated Dean from his father when he was 11, and he was bounced around among the numerous Frame cousins. He came to Bay City to live with his cousin Frankie Frame and raised a lot of hell among the Frames, who felt he was a hustler and a bad apple. Dean displayed a talent for music early on. While his dad was playing the slots in Vegas, he would mingle with the entertainers, who taught him to play the piano. There he found a surrogate family and learned quickly. With his charm and dark good looks, he had no trouble attracting the opposite sex. Dean stayed in Bay City long enough to form D&M Productions with Matt Cory, and to fall in love with Felicia Gallant's adopted daughter, Jenna. Young love personified, he and Jenna became engaged, and when Dean left Bay City for a world tour in 1993, she went with him.

The next generation of Frames is represented by Cass and Frankie's daughter, Charlie.

A consummate power broker who thrived on manipulating people, Reginald Love was a despot who lived on the edge—a very dangerous edge that earned him the nickname "The Vulture." Reginald had a brilliant mind, which he used to move the people around him as if they were pawns in a chess game. He was determined that he would control fate—not the other way around. Reginald was power personified. But he had charm—a charm that in the span of a second he could turn off, and when he did he was deadly. Reginald came from an old-line family of illustrious, monied bankers, who exuded social prestige and affluence, and he married a woman who came from the same social class, Elizabeth, who bore him a son and two adored daughters. The son, Peter, was a weak and timid boy who proved a constant disappointment to his father, while daughters Donna and Nicole were his pride and joy—that is, until he learned his wife's dark secret: she'd had an affair with Reginald's horse trainer, and Donna and Nicole were not his flesh and blood. This revelation drove Reginald mad with fury—to think that the one child he could claim as his was the child he was never able to love—his son, Peter. Enraged, Reginald went after his wife with a gun. The bullet missed, but tipsy from drinking, Elizabeth knocked over an

Reginald Love was a powerful despot, albeit a charming one, who liked to think he controlled fate and coldly manipulated his family as if they were pawns in a chess game.

ashtray and her lit cigarette ignited the curtains. Reginald took flight, while the erstwhile horse trainer, Jason Frame, saw but was unable tidentify the shadowy figure running from the blaze. The police decreed the death a suicide.

His wife's indiscretions left lasting scars on Reginald, and he ruled his children with an iron hand. His love for his daughters turned to vengeance, as they were a constant reminder of what their mother had done to him and what he eventually did to her. Hate took over as Reginald went about destroying his daughters to get back at his wife, using Peter, his only biological child, as his pawn.

Not long after Elizabeth's "suicide," Donna fell in love with Michael Hudson, the Love's stable boy. Michael's similarities to the man Reginald's wife had had an affair with were more than enough for Reginald to despise him, and he set out to destroy the relationship, driving the hapless stable boy from town before he knew that Donna was pregnant with his child. He then sent him a letter saying that Donna did not love him nor did she have any desire to see him again. "People accuse me of playing God," said Reginald. "But I don't play anything. I am." Says actress Anna Stuart, who plays Donna, "She was definitely terrorized by her father." And so Michael left Bay City and a devastated Donna believed he didn't care. Disgraced by his daughter's indiscretions, Reginald kept her locked in the basement for the duration of her pregnancy, and when she gave birth to twins he arranged for one of them (Vicky) to be adopted.

The other twin, Marley, was raised as Donna's sister, along with Peter and Nicole. Actress Ellen Wheeler, who plays Marley, explains, "She grew up thinking her grandparents were her parents and she didn't have a close relationship with them. She went to private schools, was sent away from her family. The people she thought were her parents weren't. They were very removed in her life. She probably had a life where she came home for Christmas and saw her parents at their anniversary party and things like that. And then she found out they weren't her parents and

that Donna was her mother. Her life was very protected and innocent, but it was also kind of cold."

There was a huge cultural gap between Vicky and Marley. Vicky was raised in a tough neighborhood in the mining town of Lassiter, Pennsylvania. Says Wheeler, "She grew up in a different place. Everything that Marley grew up with was cultured and refined and given to her. Vicky grew up where she had to fight for everything she got. When Vicky came, she was the one who would complain about not having anything. It seemed as if Marley had everything, but Marley really grew up without closeness within her family. Vicky didn't have her family either, but she had Bridget. She had somebody who really loved her and was there for her. So she didn't grow up with money or things, but she grew up with that kind of love that is just invaluable. The people who adopted her died when she was young and she didn't have a lot of money. She grew up on the wrong side of the tracks." But because she had more warmth in her life, Wheeler says, "That part gives her that basis, that strength she has now," whereas Marley is "still looking for the warmth she never had as a little kid. She had Donna, but Donna wasn't able to express it because of this secret." Actress Jensen Buchanan, who plays Vicky, adds, "Marley was the protected one. Vicky is the survivor. Vicky is the adaptor. Vicky was the one who was determined to have a better life. That's why she came, and that's why she adapted."

When rough-around-the-edges Victoria hit town with her lover Jake McKinnon to get her share of the family fortune, the identical twin she didn't know she had was in dire need of a bone marrow donor. Explains Stuart, who plays Donna, "Vicky comes into town and doesn't want anybody to know she is there. Marley's dying of a blood disease, and Vicky's pretending she's Marley because she wants to feel what it was like to grow up in this cushy environment. Downstairs the doctor is saying Marley isn't going to make it if she doesn't get a bone marrow transplant, and nobody in your family can do it. I think it's Marley upstairs in bed, but really Vicky's up there. So I go up

Nicole

to talk to Marley. I'm emotional and trying to hold that down so she doesn't see how upset I am. And I sit on the bed with her—who I think is Marley but is really Victoria—and I'm trying to keep from crying because this is my baby who is going to die, and she says, 'Donna, tell me about the good times.' And I say, 'OK,' and this is Vicky wanting to know. And I say, 'Remember Danny?' And she says, 'Danny?' And I say, 'I miss the puppy. You know, it was your birthday, and you drove your mother's car through the roses—messed up Mother's rose garden.' We had gotten her a puppy for her birthday, and she was being punished and she was up in her room and we're all downstairs and miserable because she's being punished and we can't give her the puppy. So I'm telling her this and the tears are streaming down her face and she's reliving something that never happened to her. And I say, 'Then we finally gave it to you,' and there is this beautiful moment when she says, 'I was so lucky, wasn't I?'"

Tormented by betrayal and guilt over the death of his wife, Reginald found comfort with good-hearted Mary McKinnon. Mary humanized him, and they had a brief affair, but Mary was married to Vince and couldn't bring herself to leave him. The night she tried to break it off, she fell overboard from Reginald's yacht. Reginald saved her, but she had developed amnesia, and no one knew she was alive.

In an effort to escape the sins of his past, Reginald staged his own "death" and took Mary to Paraguay. There he established a new identity and led Mary to believe that she was his wife of some twenty years, Marissa. Together they adopted a son, Scott. Then Reginald's scheme was exposed by none other than Michael Hudson. Forced back to Bay City and losing Mary when his scam was exposed, Reginald's hatred surfaced with renewed vigor, and he was hell-bent on destroying Michael, who had found his way back to his children and the woman Reginald had tried to keep him from.

To distance himself from his alcoholic father, Michael changed his name from Garrison to Hudson and returned, having made his fortune, to reunite with his childhood sweetheart, Donna Love. It was then that he discovered he was the father of twin girls, now young women in their teens, and he was determined to make up for the lost years when he didn't know of their existence. Says actor Kale Browne, who played Michael, "One of the things I most enjoyed early on was the fact that he met his daughters. He was learning with them and he had a great relationship with them."

Marley and Victoria had a strained relationship with their mother—they never reached the point of calling her Mom—to them she was always Donna. But with Michael it was a very different story, especially for Vicky. Browne adds, "Vicky had been

Donna

around the block, so you could be direct with Vicky in a way that you couldn't be with Marley. On the other hand, Marley had much more innocent faith and trust and belief, and Vicky you had to convince and then convince again. She was somebody you talk to but a lot of your conversation is 'Do you love me now? Do you still love me?' Because she was acting up so much. Marley seemed to be much more secure. So they were true polar-opposite twins at one point."

No matter what schemes Vicky pulled, Michael always stood by her. Buchanan says, "I loved the way he would come in and out of our dysfunctional family. He was the voice of reason and he was a very solid force in the family. All of us could just be maniacs in our own way, but Michael had a very calming and sane effect in our family. Not everybody can be nut cases. You have to have someone around who points the craziness out to you, and he was that character."

When Reginald returned, he was obsessed with taking over as head of the family, an obsession that included getting rid of Michael, who in his mind was still the stable boy who got his daughter pregnant and was responsible for ruining his idyllic life in South America with Mary. Reginald had a henchman drug Donna on the eve of her marriage to Michael. Although she got through the ceremony, she then had a nervous breakdown and was sent to a mental institution. As for the other siblings—as a reaction to his father's return, Peter would become more driven, and it was evident that there was a temper and a feisty personality lurking beneath his civilized veneer. As for Nicole, who used to be Reginald's "little girl"—the one he showed off at ballet recitals and beauty pageants, and who grew up believing that looks were her only worth—she had suffered through a drug problem and discovered that she had a talent for design. Underlying her drive to succeed was the need to prove something to her father—a man she deeply resented but whom she would love to love and be loved by. With his newly discovered granddaughter, Victoria, Reginald had instant communication in a kind of "unholy alliance," because Victoria realized she was a lot like him. She would ultimately inherit the Love fortune that she came to

scene:

The Love drawing room, about midnight, Christmas eve

Vicky sits near the tree, on the floor, and looks at her reflection in one of the glass balls, which she holds in her hands. Michael enters and watches her for a long moment. And then he joins her.

MICHAEL: Waiting for Santa Claus?

VICKY: Never believed in him.

MICHAEL: Not even a little?

VICKY: Look at this. (She hands him the glass ball)

MICHAEL: Pretty.

VICKY: Not very. Look at the date.

MICHAEL: Oh.

VICKY: Yeah. Oh. Nineteen sixty-six.

MICHAEL: It shouldn't be on the tree. Somebody goofed. I'll get rid of it.

VICKY: You can't do that. It's an old family heirloom.

MICHAEL: One that makes you very unhappy.

VICKY: Are you kidding? That's a great antique. It must be worth a fortune.

MICHAEL: Yeah. And you made the original down payment. Let's get rid of it.

VICKY: No, I'll keep it, I think. It'll remind me of where I've been all my life. Born in nineteen sixty-six right here in this house, and then out of it one day later and then Bingo! Back again. Some kids have their rattles and their teething rings. I've got this glass ball. (She looks at herself in the reflection) I can see myself in it.

MICHAEL: What do you see?

VICKY: A jerk.

MICHAEL: A real bad jerk or just a medium one?

VICKY: Pretty bad. But in spite of that, I'm a great-looking woman. Just look at those cheekbones.

MICHAEL: Inherited from me.

VICKY: Terrific eyes.

MICHAEL: From your mother.

VICKY: Men always mention my mouth.

MICHAEL: As your father, I don't think I want to hear the rest of this. OK, you're a great-looking woman who is a jerk. Why?

VICKY: Because it's Christmas. Christmas always makes me feel that it's a holiday for other people—the nice ones. The people who have been kind all year, and understanding, and patient. The people who thought about others all year long, the people who didn't muscle their way through. The people who were good to their families—(Vicky breaks off, near tears) The sisters who were—(She struggles for this word)—loving to their sisters, the daughters who supported their mom, the daughters who were—(Again a struggle)—grateful for their father's—(Vicky can't go on)

MICHAEL: Father's love?

VICKY: (Trying to put the hard shell around herself) Checkbook. Grateful for their father's checkbook.

MICHAEL: I am now going to kick your ass in. Not because you insulted me, but because you lied. You are grateful for my—what? Now dammit! Say it!

VICKY: (She's caught. Gets stubborn) OK. Your cheekbones. (Michael has had it. Walks toward the door.)

VICKY: (Con't): OK! OK! Come back! (and she holds out her arms) I love you, Dad.

town to seek. Donna escaped from the institution, and she and Michael renewed their vows, while Reginald met his deserved end when, during a fight with Michael on the roof of the Love Tower, he slipped and fell to his death.

It was around this time that Michael went to a jungle camp in Singapore to find his brother John, a Vietnam vet who had been missing in action and presumed dead. When Michael found him, he was working in a clinic for children left orphaned and devastated by the war. Because of a long-ago one-night stand with Donna, John would cause problems with the Hudson marriage, but eventually John married his soul mate, Sharlene, and became a respected doctor and Bay City General Hospital's chief of staff.

Says Browne of the brothers' relationship, "We were pretty much torn apart by the standard alcoholic-family-torn-apart stuff—disagreed on a lot of things. The relationship with John, it grew. I think what you did see was two people who came to trust each other and earned each other's trust and still retained their own very specific opinions. We could agree to disagree. I think it was a good example of brothers, because it was real. I guess you can never feel as murderous toward someone as you can toward a blood rel-

Marley grew up cultured and refined in the Love mansion.

ative or as loving. So I think we had all those polarities and yet, when the chips were down, Michael and John were always there for each other." Their mother, Clara, was still living on the family farm. Says Browne, "When I came back and I had leukemia, I went to live with Mom to kind of lay low. And she was there for both of us." Actor David Forsyth, who played John, says, "She was one of those women who would bat her boys down! And we'd go, 'OK, OK, Mom.' These two grown men just standing there in terror of this little woman." When Clara developed symptoms of Alzheimer's, the boys put her in the Green Farms Retirement Home, two miles from the farm.

Michael Hudson was soon to discover he had yet another child whose childhood he had missed, when Nick Terry came to town. An angry young man, the product of a brief affair, Nick grew up a latchkey child, much like his father before him, and reminded Michael of himself as a youth. Browne muses, "I think he saw a lot of himself in Nick. And so I think he was as judgmental and forgiving as he was with himself. He didn't want Nick to learn the hard way, the way he had, but it seemed that was exactly what

The brothers didn't always get along, but they'd defend each other to the death.

132

Victoria grew up in the tough mining town of Lassiter and had to fight for everything she wanted.

Nick had to do." Nick greatly resented his father at first, but Michael chipped away at his defenses. Actor Mark Mortimer, who plays Nick, adds, "He didn't know he had a father until Michael came along and bailed him out of jail. At first it didn't mean a whole lot. I think he rebelled against it, although he was just looking for lots of love. And Michael wasn't really the kind of guy to give him tons of love. He was a lead-by-example kind of guy—here's how I am, here's how you should be. He didn't understand the way Nick felt about things. He tried a lot of times. But it didn't come off right. So that more times than not, they ended up arguing about stuff."

Nick Terry was an angry young man who didn't know he had a father until Michael bailed him out of jail.

When Nick discovered that Michael was dying of leukemia, he repented and offered to donate his bone marrow. Mortimer remarks, "They still had tons of problems, but it showed that Nick was willing to try and willing to risk his life for his family. We just started really getting our relationship squared away when he died."

Michael's death caused numerous rifts between the three siblings, especially since it was Vicky who was blamed for the tragedy that took his life, but one thing they all agreed on—they just never had enough time to spend with their warm and loving father. A man who had grown up when he discovered he had children of his own and who died in a misguided attempt to protect his headstrong, impulsive daughter from making a terrible mistake, Michael Hudson's last words to his children rang poignant and true: "As long as you are alive ... so am I." Nephew Gregory and grandchildren Steven and Kirkland form the next generation.

the McKinnon family

The oldest McKinnon daughter, M.J., was a lot like her mother, Mary. Practical and serious by nature, M.J. joined the police force where she met and fell in love with Adam Cory.

*V*ince and Mary McKinnon had a good strong marriage. Not that they didn't endure hardship—but their major problems were almost always of a financial nature. Vince was a self-educated man, who, like his father before him, worked at any number of laboring jobs to support the family. He drove a truck, tended bar, and worked as a plumber and a coal miner before he opened Mary's Place, a bar.

Never angry or bitter, he took pride in being a working man. Intelligent but with little schooling, Vince had an Irish love for literature and poetry. He was a man of strong opinions and a great deal of pride, who ruled his family with an iron will. From behind the bar at Mary's Place, he cast a baleful eye on any guy who dared even try to make time with any of his beautiful daughters. When Mary was presumed dead, Vince did everything he could to keep the family going both financially and emotionally. Mary had been a calm and generous mother, and M.J. reminded Vince a lot of her. She had the same even temperament, the same iron will. The oldest of four, M.J. tried to take over for their mother when they thought she was dead and gave up a lot of things along the way, but she always took herself seriously, and entered the police force as a practical way to use her degree in sociology. M.J. always felt intimidated by her fierier, prettier sister, Kathleen. M.J. was the tomboy who struggled through school, unlike her beautiful and feminine sister, who received academic honors. And there was the issue of her name, Modesta Josephina, which she changed to M.J. as soon as she could talk. "You got Kathleen, I got Modesta Josephina. Our mother and father must have been on an acid trip to name me that!"

In temperament, Kathleen was more like her father, and things would have worked out perfectly if she had been a boy because in her Irish Catholic family, boys were allowed to have inquiring minds and a biting wit, both signatures of Kathleen's char-

Blue-collar Vince McKinnon and his wife, Mary, had a solid marriage until Reginald Love interfered.

...ake ...n his ...Victoria ...two ...ng ...to

The youngest McKinnon daughter, Cheryl, dreamed of being a model. Vince was furious when Cheryl took up with Scott LaSalle, Mary's adopted son with the notorious Reginald Love.

acter. Kathleen thought her mother was the most wonderful woman in the world, and she knew she wasn't a thing like her. Her mother was beautiful and kind, never brash and sarcastic, and Kathleen was sure Vince preferred M.J., who was the duplication of their mother. Fiercely independent and never good at taking second place, Kathleen kept up a fierce competition with her sister. But the love was always there, and if push came to shove, they'd die for each other. The youngest of Vince and Mary's children, Cheryl, was a sweet and sheltered teenager just beginning to set out on her own. Happy and down-to-earth, Cheryl was kept the baby but wanted very much to be like her older sister M.J. She ran away from convent school to see what it was like to be a normal teenager and reestablish her family ties, even though she knew her father would be furious at her for leaving. Cheryl worked at Mary's Place and had dreams of becoming a model. Her parents weren't pleased when she took up with Scott LaSalle, Mary's adopted son with Vince's notorious enemy, Reginald Love.

Vince and Mary's only son, Ben, was the third of the four children. Always a loner, in high school he was voted the number one man of mystery because nobody knew anything about him. Ben's first attraction was to Marley Love. Marley mistakenly got the impression that he was wealthy, and Ben worked hard to maintain the illusion, while Donna, assuming that he was after Marley's money, worked hard to break them up. When he got a football scholarship to a college in California, Ben left Bay City, leaving cousin Jake to mend his girlfriend's broken heart. A so-so student but a voracious reader, Ben went on to be a

Feisty and fiercely independent, younger sister Kathleen was more like her father, Vince. The only problem was that she wasn't born a boy.

lawyer.

Jake McKinnon grew up in the mining town of Lassiter, Pennsylvania, and it was thought that he would work in the mines and bring home money every week to help his family. But Jake had something that would take him out of Lassiter, and that was a dream of a whole other kind of life. At the time, his dream was tied to Victoria Love, and he thought they would walk away from Lassiter together. The McKinnon family welcomed Jake with open arms. Then Vicky and Jake found out about the Love family fortune and what it could mean to Vicky. Once in Bay City, Jake became torn between the twins. He fell in love with Marley and married her. Nevertheless, today he makes his home with Vicky.

After seventeen long years, Mary McKinnon returned to Bay City. Having been abducted by Reginald Love after a fall from his yacht left her with amnesia, she had lived all those years with Reginald in Paraguay thinking she was Marissa LaSalle, his wife. Indeed, she believed she loved him, and together they adopted a son, Scott. She returned to Bay City with no memory of her husband, Vince, and their four children. A beautiful woman of great charm and warmth, Mary was racked with guilt as well as with the physical trauma of amnesia, and it was with a great deal of shock that she came to comprehend her double life. A woman of deep loyalty, she had to deal with her betrayal of her husband and her children and the knowledge that before she fell from Reginald's yacht and developed amnesia, she might have had an affair with Reginald that she could not remember. As for Vince, the sight of his dear wife, Mary, made the sun shine brighter in heaven, and he alternated between elevating her to sainthood and being very angry.

scene:

Vince McKinnon and his daughter come together for the last time before she marries Cass.

Kathleen is on the sofa as Vince returns home from work. He tosses his jacket on the sofa beside her. Kathleen picks the jacket up and holds it to her. It brings back a flood of memories.
VINCE: Just like your mom. She could never stand my messy ways.
KATHLEEN: How old is this jacket, Pop?
VINCE: (sitting by Kathleen) Older than God.
KATHLEEN: I think you had it since I was a teenager.
VINCE: Why are we talking about my jacket?
KATHLEEN: When Mama died, I lay here on the sofa and I covered my head with your jacket and didn't come out for about three days.
VINCE: (his arms around her) I didn't realize that, sweetheart.
KATHLEEN: I'm leaving a lot of sad

memories behind.
VINCE: Well, hey! They can't all be bad. You're taking some good ones too. Memories don't have to make you cry. For instance, I remember the crazy things your mother did, and I start to laugh sometimes.
KATHLEEN: Mama never did anything crazy.
VINCE: Trust me. I remember once, we were so broke it got kind of scary. I was really in the dumps. We put you kids to bed and your mother went in the bathroom and stayed a long time. I got worried. And she came out looking beautiful. She had done something to her hair and had put on makeup—not that she needed any. And she had on a dress she hadn't worn in a long time. She asked me on a date! I thought the woman had gone out of her mind. But I went along with her and put

on a necktie and a jacket. When I came out, she had lit some candles and there were flowers and she had a great meal on the table and a bottle of wine. Now don't get mad, she said. Sure, I spent the last cent I had. But I had to do something for *me*. This is just my way of surviving, she said. And so we ate and put on some music and danced and she told me she loved me. (Vince has tears in his eyes, but not of sadness. After a moment he goes on.) Well, later I knew what a clever woman she was. It wasn't her survival she was talking about. It was mine. She knew I felt less of a man because I wasn't supporting my family. She wanted to show me I was still the man in her life, no matter what.
KATHLEEN: That's a beautiful memory, Pop.
VINCE: Lots more where they came from.

When Mary returned with Reginald in 1987, she and Vince divorced, but eventually they again found the love they once shared, remarried, and left Bay City to live near their children in Minneapolis, Minnesota.

the ewing family

Fred and Jeanne Ewing met at a dance in their hometown of Claxton, Wyoming. Together they had two children, Larry and Blaine. The marriage was a troubled one—he was abusive and she was alcoholic. Because of their painful home life, Larry and Blaine turned to each other and learned early on that they were the only people they could trust. But brother and sister were to lead very different lives. Blaine was a schemer, after any Cory son. When she met Jamie Frame and Dennis Wheeler on a dude ranch in Wyoming where they were spending the summer, she decided to follow them to Bay City and seek her fortune there. The money-grubbing Blaine would briefly marry Jamie and have several more affairs

The Ewing family hailed from Wyoming, and one by one they made their way to Bay City. Pictured here: Blaine Ewing with husband Sandy Cory; Larry Ewing with wife, Clarice Hobson; and Catlin Ewing, who would fall in love and marry Sally Frame.

and one more marriage before becoming Sandy Cory's girlfriend and reporting assistant and settling down. The two were married in a double ceremony with Rachel and Mac and had a son, Alex.

Larry, on the other hand, was good-hearted and uncomplicated, a conservative and law-abiding police officer who reached the rank of lieutenant. Larry married kindhearted Clarice Hobson, a waitress with a heart of gold. Through Clarice, Larry opened up and was able to trust someone other than his sister. He also formed a close father-son relationship with Cory, Clarice's son with Robert Delaney. Through Larry's marriage to Clarice, the wounds of his childhood began to heal as she became not only his lover and his wife, but his confessor and his rock. Together they had a daughter, Jeanne.

Larry and Blaine had been in Bay City for some time when their half-brother, Catlin, wandered into town. Wanting to keep his identity unknown until he had checked his siblings out, Catlin told everyone his name was Josh. Jeanne Ewing had left her husband, Fred, before she gave birth to Catlin, and Larry always felt she left because she was pregnant by some other man. He harbored a deep resentment toward Catlin for taking

their mother away from them and had little affection for the man he had become. Catlin was an angry and rebellious young man, a cowboy and a rodeo performer. He married fellow performer Brittany and had a son. It was when he believed they had died in a flood that he made his way to Bay City. His son was dead but Brittany survived, and when she found him she would cause much havoc in her husband's life. But Catlin had fallen in love with Sally Frame, and after many obstacles were thrown in their path they were married and briefly happy until Sally's untimely death.

the carlino family

*J*oe Carlino came back to his hometown of Bay City after being badly shaken by a child abuse case he was covering as a cop in New York City. Actor Joe Barbara, who plays Joe, describes his character: "He was trying to make a difference, trying to do some good, and it wasn't happening. At least he couldn't see it. Guys he'd bust for selling drugs, next day are back on the street. People who beat up kids didn't stop. All the good he was trying to do didn't seem to be working. And he was following the rules. He was doing his job as a cop. Enforcing the law. It didn't work."

When Frankie Frame asks Joe why he left the police force and came back, Barbara describes what happened: "He tells about this girl named Emelda Martinez, a five-year old girl. The neighbors kept calling the station saying that the mother's boyfriend was beating Emelda up. And we kept answering the call and going to the house. The mother would answer the door, we describe the complaint, the mother would say, 'Oh she got hurt roller-skating. She was clumsy, she's fine.' The boyfriend would always be sitting in the other room with a beer in his hand watching television. The kid would always back her up. We leave. We go to the house one day, the same thing happens. We go out in the hall and the kid fol-

Joe's little sister, Sofia, ran away from convent school to join him in Bay City. He was the typical overprotective older brother, and although she didn't always like that, the two were extremely close and protective of each other.

lows us . . . and we think *This is it. She's going to talk. We're going to nail this guy.* And she said, 'You've got to stop coming here because if he leaves Momma, she'll cry.' I got there first the day he threw her out of a fifth-floor window." That was it, says Barbara. "Packed my stuff in my car. I had a cat named Serpico. Took my cat and ended up back here at home."

Having grown up in Bay City, Joe was no stranger. In high school he had dated Rachel's half-sister, Nancy. He moved back into the family home and opened up a PI office with Frankie Frame. Joe's mother, Rose, had died a few years before; his father, Eddie, had recently moved to Arizona; and his younger sister, Sofia, was in a convent school in New York, living with their Aunt Franny.

Soon after Joe settled in Bay City, Eddie came to live with him. Barbara says, "It was so natural. They had him and me cooking." Indeed, Eddie played matchmaker when Joe was courting Paulina. According to Barbara: "Paulina would come over and she'd be sort of clueless. 'You have such a nice house,' she'd say. Eddie would reply, 'Well, Joey decorated. Joey, show her your plants. Show her your garden. Joey, why don't you have her come over for dinner!'

Family always came first for Joe, so it was a joyous day when he and Paulina welcomed son Dante into the world.

And I'd groan, 'Oh my God, you're killing me!'" However, when Eddie left for Italy to be with his brother Bruno, he was greatly missed by his son.

Eddie always wanted a restaurant, and his legacy to Joe was Carlino's. It was a legacy that Joe, now captain of the Bay City Police Department, didn't necessarily count on or even want. Barbara explains, "Pop signs a loan and has to get me to co-sign the loan. I'd been shot two days earlier. He comes in going, 'Hey, Joey! Listen, I want to start this restaurant. Could you co-sign the loan for me?' And I can't breathe and I'm signing the loan and he takes off for Italy." Today, Carlino's, run by Paulina and Joe, is a favorite place for Bay City residents to mingle and dine.

After Eddie left, Joe wasn't alone for long. His younger sister, Sofia, having had enough of convent school and Aunt Franny, ran away from school and came home. Sofia told Joe, "I can't live with the Enforcer—that's what I called Aunt Franny." Actress Dahlia Salem, who played Sofia, theorizes: "She comes from a traditional middle-class Italian-American family, and I think being in convent school, even though it was probably a great experience for her, definitely stifled her in a lot of ways, and in her teenage years she didn't have her mother." Salem describes the Carlino family as having "a real sense of loyalty to family and tradition. And respect and care for each family member. Absolutely, they stick

together. It's a strong foundation. Family is the first thing on Sofia's list." The family member she's closest to—no contest, her older brother, Joe. Says Salem, "He was overprotective because I was on my own and he was not sure if I was doing the right thing. But I finally set him straight! He always trusted her. I don't think he undermined that. I think he was just worried about the outside factors . . . and men."

Joe married Paulina, and there was a rocky period when Sofia blamed Paulina, then addicted to diet pills, for burning down the family home and putting her nephew, Dante, in danger. She felt her brother was in some kind of jeopardy, and as he had protected her, she was protecting him. Today the relationship is back on track. Says Salem, "Paulina's like a sister to Sofia. Paulina is someone she could trust immensely. She's with her a hundred percent, always looking out for her. And they're great friends as well."

Of the future, Barbara says, "Joe's dream, his ambition, is to have a family. And to raise it and do a good job. I don't think he cares really about professional goals. As long as people are safe, and they're stopping the bad guys, and his family's safe and have food and a good education and all that kind of stuff, that's really what he cares about." Will he be a good father? "I think he's going to be good, real good."

the Burrell family

Etta Mae Burrell had five children, two girls and three boys, with her late husband, Harold. They had been married twenty-five years before he passed away. The Burrells are a generational family in Bay City. Etta Mae's grandmother, her mother, and now Etta Mae all lived in the family home. Actress Elain Graham, who plays Etta Mae, recalls, "There are all those snatches of memorabilia from each time, each era, that makes it so rich. I'm proud to be a part of it."

Judy, the oldest sibling, was already out of the house when Toni, the youngest, was growing up. Toni still lives in the Burrell home. Etta Mae named all of her children after African-American authors, and Toni was named for Toni Morrison, who writes about the strength of female wisdom. Graham is proud to be playing an African-American matriarch: "She's a strong earth mother. She has a total no-nonsense approach but a very big heart. She may be truthful at times to a fault and will tell you what you don't want to know. Tell the truth and shame the devil."

The Burrells were a military family—Etta Mae's husband was a career officer, and Etta Mae was a sergeant. Of Toni, Graham says, "I think my husband wanted a boy, and you know how men can get when they have their sights on a boy, so he was really looking to make her into that. There was a lot of head-butting. That's I believe where Toni gets her doggedness. She was always trying to be right in Daddy's eyes." Rhonda Ross Kendrick, who plays Toni, adds, "Everything Toni did was for his approval. She became a cop temporarily to shut him up, but she loves being a police officer. She's no-nonsense. She's in control and she learned how to fight. She's strong, confident, sometimes overconfident, male-identified. She comes from military people. Her father loved boys, and Toni fought to be one of the boys."

Of her relationship with her mother, Kendrick says, "Toni is respectful of her mother. And she's one of all those boys, she's kind of like Etta Mae's sister. With Judy gone, they developed a relationship of girlfriends." As for her brothers, says Kendrick, "The brothers are big bad beautiful men, who are protective of me and Etta Mae. They would be enraged if a mother or sister was the victim of violence or evil." Graham adds, "During the rape trial, one of my sons, Eugene, wanted us to come to Seattle where he lived. I should bring Toni and we should just cool out at his place and be with her nieces and my grandkids."

Etta Mae has had an interesting and varied career path. When she left her army post, she became an executive secretary in a bank. And for awhile, after Bridget died, she was Vicky's nanny. Says Graham, "She was tired and wanted something else to do. And she's always loved kids." Today she owns the Lucky Lady, a popular Bay City jazz club. Etta Mae won the Lucky Lady when Dustin, a blind percussionist, who was a friend of Vicky and Shane's, decided to leave it and held a lottery. Graham thinks of the turn of events this way: "Harold kind of talked to Toni and said, 'Here, get this ticket for your mom and give it to her.' It was like the spirit guiding. So that's how I got the Lucky Lady. And I named it the Lucky Lady because it was very lucky." Recently Etta Mae turned the restaurant into a coffee bar. Music is a big part of this family. Etta Mae sang in the church choir, but Graham says, "It's really Toni who is the singer in the family." Toni disagrees: "You think I can sing, you should hear my mom's voice." Toni's music helped her cope with the aftermath of the rape.

The Burrell extended family includes Tyrone Montgomery and Chris Madison, both of whom were at one time vying for Toni's affections. Tyrone was the only child of Etta Mae's best friend. Henry Simmons, who plays Tyrone, remembers, "During the summers I would stay with the Burrell family as a way of getting out of Chicago. Toni was like a sister and Etta Mae was like a second mother. I moved from Chicago after graduation from law school and I really had nowhere to go, and I was drawn to Bay City because of the Burrells. Because my mother had passed away and I needed a sense of family." Of Toni, Simmons says, "I think that Tyrone was really lost in a way because he had no family, and being close to this woman that he grew up with, I think he just naturally needed some stability, so he went for Toni." For awhile it was thought that Tyrone might be Etta Mae's son from a long-ago affair, but that suspicion was eventually cleared up. Tyrone lived with the Burrells until Toni's rape trial, when he was defending Nick Hudson, whom Toni had accused of the crime. Then, says Graham, "Etta Mae smacked him and threw him out!" Simmons counters, "When Toni said that it was Nick, at first Tyrone believed it, but although he doesn't lead by emotion, he is very passionate about what he believes in and standing up for it, and he came to the conclusion that it could not have been Nick. From that point on that's what he wanted to prove, even if it

The Burrell family
has strong roots in Bay City.
Etta Mae and daughter Toni
still live in the family home.
Extended family members
include Tyrone Montgomery
and Chris Madison.

meant causing a rift in the Burrell family." In the end Toni respected him for standing up for his beliefs. Says Kendrick of Tyrone, "Part of the attraction to Tyrone was familiarity."

Chris Madison was another story. Kendrick explains, "Chris is a male version of Toni. He's over-confident, takes his job seriously, thrives on games and competition, is respectful." Police officer Toni Burrell met ace reporter Chris Madison at a bowling alley. Actor Eric Morgan Stuart, who plays Chris, describes the meeting: "*The Herald* and the police station had a bowling league. Chris spots her and like, boom, he's all over her. At the time, he didn't realize she was a police officer, so he starts talking about his bowling abilities and starts to impress her with the fact that he's an award-winning journalist. Meanwhile, Toni knows exactly who he is. On top of that he's talking about how badly his team is going to beat the cops and how she should come over and sit with him and watch. And then he finds out she's a cop! And he finds himself putting his foot so far down his throat it's not even funny and trying to find a way to make up for it. On top of that the police officers actually start beating the heck out of him and his team. And so this competition starts immediately. I think one of the things Toni likes the most about Chris is the fact that he is capable of going toe-to-toe with her. So they found themselves competing on everything—bowling and miniature golf, whatever they could find.

"After Toni and I had been going out for a little bit, we decided OK, we gotta tell Mom. And I was very nervous about it because I've heard all this stuff about the woman and Etta Mae is very stern—you know, 'Don't mess with my daughter!' I'm like, oh great, I've got a sarge and a cop here. Oh my God! What am I doing? So we're at Carlino's and Toni gets called into work. And I'm like, 'No, you can't go to work! I bought these tickets to the comedy club. I was going to surprise you guys.' Toni says, 'I'm sorry, I gotta go.' She says to her mom, 'Chris will take you home.' And Etta Mae's like, 'Nah, you can go to work if you want to. I'd like to go to the comedy club!' I think it was a luxury for Etta Mae to be able to sit down alone with the man who is courting her daughter and really find out who he is. I think

she felt something strong about him and felt like this relationship is supposed to work for these two."

Graham remarks, "Etta Mae was a cheating woman, and she has a problem with seeing her daughter mimic any of her bad points. So I think that may be it. 'I couldn't be faithful, but damn it, you're going to be faithful.' So she's going for Chris. I think Tyrone reminds her of the man who was in her past, that good-looking, great smile, sweep-you-off-your-feet and that kind of thing. In Etta's mind, that kind of man is nothing but trouble." But she adds, "They're both gorgeous. They both know how to treat women. So it's a good catch. Whichever part of the ocean you throw your hook, you come up with either of them, you've got something good there!"

For awhile, in the aftermath of the rape, the pendulum swung back to Tyrone. Kendrick recalls, "Right after the rape, Tyrone took Toni in charge, he was in control, made the decisions for that moment in time. This was what she needed at that time. No matter how strong we are, we all want that at some point. You're proud of what you've accomplished and you've done it on your own, but it doesn't mean you don't need the other. Chris was respectful and that was beautiful, but he was wishy-washy. He didn't know how to act. He was so gentle, didn't want to remind her of the rape. But Tyrone took charge and that was Toni's fantasy. She imaged he was the guy on the white horse. He would protect her. She had taken control, went after the rapist, but after that she was ready to collapse."

But Chris had a strong ally in Etta Mae. Says Stuart, "She's always liked Chris. I think one of the beautiful qualities about Etta Mae is she's very intuitive." Today Chris and Toni are back dating and their squabbles center mainly on their jobs. Is Tyrone a sore loser? Simmons answers, "I think Tyrone is happy as long as she is happy."

Stuart explains that for Chris, before Toni, "It was always about his job, and he would never allow a relationship to take precedence. This is the first time he's found himself in a position where if he had to weigh 'I could be at home with Toni right now and spend the day with her or be at work,' he'd go, 'Oooohhh, what do I do here?'" Stay tuned.

felicia and cass

of rascals and romance
and a circle of friends

The Friendship

Romance novelist Felicia Gallant and lawyer and resident rake Cass (short for Casanova) Winthrop are best buddies till death do them part. Actress Linda Dano, who plays Felicia, remembers, "I was the ex-wife of Louis St. George, but I had an affair with Cass in France. I came on to the show with my chauffeur, Gil Weston. I was doing it with him." Stephen Schnetzer, who plays Cass, asks, "Doing what?"

Dano: "You know, that thing."

Schnetzer: "Oh, that fine thing you do from time to time, when your body chemistry warrants."

Dano: "Cass brought me to town to sign with Cory Publishing."

Schnetzer: "But Cory dragged his feet and we decided to start our own publishing company." And they rekindled their affair.

Dano: "We were a hot item." But not for long.

Schnetzer: "Cecile had been toying with me, and one morning Felicia found out that I'd been philandering with Cecile. She confronted me with her newfound knowledge, and in a reverse of the Jimmy Cagney grapefruit-in-the-face scene, she took a grapefruit off her room service plate and smashed it in my face with great relish—a little too much relish. Grapefruit and relish . . . . And then she pulled out of the publishing company and I went bankrupt. Totally ruined me. Because not only was she my star writer, she was my only writer!"

Dano: "Kind of took everyone with me, didn't I?"

Schnetzer: "And then we became friends."

The Fun

Schnetzer describes them as "a rogue family. We were outside the law." Adds Dano, "We were outside the envelope." That rogue company of actors included Wallingford and friends. *Another World* scribe Richard Culliton explains, "We had Wallingford, we had Cecile, we had Cass, we had Felicia. We had all these people who didn't have traditional families. And they became a family and it always seemed to be the real spirit of the show that these people who had no reason to be together and were completely different in every possible way were best friends and watched each other's backs. They would yell at each other and there was no stridency. The love was always underneath it, and that's sort of like a family. After Cecile was gone, they still hung out at her place. They weren't a family, so they all went to the same place every day—it was like their clubhouse."

Brent Collins, who played Wallingford, came on as Cecile's informant. According to Richard Culliton, "It was an outrageous time." Dano remembers, "Wallingford, and the gorilla in the truck with the brakes failing . . . Wallingford driving and Felicia riding shotgun careening downhill. He went into the flour and I went into the wine—or vice-versa. We all became one person, all three of us. We were like the Marx Brothers." Richard Culliton recalls the time "Cecile and Felicia were dressed up as nuns and got pulled over by the police for some reason and Felicia said, 'We're in a bus tour of *Sound of Music*, that's why we're dressed up as nuns.' Of course, vain Cecile just had to add 'I'm Maria, *she's* Mother Superior.'"

And who could forget loan shark Tony "The Tuna" and the wooing of Krystal Lake. Schnetzer says, "I owed Tony 'The Tuna' a hundred grand and he had a henchman, George, played by a real hit man. He was going to break my kneecaps. So in order to go out in public to scare up the money to

*T*hey were
lovers first, then
best friends.

Look closely and you'll see Cass, aka Krystal Lake, in a getup meant to throw loan shark Tony "The Tuna" off the track. Unfortunately, Tony fell for Krystal in a big way.

pay the debt, my first concept was to dress up in Krystal's rags and go out. I had scenes with Jamie Frame at Cory, where I'm grabbing him by the lapels, dressed in drag, and saying, 'You gotta give me a job. I'm the man for your company!' And Tony 'The Tuna' saying, 'Would you like to dance?' and me saying, 'I can't dance, don't ask me!' Then there was the reveal at New Year's when Tony went to kiss me and Krystal's wig got caught on the chandelier. I get hung up on a decoration, a Christmas decoration."

Schnetzer continues, "We've talked about our comedy, but I think some of our drama has been right up there." Felicia helped Cass through his bout with manic depression. He helped her recover from her descent into alcoholism after the death of her beloved Lucas. Dano recalls, "Lucas died, and she hit a brick wall." Cass was a major part of the intervention that led to her recovery.

The Romance

Dano: "We've never gotten back together romantically."

Schnetzer: "After that it was just a series of Zane, Mitch, Lucas, John, and Nikos for her, and for me it was Cecile, Kathleen, Nicole, Frankie, and Lila. We flirt like crazy—and then, of course, I'm overprotective with Nikos, and she's overprotective with Lila, there's always that possessiveness: 'You're not good enough for him. Nobody is except me.'"

Dano: "Some of the mates resented each other."

Schnetzer: "Zane I was supportive of, Lucas I was supportive of. Nikos, right from the get-go, 'Stay away from him! What are you doing?'"

Dano: "I came around to Kathleen. I hate Lila, the latest."

Schnetzer: "And you hated Cecile."

Dano: "She's dark. Cecile was very bad for him. So is Lila."

Schnetzer: "The sex is good."

Dano: "But you're going to get your heart broken. If she hurts Cass, it's like she hurts me, and that's the bottom line—if you hurt him, I will have to hurt you. We're relentless. We fight about it as only friends do. We get into brawls over stuff like that because we're both right and we know it. I can go full-out mad, screaming, stomping out of a room, slamming a door, and half an hour later, he'll be back or I'll be back saying, 'OK, I'm sorry, I shouldn't have probably yelled at you. You're right.' And before you know it we're back at it again."

Richard Culliton adds, "If they were going to save Kathleen and they would do anything in the world to save Kathleen, they would argue about who should drive while they were doing it."

Dano: "Stephen has always said, 'If we stay to the end, he and I will lock eyes.'"

Schnetzer: "And the lightbulbs will go out and we'll say, 'My God! It's always been you.'"

Dano: "And we will walk off through gauze."

Schnetzer: "No, the gauze will already be on the lens."

Dano: "Either that or we'll go off on our walkers!"

Schnetzer: "Or we'll fall back over in our rockers on the porch!"

the life and loves of felicia gallant

Felicia Gallant is the most glamorous and outrageous person in Bay City. Her fashion statement has always been "If you've got it, flaunt it!" Born and raised as Fanny Grady on Gold Street, she went to Europe and reinvented herself as glamorous romance novelist Felicia Gallant. Linda Dano says of the character she has come to inhabit, "I think of Felicia as a lot of different women. For me, she's always been so fascinating because she's a woman who did it all on her own. She didn't kill a husband, she didn't inherit the money. She came from such poverty and worked her way up. And that makes her fiercely independent. She doesn't have to ask anyone if she can buy this or do that. She's the absolute boss in her life. She's fiercely loyal to people she loves. When she loves you, she really loves you, and that makes her fearless. Everything she does, right or wrong, is from a place of caring. She's one of those great broads that if you're her friend and you're in trouble, she will go to battle with you and afterward ask why we did it. She's funny. She has claws. She has weaknesses. She worked though alcoholism, but somehow, some way, her strength is to get back up, dust herself off, and go out again."

Romance Novelist and Entrepreneur

And how did she become Felicia Gallant, romance novelist? Dano explains, "I went to Europe where I met a man named

*W*hen Felicia joined forces with Wallingford, you knew you were in for outrageous adventure and comedy galore.

They've helped each other through some dark times and haven't always approved of the other's mates, but it is a certainty that these two will be friends forever.

writer. It would make perfect sense that if you have more money then God, and you write books like people change their underwear, why not own a restaurant? I think for five minutes she owned a gym. [Actually, it was a spa called Gallant's.] She had a restaurant, Tops. She also had a talk show—*Breakfast with Felicia*—that became *Jam Sessions.* "The bookstore, Wallingford's, came out of a real love affair between Stephen and Felicia. And that made perfect sense. The two of them were tired of their lives. He was tired of being a lawyer. She was tired of being a writer. 'What can we do?' Why not go into business with your best friend? And they came up with a bookstore. Wallingford's was perfect because it was about Brent. It was the friendship. The three of them were together again, in spirit."

Edward Gerard. Never had I written anything. He's the one who helped Felicia begin a writing career. And he's the one who helped name her Felicia Gallant—because no one ever heard of a romance writer called Fanny! She had to have a more glamorous name. He was her mentor and she discovered herself." Of an output that rivals Danielle Steel's, Dano says, "She's prolific because she lives her life as if at any minute nobody's going to want to buy one, no one's going to like her anymore. So she just keeps churning them out. It can't be about money, because she's very wealthy, but she needs to constantly feel like she's wanted. It goes back to that childhood thing of not having a parent."

THE **ROMANCE NOVELIST** *OF THE* **YEAR**

FELICIA GALLANT

And She's Had Other Careers As Well

"Felicia is a social person, she kind of likes all of that," Dano remarks. "And I think it's a diversion from the writing. Remember, she's an enormously successful

Felicia in Love

"She's always looked for love and sometimes in the wrong places," Dano says. "She didn't have enough of it as a kid and she made mistakes. Her Achilles' heel is the men she picks. She's always been somebody who jumps in no matter what. And I don't think she ever

Felicia Gallant's romance novels are best-sellers in Bay City and throughout the world.

regrets it. I think it makes her who she is, and they all have a special place for her. I don't think she ever throws them away. And I don't think it's because she's a writer. I just think that's how she operates. She always finds the goodness in everybody—unless it's Lila."

Felicia was responsible for introducing the notorious Carl Hutchins into Bay City society, but the liaison didn't last for very long. After art dealer Louis St. George, whom she had married abroad, and who was coincidently Cecile de Poulignac's father, Felicia chose simple fisherman Zane Linquist as her next mate. Says Dano, "He was such a hometown kind of guy. She'd been through those years of glamour in Europe and suddenly here was this guy who was simple and honest and direct. And I think she really kind of felt he was sweet. There were no agendas with him." Zane died in 1986, the victim of a stray bullet. His last words were, "I love you, Fanny Grady. One classy lady."

Her next bridegroom was a reformed Mitch Blake, who had returned to Bay City to get to know his son, Matthew Cory. Dano says, "He was like an enigma. He was a guy who didn't talk much. He made Felicia work hard—that was a new experience for her—because he was shy and he was almost afraid of her and somewhat intimidated. I don't know that it was an equal marriage. I think Felicia had to work her heart into it. I think all of them were about Lucas. She was looking for Lucas, and those two men had parts of Lucas in them, because Lucas was sweet and quiet."

*F*ashionable Felicia Gallant considered her feather boa a lucky charm and never sat down to write without it.

Lucas was Felicia's childhood lover. He left her immediately after she gave birth to their daughter. Dano says, "My stepfather got him to leave town, made up some story and I never saw him. I never saw the baby." Lucas went out into the world and made his fortune. And Fanny "went on to discover herself and become this independent woman. She lived in Europe, met Louis St. George and married him and divorced him, and then met Cass. Had an affair in Paris with Cass, and it was Cass who was involved with Cory and brought her to Bay City. She came home again because she needed to touch base. She didn't go back to Gold Street or Chicago. She came to Bay City. Maybe she was there to look for Lucas. I like to think that. Maybe she came back hoping she'd see him again, because she had one love affair after another, but they were all parts of Lucas. Lucas was the greatest love of her life—that unrequited love."

However, when Lucas returned to Bay City and tried to win Felicia back, she told him she was happy with Mitch, and they agreed to be friends. When Mitch left for Africa on a photography assignment, Lucas and Felicia found themselves drawn to each other and they made love. When her divorce from Mitch was final, they resumed their relationship. Lucas had been a gangster during his time away from Felicia, but once he was back in her life, he promised her that he'd put his criminal days behind him, and except for a few minor indiscretions, he remained true to his word. They were married in July of 1991. Dano muses, "He was her dream. She had her only child with him and she didn't know that this child was alive until he came back into her life. He never married, and it's every woman's fantasy that the great first love of your life never married anyone because no one ever was you."

Tragically, one year after they wed, Lucas was shot by a jealous ex-lover. Devastated by his death, Felicia turned to drink. Dano says, "When Lucas died, she completely shut down."

Several years later, Felicia found love in a very unexpected place, the arms of John Hudson, her good friend Sharlene's husband. They had become close during Sharlene's frequent absences from Bay City,

Felicia and Cass were at low points in their lives when they decided to go into business together and open a bookstore, Wallingford's. The store was a tribute to their dear friend Wallingford and the friendship they had shared.

and both were shocked and confused by the intensity of their feelings. Dano explains, "John was all the things that Felicia never felt she was worthy of. He was a doctor. He was very educated. She'd married people from the streets in one form or another until John. John was respectability. And there was a kindness about him, like Lucas. There was also some part of Felicia, whether she admitted it or not, that he was untouchable because he was married to Sharlene. And as much as she hated herself for it, there was an attraction because of it. Felicia had nothing to lose. She'd lost everything. She'd gone down the road with alcohol. There was nothing you could do to her that was going to scare her at this point. And then there was John, and I think she just said, 'Why not?'"

After sharing just one passionate kiss, they resolved to ignore their feelings. Ironically, when Sharlene found a woman's handkerchief in her husband's pocket, it was to her good friend Felicia that she ran for emotional support. One night, while John and Felicia were stranded in their stalled car during a snowstorm, John began to relate some of his experiences in Vietnam, which culminated in the death of a young child in his arms. He broke down and Felicia comforted him and they fell into each other's arms and made love. When Sharlene discovered the affair, she kicked John out. Felicia welcomed her newfound lover, despite the condemnation of their families and friends. Says Dano, "She was like a pariah for awhile." However, John and Felicia were ecstatically happy, enjoying their rediscovered sexuality, and planning to marry. A few weeks before the ceremony was to take place, John spent a bittersweet night of lovemaking with Sharlene. Despite his reassurances, Felicia refused to accept what had happened. Dano explains, "Having a man cheat on you is like you know the rest of your life every time he's late you'll go, 'Where have you been?'" Felicia broke their engagement and soon moved on to a new relationship with Alexander Nikos.

They were on a plane, sitting next to each other in first class, when he turned to her and said, "I believe you're looking for me." Felicia was stunned because he bore an uncanny resemblance to Lucas. Nikos was a man who loved women—he'd already been married seven times, and according to him, each time was for love. His second marriage lasted six months. His third, six weeks. Immediately smitten with Felicia, he proposed the day after they met. Dano says, "With Nikos, it was back to glamour and power, and why fall madly in love? She's had that. I don't think through the whole Nikos thing she ever really got over John. What attracted her to him was his power. She wasn't going to go to that other place, but his power was intoxicating.

"She also likes people in her life who are like mutts, the people who no one else likes. She was one of those kids I'm sure who brought home stray animals and birds with broken wings. Nikos was damaged. He was damaged from his past, his childhood, and his hatred of Carl Hutchins. If you're damaged, Felicia will take you on. She tried to make him whole, and he almost killed her in the process. But she never believed for a second that he would have hurt her. She's got a really big heart, and she'll forgive you a lot. But he crossed the line with friends. You could have beat the hell out of her, but if you start going after her friends ... That's the one constant with this character, her loyalty." She would have to find a way to heal and move on, and she did.

cass's women

"The women traditionally for Cass have been very spirited, somewhat high-strung, strong-minded, and capable," Schnetzer states.

"Cecile," Schnetzer continues, "was a magnificent obsession." Alluring, conniving Cecile de Poulignac thought nothing of employing blackmail, treachery, or her feminine wiles to get what she wanted. Says Schnetzer, "She was just too driven by her ambition and greed to ever appreciate what she might have had until it was too late. But we had great fun." What motivates Cecile? Actress Nancy Frangione, who played her, says, "She's dynamic, energetic, and has

Felicia & Carl

Felicia & Zane

Felicia & John

Felicia & Alexander

Mitch Blake was a reformed man when he returned to Bay City and fell in love with Felicia. In honor of her friend Wallingford, who found great pleasure in betting on the horses, the two chose a racetrack as the setting for their wedding.

Close family friend Mac Cory gave the bride away. In a romantic grand finale, dozens of white doves were released when Mitch and Felicia said, "I do."

Felicia & Mitch

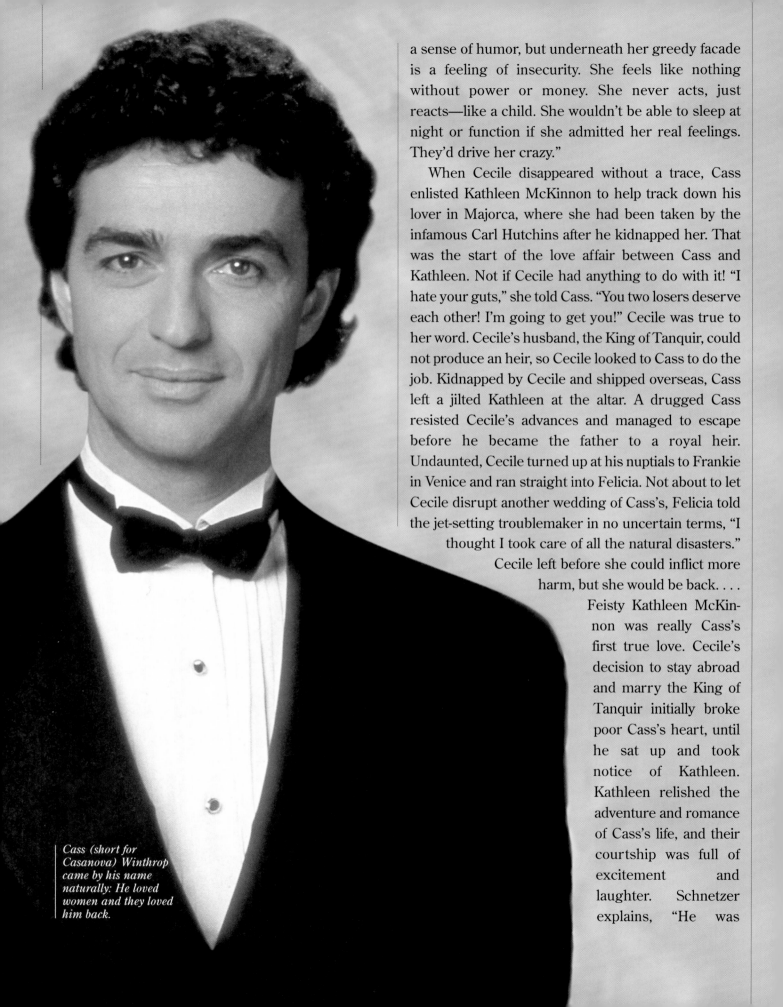

a sense of humor, but underneath her greedy facade is a feeling of insecurity. She feels like nothing without power or money. She never acts, just reacts—like a child. She wouldn't be able to sleep at night or function if she admitted her real feelings. They'd drive her crazy."

When Cecile disappeared without a trace, Cass enlisted Kathleen McKinnon to help track down his lover in Majorca, where she had been taken by the infamous Carl Hutchins after he kidnapped her. That was the start of the love affair between Cass and Kathleen. Not if Cecile had anything to do with it! "I hate your guts," she told Cass. "You two losers deserve each other! I'm going to get you!" Cecile was true to her word. Cecile's husband, the King of Tanquir, could not produce an heir, so Cecile looked to Cass to do the job. Kidnapped by Cecile and shipped overseas, Cass left a jilted Kathleen at the altar. A drugged Cass resisted Cecile's advances and managed to escape before he became the father to a royal heir. Undaunted, Cecile turned up at his nuptials to Frankie in Venice and ran straight into Felicia. Not about to let Cecile disrupt another wedding of Cass's, Felicia told the jet-setting troublemaker in no uncertain terms, "I thought I took care of all the natural disasters."

Cecile left before she could inflict more harm, but she would be back. . . .

Feisty Kathleen McKinnon was really Cass's first true love. Cecile's decision to stay abroad and marry the King of Tanquir initially broke poor Cass's heart, until he sat up and took notice of Kathleen. Kathleen relished the adventure and romance of Cass's life, and their courtship was full of excitement and laughter. Schnetzer explains, "He was

Cass (short for Casanova) Winthrop came by his name naturally: He loved women and they loved him back.

manipulative and driven by ambition. There was a softening through the love of Kathleen." *Another World* scribe Carolyn Culliton puts it this way, "At bottom, Cass does not have a heart of gold, and they were so atypical, which made them romantic and fun to write. They were both so self-interested and surprised themselves by falling in love with each other."

They had finally given in and decided to trade their treasured independence for a lifetime commitment, but their wedding was postponed when Kathleen suffered a paralyzing injury at the hands of Carl Hutchins. She was confined to a wheelchair for six months, during which time Cass had to reassure her that he still loved and desired her. They set another date. Kathleen exercised every day to be able to walk down the aisle on her wedding day. She was able to accomplish her goal, but when she arrived at the altar the groom was gone! Cass had been kidnapped by his old flame, Cecile, who wanted him to father her child. Kathleen thought Cass felt sorry for her, that she was an obligation because of her paralysis, so when she managed to walk down the aisle, he thought he was free. When Cass finally made it back to her, she rejected him, thinking he had run off with Cecile. It took a few months and a few more escapades before Cass and Kathleen finally tied the knot and left for an around-the-world honeymoon. Six months later Cass returned to Bay City and broke the tragic news that Kathleen had been killed in a plane crash.

Although ambition and greed were what motivated Cecile, Cass found himself obsessed with her.

It took Cass several years to recover from his tragic loss, but eventually he found love with Frankie Frame and they were married. They weren't married long, however, when Kathleen returned to Bay City! Because of her testimony against Hutchins, Schnetzer explains, "She was in the witness protection program and presumed dead. I had grieved and gone on, and then she appears and I had to annul the marriage."

When Cass's marriage to Frankie was deemed invalid, he found himself between two loves. Because of their shared history and because he thought it was the right thing to do, Cass returned to Kathleen. Dan Griffin, *Another World* production coordinator and longtime fan, describes the couple: "They had spunk and they had character. They had a lot of fun." But they had changed. Cass was no longer the adventurous thrill-seeker he once was. Kathleen missed the man she'd fallen in love with, and in his heart, Cass longed for Frankie. It was over.

Fashion designer Nicole Love, calculating daughter of the unscrupulous Reginald Love, was the next fair lady to capture Cass's heart, when he signed on to handle the legal end of Love Fashions. Spirited, sharp, quick to speak her mind, Nicole was vulnerable and insecure about herself and with the people she loved, particularly men. She was Reginald's little girl, and he instilled in her a feeling that she was pretty but not bright, so she grew up believing that looks were her only worth. Her you-can't-get-to-me-cuz-nothing-bugs-me attitude was merely a defense. While a fashion model for *Brava,* working exhausting twelve-hour-a-day shoots and

*W*hen Cass enlisted Kathleen McKinnon's help in tracking down his errant love, who had been kidnapped and taken to Majorca, Cecile was in for some serious competition.

partying at night with the beautiful people, Nicole succumbed to what everyone in her crowd was into—cocaine—and became addicted. She kicked the habit, but the memory of her addiction stayed with her as a reminder of her continued struggle to come to terms with who she is.

At a time when Cass was working hard not to be hung up on Kathleen, and it was much too soon to allow another woman in his life, Nicole was aware that Cass's affection for her was as a friend and business partner, but she couldn't shake off the residual feeling she had for Rex Allingham, who she thought was Cass! To complicate matters and aggravate her dilemma, she and Cass had a clash of creative and business styles, which led to constant conflict in their business relationship. A part of her fought against loving someone she thought wouldn't love her back, and another part of her couldn't deny those feelings. And Nicole was getting to Cass, more than he cared to admit. It didn't take long for them to realize that no matter how much they clashed, deep down inside they needed and loved each other.

Cass and Nicole set a wedding date and almost made it down it down the aisle. But she had secrets and they would come back to haunt her. Enter Frankie.

Frankie was Cass's second true love. While Kathleen ended his womanizing streak, Frankie's love enabled Cass to become the devoted husband and father he is today. They met when Frankie revealed to Cass, on the eve of his wedding to Nicole Love, that his fiancée had killed her uncle Jason Frame. Needless to say, the relationship got off to a rocky start. But Cass had never met anyone quite like Frankie. Her eccentric nature and kind and loving spirit totally intrigued him. Actress Alice Barrett, who played Frankie, describes her character as "spunky, spiritual, and loving."

Cass and Frankie spent a good part of that first year investigating supposedly reformed criminal Lucas. Cass was worried about his best friend, Felicia, who was Lucas's childhood love. Frankie got a job working for Lucas at his apartment in Love Tower and Cass spied on them from across

*F*rankie and Cass were happily married when Cass's first wife, Kathleen, returned from the dead.

the street. Says Barrett, "I was sneaking around Lucas's apartment and diving in and out of closets. Cass was convinced he had to rescue me or Lucas would kill me. So he came in as an exterminator—Bug Man!"

According to Barrett, "Frankie had a boyfriend who died while they were making love, and she believed she was a jinx, that his grandma had cursed her. Frankie and Cass had just decided that they were going to give themselves a shot as a couple and take a trip together to Las Vegas, but everything led her to believe that she was cursed. He had allergic reactions to the food, he hurt himself somehow, he's losing at the tables like Cass has never lost before. At one point he yells at her, 'Go away!' and she tells him, 'I'm cursed by Grandma.' And that's just the beginning of the courtship." Barrett adds, "The first year we were always back and forth. I love you. I hate you. I love you. I hate you. I love you."

Their first try at marriage ended when Frankie, having been mistaken for her Aunt Sharlene, was kidnapped by Ryan Harrison on her wedding day. She was rescued within the week, and they promptly set another date to wed quietly in their new home. "We had already bought a house, and we wanted to get married on the spot," Barrett remembers. "We needed music, and Reuben Lawrence came in with a bunch of rap singers and they were going, 'Yo Frankie, Yo Frankie,' and we were like, no, we don't want to get married to 'Yo Frankie'! And so they wound up singing from the score of *West Side Story* and it was gorgeous. It was beautiful. That was our first wedding."

The return of Cass's first wife, Kathleen, rendered that marriage null and void and threatened to separate them for good when Cass returned to Kathleen. Says Barrett, "They were broken up. He had left me for Kathleen. I had had a miscarriage and not even told him I was pregnant. He and Kathleen were living together. And the explosion happened: Carl was using a special effect on Dean Frame's rock video as an excuse to blow Kathleen up, to kill her. And Frankie, being Frankie, figured that out and went to the rescue and pushed Kathleen out of the way. Frankie got caught in the explosion. So Frankie saved Kathleen's life and then 'died' of internal bleeding. Cass was away at the time. After he left Frankie for Kathleen and they were living together, he was just too miserable. Something wasn't working and he felt guilty and torn and felt it had been the right thing to do to go back to Kathleen but he wasn't really happy. So he went away to sort out his feelings, while Kathleen was working on the video and Frankie was investigating Carl Hutchins. He came back to declare his love for Frankie and found her 'dead' in the hospital. It was her miscarried son who was instrumental in sending Frankie back. She goes to heaven and meets a little boy whom she doesn't at first recognize as her child

The next woman to capture Cass's heart was unpredictable Nicole Love, daughter of the notorious Reginald Love.

and then she figures out who it is. He says, 'Go back. You're not finished down there.' And then she says, 'But I don't want to leave you,' and he says, 'We'll meet again.' And she goes back."

Frankie recovered, and she and Cass set another wedding date. It was around this time that Frankie's childhood friend from Oklahoma, Christy, came to Bay City with her terminally ill husband and quickly fell in love with Cass. Christy plotted to kill her husband, frame Frankie, and have Cass all to herself. Says Barrett, "Christy killed her husband on the day we were supposed to marry, and I got put on trial. We decided that we were jinxed and that we weren't going to get married. We were going to live together forever, and that's when we got kidnapped to Venice."

Despite their past experience with trying to get married, this time it was clearly meant to be, and Felicia was going to make it happen! Schnetzer recalls, "It was just beautiful and very loving and fun and spiritual. The females kidnapped Frankie and the guys kidnapped me, because we weren't going to get married if left up to our own devices. So they said, 'You guys are so meant for each other,' and they prepared everything for us with Felicia being the grand architect." And so the reluctant bride and groom were married in a courtyard in Venice.

It was Frankie who discovered, on the eve of Cass's wedding, that Nicole had killed her Uncle Jason. She would become Cass's second true love.

scene:
Venice courtyard/day

FRANKIE: Do we dare?

CASS: I think the two of us can take on almost anything. I say we go for it.

I take you, Mary Frances, to be my lawfully wedded wife. To share the secrets of my soul. To love and honor with my whole heart.

FRANKIE: I take you, Cass, to be my lawful husband, my friend for life, my inspiration and my spiritual partner. To grow with you, and love you with every ounce of my being until the end of time.

FELICIA: (handing a ring to each of them) We're almost home free.

CASS: (placing a ring on Frankie's finger) With this ring, I thee wed . . . again.

FRANKIE: (placing the ring on his finger) With this ring, I thee wed, again and for good!

FELICIA: It's done!

FRANKIE: We're really married this time?

CASS: We're legal, Mary Frances.

The final toast was reserved for Felicia.

CASS: As usual, Felicia was right. She made it happen, just like she's made so many other wonderful things in our lives happen. (lifting his glass) To Felicia, my best friend.

---

the tempestuous triangle

Alice, Rachel, & Steve

Scheming Rachel Davis married Dr. Russ Matthews to better her social status, but soon grew tired of being a doctor's wife. Enter magnetic, ambitious, self-made millionaire Steven Frame. Never mind that he was falling in love with Rachel's sweet, innocent sister-in-law, Alice Matthews. Make no mistake about it, Steve Frame was the love of Alice's life, although Rachel would almost always stand in the way of their ultimate happiness. Actress Jacquie Courtney, who played Alice Matthews Frame, described these tortured lovers as "a wonderful combination of the blond good girl, the brunette villainess, and rough-and-tumble Steve."

Alice's love softened Steve, but his stubbornness often got them into fights. During one of their separations, Rachel showed up at Steve's apartment with seduction on her mind and Steve did not resist. By the time Rachel realized that she was pregnant with Steve's child, Alice and Steve had reconciled and planned to marry. When Rachel confronted him with her pregnancy, Steve refused to believe that the child she was carrying was his, as Rachel was still married to Russ. Steve coldly told Rachel not even to think about spoiling his happiness with Alice, which sent Rachel reeling with jealousy and rage.

At the time, Rachel's mother-in-law, Mary Matthews, was planning an engagement party for her daughter and asked Rachel to act as hostess—a chore Rachel not only didn't relish but despised! As the party was about to begin, Rachel maliciously told Alice that Steve was the father of her unborn child.

Alice quietly endured the evening, leaving Steve to wonder why she was so withdrawn. The next day when Alice confronted him, Steve had to admit that it was true, he had spent a night of passion with Rachel when it seemed that he and Alice were through. Devastated by this betrayal, Alice broke the engagement and moved to Paris. Before she left, however, Rachel told Alice what she thought of her and Alice responded in kind.

But Steve never gave up, and went so far as to build a dream house for Alice in hopes of her return. In time Alice forgave him and came back, and their long-awaited nuptials took place on the terrace of the dream house he had built while she was gone. But this was not the end of their story.

Rachel divorced Russ and married loser Ted Clark, while Steve remained close to his son Jamie and tried to keep Rachel—who never stopped conspiring to win him back—at arm's length. Newlyweds Alice and Steve were overjoyed with the news that Alice was expecting their first child. One day Rachel made her presence a condition for Steve to see their son. Not wanting to upset his pregnant wife, Steve made up an excuse and left. While he was gone, Alice fell off a ladder and miscarried. Because Alice didn't know that Steve was with Jamie and Rachel, she couldn't reach him in her time of need. The miscarriage left Alice barren—she would never be able to give her beloved Steve a child.

It was Rachel's errant father who decided to help his daughter win back her reluctant lover. He lured Alice to Steve's office when he knew that Rachel would be there discussing Jamie. Alice misread the situation and, without a word to her husband or her family, packed her bags and moved to New York City. On the rebound, a heartsick Steve proposed to Rachel. Ecstatic, she said yes.

Rachel relished the thought of moving into the dream house Steve had built for Alice, and constantly gloated about being the new Mrs. Steven Frame.

Steve knew right away that he had made a mistake. His longing for Alice led him to negotiate an illegal divorce in an effort to win back his true love—

an effort that failed and landed him in jail! The night before he went to prison, Steve and Alice married for the second time.

While her husband was incarcerated, Alice's mental health deteriorated, a fact that wasn't lost on Rachel. Taking advantage of her rival's fragile mental state, Rachel tortured her with the blatant lie that she had visited Steve in prison and that he had demanded Alice leave the house so Rachel and Jamie could move back in. This sent Alice over the edge—she had a nervous breakdown and was sent to an institution for psychiatric help. Steve was released and Alice recovered, but she refused

to see him and continued to stay at home with Mary and Jim. Alice knew how much Steve wanted children, and for that reason, she felt she was not the woman for him. Always scheming to outdo her rival, Rachel discovered that Alice could not have children, and in a last-ditch

To escape the pain of Steve's betrayal, Alice ran away to France. But distance could not erase her love for Steve, and when she returned they married.

prologue:
Alice's bedroom

ALICE: (dumbfounded) When you came in here, you didn't just come in to chat, did you?

RACHEL: (grim) No.

ALICE: I thought for a couple of minutes we were just having some girl talk.

RACHEL: Girl talk. Before the party. Before your wonderful engagement party to wonderful Steve.

ALICE: Well . . . yes.

RACHEL: Girl talk. Well, Alice, I did come here to have girl talk with you, oh my, yes, I guess you could call it girl talk, all right. But not the kind you think. And not the kind you're going to like either.

(take Alice and fade out)

(ACT 1) *(continue it)*

ALICE: Well, Rachel, whatever it is . . . go ahead and tell me.

RACHEL: All right. I will. (Only Rachel's face in close-up, full of venom, intensity, and murderous intent, should show. She speaks quietly, knowing that the impact of what she is saying is quite enough to produce the desired effect) The man you're going to marry, Alice, . . . is the father of the child I'm going to have.

ALICE: (not absorbing the words really—just sure Rachel is unbalanced) Now, Rachel . . . Rachel . . . Are you all right?

RACHEL: I'm fine. Perfectly fine. Of course, I'm pregnant . . . pregnant with Steve Frame's child.

ALICE: (still not believing she's hearing what she's hearing) Now, Rachel . . . you'd better not say that because . . .

RACHEL: There's no reason not to say it. It's true.

ALICE: It can't be true.

RACHEL: It can be true and it is true. Steve Frame is my child's father.

ALICE: (starting to tremble with both anger and fear) Now, Rachel . . .

RACHEL: Alice, I am trying to tell you a simple fact of life and you'd just better face it. You want to know how it happened? Well, you remember when I left Russ for a while there—the second time. I went to Steve's apartment. I spent the night. And I got pregnant. I'm just telling you plain simple facts. That's all. Well, after I spent that night with Steve, I went to live with my mother for a while. You may remember that. Do you?

ALICE: (very quiet) I remember that.

RACHEL: And . . . while I was living at my mother's, I found out I was having Steven's baby. You see, Alice, I love Steve, do you understand? I've loved him for a long time! A lot longer than you have!

ALICE: Go on.

RACHEL: (subsides, a bit calmer) When I told Steve I was going to have his child, he . . . he . . .

ALICE: He what?

RACHEL: He wouldn't admit what was perfectly obviously true. I don't know why he wouldn't because I know he loves me . . .

ALICE: (now sure Rachel is mad) Rachel . . .

RACHEL: (slightly hysterical) Oh yes . . . he loves me . . . just the way I love him. But maybe he didn't like the idea of my having his child while being married to Russ. Anyway, he wouldn't take any responsibility for the child or for me or for anything. So I went back to Russ. (before Alice can say anything) Well, there wasn't anyplace else for me to go—nobody wanted me, except Russ. Nobody cared what happened to me, except Russ. I had to go back to him—there wasn't anybody else. And since we've been back together we've been happy . . . well, anyway he's been happy, and that's because I've about broken my back to make him happy, but he is happy and he thinks the baby is his and he's very happy about the whole thing . . .

ALICE: (quite gentle) Rachel, you can't really expect me to believe any of this.

RACHEL: Oh, Alice, you never want to believe anything that isn't all sunlight and roses and sweetness and light. You're so stupid, you're so sweet and sanctified, you think everything's easy for everybody just because it's easy for you. Well, it isn't. Things are very different for other people from what you think they are.

ALICE: Rachel . . .

RACHEL: Alice, I'm the one Steve Frame should be marrying. I'm the one he loves. I'm the one who's carrying his child. I'm the one who's absolutely sick with loving him . . . for months and months and months now. I'm the one who's had to stand around and watch him make a fuss over you— yes, and you falling all over him and kissing him and making a big spectacle of yourself, talking about love and how wonderful it is and how happy you are and he is, and isn't life grand and wearing that big diamond on your finger and showing it off to everybody like you'd won first prize. All that—the ring and this party and all that kissing and carrying on—that all belongs to me, not to you, because I love him and I'm going to have his baby.

ALICE: (quite shocked by Rachel's display. Pitying her a little, also disgusted at her revealing herself) Rachel . . . Rachel . . . you just don't know what you're saying . . .

RACHEL: I know perfectly well what I'm saying. There's nothing wrong with what I'm saying because it's all true. What's wrong is you don't want to hear it—and most of all, you don't want to believe it. But it's true.

Alice mistakenly thought Steve had betrayed her again and left him, so Rachel finally got her man when Steve proposed on the rebound.

effort to win Steve back, she broke the news to him, thinking this would break them up for good. Fortunately for these star-crossed lovers, it had the opposite effect. Steve convinced Alice he could live without children but not without her. They celebrated their love on a second honeymoon at Steve's vacation getaway in St. Croix.

Soon after, Steve left for a business trip to Australia. They had had precious little time together when Alice received the news that his helicopter had crashed in the wilderness and Steve was presumed dead. Unbeknownst to her, Steve had not died in the crash, but he was horribly scarred and suffering from amnesia. A few years later he remembered his true identity and returned to Bay City using the alias of Mr. Black. He had come back

MINISTER: Alice? Steve? Surrounded as we are, here, by the beauty of God's nature and by those we most love, let us turn our hearts and minds to the two before us, who wish to bind their lives together in peace and love. Our world is not an easy one; we have much pain to answer for from day to day, and we have tragedy, which seems to strip us of all hope, again and again. But we are together through all of this in love. As it has been said, "No man is an island, entire of itself; every man is a piece of the continent, a part of the main." We are involved in all mankind. And each time two people come together before God to bind their lives as one, it is a reaffirmation of all mankind; a reaffirmation of human faith and courage.

The human heart is boundless. And God's love for us, eternal—imperfect as we are. May I add . . . that the courage to love is the greatest of human strengths, the most difficult. And now we have Steve and Alice before us, who wish to take their places among those who have said yes to living. Yes to the hard task of loving. Yes to all the best that mankind stands for. Steve, do you love this woman?
STEVE: With all my heart.
MINISTER: And Alice, do you love this man?
ALICE: Oh, yes. Yes, I do. Very much.
MINISTER: Steve, will you care for Alice with gentleness, and strength, and understanding, to the very best of your own human capabilities?
STEVE: I will.
MINISTER: Alice, will you match Steve's gentleness, his strength with you own strength, his understanding with yours, to the very best of your own human capabilities?
ALICE: Yes, I will.
MINISTER: And will each of you deal with the other honestly, and with compassion? Steve?
STEVE: Yes.
MINISTER: Alice?
ALICE: Yes. Oh, yes.
MINISTER: And leave room for joy to flower in your growing love?
ALICE AND STEVE: Yes.
STEVE: Yes. Yes, we will.
MINISTER: I see no reason before God or man that these two young people should not be joined in marriage. If any man or woman feels strongly otherwise, let him speak now, or forever hold his peace. The rings? With God as our witness place the rings on each other's hands. Since you love each other in your heart of hearts, and have promised to help each other live and grow in wisdom and compassion, may God bless this union. With these rings, you, Alice, and you, Steve, bind your lives and loves together . . . forever. I now pronounce you man and wife.

scene:
Terrace of a country home

for Alice, but this time it was Rachel who won his heart.

At this time, a reformed Rachel was separated from Mac. Ironically, when Steve returned, Alice was engaged to Mac, but she broke it off to return to her first love. The day before Alice and Steve were to remarry, Rachel and Steve were trapped in the collapse of a building at a construction site. Amid the crumbling debris, their passion was reignited into a love now tempered with admiration and respect. The battle of the good girl and the bad girl for the heart of a flawed hero had come to an end. Alice, realizing that Rachel would never be out of Steve's blood, left Bay City, this time for good. Rachel and Steve were on their way to be married when Steve's car crashed. He was killed, and Rachel was blinded. It was the end of a love affair, and Rachel eventually returned to her beloved Mac.

❧

Rachel & Mac

He was the first man to accept her for who she was, to understand her darker moments and delve deeper to reach her soft side. A man of generosity and compassion, Mac Cory was able to see the good points underneath Rachel's rebelliousness, and her feisty temperament intrigued him. Rachel had never had that kind of unselfish attention from a man before, someone who was willing to make her a project, who seemed to understand her mistakes and make little of them. She just needed someone to bring her out, and Mackenzie Cory was that someone. Finding a man who could cherish her, as only her mother could in the past, was the missing piece of the puzzle in Rachel's young life. She'd never had a respectable father figure. She'd never had any money. And she didn't have a decent family background. The other men in her life hadn't been able to look beneath that surface. When Mackenzie Cory played Pygmalion to Bay City's bad girl, everyone who knew Rachel marveled at the transformation.

Publishing magnate and millionaire Mackenzie Cory was a man who loved women and he was fascinated by this exasperating young woman who didn't quite fit the mold of the society ladies he'd dated. Mac was a bon vivant and here was this little girl with rough edges. They became fascinated with each other—she was fascinated with his world and he was fascinated with her issues. And so their relationship deepened and evolved. Mac became Rachel's father figure and mentor—a lover who loved her as much as she loved him. He gave her an emotional security she'd never experienced before. Once he began loving her, Rachel's rebellious behavior became unnecessary—but if anything was taken away from her, the old Rachel would reappear and fight to the death for what was hers! This was a woman with temper and humor and moods, and every inch as strong-willed as her husband. They were two stubborn people in love, who were to divorce twice and marry each other three times.

Their first wedding took place in Mac's New York town house, where the groom lavished his young bride with a floor-length mink and exquisite jewelry. He just went for it—the total fantasy—and it didn't stop there. When Rachel recognized the Clayton estate as the house she'd passed on her way to school and dreamed about living in, Mac bought the stately mansion for his bride. The new Cory home would have "seventeen acres . . . lawns and a formal garden, carriage house with living quarters above, stables, wooded area with spring-fed lake." Rachel was thrilled as she recalled the mansion and its elegant owner: "Mrs. Clayton! In the spring, I'd get off the bus near the house and sneak through the woods to the wall of the property so I could look at the gardens. It seemed like there were flowers as far as you could see. And usually at that time of day, she'd be there."

A major obstacle would threaten the Corys's wedded bliss in the form of Iris, Mac's incestuously possessive, insanely jealous daughter. Iris simply couldn't accept her daddy loving anyone but her, especially when that someone was her own age! Rachel was equally strong-willed but did not have

It would be the third and last time for Rachel and Mac when they were married in a double ceremony with Mac's son Sandy and his bride, Blaine. Mac died a few years later, leaving his wife a legacy of his unconditional love.

Iris's panache. Here were two women fighting for the love of a good man and one of them was his daughter! It was a long testing period for Rachel, as she watched her husband give Iris chance after chance to claw her way back into the fold and saw the toll it took on him to watch his daughter do everything she could to thwart his new marriage. But love won out, and Rachel and Mac welcomed their daughter, Amanda, into the world.

It was Rachel's independence that cost her Mac the first time. He encouraged her career as a sculptress, only to feel that he had created this woman, given her a sense of herself, and now she was getting away from him. Mac became wildly jealous of Rachel's art teacher, even though there wasn't any reason for him to be. The two divorced, and Mac married money-hungry Janice Frame.

*M*ac's unconditional love for Rachel transformed her from a selfish vixen into a mature and loving woman.

When Rachel discovered that Janice was trying to kill Mac for his fortune, she made a fateful decision. In return for information, she slept with Janice's partner in crime, Mitch Blake, and became pregnant with his child. Soon after she saved his life, Mac and Rachel remarried, but the situation proved too much for the couple to bear. When he learned that the child Rachel was carrying wasn't his, a devastated Mac let the hurt outweigh the love he felt for his wife and they divorced once more.

Just as Rachel was enjoying life as a single, independent career woman and mother, she was jolted by a ghost from her past—Steven Frame. They were about to marry when the car they were riding in crashed. Rachel was blinded, and Steven was killed. Rachel's blindness made Mac realize how very deeply he still cared for her. Knowing full well that Rachel would interpret any comfort from him as pity, Mac posed as "John Caldwell," a British hospital administrator, and became an integral part of Rachel's recovery. When she regained her sight and discovered Mac's sweet deception, Rachel knew in her heart that there would never be another man for her.

In a double ceremony with Mac's son Sandy and his bride, Blaine Ewing, Rachel became Mrs. Mackenzie Cory for the third time and remained so until his untimely death. His legacy to her remains his unconditional love, the love that redeemed her. She was a woman who came from nothing, who suddenly became the lady of the house, the quintessential vixen changed by the love of a good man. Rachel Cory became a better person through love—and isn't that every woman's fantasy?

✦

Rachel & Carl

One would be hard-pressed to find a stranger pairing than Carl Hutchins and Rachel Cory. He was a former mafioso who was her family's arch-enemy and she was Bay City's preeminent society matron. But despite their differences, their love affair flourished through family opposition, wedding-day shootings, a crazy look-alike named Justine, and the birth of twins.

Carl Hutchins arrived in Bay City in 1984, blaming Mac Cory for his father's death and vowing to seek revenge on the entire Cory clan. The following year he went on the run, taking Rachel hostage. When Mac attempted to rescue his wife, she took a bullet meant for him. Years had passed and Mac had died, but still, was it any wonder that when Rachel began being seen around town with Carl, the people of Bay City were sure she had made a deal with the devil?

It started when the hitherto diabolical Carl cut a deal to save Cory Publishing. Carl owned 10 percent of Cory stock, which Rachel desperately needed to fight a hostile takeover. He agreed to give Rachel his shares if she agreed to help him gain respectability by consenting to be seen with him in public. When the Cory deal failed, Rachel stepped down as CEO and fled to New York. The now love-struck Hutchins followed. There he wooed her with words as the two strolled the streets. Actor Charles Keating, who played Carl, explains: "He opens a book and he reads her a poem and they woo each other with poems—'Not even the rain has such small hands.'" According to Victoria Wyndham, who plays Rachel, "She found the love of her life a second time—lightning struck twice. She was much too pessimistic to think that that would ever happen again, especially at this age, and to be head over heels in love in your 50s—what fun!"

Many people questioned the union. Was this Carl's ultimate revenge? Wyndham answers, "It's really the reverse of Mac and Rachel's love story. This was the first man who was her contemporary, and even bigger villain than she had been when she was young. And a much more difficult personality to deal with than Mac had been." She had been a strong businesswoman, used to managing on her own. "She's a softer Rachel now, more vulnerable, more of a partner. Love makes you different." As for Carl, Rachel was the great love of his life. Says Keating, "Nobody else filled that or was able to soften him that much."

They tried to marry in 1994, but the ceremony was halted when Iris Wheeler, shocked that Rachel would marry her beloved father's arch-enemy, shot

Rachel didn't think it was possible, but in Carl she found the love of her life a second time.

Carl (albeit by mistake). Soon after, they tied the knot for real. This was a union that was to be constantly tested, especially when Carl's old lover Justine Duvalier returned. A dead ringer for Rachel, Justine kidnapped her nemesis and proceeded to take her place in Carl's life. Carl even slept with her! When Carl and Rachel were reunited, he never told her of this lapse with Justine.

Soon after, with the death of his son Ryan, Carl's obsession with Grant Harrison took over his life and brought with it the possibility of irrevocable violence. Despite her love for him, Rachel ordered Carl out of her life, only to discover that she was pregnant with his child. It was then that she came to the realization that she wanted to be with him no matter what the cost. She told her closest friend, Felicia, "I just have faith in the man that I promised I'd share my life with. I love him." Under difficult circumstances, both physical and emotional, Rachel gave birth to twins, Cory and Elizabeth.

"Rachel believes in the redeeming power of love," says Wyndham. "That's what Mac taught her, that's what saved her life, and that's what she believes is her mission in life. So she turned around and performed the same miracle for Carl that Mac did for her."

Toward the end, when everyone doubted Carl's motives, Rachel tenderly remembered Mac: "Your love saved me, Mac, and I'm determined to save Carl. Everyone is turning against him. They want me to choose and the choice is so easy—I choose Carl. Just as you taught us we live with our mistakes, in order for love to be true it must be unconditional, and I do love Carl beyond reason. Certainly that love will heal whatever is wrong with him, but I can't give up on him any more than you gave up on me."

Carl died in a mysterious plane crash, and mourning the loss of the "man that understood the music of my soul," Rachel scattered his ashes on the anniversary of Mac's death.

y o u n g   l o v e

Amanda & Sam

Amanda Cory is beautiful and glamorous and more sophisticated than her years would indicate. Add to that charming, vivacious, and infinitely likable.

*H*e
wooed her
with poetry
on the streets
of New York
and she
responded
in kind.

Amanda is her own person. Actress Sandra Ferguson, who plays Amanda, states, "She's got a very strong backbone." Although she is used to getting what she wants, Amanda is not a spoiled brat. So when she decided to go into the family publishing business, she decided to learn from the bottom up without the privileges she'd otherwise be privy to as Mac Cory's daughter. And it didn't take long for her to discover that publishing was her field and that she had a real talent for writing.

It was at Cory Publishing that Amanda met darkly handsome aspiring artist Sam Fowler. Sam came to Bay City to get to know his older brother, Mitch Blake, and was working as a graphic artist for Cory. Sam didn't talk much about himself, and his aloofness gave him an air of mystery, which Amanda found intriguing. One of the qualities she immediately found attractive was his fierce passion for his work. But Sam went to great lengths to protect himself from this woman he knew would touch him emotionally. Hell-bent as he was on keeping his concentration on his work, he knew he was susceptible, and he didn't need the distraction.

Not wanting to scare him off by admitting she was the boss's daughter, Amanda told him her name was Mandy Ashton. When she assumed this identity, she found herself exploring another side of life she'd never had to think about, and she developed a strong appreciation and respect for Sam, whose passion about his work gave her new insights into herself.

Though their backgrounds were vastly different, they were drawn together and discovered they had much in common. Amanda was attracted by Sam's determination to make it against all odds, and his talent and cultured taste for the arts. The more time she spent with him, the more she began to see with new eyes the things she'd always taken for granted. The priceless paintings on her parents' walls were no longer just that but became great works of art to be appreciated and interpreted. The fact that Sam was a challenge, unlike most other men she had known, was also an attraction. And so Amanda

worked hard to understand him and win his love. As they gradually came to know each other outside the office, they experienced a meeting of the minds that had an undeniably strong effect on Sam. A one-woman kind of guy, he wanted to share his passion and his work with someone he loved, and he thought he'd found that someone in Mandy Ashton.

But when Sam discovered that she had lied about her true identity, he felt that she had betrayed his trust. It didn't help that Amanda was a Cory, someone he felt was as different from himself as she could get, and also part of a family Sam believed had done his brother, Mitch, a great injustice. Deep down, Sam knew that Amanda was no different from Mandy, but he had to overcome the distrust and the deception. When they were able to overcome this hurdle in their relationship, they knew that they'd found love.

Then Amanda accidently became pregnant. Not wanting to disappoint her family, feeling confused and alone, Amanda went to

Sam and Amanda were married for a second time on New Year's Eve in 1991.

New York to have an abortion. Sam tracked her down before the operation. He convinced her that he loved her and asked her to be his wife. And so this young couple were compelled to tie the knot sooner than they had planned, and Amanda put her budding publishing career on hold to become a wife and mother. Their daughter, Alexandra (Alli) Cory-Fowler, arrived a few months after they were married.

Now differing priorities began to drive Sam and Amanda apart, as Sam focused more on his painting, and Amanda, now back at work, on her family's business. They were two years into their marriage when Amanda cheated on Sam with Evan Frame. Guilt-ridden, she confessed to Sam and they reconciled. But desperate to win her back, Evan devised a cruel plan—he made it look as if Sam was plotting to kill her, and then he told Amanda Sam was dangerous and could harm her. Evan's warnings began to act on Amanda and she started misinterpreting Sam's most innocent acts as sinister ones. Believing that her life was truly in danger, Amanda left Sam and went to live with Evan. It didn't take long for her to realize that she'd made a mistake. Sam began to do some sleuthing and uncovered Evan's treachery, but the damage had been done, and Sam and Amanda, unable to patch things up, decided to divorce. They found themselves drifting closer after the divorce, but Sam was too hurt to forgive Amanda's indiscretions and he left town. When he returned, despite his hurt feelings, he found himself drawn again to the woman he had married.

Donna Swajeski, who was head writer at the time, explained, "Amanda made a big mistake. She slept with Evan and lied about it. She was a young girl who had motherhood and wifehood thrust upon her and she had not sown her wild oats. She's Rachel's daughter and she has a rebellious streak."

No matter what had happened, it was never really over—"They still had their wedding rings." Sam and Amanda married for the second time on New Year's Eve in 1991. Always intense about his work and his art, however, Sam's obsession with his new career as a country singer now began to take a toll on the mar-

scene:
Sam's loft-studio.

Amanda and Sam are now in love, but it has remained unspoken between them. Amanda is dripping wet, having come to the loft through a heavy rainstorm. She has taken off her wet clothes and now stands in her panties and a man's shirt. The chemistry is very strong between Amanda and Sam, as he has tried not to watch her as she undressed.

SAM: (not moving) I guess I had better find my robe for you.
AMANDA: OK
SAM: It's probably in the bathroom.
AMANDA: (not moving) I'll get it.
SAM: Good.
AMANDA: (trying to get out of the shirt by taking it over her head) Except I can't get out of this darned thing. It's so wet . . .
SAM: Yeah, it's clinging to you, it's like a second skin. Here, let me help. We need to unbutton it more. Why did you think you could take it off over your head? (Sam begins to unbutton the shirt)
AMANDA: Just wasn't thinking, I guess.
SAM: There, you can take it off.
AMANDA: OK. (She takes off the shirt and it drops to the floor)
SAM: Now you can dry off.
AMANDA: OK.
SAM: (Takes a towel from the bed and hands it to her. Amanda begins to dry her hair) You missed a spot.
AMANDA: Did I?
SAM: (moving to her once more, taking the towel) Yeah. You're still dripping right here. And your back is wet, too. (Sam now dries Amanda off) You cold?
AMANDA: No.
SAM: You ought to be.
AMANDA: Nobody's done this since my mom stopped giving me a bath.
SAM: Just think what you've been missing.
AMANDA: Yes. I was just thinking that.
(They are now very close, very drawn to each other, and Sam stops drying Amanda off.)
SAM: Amanda?
AMANDA: Yes, Sam?
SAM: I'm crazy about you. I have been for weeks.
AMANDA: I know. I feel the same way about you. I want you to make love to me.
SAM: You sure?
AMANDA: I have never been more sure of anything in my life.
(They kiss with growing passion)

scene:

Smiley's. Afternoon.
We open on Sally, seated in a booth.

She's lost in thought. Catlin enters, looks around. He sees Sally. He is surprised and happy to see her. He moves to the booth, remains standing.

CATLIN: Hello, again. (She looks up, not recognizing him) We met at the airport a couple of weeks ago. Your plane was late . . .

SALLY: Oh yes, I remember.

CATLIN: How was your trip to Boston?

SALLY: Fine.

CATLIN: How's your mama?

SALLY: She's fine. (She looks at him, puzzled)

CATLIN: You don't remember me?

SALLY: Yes, I do. I'm just surprised to see you. You told me you were on your way to California.

CATLIN: I changed my mind. (smiles) Too much sunshine. (Sally smiles) The coffee's much better here than at the airport. (She nods) Would you like some company?

SALLY: I'm waiting for someone . . .

CATLIN: Your boyfriend?

SALLY: My cousin.

CATLIN: You don't come here much, do you?

SALLY: No. (He holds, then sits opposite of her)

CATLIN: The hot dogs are terrific.

SALLY: Are you a connoisseur of hot dogs? (He looks at her, puzzled) An expert?

CAITLIN: Well, I've had hot dogs in about every roadside diner in the West and Southwest, but Smiley's are the best. (smiles) Want to try one?

SALLY: No. Thank you.

CATLIN: Do you have a job?

SALLY: Yes. I work at Cory Publishing. (He looks at her, waiting for more) I'm the art director. (He has no idea what that is, but nods, impressed)

CATLIN: You like it?

SALLY: Yes. Do you work?

CATLIN: When I can find it.

SALLY: What do you do?

CATLIN: Just about anything. I cowboyed for a while, rode the rodeo circuit till I busted my ribs—would you go to a picture show with me sometime?

SALLY: No, I don't think so.

CAITLIN: You don't like cowboys?

SALLY: (lying) I'm engaged.

CATLIN: So? That doesn't mean we can't have a little fun.

SALLY: (smiles) Thanks anyway, but no thanks. (He looks at her, then nods, rises, smiles, moves off. She looks after him, intrigued, and we ...)

Fade out

Sally and Catlin's love was deep but their happiness short-lived.

riage. Amanda gave him a choice—his career or his wife and daughter. Sam pleaded with her, "Please don't ask me to choose between you and my work." But he chose his career and left town for a world tour. Later that year they obtained their second divorce. According to Ferguson, "When it comes to men, Amanda can't pick them to save her life!" Was Sam the love of her life? Says Ferguson, "So far . . ."

❧

Sally Frame & Catlin Ewing

Sally Frame, adopted daughter of Alice and Steven Frame, had a rebellious adolescence and returned to Bay City as a teenager, having run away from boarding school. After a disastrous marriage to Denny Hobson, who went to prison, Sally met wealthy Peter Love, who was instantly smitten. His sister Donna, appalled that her brother would contemplate marrying beneath his station, had other ideas and joined forces with Bay City's schemer extraordinaire, Cecile de Poulignac, to break them up.

Around this time, David Thatcher, an older married man with whom Sally had had an affair and a child during her rambunctious years, arrived in town. Unbeknownst to Sally, Thatcher and his wealthy wife had adopted her baby on the black market.

When Donna found out that Sally had an illegitimate child, she held it over her head like a sword. It worked, and Peter and Sally's engagement was soon history.

Enter Catlin Ewing, half-brother of Larry and Blaine. Independent, strong-willed, and carrying a major chip on his shoulder, troubled, handsome, brooding Catlin Ewing was the sort of man most women find very attractive. *Another World* producer Scott Collishaw says, "He was the typical soap opera antihero. He had a rough side and was sort of dangerous. He and Sally fell in love and they had all kinds of ups and downs and turns. It was a wonderful love story."

Catlin worked at the Love stables and had a brief affair with Donna, but when he met Sally Frame he fell in love, and although Sally's life was complicated at the time, she was definitely attracted.

Their friendship blossomed while Catlin was giving riding lessons to Sally's son Kevin at the Love stables. He might have been fiery and suspicious of life, but Catlin had a gentleness and a soul, and he was great with Kevin. It was his kinship with Kevin that first let Sally see what kind of man he really was. It was the beginning of a turbulent relationship—one that took a long time to develop and grow. Sex and love were two very different things for Catlin, and Sally was the first person who would combine them for him.

But at the time, Sally was determined to marry David Thatcher in order to secure custody of Kevin. She was literally at the altar when she had a change of heart and canceled the ceremony. A livid David threatened to keep Kevin away from her, and they were in the middle of a fierce argument when a gun went off and David fell the ground—dead. Sally fainted, and when she came to, Catlin was holding the smoking gun. Catlin was arrested and charged

*W*hen Catlin was charged with a murder he didn't commit, the trail to find the killer and clear his name led the young lovers to the island of Majorca.

The couple's happiness was shattered when Catlin's wife Brittany, presumed dead in a flood, found her way to Bay City, determined to win her husband back.

with murder. He was thought dead when a police car he was riding in was forced over a cliff, but to Sally's great relief, he was found alive, and together they determined to clear his name. The trail led them to Majorca, where they discovered that the shot that killed David had been fired by Nurse Emily Benson, under orders from the villainous Carl Hutchins.

A joyous Catlin and Sally finally wed, but their happiness was shattered when Catlin's first wife, Brittany, presumed dead in a flood, arrived in town, her mission to find Catlin. The accident had left her deaf, but even after she was cured she continued to fake it, hoping to win him back. Their backgrounds were more similar than his and Sally's—Catlin was a cowboy and rodeo performer and that was where he and Brittany had met—and Brittany never missed a chance to remind him of the great times they'd had. Sally's world was very different—a world that Catlin loved but sometimes had difficulty accepting. But he was in love with Sally and Brittany's tactics failed to work. Realizing this, Brittany changed course and

decided to seduce Peter Love, Sally's one-time fiancé, in hopes of making Catlin jealous. It was Peter who helped her search for Evan, the son she'd had with Catlin, although Catlin was sure the boy had drowned in the flood—and he was right.

Although Brittany eventually gave Catlin a divorce, she never stopped loving him, and one drunken night she managed to get him into bed. Unfortunately, Sally walked in on their tryst. Soon after, Brittany, now pregnant with Catlin's child, married Peter Love. Sally and Catlin's love was now so deep that it transcended past transgressions and they made plans to marry. This time they hoped it would be forever. Shortly after they wed, Brittany and Sally got into a bitter confrontation. Soon after, Sally died under mysterious circumstances in a car accident, which many believed was plotted by Brittany, although this was later disproved. Sally's last words were to her beloved Catlin: "I love you . . . I'm not scared. Tell Kevin I love him. And remember me."

the trials and tribulations of young love

Thomasina Harding & Carter Todd

Thomasina was the adopted daughter of successful businesswoman Quinn Harding. Quinn discovered Thomasina in a class she was teaching to help young black girls "get out." Thomasina was intelligent, street-smart, and surly. Under Quinn's guidance the intelligence stuck, the surliness went, and ambition took hold. Thomasina explained the way she felt about her new circumstances to high school buddy Perry Hutchins: "I don't need that scholarship for the money, but if I win it, it says that I'm different. I am a black woman who can make it on their terms. I had a lot of things given to me. I'm going to make the best of them." In many ways she was her mother's daughter.

Young Carter Todd's mother left him and his dad when Carter was very young. His father, Grant, was a smart and energetic man, but a combination of circumstances left him stranded in dead-end jobs, struggling just to get by. When it became evident that Carter was a phenomenal football player, Grant poured all of his ambition and energy into his son, becoming a constant and demanding coach. Carter was driven to resolve the demons in his father's life, a task he would never be able to complete, but he was a young man with a great sense of responsibility. He would have a lot to bear when he entered into a relationship with Thomasina Harding.

They were high school sweethearts, enjoying the flowering of romance and tentatively taking the steps that define young love while giving equal time to their hoped-for careers. Carter was tapped to become a star football player, and Thomasina had her heart set on attending medical school. But Thomasina got pregnant, and decisions had to be made.

Thomasina Harding and Carter Todd were teenagers in love until an unplanned pregnancy changed their lives forever.

Quinn Harding pressed hard for her daughter to opt for abortion, so she would not have to postpone her dreams indefinitely, maybe for good. Being a solid and decent young man, Carter struggled to do the right thing. They were barely eighteen. The crisis prompted many family conflicts.

Thomasina came close to taking her mother's advice, but Carter stopped her, and together they decided to make a commitment to each other and to their unborn child. Seeing how devoted their children were to each other, Grant and Quinn eventually gave their blessing to the union. It was a moving moment when Thomasina reworked tradition and asked her adoptive mother to give the bride away. Amid family and friends wishing them happiness and joy, Thomasina and Carter became Mr. and Mrs. Todd.

sometimes love is not enough

John & Sharlene

She was married first to Floyd Watts in the early 1970s. They were barely teenagers in love when Floyd was drafted into the Vietnam War. A few months later he was killed in action. Haunted by memories of her young husband dying in foreign jungles in a senseless war neither understood, Sharlene began sleeping with army officers. It was the start of her life as a prostitute. When she married Russ Matthews in 1976, Sharlene kept her past a secret, and when Russ found out, he divorced her. Taking back the name of her first husband, Sharlene left Bay City, without telling Russ she was pregnant with his child.

Sharlene returned with her daughter, Josie, in 1988 and went to work at Frame Construction for her brother Jason Frame. It was there that she met construction worker John Hudson. John had a past scarred by his experiences in Vietnam. Unlike Floyd, he had survived, but it was not an easy existence. Slowly they began a relationship, and it was she who transformed

him from a bitter, cynical war vet into a loving and open man, but because of her past, Sharlene was still hesitant to commit herself.

When that past was revealed, she gave John his freedom to leave. But John loved her and he didn't care—they made love for the first time that very day.

Anna Holbrook, who plays Sharlene, explains that she was "a woman who didn't know how to allow love into her life again in a romantic way, but that changed through John Hudson. It was a sweet beginning. When John took Sharlene, dressed in white, to the Snowflake Ball, it was such a Cinderella kind of story." They married in November of 1989 and then the trouble began.

Soon after the wedding, Sharlene's split personality made itself evident in the person of Sharly Watts. David Forsyth, who played John Hudson, describes the time: "When all of this weird behavior started coming out, it really floored John. It was like, 'Where's my wife and what is happening to her?'" As Sharly, Sharlene almost had an affair with nefarious mayor Grant Harrison. Because she loved John so, she considered leaving rather than cause him further pain. But instead she stayed and went into therapy to fuse her personalities. She was making progress when another obstacle reared its ugly head—Sharlene's psychiatrist, Taylor Benson, was falling in love with John!

It was around this time that Sharlene gave birth to a son, Gregory. According to Forsyth, "The birth of a son gave John even more purpose. It solidified his purpose for living." With Sharlene's help, John, who had been trained as a doctor in Southeast Asia, took his U.S. medical exams and returned to his first love, medicine. Soon afterward he joined the staff at Bay City General Hospital. John and Sharlene's happiness was short-lived, however, because a jealous Taylor Benson kidnapped Sharlene on a boat that exploded. When her body wasn't found, it was presumed that she had been killed in the blast.

Sharlene returned to Bay City with her teenage daughter, Josie, and went to work for her brother's company, Frame Construction. It was there that she met John.

Although they'd helped to heal each other's wounds, love was not enough for this troubled couple, and eventually they went their separate ways.

scene:
Frame parlor/dusk.

A single packed bag sits next to Sharlene as she writes a note. We hear her in voice-over.

SHARLENE: My love . . . and you are my love . . . this is the hardest thing I've ever had to do. . . . You're the most wonderful, loving man. . . . I know you'd stand by me. . . . I also know how much it would cost you . . . and you've suffered enough because of me. . . . I couldn't bear to see you hurt anymore. . . . So, my darling, . . . I'm leaving you, . . . going away by myself in the hopes that I'll get well. . . . I want you to go on without me. . . . I'll come back to you if I can. . . . Pray for me as I will pray for you. . . . I'll call Josie and Frankie later . . . and tell them . . . but now all I can think of is you . . . and how much I love you . . . and always will. . . .
That's why I know I'm doing the right thing. Good-bye . . . and God bless . . . (The tears streaming down her face, she puts down her pen, stares at the page a moment, then picks up her bag and moves to exit through the door as we . . .)

Fade out

After a long period of mourning and grief, John moved on with his life and married Dr. Kelsey Harrison.

the second time around

In 1994 Kate Baker moved to Bay City and John was shocked by her resemblance to Sharlene. He soon discovered that Kate was another of Sharlene's personalities. Says Holbrook, "John knew who she was before she did and tried to help Kate. The potential of it was so sweet. Kate fell in love with John, and John had to very gently say no to Kate because he was trying to be healthy about it

When John and Sharlene married again, it was simple and sweet like the first time.

and help her figure out who she was, and he was married to Kelsey at the time. It was because it was such a sweet thing that when he finally realized who she was and they'd see each other in the hospital and there would be those little glimmers to Kate, but she really didn't know who he was (and if she did, she wasn't telling Sharlene), when John finally realized that it was Sharlene, he had to sit on his instincts to go over and shake her awake. It took months for him to finally help her figure out who she was. But John and Sharlene did find their way together, and it was that fresh sort of high school love scene all over again, and it's always nice to know that you can resurrect that."

When John was laid up in the hospital after being hit by a car, Sharlene emerged and they had a tender reunion in his hospital room. They got engaged, but the marriage was delayed by the arrival of Bailey Thompson, the man who had raped Sharlene when she was a child, causing her personality to split, and who was by a strange twist of fate now John's boss at the hospital. Bailey delighted in tormenting Sharlene, but happily, he was soon arrested. And so, in the Frame living room in a simple ceremony reminiscent of their first, John and Sharlene remarried. Says Forsyth, "It was simple and sweet like the first time."

It was when Sharlene began making frequent trips out of town that John found himself drawing closer to his good friend Felicia Gallant. Both were shocked at the depth of their feelings and tried to end the relationship before it began. Forsyth recalls, "The relationship with Sharlene was a little rocky, but nothing that would take it over the top. What happened was that something came up about Vietnam that John had suppressed completely, and it came back to him and he broke down and was completely vulnerable, and they were stuck together in this snowstorm, and it was one of those things that just sort of happened. Both of them felt really bad. Felicia felt horrible because she loved Sharlene. They went back to the house to own up and say, 'Look, this is what happened,' and the words never got out, and it became known before they could explain, and the hurt had already happened, and Sharlene never got an explanation.

"John had just been kicked out of the hospital because he took responsibility for the death of a child, and the hospital won a lawsuit that cost him seven million dollars. He was literally up the creek without a paddle. He felt horrible about the death of this child, and he was taking that on, and then he found out he was bankrupt. He had no job—and then this incident about Vietnam came up—and all that happened at once. And Sharlene was going through her therapy and had taken Gregory away to go and find herself, and John tried to call her. He needed Sharlene's support after all those years of supporting her, being there for her. He needed to connect with her, but he could never get her on the phone—she was just too busy taking care of herself. And that's when Felicia was there. She was just talking to John as a friend and it just happened."

Sharlene sensed a distance between herself and John and began to suspect that another woman was the cause. Says Holbrook, "Sharlene's strength was her loyalty. But her weakness was that she had such an intolerance for injustice, all she could resort to was anger. She was so angry that there was no way there was room for John to even try to come back in. The damage was done." Forsyth adds, "John was sleeping on the operating room table in the hospital and changing his clothes in his office, and Sharlene was just bitter and angry and wouldn't have anything to do with him."

a bittersweet good-bye

Felicia and John eventually broke their engagement. Stuck in a storm at the Cory cabin, John and Sharlene talked through their feelings and realized that while their relationship was over, there were unresolved emotions. As a kind of closure, they made love one last time. Holbrook says, "It reignited what was true about them. It was like a part of Sharlene and a part of John had been dead and she kept screaming to it, 'I know you're in there! Wake up!'" And then they went their separate ways.

flawed lovers find a common bond

Josie & Gary

Her first love was young Matt Cory. They were teenagers when they fell in love after getting to know each other on a teen chat line—he was "Captain Cool" and she was "Rivera." They were engaged in 1990 but backed out at the last minute during the ceremony. Before she left Bay City to try her luck at an acting career in LA, Josie told Matt she knew he would find the perfect woman, and "whoever she is, she's gonna be lucky."

Upset at the lack of jobs in LA and devastated by the loss of her mother, Josie found herself slowly sucked into the world of high-class prostitution (as her mother had been years before, although not so high-class). When she returned to Bay City, it was Ian Rain who helped her to break free of that past and to whom Josie opened up her heart. But when Josie decided she wanted to become an officer of the law, Ian couldn't handle the thought of her in constant danger. He proposed. She said no. Ian went back to Australia and Josie met Gary Sinclair.

Josie met Gary when they struck up a conversation at Wallingford's Bookstore. Later she was aghast to learn that he was her instructor at the police academy! Gary was tough and strict and Josie took it personally. But when she discovered that he was an alcoholic, trying desperately to stay sober, her heart softened and she began to care for this sensitive, troubled man. Because of her background, not many people took her desire to join the force seriously, but Sinclair recognized her inner strength and fell in love. And so the romance between this boozing cop with a painful past and the young cadet with her own closet full of dark secrets began.

Because he was her superior officer, Gary insisted they could never be more than friends. But their desire soon overwhelmed them, and throwing caution to the wind, they embarked on a steamy affair.

Their second try proved successful, and on her wedding night, Josie told her groom that she was pregnant with his child.

When the burden of arranging secret liaisons became too much, they admitted their relationship to their Captain, Gabe McNamara. The captain reminded Gary of a painful incident in his past, however, and Gary quickly broke it off with Josie. This incident involved a woman, a lover and fellow police officer, whom he had sent to jail for corruption and who was now out and seeking revenge. Gary tried hard to protect Josie, but in the fallout, Josie was shot and later traumatized when held hostage by an escaped con who hated cops. She was rescued by Gary and, despite what she had been through, they pushed ahead with plans to marry. Because of the imminent danger, they chose to wed secretly at the Hudson barn, but con man Cody showed up, and the wedding turned into a shoot-out, paralyzing the mother of the bride, Sharlene.

But this is a love story, and love stories have a happy ending. In July of that year, Josie and Gary tied the knot in a police ceremony on the steps of the precinct. They did not do things the traditional way.

She entered on a motorcycle, he on horseback. Their "something blue" was the sea of police officers in attendance. Josie asked her good pal, current police captain Joe Carlino, to escort her, and Gary chose Felicia, his AA sponsor, to be "best person." On their wedding night Josie broke the happy news—she and Gary were going to have a child.

And how is married life? He calls her "J" and tells her he loves her, while she answers "I love you more." Sadly, they lost their child. Actress Nadine Stenovitch, who currently plays Josie, describes her as "a very strong person, but she's vulnerable. She's driven to be the best, and despite things in the past that have happened to her, she is able to use them in order to grow." Right now, "she invests a lot of her life into Gary. They exist as one together." But it isn't easy being married to someone who's addicted. Says Stenovitch, "Anybody who's an addict, they need to help themselves. To see someone suffer like that, it kills you too, because there's nothing you can do."

But it works both ways, says Josie, "—the healing, helping each other, accepting and loving each other, because Gary was able to do that with me, with who

*J*osie had been held hostage by an escaped con. Because of the imminent danger, they decided to have a secret ceremony and chose the Hudson's barn. The wedding never happened.

Their relationship would be sorely tested when, thinking Gary dead, Josie turned to his brother, Cameron, for comfort and became pregnant with his child.

I was, with my past. I thought nobody could . . . and he did." Though Josie is a member of one of the oldest families in Bay City, the Matthewses, right now, says Stenovitch, "Gary's pretty much her family."

And is he her soul mate? Stenovitch answers, "Yes, he's definitely the one. I think their bond was that they're both sort of misfits in the way that they were down and out and vulnerable, and meeting each other and being accepting of those faults, because not everybody is perfect, and loving them for their faults and growing."

John Littlefield, who currently plays Gary, adds, "He's a troubled man. Having to fight the booze and the demons and the horrors and the voices and the screams and everything that he's learned to stifle and deal with. He could get lost, but he's got a second chance at life with his love for Josie. He's not going to blow it this time." He continues, "It's a healing kind of love. This is pure. This is true. It's right. It comes from such an organic, visceral, wonderful place. It's not forced. If Josie died, he'd probably riddle Bay City. He wouldn't care, because that's his life. That's

his nucleus. He's just a mere electron or proton that magnetically and scientifically falls and rotates and orbits around her. And without that, there's absolutely nothing. It's not to say that he relies on her. He doesn't. It's just that he lives for her. She is the reason that he breathes oxygen. Alone, Gary with his demons and his thoughts would not be able to justify why he breathes."

Their love was about to be sorely tested. When Josie thought Gary had died in a cave, consumed with grief and seeking comfort, she slept with Gary's brother, Cameron, and became pregnant with his child. Distraught, and not knowing whether or not to tell him, Josie poured herself out to Cameron: "Gary is a drunk. I'm an ex-hooker. We were two world-class liars before we met, but the thing we learned was to be straight with each other. That's what holds us together—at least that's what used to hold us together."

Cameron's girlfriend, Amanda Cory, unaware of the situation and upset with Cameron for keeping secrets, had this to say about Josie and Gary's relationship: "He loves his wife and that's his essential truth. He holds to that. He doesn't screw things up by demanding perfection or judging or asking a million questions."

And what does Stenovitch think about the future of this troubled pair? "You think about people who have been married for fifty years, and it hasn't always been easy. If they get through this, I think they could probably be married for fifty years."

married four times until death do us part

Donna Love & Michael Hudson

Donna Love and Michael Hudson—the stable boy and the heiress. Theirs is a story of first love . . . and last. She was a spirited teenager and her attraction to the unthinkable led her into an affair with Michael Hud-

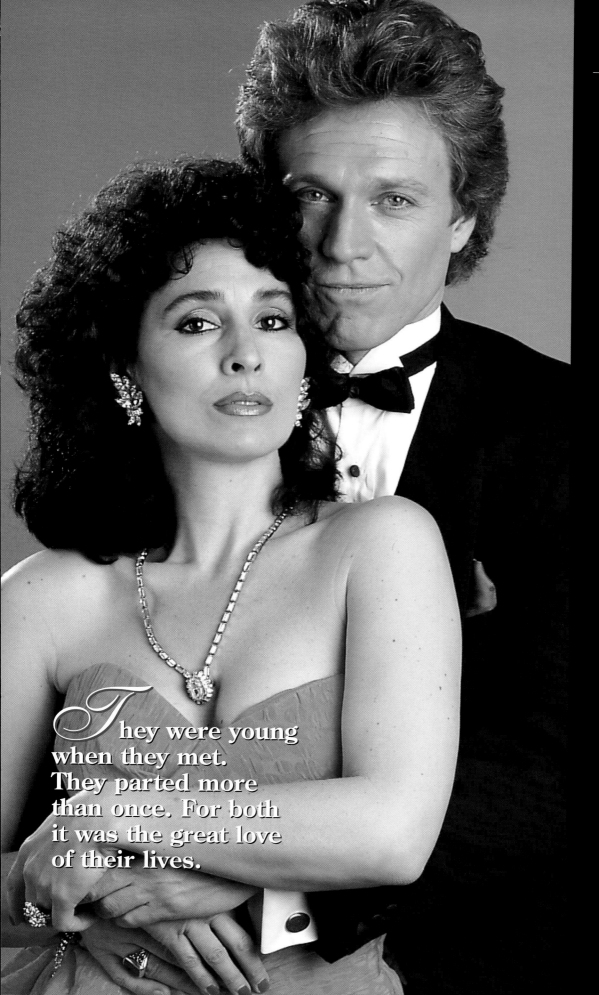

They were young when they met. They parted more than once. For both it was the great love of their lives.

MICHAEL: Now do you remember?

DONNA: Yes . . . We're here because I won the honesty contest.

MICHAEL: What?

DONNA: You had to pay for my trip and you also had the incredible good fortune to be chosen the man of my dreams.

MICHAEL: Honestly?

DONNA: You want the truth? We're here because I love you so much I've changed.

MICHAEL: And I'm crazy about it.

DONNA: I feel so strong when I'm with you, Michael . . . strong and safe. Even my father couldn't hurt me.

MICHAEL: He can't.

DONNA: (twirls happily) This is paradise.

MICHAEL: And tonight is going to be perfect. (He kisses her again)

DONNA: (gently breaks away) My plans—I have to get started on them. Room service . . . (She goes on the phone)

MICHAEL: You're too late, Donna.

DONNA: Surely room service is open twenty-four hours.

MICHAEL: It's all taken care of.

DONNA: What is?

MICHAEL: Dinner . . . alone here in the room . . . music, flowers, the sound of the waves lapping at the beach . . . and love. It's all set.

DONNA: (puts her arms around him) You think of everything.

MICHAEL: All you have to do is enjoy it.

son, who was working as a stable boy on the Love estate. She was barely sixteen. When her tyrannical father, Reginald Love, found out about the affair, he ran Michael out of town, telling him that Donna never wanted to see him again. Michael left unaware that Donna was pregnant and expecting twins.

Michael returned to Bay City in 1986. During his time away, he had amassed a fortune in his own right and he intended to resume his romance with Donna Love. They had been separated for twenty years. Actress Anna Stuart, who plays Donna, describes her feelings: "The falling back in love again and trusting him again and discovering that it was my father that wouldn't let me have any of his letters … I thought he had just disappeared. I thought he had totally abandoned me. Rediscovering all that was nothing short of glorious."

To consummate their love after twenty long years, Michael whisked Donna away to romantic Hawaii.

There he fulfilled her wish, expressed on the night of their engagement, that he sing for her. While she stood on the balcony, he serenaded her. The song was "I Can't Help Falling in Love with You," and it aptly expressed their love. They were married in a judge's chambers in November and renewed their vows in a lavish church ceremony several

When Michael was working undercover, he had to lie and say he was having an affair so that Donna would be safe. She believed him and turned to son-in-law Jake for comfort and support.

months later. Although this renewal wasn't a true wedding because they were already married, they both referred to it as their "second marriage."

Donna and Michael are not what you would call a compatible couple. She's selfish and self-absorbed. He's intense and devil-may-care and has strong moral convictions. She can be fun and make him laugh, and

he's a stabilizing element in her life. Stuart explains, "It's the classic *Taming of the Shrew*. It was so much fun—getting stuck in a barn overnight, her falling through a hayloft and getting drenched and sopping wet in the rainstorm in her beautiful dress and her beautiful hair and she looked like a drowned rat! There's love, hate, humor, and gentleness. When Michael bosses Donna around, everything is done out of love."

And despite their squabbles, they always have a passion for each other. Actor Kale Browne, who played Michael, remembers, "The energy between Donna and Michael was always very sexual and very funny. They never took themselves or each other all that seriously except when it mattered."

When Michael discovered the truth about Donna's past and present relationship with his brother, John, he divorced her immediately. And at one time he turned briefly to his sister-in-law, Sharlene, when John was with Felicia. But because he and Donna truly loved each other, it was a short-lived divorce and they remarried within the year.

While working for an organization called The Club, Michael was forced to tell Donna he was having an affair, in order to keep her from harm. Because she knew nothing of his undercover work, she believed him, and once again they signed the divorce papers on the dotted line. Donna then turned to son-in-law Jake for solace and support. Stuart says, "It was very sweet, very gentle, not sleazy. I was in the bedroom and I was crying on the bed, and he came in and he comforted me very, very gently, and from there we ended up in this very delicate situation. I don't believe there was a morning after." At the end of the investigation, Michael returned and confessed all and Donna accepted him back. But she never said a word about her own affair with Jake. When it was finally revealed, the feuding Hudsons divorced again. Finally they signed an antinuptial agreement barring them from marrying each other ever again!

Then Michael left town, and Donna entered into a May/December relationship with young Matt Cory. Actress Anna Stuart describes their affair as one of "incredible sweetness." Michael returned and professed to wish them well, but on the night before Donna and Matt were to marry, she paid a fateful visit to her ex, and caught up in the moment, they made love. She wanted him back, but he had no intention of reigniting their romance. In fact, he was so intent on Donna marrying Matthew that he took it upon himself to hire a priest! But the marriage fell apart, and Donna stopped fighting the attraction she'd always felt for Michael and began to pursue him despite his supposed disinterest.

Why did she keep coming back to him? Why did she marry him so many times? Stuart says, "Sometimes in a lifetime there's a person that you're so inexplicably bound to historically, past lives, future lives . . . and it never finishes. And even though there might be hate and spite and all that stuff, it's a thread, it's like steel, and you can go away from it, but it's always there."

Browne describes his relationship with Donna, or "Blackie" as he liked to call her, "as multilayered and multifaceted and colorful. Here are two people who have known each other most of their lives—have tried any number of relationships in the course of trying to find the one that worked. You know, friends, lovers, and everything in between. And so I think they were still trying things on for size when Michael took a header over the cliff. We had a certain thing that just pops, and you know it's that kind of unspoken chemistry

that also attracts people to each other. She wasn't particularly awed by Michael's success or prowess or anything like this. I mean fundamentally her concern when she walked into her room was Donna. And there was the ease—they could talk about just about anything and they were both very direct and out there and honest with each other most of the time. I think they learned, they went through the training wheel period together, and they went through this and they went through that. It's pretty hard, you just can't take all that experience and throw it away. I think there is just something indefinable about the great loves. Can you really quantify it? I don't know. Why do people choose to love one person or love a person in spite of all the differences and all the stuff that goes on and all the garbage in the history you pick up along the way. There are still some people who for whatever reason live in

Separated from Michael yet again, Donna entered into a sweet May/December romance with young Matt Cory and the two were briefly married.

your heart forever, and that just happens to be my relationship with her."

When Michael's son Nick became engaged to Sofia Carlino, Donna asked him if he and Sofia were soul mates. Nick's answer was "Everyone just tosses that word around. I'm not sure I know what it means." Donna's response was an obvious declaration of her feelings for her soul mate Michael: "Let me see if I can describe the indescribable. It's like when you meet somebody for the first time and you feel like you've known them forever. Maybe you had a past life together. Maybe it's just chemistry, electricity, but your soul mate is that other half of your heart, the missing part of you that you didn't even know existed. Sometimes when you finally meet each other, you can't even stand the sight of the other person, but there are always sparks. Definitely sparks. And when you find your soul mate, nothing can ever tear you apart . . . not really."

Michael had intended to propose again to Donna when he was tragically killed in a car crash on an icy mountain road. Later that night, Donna found the ring. It didn't end there. In his will, Michael

Right before the second wedding, Paulina found out that Jake was planning a hostile takeover of Cory Publishing, so instead of saying "I do," she punched him out and walked away.

left her with this tribute to their love: "To Donna. You are the love of my life. I leave you the greatest gift—our children."

a walk on the wild side

Paulina & Jake

He was known in those days as Jake the Snake and he was Paulina's errant knight. Women have a tendency to fall in love with Jake—he's the one you can't quite get out of your system. Jake and Paulina took three trips down the aisle, but only managed to marry twice. It went something like this: Jake was trying to get some dirt on her. He bugged her phone to prove she wasn't a Cory and blackmailed her (as it turned out, she was a Cory). She got mad and shot him. Then married him, divorced him, and fell in love—in that order.

According to Judi Evans Luciano, who plays Paulina, "They fell in love, but they didn't want to admit it to each other. So they got divorced. And then they fell in love again and decided to get married." Finally happy, Jake followed his typical MO—he screwed up.

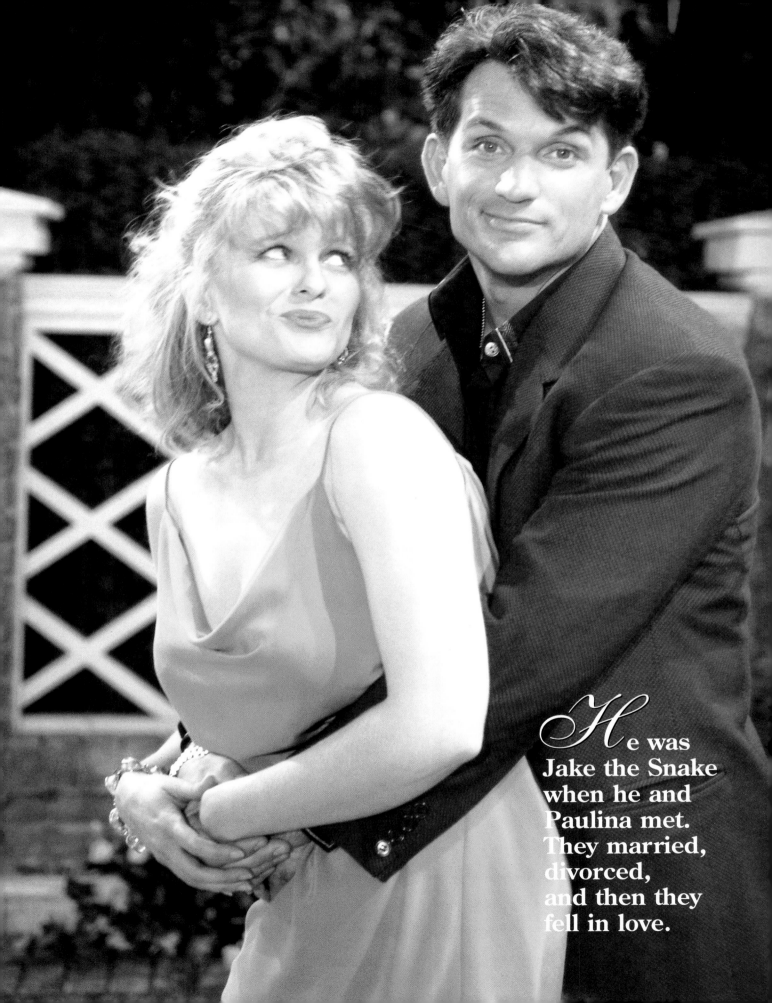

*H*e was Jake the Snake when he and Paulina met. They married, divorced, and then they fell in love.

Wedding number three went smoothly, but the honeymoon did not. Vicky put a baby in the backseat of their car. The couple thought it was abandoned and spent their honeymoon taking care of it.

Wanting to prove himself, he tried to stage a hostile takeover of Cory Publishing. Paulina found out right before the wedding, and instead of saying "I do," she punched him out at the altar and walked away!

It was up to Jake to prove himself all over again. Luciano says, "Before they got married the third time, they were kidnapped and dropped off in the middle of nowhere. At this point they were still mad at each other and hating each other, or Jake loved Paulina, but Paulina was sort of hating Jake. While they were almost dying out in the woods they fell in love again and got married."

Like the couple themselves, the honeymoon was anything but typical. Vicky put a baby in the backseat of the car Paulina and Jake were going to use for their honeymoon. They thought it was an abandoned baby and spent their whole honeymoon trying to appease the child. Then Jake found out it was Kirkland (Vicky had

They were barely on speaking terms when they were kidnapped and dropped off in the middle of nowhere. While almost dying in the woods, they fell in love again.

pulled a baby switch to keep her son from Grant) and he didn't have the heart to tell Paulina, because Paulina had started to fall in love with the baby and was thinking about adopting him. It was a big mess!

Right before they married the third time, to prove to Jake that money didn't matter, all she wanted was to love him, Paulina put her Cory fortune in a trust fund for the community center. Deep in debt from his latest business venture, Jake borrowed money from a loan

190

shark. Threatened by hit woman Bunny Eberhardt, Jake was trying to push Paulina away because he didn't want her to get killed. As it happened it was Jake who "died," or so they thought when a charred body was found beside his car. Actually, amnesiac Jake attended his own funeral and then went to San Francisco, thinking his name was Bunny Eberhardt, while Paulina, along with his good friend Vicky, spread his ashes at the swings in Lassiter.

Why the attraction between these two people who obviously spelled trouble for each other? Luciano says, "It was the combustible energy and passion and humor. They both knew they always did the wrong things for the right reasons. And they were cut from the same cloth, so they understood each other, which was one of the things that drove them crazy—they almost knew too much about each other. But it was exciting and it was fun, Jake and Paulina having mud fights. She pushed Jake in the pool. Jake pushed Paulina in the pool. Jake threw Paulina over his shoulders. Jake spanked Paulina. Paulina spanked Jake. It was wild!"

But now Jake was gone, or so she thought. Enter Joe . . .

✤

Paulina & Joe

Of her character Paulina, Judi Evans Luciano had this to say: "She's gutsy and spur-of-the-moment. Paulina thinks with her heart. It's like boom! There it goes. And then she's like, 'Oops! I'm in trouble.'" As Luciano describes Joe's character, "There's just black and white. There's very little gray. You're either good or you're bad. You can't be good and bad. He's very opinionated, and choices are pretty simple."

Joe Barbara, who plays Joe, adds, "Joe's sort of a no-nonsense guy. He's a very straight shooter with a big heart, which gets in the way sometimes. He has a bit of the nineties thing going on, but underneath the surface there's an old-fashioned side."

An interesting match of temperaments to be sure. They met when she asked his help in finding out the circumstances of her husband's death. Barbara says,

Before she arrived at his office, Joe was having a fantasy that he was Humphrey Bogart and Paulina was this blond with legs that made him start thinking about a joint checking account.

"As far as she knew, Jake was dead. But the night he 'died' he was supposed to be meeting her somewhere.

And when they found him they found his car heading out of town at a very high rate of speed and he had all this money with him. So everyone was saying, 'You know, Paulina, he was driving away with thousands in cash—he was leaving you.' And she didn't want to believe it. 'Was he leaving me or did he love me?' She couldn't go on until she had that question answered. She came to me as a private eye and said, 'I want you to find out.' I happened to have seen her the night before at some party, and I was thinking about her and I never got to talk to her. She had disappeared before I could find her.

"Frankie and I were unpacking our PI office—all these books, all this Bogart-like stuff. I'm reading and I'm having this fantasy about her coming in, and

I was Bogart, and she was blond and I don't like blonds much, but this one had the kind of legs that made me start thinking about a joint checking account. I'm having this fantasy about her, and then all of a sudden I look up and she walks in—the real-life Paulina walks in the office! And we start talking and I'm asking her, 'What was your name again?' And she goes 'Paulina.' And in my mind I go, 'Paulina Carlino.' And she goes, 'Paulina Cory McKinnon.' And in my mind I'm going, 'Married, my luck,' and she says, 'I need you to find out what my husband was doing when he died.' I go, 'When he—you're a widow?' And she hired me to check it out.

"I started investigating, and all the information that I got said he had taken off. And I had to tell her, 'Look, he was leaving you,' but I knew that would kill her. And I'm thinking, 'You know the guy is dead. He's not coming back. What good is it going to do to tell her he was running away? Why not just tell her he loved her more than anything.' And I made up this story: 'He was going to buy you a necklace. It was a very special necklace. He saw it in the store—I talked to the store owner. He was going to buy it and bring it you. That's where he was going that night, because he loved you more than anything.' I gave her the necklace and she cried, 'That's a beautiful thing. Thank you so much.'

"I'm totally in love with her at this point, and she wants to reimburse me for it because she feels obligated. She goes to the store to find out how much it was and finds out that the story I told her wasn't true. It was a big thing, but as time goes on she starts to fall for me, and then I get shot. That's when everything changed. She thought, 'I can't lose you too! Let's get married.'

"But I had started to put things together. They never found Jake's body, and they never identified it with the dental records. I went to San Francisco to find out if he was alive. I had a picture of him and I found the girl that he was living with, and she lied to me too. She said he left his wife and tried to change his identity so he didn't have to go back to her. I was thinking, 'Great, now I've got to tell her the guy's alive and he doesn't even want to see her again. How can I tell her that?' So I said, 'You know what, he's gone, out of the picture completely. Why tell her, it's only going to kill her? I'll never mention it to her and we'll get married.' It was totally out of love. I thought he was in San Francisco. I had no idea he was back in Bay City.

"The first time we actually saw him was when he

walked into the church in the middle of our wedding! I grabbed Paulina and took her out the back. And Jake got punched out again—this time by Matt. But they moved back in together, and I was kind of hanging around wanting her and longing after her.

"And then Justine comes to town and we think she's coming after all the Corys. At the police department we drew names because we had to protect all the members of the Cory family. I happened to draw Paulina's name and was assigned to be her bodyguard. So I had to stand outside her and Jake's house guarding them—sheer torture—and he's torturing me trying to woo her with all this fancy stuff. And I'm standing outside trying to foil their plans. At this point, after everything that had happened, they still weren't together emotionally or physically. She just couldn't get over the fact that she'd mourned him and gotten over him and there he was again! And Joe was more of what she'd looked for all her life in the sense of a stable family."

Then Jake did something stupid—he tried to make Paulina jealous by pretending he was after another woman, thinking that would bring her back. Instead it pushed her further away. When Paulina went to Reno to get a divorce, a desperate Jake donned a wig and pantyhose and, claiming to be a kindly old lady named Doris, he befriended Paulina and counseled her not to give up on her husband. It didn't work, and Paulina went back to Joe.

"We had this one night of bliss," says Luciano—the night Dante was conceived. Since Paulina was pregnant, the couple was anxious to make it official. Unfortunately, they were short on cash, as Carlino's was proving to be a huge drain on Joe's finances. So they decided to postpone the wedding. But not if Sofia had anything to say about it. She took her life's savings and threw a surprise wedding at the Cory chapel, followed by a reception at Carlino's. Luciano says, "When we came out of the church, Jake was there saying, 'The best man won. Have a wonderful life, you two. I'll always love you,' and he went away crying."

Today Jake and Paulina are confidants and best friends. All was not smooth sailing for the newly married Carlinos. Haunted by the demons of inadequacy and low self-esteem dating back to her days as an orphan on Gold Street, Paulina struggled with weight loss after the birth of her son, Dante. The struggle led her to abuse alcohol and pills and threatened her newfound family. Through it all, Joe tried to be supportive—that is, until their house, the house that

The first time Paulina saw Jake and knew he was alive was when he walked in during her wedding to Joe!

When Ryan became overly judgmental, Vicki rebelled and turned to Grant, who accepted her for who she was and offered her the glamorous life she'd always coveted.

he grew up in, burned down and Paulina tested positive for drugs. Luciano remembers, "He was supportive at first until he really felt that Dante was in danger. Then he was afraid for his wife and afraid for his son."

Barbara claims that's when Joe drew the line: "That's it. You almost killed yourself. You almost killed our kid. You wiped out every memory of my parents that I had. I can't deal with this anymore." Luciano adds, "At first he said, 'You've changed, but I love you, it doesn't matter.' And Paulina's thinking, 'Are you blind? Are you stupid? Do you think I'm stupid?'" His answer to his troubled wife when all was said and done was "I loved you more than I cared about how you looked."

The family's back together now. Says Luciano of Paulina's two loves: "It's mixed. They're both the loves of her life. Jake was the love of her life for that period of her life and who she was then. And Joe is definitely the love of her life for this period now."

✤

Vicky & Ryan

When he happened into her life, she was ready for Mr. Right. They met when he rescued her from a runaway horse. It would be the first of many rescues. Their courtship got off to rocky start, since Ryan was a by-the-book type of guy and Vicky bristled under the restraints he tried to impose on her. They spent a lot of time disagreeing with each other, and Vicky was afraid of messing up yet again. But in the end they fell in love, and in the fall of 1991 they got engaged.

That fall Vicky also went to work for Ryan's half-brother, Grant Harrison, as a political aide. Grant was immediately attracted to her and set out to make her his own, even though she was engaged to his brother. Actor Mark Pinter, who plays Grant, describes what attracted him to Vicky: "Her spunk, her ambition—it matched his, her energy, her intelligence, her drive. All those things that he would demand in a woman. Grant would not want a placid woman. He would want somebody who's really in the thick of it, and Vicky was all of that and yet she was not his. And so it was hands off, and it was almost that that made it even more interesting and attractive for him. He could work with her. She shared his passion as a senator and she drove him on. She did the research for him. There was almost a sexual kind of thing between them that was never sexual but it was passion. And so you know he had to have her. He just couldn't control it. That was it. He did the unspeakable thing. He coveted his brother's woman and took her. And then did all the wrong things to keep her."

Actress Jensen Buchanan, who plays Vicky, recalls, "Ryan was doubting her and judging her, and that brought up some things in Vicky that just made her lash out in a kind of behavior that was very typical of her past. She turned to Grant because he accepted her and offered glamour and a carefree

scene:

RYAN: I know all about you . . . and I buy the whole package. I love you, Vicky, and I know you love me.
VICKY: But for how long?
RYAN: Give us a chance—we'll see.
VICKY: If you weren't so perfect—
RYAN: I'm not perfect.
VICKY: Come on . . .
RYAN: And neither are you. But that's what's so great about us—we're such a match for each other.
VICKY: Too close a match.

RYAN: There you go being irrational again.
VICKY: I can't help the way I feel.
RYAN: I know what you're really afraid of—you'll commit to me, and I'll leave you.
VICKY: Maybe.
RYAN: That's not going to happen.
VICKY: Honey, it's what always happens.
RYAN: (about to blow) Vicky . . .
VICKY: And this time—this time

I couldn't take it. I couldn't take losing you.
RYAN: So you're just going to run away.
VICKY: (fighting tears) I can't . . . give you what you want. I can't.
(Ryan looks at her, then turns and walks to the door. He stops and looks back)
RYAN: You've done it to us, Vicky. What you were afraid of doing, you've done. Congratulations. (He opens the door and exits)
Fade out

kind of whirlwind sort of life. He was the politician and he offered an exciting and forgiving life. Whereas Ryan was very judgmental at the time." Vicky's feeling was, "You don't accept me the way I am, fine, this is the way I am. You think I'm a bad girl, just watch how bad I can be!"

Vicky married Grant. On her honeymoon, she was kidnapped by Carl Hutchins, who thought that she belonged with his son Ryan, not with Grant. Never giving up on his love for her, Ryan rescued Vicky and they made love. Devastated, Grant tried to make the marriage work, but when Vicky was kidnapped a second time, aiming for her kidnapper, Grant tragically and accidentally shot her in the back. Desperate to keep her separated from his brother, Grant shipped Vicky off to a remote Swiss sanitarium to recover from her wound.

When Vicky realized how manipulative and tyrannical Grant could be, she left him and ran into Ryan's waiting arms.

Locked in her room and kept under sedation, Vicky came to realize how manipulative and tyrannical Grant really was. As soon as she could, she left him and ran straight into Ryan's waiting arms, only to discover that she was pregnant with Grant's child. Afraid that Grant would take her son from her, as he had threatened, Vicky took her newborn far away from Bay City and his powerful father.

At first Ryan refused to forgive Vicky for abandoning him, but then Grant pulled his lowest of dirty deeds, shooting himself and framing Vicky for the crime so that he could get custody of Kirkland. To protect her, Ryan confessed to the crime that neither of them had committed, and when it was resolved, they reaffirmed their love.

They were briefly happy until Ryan's psychotic mother, Justine, arrived and created havoc. Justine kidnapped Vicky and hid Kirkland so that she could return him to Grant. Once again it was Ryan to the rescue. When Ryan caught up with Justine at the train trestle, Grant was already there. In the confrontation that ensued, to protect Justine and learn the whereabouts of his son, Grant shot his brother. Ryan lay near death on the very spot where he had proposed to Vicky.

Devastated, Vicky maintained a bedside vigil as Ryan lay in a coma. She insisted on no tears in the hospital room, only laughter, hoping that good vibes would bring Ryan back. But fate had other plans. Ryan briefly awoke, professed his love for her, and then succumbed to his injuries. Ryan's restless soul returned to look after Vicky, however, as Grant plotted yet again to kill her and gain custody of their son, this time by planting a bomb in a truck. Ryan's celestial

The year Vicky and Ryan got engaged, she went to work as a political aide for his brother, Grant Harrison. Grant was immediately smitten.

When an explosion left Vicky hovering between life and death, she left her body and joined Ryan in heaven, where they reaffirmed their love and exchanged their long-awaited vows.

warning saved her, but in the shockwave of the blast, Vicky hit her head. Hovering between life and death, she left her body and was able to join Ryan briefly in heaven.

Overjoyed at being able to look at each other and touch each other, they reaffirmed their love and exchanged their vows in heaven. "Part of me wants to stay like this forever," said Vicky. Her heart broke as Ryan gently showed her how much she was needed on earth, especially by her children, and she knew she had to say good-bye forever.

Buchanan remembers, "That moment when he sent her back to take care of her children and live her life—it wasn't time for her—it was heartbreaking." Of the romance, Buchanan says, "Such highs and such lows. The great feelings were just out of this world, and the pain was deeper and darker. There was a romantic quality to the relationship that hasn't existed since."

Vicky was a wild thing when she came to Bay City with Jake to seek her fortune.

love comes full circle

Vicky & Jake

Even when married to other people, Vicky and Jake always had each other. While growing up in the coal-mining town of Lassiter, Pennsylvania, they were childhood crushes, then teen lovers. Once they hit adulthood, they lost sight of their romance—for a while. He was her first love and she thought nothing could tear them apart. Then they came to Bay City with the intention of claiming Vicky's part of the Love family fortune, and Jake fell in love with Vicky's twin, Marley. Jake and Marley married and Vicky moved on with her life, or so she wanted people to believe. Actress Ellen Wheeler, who played Vicky/Marley at the time, recalls, "Vicky said she was OK with it, but she was crushed. She showed up at the wedding crying."

Sometime later, Vicky and Jake were trapped in a cave-in. Facing imminent death, Jake admitted that he loved her and always would. They made love, but

he returned to Marley. Then Vicky discovered she was pregnant. For awhile Jake thought her son, Steven, was his. But Vicky married Steven's father, Jamie Frame, while Marley sued Jake for divorce. Subsequently Vicky and Jake forged intense relationships with other people—he with Paulina, she with Ryan. The turning point came when Ryan died and Paulina left Jake to marry Joe Carlino. Finally it dawned on Jake—his partner for life, someone who could accept him for himself was right under his nose, and they began to find their way back.

Then there was Shane. Shane had received Ryan's eyes in a transplant. He was about to capture Vicky's heart. "Best friend" Jake helped Vicky clear Shane—saving him from death row—because he couldn't bear to have Vicky pine away for Shane but still marry Jake because he was the next best thing. As it happened, it was Vicky who proposed at their special place, the playground swings in Lassiter. Tom Eplin, who plays Jake, says, "It's a place that Jake and Vicky hold dear to their hearts. It's not just the swings. It's symbolic of a time in their lives when they were confused and forming opinions, and each time they come to renew a promise or explore a new future. That spot is like a time machine for Jake and Vicky."

They dreamed their dreams there. They fell in love there. It's their special place. Like the Lassiter swings, Jake's the one constant in Vicky's life—the man who's stayed by her side through everything. He kept her children safe from Grant when she hid out in Europe after Ryan's death. And as best friend and former partner in crime, he helped her with the baby switch to the extent that he took Kirkland on his and Paulina's honeymoon!

Jake and Vicky's relationship started a lifetime ago in Lassiter and has come full circle.

From friends to lovers to friends and, finally, to husband and wife. When they exchanged their wedding vows, Vicky expressed her feelings this way: "Thanks to you I know what real love is. It's been standing right here next to me my whole life."

For other couples, the opposites attract thing might work, but for Vicky and Jake, it's their similarities that are key. They are both smart, opinionated, sexy, tough on the outside, tender on the inside, and flawed. Others may have tried to change them, but

Vicky was crushed when Jake fell in love and married her gentle, refined twin sister, Marley.

After Ryan died and Paulina chose Joe, Vicky and Jake started to find their way back to each other...and then Shane Roberts came to town.

these two accept each other as is. Jake didn't run when Vicky had unresolved feelings for Shane. And although she was tempted, she never slept with Shane. Vicky accepts Jake's (very!) colorful past with both Marley, whom he married first, and her mother Donna, with whom he had an affair.

After Michael's and Shane's deaths their love was tested, but they never stopped loving each other, and in the aftermath their love went to another phase. Jake understands her and he's passionate. Eplin says, "Jake and Vicky turned from a postjuvenile story into a mature love story." When Jake is with Vicky, life is good.

Buchanan speaks about their love: "There's depth to the relationship with Jake—maybe because they're older or because they've been friends for so long. They've worked through the betrayals. Secrets and lies have run rampant in this relationship, but over the years they have somehow worked through

fade:

VICKY: I'd be sitting in Bridget's house waiting for you and I'd hear your bike pull up, it was the best sound in the whole world. I used to come running out of the house. I would just jump on the back of that bike and wrap my arms around you. I'd like that again—the bike, adventure, sex, rebellion. I want that all again. Just want to feel the wind in my face. I don't think I've ever felt as completely free as that.

When Vicky married Jake, love came full circle.

An outing in Central Park with Jake and the boys made Vicky see him in a whole new light.

this and come to a point where they can be together. I think that's pretty miraculous! I think what Vicky sees in Jake is a strong aphrodisiac. They have triumphed over an enormous number of obstacles, and I think every time you struggle through something and make it, it's like a mini victory. In some ways, I think this relationship is Vicky's prize for making it through so many difficult times. And he is struggling so much to be a better person. They're tickled and charmed and amused by each other, and that's exciting and it's titillating."

generation x looks for love in all the wrong places

Maggie Cory, daughter of the infamous Cecile de Poulignac and Mac's illegitimate son, Sandy, is a chip off the proverbial block. She returned to Bay City in 1993 in amorous pursuit of Ian Rain and took up residence at the Cory mansion. She soon trans-

ferred her affections to the darkly handsome and sensitive Tomas Rivera, himself a single father of a daughter from a childhood romance. After awhile, feeling restless in her relationship with Tomas, Maggie lapped up the attention given to her by Nick Hudson when he blew into town, but she still wanted Tomas as her boyfriend and schemed to keep them both. Tomas and Nick were no dummies and Maggie was no Cecile. When the boys found out, they wasted no time in dumping the hapless manipulator.

Not one to go down in defeat, Maggie honed in on Nick and professed undying love. At the time, Nick was discovering a relationship with Catholic schoolgirl Sofia Carlino and wanted no part of Maggie. Undaunted, Maggie did everything she could to come between them, going so far as to use her position as Sofia's "best friend" to counsel her to hold on to her virginity, especially when it came to Nick. While Nick was on the outs with Sofia, Maggie begged him to make love to her, and he did. It was not a wise move on his part. Maggie pressed her advantage by claiming she was pregnant with Nick's child, and for the sake of the baby he agreed to tie the knot.

Enter Rafael Santierro, Nick's best friend from the old rough-and-tumble days. When he tipped off his buddy Nick that Maggie was faking the pregnancy, Nick dragged Maggie into Carlino's and treated her to a very public display of humiliation. As for Maggie, she would do it all over again, just to win her man! As it happened, she ended up with her betrayer, Rafael, whose main attraction to his best friend's ex was her hefty trust fund. He soon smooth-talked Maggie into marriage, sans prenuptial agreements. "Let's run away and never look back," Maggie told her husband-to-be. They left Bay City behind and said "I do" in Spain.

Child of a single working mom, Nick Hudson discovered his father, Michael Hudson, only when his mother, Diana, died. Nick liked to play the tough guy with an edge. Actor Mark Mortimer, who plays Nick, says, "Without parental guidance, when you're a youth, you're going to get in trouble. He was in and out of jail a couple of times and hanging with a bad crowd—he was a tough kid." But Mortimer adds,

*G*eneration X
searches for love.

"He's a very caring person and he tries to care about everybody, but he's too reactionary, he doesn't think about the consequences before he does stuff—he's still young."

Nick met innocent Sofia Carlino when she broke into Carlino's Restaurant looking for her brother Joe and nearly knocked him out with a two-by-four. Actress Dahlia Salem, who played Sofia, recalls, "I was frightened. I didn't know who the hell that was, and I grab a club and I'm about to knock him over the head, and that's how we met. He was determined to make sure I was safe and invited me back to his farmhouse, where I stayed with him and Michael." Salem adds, "She was very sheltered, and he was sort of the bad boy with a good heart—vulnerable with a twist of danger. She was intrigued by his life and his experiences and wanted a taste of that."

Maggie set her sights on Tomas, whose childhood romance with Angela produced a child now under his care. To complicate matters further, Angela wanted her lover back.

On New Year's Eve they shared a kiss. Salem says, "They fell in love and it was exciting for her. First love— she was the young innocent, very open and understanding, very honest and direct, a feisty type willing to give everybody a chance. When she first came into town, she was sort of rebellious. She has a fiery streak, a real passion for life and experience."

As for Nick, he couldn't seem to stay out of trouble with the law, and Sofia's overprotective brother Joe's constant disapproval prompted them to run away. Salem remembers, "Part of the excitement was doing something that her brother didn't want her to do and being involved with this person he wasn't too fond of."

Nick's Uncle John's illness brought them back to Bay City, and Joe warned Nick to stay clear of his little sister. Nick agreed, but he and Sofia continued to see each other secretly until the Maggie mess led her to date Tomas, however briefly.

Reunited, Sofia and Nick made plans to elope, but a jealous Maggie threw a wrench into their romantic plans again. Salem explains, "She was able to manipulate the situation to make Sofia feel that she wasn't in the picture." Nick married Maggie briefly, and

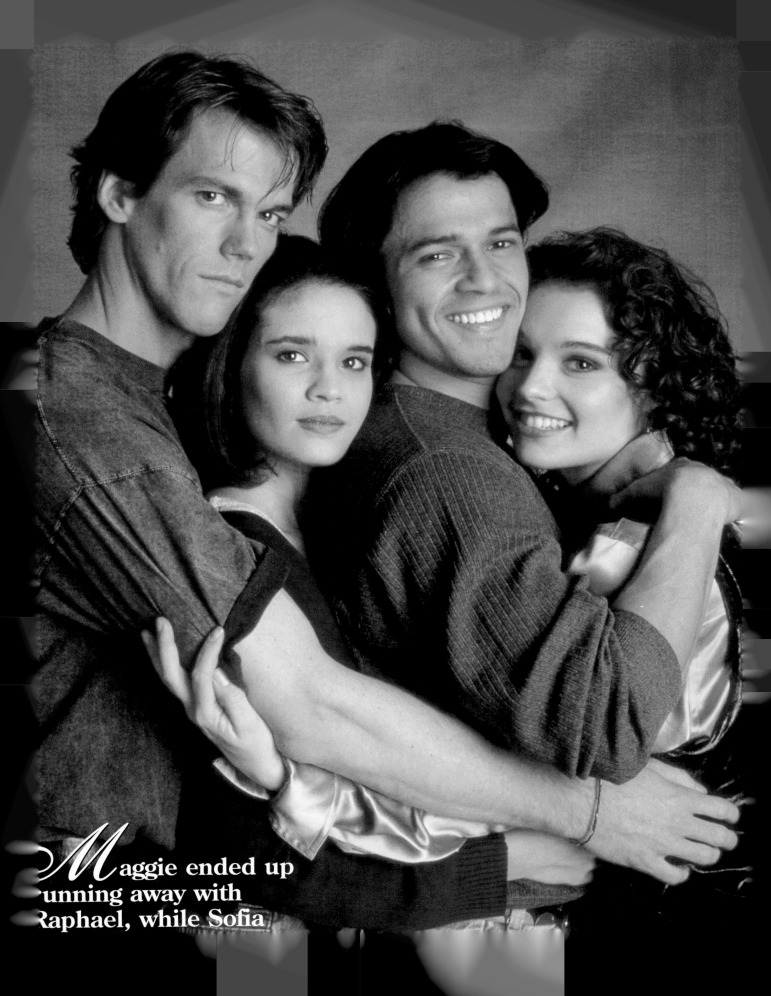

*M*aggie ended up running away with Raphael, while Sofia

The Maggie mess led Sofia to date Tomas briefly. Although Tomas and Sofia were roommates, there was nothing more than friendship between them, and she soon went back to Nick.

Matt Cory entered Sofia's life. When his efforts to regain Sofia backfired, Nick found refuge in the bottle. Mortimer says, "I was trying to win her trust back. We had so many fights, but it was always the underlying feeling that I loved her, always." His drinking led to an unfounded rape charge, and, knowing he couldn't be capable of such a violent crime, Sofia stood by him through the trial. Mortimer remarks, "Nick felt betrayed by everyone. Sofia was his salvation."

So a wonderful bond was created between them of trust and friendship, and for awhile they found their way back to one another and planned to marry, this time in a church with family present. But on the eve of the wedding, Nick's father, Michael, was tragically killed in an automobile accident. Wedding plans were put on hold. And eventually, as Salem describes it, "Sofia realized they were

Although they'd planned to wed, Nick and Sofia drifted apart. She became involved with the more worldly and sophisticated Matt Cory when they went into the music business together.

really in different places, and Nick in a sense wanted to hold her down, stifle her—didn't really want her to go out and experience different things. They were different people with different goals. She had high expectations and aspirations for certain things, and they just couldn't see eye to eye anymore. She grew out of him."

Sofia turned to Matt. Says Salem, "Matt was so cultured, he'd lived life, seen the world, and that intrigued her. He inspired her, turned her on to something totally different and she was able to find a new direction and purpose—that was the attraction. Things are not what they were. It's not such a fairy tale for her anymore. She has to deal with life." Sofia and Matt had not even discussed marriage when she lost her virginity to him while on a business trip in New York.

Mortimer's last words on Sofia and Nick: "He'll always love Sofia, he'll never give up hope on what's there. But if it doesn't pan out, and it's not going to pan out, Nick's ready to move on with his life."

❧

It was Nick's turn to be intrigued by someone else when Remy Woods decided to try her luck in Bay City. She made quite an entrance. First she spied on Nick in Carlino's. Then, when he accidentally almost ran her down with his motorcycle, the first thing she said to him was "Ow! Don't slap me anymore, OK?"

To say that she had a mysterious background was an understatement. All that is known of Remy's past is that she is a child of foster homes, who sometimes experiences psychic powers. Actress Taylor Stanley, who plays Remy, says, "She's still very much a mystery. She's quite bubbly, but she could stop on a dime and turn around and be a different person. That's what she's learned to do. Make whoever is in the

*N*ick thinks
his romantic future lies
with Remy, and Remy
is definitely interested.

room like her and feel comfortable with her, depending on who they are. She sort of feels them out and will adapt for them, so she ends up on everybody's good side. It comes from having to deal with so many different people and never having something solid to hold on to or any one particular person to hold on to. She's vulnerable, but very headstrong. She would never let her guard down for a second. So no matter what she does, whether she wants to be doing it or not, she's manipulating the situation. No matter how close she gets to Nick, who's to say that she'll ever be able to let that go?"

As for the other people in Bay City—Joe distrusts her, Paulina adores her, and Sophia considers her a

friend. And Nick—well, he fancies himself in love. Mortimer muses, "I think Nick is falling in love with Remy. I see that going all the way. I think it's going to take some time to develop, but Nick's immediate future is in Remy."

And is she romantically interested in him? Taylor answers, "I think she would have to have some sort of crush on him because he's probably nicer to her than anyone has ever been. Sincerely nice to her, not nice because he wants something, but nice because, unbelievably, he wants to spend time with her. And that has to conjure up some sort of emotion for her. I don't know if in her life she's ever felt romantic toward anybody. So I don't know if she would know what those feelings were like. No one who's on their own when they're young can have a positive outlook, especially a young woman on the streets. Their experiences with men are generally negative. But he's really a good-looking guy and he's being really, really wonderfully sweet to her."

Will she fall in love? Says Taylor, "The opportunity is definitely there." Stay tuned.

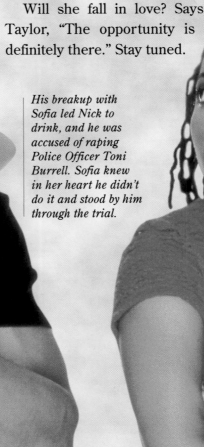

His breakup with Sofia led Nick to drink, and he was accused of raping Police Officer Toni Burrell. Sofia knew in her heart he didn't do it and stood by him through the trial.

b a y   c i t y   b l a c k g u a r d s

Carl Hutchins

A Shakespeare-spouting villain known for his brilliant treachery, Carl Hutchins was a mesmerizing egomaniac. Behind the silky voice, the acid smile, and the rapier wit lay a worldly rogue, a prince of players. Says Charles Keating, who played Carl, "The character was very rich. He listened to opera and played chess. He was a gamesman. He was Machiavelli."

Crafty, ruthless, depraved, and sinister, Carl burst on the scene in 1983 as a vicious criminal acknowledging no societal constraints and pursuing a dangerous vendetta against Mackenzie Cory and his family. According to Keating, "The vendetta had to do with Carl

He was a man of many disguises.

Hutchins's father. In those days Carl believed Mac Cory had been responsible for his father's undoing. He came to town to romance Felicia and to attack and undermine Mac Cory. During that period of time, he did everything he could. And he was fantasizing about Mac's wife Rachel. The collective verse of Shakespeare sat on his desk. There was Carl sitting at his desk musing with his glass of brandy, reading his *Richard the III,* and he fantasized himself as Richard, Rachel as Queen Anne."

The list of Carl's dastardly deeds is long. He kidnapped Rachel, turned Sandy Cory against his father after Jamie was named CEO, and then poisoned him. He murdered Daphne Grimaldi, kidnapped Marley, and swindled Donna, to whom he had once been married. He was also responsible for paralyzing Kathleen McKinnon and almost killing Frankie Frame when he detonated a bomb on board a boat. Carl went over a cliff in Arizona after being shot by Nancy McGowen, Rachel's half-sister, and her lover Chris Chapin, during another vendetta aimed at the Chapins.

Keating says of his character, "When he was a bad guy, I did my best to make him as pleasant and likable as possible. All of the villains have to be loved and liked; otherwise, they could never get away with every little thing. You must find the human aspect."

Actress Ellen Wheeler, who plays Marley, remarks, "Carl was a wonderful villain. When Marley was growing up, Donna and Carl had been together, so Carl was like Uncle Carl to Marley. When it came to his being evil, that was hard on Marley because he had been a father figure in her life. That was at the same vulnerable time when she and Jake were starting to fall in love and Carl kidnapped her. He was a wonderful villain. I think what we loved about

Carl Hutchins was an infamous villain known for his brilliant treachery and deceit.

The fact that they'd once been man and wife didn't stop Hutchins from swindling Donna Love.

She knew him as Uncle Carl, but that didn't deter Hutchins from kidnapping Marley in the Arizona desert so he could get his hands on her money.

him was that he was one of those villains who was just delicious. You love to watch him be bad, but you also always felt for him—just a little bit. You didn't want him to accomplish what he was doing, but you did. You rooted for him just the tiniest bit because he was just deliciously evil, and it's hard to be that."

When Carl resurfaced in 1991, he discovered more of his "human aspect" when he discovered Ryan, his son by Justine Duvalier. He adored the boy so much that it led to an attempt to mend his wicked ways. When Ryan was killed by his brother, Grant Harrison, in a struggle

on a train trestle, it led to a hatred even deeper and more dangerous than the one Carl had harbored against Mac. Years before, Carl's son Perry had died under mysterious circumstances in Donna Hudson's barn, and now Ryan—it was more than he could bear. Grant and Carl had tangled before. Indeed, Carl had shot Grant some years earlier, when he discovered Grant's role in his imprisonment, and there were other incidents. But, says Keating, "Killing the boy was the thing," and Carl became obsessed with revenge. Grant in turn took pleasure in tormenting him.

The vendetta almost destroyed Carl's marriage to Rachel, and she became fearful that this tragedy would cause her husband's villainous past to rear its ugly head. The marriage survived—that is, until Carl disappeared under mysterious circumstances at the same time Cory Publishing's bankroll was discovered missing.

Grant Harrison

Grant Harrison has always been defined by ambition and elegance. Mark Pinter, the actor who plays him, says, "He goes to extremes. He's outrageous, he's hilarious, he's neurotic, he's compulsive. He's lost his power base over the years because he's made so many mistakes in his life. He lost his chance to be Congressman and lost his Senate seat. He's lost everything. Everything that he's loved, he's frittered away.

Ryan's death at the hands of his brother, Grant, left Carl bereft and vowing revenge.

It happens to a lot of men, especially men of power who have a lot of responsibility. They walk a dangerous line and they're that close to toppling over. It's so sad. He could have it all and he's always wasted it all."

How did he get to be Bay City's mayor? Surprisingly, he didn't rig the election. What he did was set his opponent, Donna Hudson, up for a possible sexual harassment suit from a male employee. Pinter describes Grant's struggle as "an internal battle within him to try to figure out whether he's a good person. He was taught to manipulate and taught to go after what he wanted and he had blinders on. His father wanted him to be the president, wanted him to succeed in politics, and he raised him with blinders." His biggest weaknesses, says Pinter, "are women—this great need for somebody to love him, which goes right back to his being raised by his father. There were no women in his life. His mother was an insane person who left him very, very early. He doesn't know how to love, because no one was there to love him, pick him up and hold him and just be with him. Grant is a character with an enormous amount of pain, unrecognized pain. He does the wrong things. He makes the wrong choices in relationships, in ambitions, in desires. It's gotten him in trouble with the law. He's been in jail. He killed his brother."

Grant grew up believing that their mother died in childbirth and he always blamed Ryan. While the boys were growing up, says Pinter, "Grant had all of his father's attention. He was the one who was primed for success. Ryan wasn't. Ryan was almost the antithesis of Grant." He was the good cop. Grant was the politician.

Any familial bond they had fell apart when Ryan learned that Carl Hutchins was his father from an affair he'd had with Justine. According to Pinter, when Grant killed Ryan, "He was trying to find his son, Kirkland. Justine had hidden him. His son was missing and he was frightened to death that she had done something to him. They were on a railroad bridge, and he was trying to protect her as well because he had reestablished this kind of absurd relationship with her. Remember that she was mad, but a part of him wanted his mother. Everybody had a motive for being up on that bridge, and everybody had a gun in their hands. It was almost a Greek tragedy playing out on that bridge. Grant didn't murder Ryan. He tragically got in the way of that gunshot. Obviously it was a case of manslaughter, and Grant should have gone to prison, but it was not premeditated murder. It was a terrible, tragic mistake—and what terrible haunting grief he felt for the loss of his mother and his brother."

After Ryan was killed, the vendetta between Carl and Grant intensified. Says Pinter, "We were at odds with one another constantly. "We were two people with the same kind of motives, the same kind of ambitions, the same kind of drive, and the same kind of we'll-do-anything-to-get-what-we-want mentality. And so they would butt heads." Ryan's death, says Pinter, "changed the whole dynamic. Carl's objective then certainly was to get Grant for killing his son. To make Grant pay."

Pinter describes more of Grant's dastardly deeds: "He actually shot Vicky in the back. Again, it was a tragic accident. He was attempting to shoot her captor and she stepped in the way. The most devious thing he ever did was to shoot himself and frame Vicky because he wanted custody of his son." Says Pinter, "It was a desperate act. He really had to slither on the ground like a snake to get to that point. That's a hideous thing. I can't imagine that Grant did anything worse than that. He's had a lot of affairs. Lorna—she was his campaign manager—he used Lorna. He used a lot of people. I remember we played a series of scenes where there were so many people who hated Grant that everybody came to the door and took a shot at him."

But like his nemesis, Carl, Grant does have a saving grace, and that's his love for his son, Kirkland. Says Pinter, "Ever since Kirkland was born, it was Grant's objective to have his son—physically have his son." This led

The brothers were the antithesis of each other—Grant the manipulative politician, Ryan the good cop.

Vicky to pull a baby switch in fear that Grant would gain custody. Several years later, realizing that Paulina, whom he'd gotten addicted to drugs, could testify against him in a custody hearing, Grant determined to destroy her credibility. He drugged her drink, set a small fire in her house, and left. The house burned down, but happily, Paulina and her infant son, Dante, were saved.

Pinter describes the situation now: "Grant had to recognize that Vicky was a good mother, and he had to stop persecuting her, stop torturing her, stop threatening her." His love for his son knows no bounds. As Grant has said, "Not seeing him is like not breathing. He's my life. If I do anything with my life ever again, all I really want to do is to make my son love and respect me." And Kirkland does love his father.

The death of his brother and his mother would haunt Grant's dreams for many months.

Carl and Grant were villains cut from the same cloth and they would constantly have to watch their backs.

There is someone else who loves this flawed man, and that's Cindy Harrison, the ex-Mrs. Mayor. At the height of their vendetta, Grant had been slipped a mickey by Carl that made him literally mad. He met Cindy in the psych ward. Pinter recalls, "It started out to be total manipulation. Total use of one another. They bring out the worst in one another." He married her so she couldn't testify against him. Actress Kim Rhodes, who plays Cindy, describes the wedding: "It was a thirty-second wedding—I do, she does, we're gone, good-bye. He didn't even kiss me.

It was the saddest wedding in the whole wide world.

"They tried to kill each other, but then they had sex and the sex was too good. That's what kept happening. They kept setting up plots to kill each other and then they'd end up in bed together, and they'd say, 'Oh, okay, maybe not quite yet.'"

Rhodes adds, "Cindy's a wild card—she's smart, she has an individually tailored set of morals. She's multitalented, loyal, and slightly psychotic. I don't think she should be locked up in an institution, but she definitely deals on a different plane than the rest of us." But Rhodes says of Cindy's feelings for Grant, "I really think she has the ability to see something in him that no one else can. That's the part she loves, and that's the part he won't give to her. I think

It was a marriage of convience for Cindy and the Mayor. They tried to kill each other several times, but the sex was so good that they're still among the living.

Among Grant's most dastardly deeds were marrying Amanda Cory after she was paralyzed in a car accident and then torturing her for an affair he thought she'd had with Evan Frame.

that it is genuine and I think this is love. This is the first time in her life that she's been in love and she's in love with a bad man. That's the part that he works like hell to hide, which I personally am convinced is the reason he wants to get rid of her so badly, because she knows it exists. She knows his vulnerabilities. I also think they are of a like mind: They think alike. They act alike. They understand each other. They're kindred spirits. It's just that she's not allowed herself to hate as much as Grant has."

Grant's unconditional love for his son Kirkland is what saves his soul.

Is he the devil incarnate? Rhodes insists, "Absolutely not. You've seen over and over how much he loves his son. He did have genuine tenderness for Cindy. He has moments of extreme vulnerability and loneliness. He loves his father. He's just a very lonely, angry man, and he's taking it out on the world around him. He's going after what he wants because he's never gotten what he wants."

femmes fatales

Iris Cory

Iris came to Bay City in 1972, intent on destroying the relationship that was growing between her estranged husband, Eliot Carrington, and their son's governess, Alice Matthews Frame. Scheming with her maid Louise to get rid of Alice, Iris tracked down Alice's brother, Russ, to be her son Dennis's cardiologist. She then maneuvered the family to relocate to Bay City, using Dennis's heart problem as an excuse for reconciliation. Actress Beverlee McKinsey, who played Iris, describes her as "unbelievably self-centered and manipulative and conniving, but at the same time she was very loving and very vulnerable." As a mother, "She was very possessive of Dennis, which of course we know is not good, but in her mind she was just trying to do the best thing for him, and she was always a good mother to him."

Iris idolized her father, publishing magnate Mackenzie Cory, even though she had spent her childhood not with him but in fancy European boarding schools. When Mac moved permanently to Bay City in 1974, to Iris's horror he became enamored of and married Rachel Davis Matthews Clark. McKinsey says, "In Iris's mind, Rachel was trash compared to her. Rachel has become this elegant lady, but she was trash, and Iris just couldn't deal with that, she couldn't handle it. She wouldn't have objected to her father being with Liz—at least I don't think she would have, because she and Liz were very good friends. Also the fact that Rachel was younger than Iris really bugged Iris a lot."

The schemes of self-centered jet-setter Iris Cory Carrington would disrupt the lives of many Bay City inhabitants.

Iris was constantly scheming to break up the happy couple. First she hired European acquaintance and womanizer Philip Wainwright to put Rachel in a compromising position, but those plans were foiled. Iris's growing overprotectiveness toward Mac backfired on the people she cared about: Philip caused Mac to have a riding accident that left him temporarily paralyzed, Liz nearly had a nervous breakdown, and Rachel's son, Jamie, and Dennis missed each other's company. Tensions escalated when Iris discovered that Rachel had replaced her as chief beneficiary in Mac's will and she feared that Rachel would plot to kill Mac in an effort to get the inheritance. Nothing could have been further from the truth.

Iris became engaged to Russ Matthews, Rachel's first husband, while trying to set Rachel up as an adulteress yet again. That plot collapsed and so did Iris's wedding plans. Despite her desperate begging, an outraged Mac vowed to have nothing more to do with his scheming daughter. Fixated and paranoid, Iris shut herself in her house in a frenzy that led to a suicide attempt. Dr. David Gilchrist helped her recover and the two were briefly involved until news of Rachel's pregnancy drove Iris back to her old manipulative ways.

Iris then maneuvered a short-lived marriage to architect Robert Delaney, after which she met and married Brian Bancroft. Says McKinsey, "She certainly loved Brian Bancroft. He was really a father replacement for her. He was older, and my husband in real life had the idea that his character should call me 'Baby' and that this would highlight the fact that he was like a father as well as a husband to me. And it was enormously successful. She was always convinced that he, like everybody else, would leave her, but he never did." It was Iris who would leave him, and his last words to her were, "No matter where you go or what you do, there will always be a special place in my heart for the love I have for you."

Iris's next move was to enlist Gwen Parrish to make a play for Mac (she had also tried to get David Gilchrist to seduce Rachel but to no avail). Then a plot involving Sven the butler backfired for Iris, leaving Rachel to bail her out. Sven ended up terrorizing Mac and Rachel, and the incident brought them closer together than ever, with Iris foiled yet again. With all of her closest relationships deteriorating, Iris left Bay City to visit friends on the Riviera. When she returned home a month later, no one was particularly happy to see her.

When Amanda was born, it was revealed that Iris was not Mac's natural daughter—she had been adopted. Crushed by this startling revelation, an hysterical Iris fled with Brian to their villa in St. Tropez. Iris no longer referred to Mac as "Daddy," and Mac felt guilty when Brian reported that she was behaving in a childlike manner, neither eating nor sleeping and wishing him dead. Brian was loving and supportive, but Iris's behavior continued to be oversensitive and erratic. Finally she pretended to reconcile with Mac and Rachel, hoping somehow to make Mac pay for all the heartache she'd experienced.

While causing dissension in the Cory household, Iris seemed to be all sweetness and light. Her unpredictable and spoiled behavior kicked back into gear, however, and she managed at last to split up Mac and Rachel. Anxious to keep them apart, Iris encouraged Janice Frame's romance with Mac. It worked, although ironically Janice was the one who wanted Mac's inheritance and tried to poison him to get it. He was saved by Rachel, after which the two reunited, and Iris moved to Houston with Dennis to rekindle

When her adored father, Mackenzie Cory, married Rachel Davis, Iris became obsessed with breaking up the happy couple.

Cecile used lover Peter Love and Cass Winthrop to further her ambitions.

shot Carl during his wedding to Rachel. She believed there were blanks in the gun, and all she intended to do was scare Carl into not going through with the wedding. But real bullets were placed in the gun by a henchman working for Evan Frame, who used Iris as a means of getting back at Rachel for killing his mother, Janice. Iris was brought to trial for attempted murder. During the proceedings she uncovered Evan's guilt, but she had no proof. Iris was found guilty and sentenced to eight years in the state penitentiary, where she remains today.

A forgiving Rachel and a not-so-forgiving Carl paid Iris a visit in jail. The last thing she said was, "Life is too short for regrets."

Cecile de Poulignac

When Cecile de Poulignac arrived in town from Europe, her mother, Elena de Poulignac (who she thought at the time was her stepmother), was having an affair with the much younger Dennis Carrington. When Dennis and Cecile became attracted to each other, Dennis's scheming mother, Iris, was overjoyed—Iris despised Elena. However, Cecile became interested in Jamie Frame, and in an elaborate scheme to get her back with Dennis, Iris brought Cecile's old flame Philip Lyons to town. Iris thought that bringing the womanizing Philip back into Cecile's life would certainly destroy any permanent relationship between Cecile and Jamie, and when Philip jilted Cecile, the way would be paved for her to run into Dennis's waiting arms. But like so many of Iris's schemes, the plan backfired, and Bay City's most notorious femme fatale emerged from the fray.

According to producer and show historian, Scott Collishaw, "Cecile started as a sweet young thing—a very sweet, innocent girl, and she was supposed to marry a guy whom the audience knew was bad. We knew that he was stringing her along. It literally got to the wedding. She was walking down the aisle. She got to the end of the aisle. He stood there. She was beaming up at him and he just looked down at her, and I don't remember the exact words, but the gist of his speech was, 'I'm not marrying you. This was all a

her romance with Alex Wheeler, a poor seaman whom she had loved for three short days in 1955 and who was now head of World Oil. It was then they discovered that Dennis's natural father was not Eliot Carrington but Alex. Iris and Alex planned to marry, but as they stood at the altar kissing after they were pronounced man and wife, Alex was shot in the back. Although Iris nursed him back to health, he died soon after of a stroke.

Iris returned to Bay City claiming that she wanted to help her father fight a hostile takeover of Cory Publishing, but Rachel discovered that Iris had orchestrated the takeover and insisted she tell Mac the truth. Iris tried to explain to Mac that she was just trying to get his love, attention, and respect, which she felt she'd never had. Mac didn't buy into her excuse: "You're dead to me, Iris. You're not my daughter anymore," he told her. Iris was devastated, but never stopped protecting Mac, even after his death. Outraged when Rachel took up with Mac's arch-enemy, Carl Hutchins, she constantly voiced her disapproval. In June of 1994, Iris inadvertently sham.' It was all boom, boom, boom, bang, bang, bang, blah-blah-blah, see you later, honey, and he stormed out of the church. But it wasn't anything she had done.

"Then what happened was just brilliant. In that moment they gave her a Scarlett O'Hara speech, where she said, 'I've been good. I've been sweet. I've always done the right thing. Well as God is my witness, I will never do the right thing again. I will scheme. I will connive. I will do whatever I have to, and no man is ever going to humiliate me like that again.' And from that moment on, Cecile became a conniving little bitch who just did whatever she did to get what she wanted. I thought it was brilliant because this was an instance where you saw a character was good, saw something happen to her that was devastating, and saw her make a willful decision to change, and say 'I'm not going to be the little stepped-on throw rug anymore.'"

Cecile was hurt—so hurt that no one would ever be allowed to enter her little world again without sharing some of her pain. Nancy Frangione, who played Cecile, said, "The character's resultant behavior was extreme, yet hardly unrealistic, considering the feelings Cecile experienced in her disastrous encounter with Philip. She felt terribly betrayed and from then on she didn't trust people. She decided that the hurt was strong enough to seek revenge. She was so hurt that she didn't care who she hurt back to make her feel better.

"In the months that followed, Cecile became a one-woman bulldozer. When she wanted something, she came out with guns blazing, and what she wanted was power, money, and respect. She lied, cheated, and married to get her hands on it, and she did quite well, marrying Jamie Frame, Sandy Cory, and the King of Tanquir. Not a one-man woman by any means, Cecile used lovers Peter Love and Cass Winthrop to further her ambitions.

"There's very little this woman won't do, and kidnapping seems to be a specialty. Years ago she kidnapped Cass on what was supposed to be his wedding day to Kathleen and brought him to Tanquir—she wanted him to father a child because the king couldn't. Only recently she kidnapped her own daughter, Maggie, in a scheme to collect ransom money, and that was after she tried to pass her off as Cass's child. Who knows what she'll try next. . . ."

Lila Roberts Cory

Lisa Peluso, who plays Lila, describes her as "a strong-willed, very determined, deeply wounded femme fatale, who wants nothing more than to have the love of her life love her back, have the nice warm home that she never had, and some money wouldn't be too bad either, since she was raised in a brothel. However, Miss Lila doesn't have a clue how to go about it in any sort of proper fashion. No, she finds it much easier to lie and scheme and manipulate, having absolutely no faith that things would ever truly work out in her favor if she'd just let them be. No inner peace for poor Lila.

"She grew up on Bourbon Street. Her mother was killed—stabbed—in front of her when she was eight years old. In the rain. To this day Lila has a real phobia about rainstorms. Bad things always happen when it rains. Another time she was walking along the river walk in the rain, coming home from secretarial school, which she worked hard to put herself through, and these drunk college boys jumped out and took turns trying to fondle and molest her. Then Shane came out of the mist dressed in his air force uniform—her knight in shining armor and thus her savior. Hence her obsession with Shane, the only man she's ever slept with"—until Matt.

"Lila learned at a very young age that she never had to sleep with men to get what she wanted from them. All she had to do was smell pretty and charm her way and flatter them, and men often were putty in her hands. She loved Shane so much. She worked very hard to help put him through medical school because she was hoping that he being a doctor would be their ticket out of poverty."

But while they were married, Peluso continues, "Lila became clingy and needy. She was pregnant and she had a miscarriage. She blamed Shane for not being there more for her, and this is what drove a wedge between them—then he had an affair with the chief of staff's wife and she ended up dead. The chief of staff had figured out a wonderful way to do in both his

wife and Shane. He gave her a lethal injection and pinned the murder on Shane."

Lila fled, with a letter from the chief of staff that she never opened. Peluso says, "Shane believed Lila did it because of her hot temper and that she found out about the affair. So Shane confessed to a murder he never committed to protect Lila, and ended up on death row.

Meanwhile, she read this letter and had proof that Shane didn't kill anyone. Just as she was ready to go to the jail and tell him, the prison burned down and Lila was told that Shane was dead. She tried to kill herself, and ended up in Sister Patricia's clinic, where Shane's sister nursed her back to health.

"Meanwhile, nobody else had the proof that Lila had to release Shane—who didn't die in the fire—so Shane went on the lam thinking Lila had just gone mad, and he showed up in Bay City and meets Vicky Hudson. He couldn't admi that he was a doctor because they might find him and put him back on death row, so he became

Bobby Reno, a racing car driver. Time went by and he fell totally in love with Vicky.

"Around that time he was arrested and they found out he wasn't Bobby Reno. Vicky teamed up with Jake and they tried to get him released because she knew the kind of man he was and that he wouldn't kill anybody. Lila realized that no matter how sick she was, she had to get this letter into the hands of someone who could help. She went to the airport and managed to drop the letter so that Detective Sinclair found it. This letter, coupled with Vicky's efforts, released Shane from prison. Vicky got the victory, Shane and Vicky went off together, and there was poor Lila. In that first year, she did nothing but try to get her husband back."

When Shane died in a car crash, Lila blamed Vicky and set about to destroy her marriage to Jake and let her see how it felt to lose a loved one. Peluso says, "I think there will always be something against Vicky in her heart, but right now, the attention has shifted. She doesn't really believe that love is out there for her. She's awful tired living this life of being one of the have-nots, so Matt Cory and this baby are her ticket to Easy Street. She does genuinely believe that the baby needs two parents because she knows what it means to be a bastard child. But she wants the whole package, not only for her baby, but very deeply for herself." It was supposed to be a christening for their daughter, Jasmine, but when Matt Cory surprised her and proposed, Lila thought she'd finally achieved the respectabililty she longed for and she said yes.

Of Lila's union with Matt, Peluso says, "She was genuinely fond of Matt, but no one has taken her heart like Shane." Enter Cass. "Cass is the only one she can charm some of the time but not all of the time, and most of the time he calls her on her stuff! Tells it like it is! This is brand new for Lila. A strong man she can't manipulate? 'I hate you, but I really like you, but I hate you!' What does she do with him? What she does is confide in him, because those few times she has tested him to see if he would give her up, he hasn't. Cass is the one person she genuinely trusts, because in spite of the fact that he knows her,

Lila Roberts, now Cory, would sell her soul for respectability and wealth, and recently she did just that.

she can't pull her stuff on him, he's still hanging around. And she always asks him, 'Well, what do you care anyway? Why are you so interested in who I marry and what I do? It's my life, leave me alone!' And he doesn't go away. But at the same time, because she feels she's trash, I don't think she can see that maybe he really cares. He must want something like all men do. So she's on the fence. I don't think she really even knows how she feels about him, but he's definitely intriguing. Cass has been the one person who says to her, 'I believe in you.'"

But Lila's "got to take care of business, got to get the house and the money. She's alone in the world, and what's she going to do on a secretary's salary? It's not just that Lila's greedy and that she wants a father for Jasmine—she definitely wants to live in the house on the hill like her mamma talked about. She was illegitimate, and marrying someone legitimate will legitimize her. If she marries a Cory it will validate her. She's no longer Miss Lila Roberts from New Orleans who grew up in a brothel where her mamma was a whore and she never knew her daddy. Now she's Mrs. Lila Cory and you better not mess with her! She'll have respect. That was part of her drive behind getting into this family and why she does it so shamelessly!"

Lila *is* Mrs. Cory now, and she lives in the house on the hill with her husband and child, but her nights are lonely and filled with longing for Cass.

The Executive Branch Celebrates 35 Years of *Another World*

P & G

Bob Wehling, Senior Vice President

Wehling remembers *Another World*'s highlights over the past 35 years: "The whole saga of the Cory family and particularly the initial coming together of Mac and Rachel is just absolutely what soap opera is all about. Vicky (Wyndham) has done a terrific job in developing Rachel and keeping the audience enthralled through lots of trauma and changes over the years. Some of the Cass and Kathleen episodes were tremendous fun. And then Felicia through the years—Linda Dano has done a great job in keeping a somewhat zany character in and out of mischief and fun. Another wonderful thing about this show is the quality of the cast: Vicky Wyndham, Linda Dano, Stephen Schnetzer, Jensen Buchanan—all of them have brought so much to this show and we're grateful for that."

Wehling concludes, "I am personally optimistic about the future of this show and very hopeful that we can get some magic out of this production and writing team that, together with our wonderful cast, can build the ratings and set the stage for the 40th anniversary book."

Phil Dixson

Senior Vice President
Managing Director for Daytime Programs, TeleVest, Inc.
"Before joining Benton & Bowles' Media Management group, I was head of CBS Operations' Design Services department. So naturally, I had more than a passing familiarity with the Procter & Gamble CBS soaps. But I had no clue about *Another World* over on NBC, except that it was my wife's favorite show—Alice Matthews with her big beauty-pageant hair, the complicated Steve Frame, and low-class Rachel were a wildly popular triangle at the time.

"When I started watching *Another World* in 1980, I was immediately struck by the dark, edgy, theatrical feel and the unbelievably accomplished acting. Today, all the best characteristics of New York theatricality remain firmly embedded in *Another World*."

Mary Alice Dwyer-Dobbin, Executive in Charge of Production

"*Another World* has always had humor as one of its hallmarks. And interestingly enough, although right now we're doing sort of a far-out story line, *Another World* has also always been known for its more realistic approach to material. The acting is superb on this show. We've been blessed with that and that talent has helped to make things happen."

"We have a great quadrangle that's going on with Lila and Cass and Matt and a new character, who's recently returned, who just so happens to look exactly like Cass's late wife. It's a typical quadrangle on the one hand, but on the other hand there are many complexities that are going on. That's also been one of the hallmarks during the glory days of *Another World*. When Pete (Lemay) was writing there were many complexities to his storytelling.

One of the wonderful things in soap opera is that you can go back and dig into the history of the characters. That's interestingly enough one of the other things that I think we're getting back to now. Of course the standard-bearer over the last 25 years has been Rachel and she continues to be—she's a character that has spanned the generations and continues to delight audiences.

"I'm thrilled with the fact that Vicky and Jake have become such an effective super-couple. Vicky is one of the very special daytime heroines, and it's been fun to get the Marley character in there, too—two sisters in love with the same man. I'm very pleased that we've been able to restore the Cory family to what it looked like a few years ago, with the return of Sandra Ferguson and Matt Crane. People like Judi Evans Luciano and Joe Barbara bring an awful lot to a very traditional type of soap couple.

"I'm also glad that we've got a writing team in place, several of whom know the history of the show. We can't forget what the soap opera genre means to the viewers—they need more than just a surface story. They know these characters better than some of their own family members, so they need to get more from the storytelling, and I think that's what we're finally able to deliver to them."

Bill Graham, *Director of Creative Affairs*

"I look at soap operas as being different than almost any other form of storytelling except books. They are more analogous to books than they are to other entertainment mediums, and I look at every episode as a page. The nature of our audience is that they want to get involved in picking up their book each day and escaping into it. So every day needs to be filled with characters that they've been involved with for years, because if they've been watching for four or five years, they've read 1,200 pages.

"The other interesting thing about daytime is that in the male-dominated world which we live in, the female fantasy has to be women taking action. That is why I believe the Vickys and Rachels. These women of action become so important to the audi-

ence because if they do crazy things to get what they want and yet remain appealing people, people I want to root for, I can do the same thing. Look at Paulina's history, look where she could go. Lila, Cindy, Vicky, Marley, Donna, Remy, Rachel, Amanda. We're talking not only about fascinating characters and women who are very capable of taking action, but really spectacular actresses. This may be the finest female cast in daytime."

Gillian Strum, *Publicist for* Another World

I am the liasion between the actors and the press," Strum explains. "As *Another World*'s media advisor, not only am I here to promote the show, but to protect it as well."

Strum's main focus is securing coverage about the show and the actors in mainstream magazines and newspapers, as well as on radio and television. "My six years at *Another World* have taught me to be a shrewd and innovative thinker—to use creative angles to promote our show," she reveals. For example, a show idea that she pitched to E! Entertainment Television's *Fashion Emergency* ultimately resulted in an exclusive episode, which featured the talents of *Another World*'s behind-the-scenes staff and fashion expert Linda Dano, and made the dreams of an aspiring actress come true.

Strum concludes, "Effective communication and a passion for publicity are the keys to success in this job. I have been fortunate to have the opportunity to work with actors who are so totally accessible and excited about doing publicity."

N   B   C

Kathy Talbert, *Director of Daytime Programming, East Coast*

"*Another World*'s distinction is that our audience has always counted on this show for a certain amount of

reality. They also clearly like the humor, so that would be the second distinguishing element. We have an extraordinarily talented group of people—phenomenal.

Kathy Talbert congratulates Victoria Wyndham on her 25th year as Rachel on Another World.

Douglass Watson, who played Mac, was astonishingly charismatic. He was a great partner for Rachel. Donna and Michael, and Reginald taking those twins—that was huge. Since I've been around, those twins have grown up and gotten together, and I love Vicky and Marley. I also loved Jake and Paulina and Lila and Cass. Another relationship I should add is Frankie and Cass, because she's the one that nabbed him. Cass's relationships were big, fun, and there was always humor and a bit of the melodrama.

"You can see the humor in certain characters: Felicia and Wallingford were wildly popular; Felicia and Cass; Cass and whomever he is with. Somehow the wit really comes through. And I did love when Charles Keating was a villain on our show—it was amazing that they cast a British actor, so elegant, a wonderful, delicious villain. I've always liked the friendships of Vicky and Paulina and Rachel and Felicia.

"*Another World* has been a very important part of NBC's lineup for a long time, because, remember, this show was the number one show when it was a half hour. And then it went to the hour and it was still number one, because Pete Lemay was breaking

ground with his stories. I've always loved this show. It has a lot of depth, a little more maturity, and a kind of uniqueness. *Another World* has never been superficial and that's always been important to this group."

Another World's Executive Producers

Allen Potter: 1964–1966
Doris Quinlan: March 1965–July 1965
Paul Robert: 1965–1966
Mary Harris: 1966–1969
Lyle B. Hill: 1969–1971
Paul Rauch: December 1971–1983
Allen Potter: 1983–1984
Stephen Schenkel: 1985–March 1986
John Whitesell: 1986–1988
Michael Laibson: 1988–1993
Terri Guarnieri: 1993–1994
John Valente: 1994–1995
Jill Farren-Phelps 1995–1996
Charlotte Savitz: 1996–1998
Christopher Goutman: 1998–present

Paul Rauch, Executive Producer, *1972–1983*

"*Another World* probably had the finest assembled cast of New York and Broadway actors in our business: Brian Murray, Charles Durning, and Morgan Freeman. I cast Vicky Wyndham in 1972. The story that made us number one was the development of the Mac–Rachel–Iris story. We had a lot of theater directors, too—a special combination of actors and directors and writers. I think the key ingredient was the relationship between Pete Lemay and myself. We worked seven years together on that show. Pete and I did all the development and the casting; we collaborated on all the creative duties on the show. Doug Marland was the chief breakdown writer for Pete for a while, and it was just that wonderful symbiotic joining of talented people. It was really the golden age of that show."

A landmark first for *Another World,* and a defining moment in the history of soap opera, was the expansion of the show to an hour. Rauch remembers, "In 1974 I went to NBC and asked if they could give us another half an hour—the time period of a show called *How to Survive a Marriage*—so we could do the Steve–Alice wedding. Already Pete and I were feeling that the show was bursting out of its seams at half an hour. They gave us a half an hour in June of 1974 and we produced an hour program that was huge in the ratings. On the strength of that, I recommended to P&G and to NBC that they go to an hour for the program, which was unheard of at the time. In January of '75 we went on with an hour and we were an instant success. Then Fred Silverman (president of NBC) wanted us to go to ninety minutes. So we went to ninety minutes for a year and a half. And we produced the show at both studios in Brooklyn, put it on the air, and at its height it did very well. But eventually we just couldn't sustain that much viewer interest. So NBC reduced us back to an hour and then they asked the Corringtons and me to develop a new program and it went on the air as *Texas* in 1980."

Christopher Goutman, Executive Producer

Goutman brings impressive credentials to his position. As an actor, he had roles on *Search for Tomorrow, Edge of Night,* and *Texas,* and he has been a director in daytime for the past 17 years, including five years on *Another World* in the mid-eighties. One of the first shows he directed here was the double wedding between Mac and Rachel and Sandy and Blaine. Goutman remembers, "From that moment on I was just really taken by these people—it's such a rich show." Goutman was the recipient of an Emmy for his work on *All My Children* and before he took over at *Another World,* he received a nomination from the Directors Guild of America for his work on *As the World Turns.* Says Goutman, "As an actor and as a director, I've been trained to understand story from a character point of view. I love big events. I love splashy things. I love gimmicks. But they don't mean anything unless they are all character-driven. So hopefully that experience will allow me to approach story from that standpoint and to allow me a fairly unique way of looking at things.

"We're using old formulas and we're constantly developing new formulas all the time, reinventing as we go along—using what we have already created, but then re-creating that and topping ourselves with this. That's where I want the show to go. I'm very optimistic about everything. There are many assets: Vicky Wyndham, Linda Dano, Stephen Schnetzer. There's no other show like it on the air! It's an acting company that has great range. Stephen Schnetzer can do a very emotional thing, but can also do something very comedic. Most shows have actors who are slotted to do one thing and repeat that one thing over and over again. If we take advantage of our actors' range, and if we apply our imagination to the storytelling, we can go a lot of places, a lot of fun places. Every character that you have in your cast has a story to tell. It's something that I've told each actor: Every day you have a story to tell, no matter if you're in the background or the foreground.

"My mantra is if it's not romantic, we're not going to be doing it. Romance is the heart of daytime. Romance is not two people jumping into bed together. Romance is searching for that person who complements you, helps you grow, defines you. Every person's looking to complete his or her identity. And that's what romance is about. If it's truly romantic, one never truly finds it and that's why we have these things going on and on forever. But the journey is the fun part. The journey is what we're dramatizing. I find that audiences—if you're true to do what you are doing—are eager to take these journeys with you. They want to get carried away. I want the thrill and surprise. The core of *Another World* is tradition and potential and I don't think that any show has greater assets in either of those areas. I'm terribly excited about it and I'm very confident. This show has strength and this show has a future."

The Storytellers

Irna Phillips: May 1964–1965 (with Bill Bell)
James Lipton: 1965–1967
Agnes Nixon: 1967–1968
Robert Cenedella: 1968–August 1971
Harding "Pete" Lemay: August 1971–April 1979
Tom King: April 1979–end of 1980
L. Virginia Brown: end of 1980–spring of 1981
Corinne Jacker: 1981–1982
Robert Soderberg: 1982
Dorothy Ann Purser: 1983
Richard Culliton: 1984–1985
Gary Tomlin: 1985
Sam Hall: August 1985–1986
Margaret DePriest: 1986–January 1988
Sheri Anderson: February 1988–April 1988
Harding "Pete" Lemay: September 1988–October 1988
Donna Swajeski: November 1988–November 1992
Peggy Sloane: November 1992–November 1994
Carolyn Culliton: November 1994–August 1995
Tom King and Craig Carlson: August 1995–May 1996
Margaret DePriest: May 1996–January 1997
Elizabeth Page, Tom King, and Craig Carlson: January 1997–March 1997
Tom King and Craig Carlson: March 1997–April 1997
Michael Malone: April 1997–December 1997
Richard Culliton: December 1997– May 1998
Richard Culliton and Jean Passanante: May 1998–July 1998
Jean Passanante: July 1998
Leah Laiman: July 1998–present

*K*nown as the mother of soap operas, the late **Irna Phillips** created *Another World* while she was still writing *As the World Turns*. *World Turns* was so successful that Irna originally conceived her new serial as a spinoff, and the original scripts had mem-

bers of the Hughes family from Oakdale visiting the Matthews in Bay City. The new show was originally planned for CBS, but was turned down because their afternoon lineup was full, but was quickly picked up by NBC. As the story goes, the title *Another World* came about because NBC, seeking a hit as big as *As the World Turns,* wanted another "world," and the show's title was Irna's droll way of exploiting that show's success. Irna knew that she had to live up to her reputation and wasn't about to take any chances with a prolonged wait for ratings, which often happens when a new soap goes on the air. In that vein, she opened the show with a terrible family tragedy, the death of Bill Matthews, patriarch of the Matthews family, and followed with an out-of-wedlock pregnancy, a septic abortion, a murder trial, and a story of young love between a beautiful orphan and a wealthy young man that was thwarted by his meddlesome, social-climbing mother. This type of high melodrama was a radical departure from the domestic drama and homey philosophy of daily living and family values that characterized Irna's other shows and it was clear that she was out of her element. For the short time that she wrote *Another World*, the ratings were horrendous and the show was almost canceled. It was the vision of Procter & Gamble's Bob Short, who saw the show's possibilities and wanted to give it a chance, that saved the day. Unable to live with the failure, Irna left and was briefly replaced by James Lipton.

When daytime legend **Agnes Nixon** took over as head writer in 1967, the first thing she did was to kill off all of James Lipton's new characters in a plane crash and bring back the exiled Matthews family. Then she put orphan Missy Palmer in dire jeopardy by having Missy lured into marriage by sleazy Danny Fargo, and then being tried for his murder. The ratings soared to 10! But it was the love story that Agnes Nixon created for Alice Matthews that was to become one of daytime television's most powerful romances. Noting how well Jacquie Courtney (Alice Matthews) and George Reinholt (Steve Frame) worked together, Nixon fashioned a triangle with Alice, Steve, and Alice's scheming upwardly mobile sister-in-law, Rachel. Nixon had already written the bible for *All My Children* and she patterned Rachel after Erica Kane. Nixon has written that "Rachel was a character with doom potential—meaning that she is destructive, but was ultimately a greater threat to herself than to other people." By creating a love triangle between a handsome, self-made millionaire, a destructive young woman from a similar background who appealed to his sexual longings, and a gentle and kind young woman with good upbringing, Nixon fired the imaginations of viewers with a drama that ultimately fulfilled Irna's original promise of a story encompassing different psychological worlds.

*H*arding Pete Lemay, *Another World*'s head writer from 1971 to 1979, was an author, a teacher, and a man of the theater, and his years on the show were characterized as the Golden Age of *Another World.* Lemay says, "I think one of the things that worked in those days was that Paul Rauch was the producer I worked with mostly, and I had been trained from the theater, so we both used the same vocabulary of subtext and motivation. I was allowed a great deal of freedom in those days because the ratings were high and I'd been on the show for about a year."

One of the stories Lemay was most proud of was Ada's late-in-life pregnancy and how that contributed to the transformation and deepening of Rachel's character. Lemay explains, "She came to be her mother's mother in a way. She comforted her, took care of her during her pregnancy, because Ada was very concerned about it. We were trying to change Rachel from being the worst bitch on television to a more sympathetic character, because I wanted Beverlee McKinsey to be the bitch and I didn't want two. And I

didn't want a brunette bitch, I wanted a blond!" Says Lemay of Beverlee McKinsey: "She was a very good actress . . . on a level that a lot of actresses aren't. You never knew what she was going to do next and she was so sophisticated, she was so subtle in what she did and she was so vulnerable. Iris came on as a heavy. And then we brought her father in because she was supposed to have a fortune. A very good actor named Bob Emhadrt played it but he was not romantic. He played it for three weeks and then I saw Douglass Watson in a play with the Andrew sisters and I called Paul and I said, 'Look I know who we need for Mac Cory. Go see that show and let's talk.' He agreed with me and we asked Douglass to do it, because I wanted a romantic older man."

In terms of family, Lemay says, "I wanted the upper-class jet-set that was what Iris and Mac represented, and I wanted the working class that the Perrinis represented. Because you get more conflict, you get different values, and you can do scenes like Iris taking the girl who's going to marry her son out to lunch and correcting her grammar—all kinds of things that you don't normally do on television because you're playing off different levels of economic and cultural backgrounds. That's always been the fun in writing." Lemay was responsible for bringing on the Frames, a family patterned closely on his own: "They're all farmers. I brought on Sharlene, Willis, Vince, and Janice. Aggie had set up Steve Frame as an only child. It had been in the scripts and I decided I didn't want to go that way with it. There were too many mysteries about it. He was too ambiguous a character, so I wanted to play off both sides of him. He was so ashamed of his family, he pretended he was an only child, and I made that the story. They all did show up to use him—one by one."

Lemay recalls expanding the show to an hour: "I wanted to do the hour because I wanted to write five-minute scenes. The first one had an enormously long scene, perhaps seven minutes, between Steve and Alice, and that was their reconciliation. Coming from writing plays was very interesting to me. I decided, because I didn't know how to write a soap—

I'd never watched them or anything—I would write a one-act play every day. That was when it was a half hour, with a beginning, a middle, and an end. One straight line going through it. Then the next day I'd pick up a different story and I'd write that as a one-act play and sometimes thread a little of one story into another. When we went to the hour, I insisted they shoot it in sequence, because I wrote counterpoint scenes a great deal. It gave a much more interesting story design."

Lemay left during the show's ninety-minute run and returned briefly in 1988. His experiences as head writer are chronicled in his book, *Eight Years in Another World.*

Both **Richard** and **Carolyn Culliton** have long associations with *Another World*. Carolyn's first job in New York was for *Another World*'s executive producer, Paul Rauch. Carolyn was on *Another World*'s writing staff for seven years, 1984 to 1991. Richard was head writer from 1984 to 1985. Then Carolyn came back as head writer in 1994. Presently Carolyn is script editor and Richard is writing breakdowns.

"We watched *Another World* because there were all these fabulous actors on it," Richard explains. "These New York actors like Douglass Watson, Kathleen Widdoes, Ray Liotta, Irene Dailey. It had an edge and a wit that was unique." Richard wrote scripts for *Texas,* went on to become head writer on *Guiding Light,* and then cameback to *Another World*. "They were years of wonderful humor, which is one of the hallmarks of this show." The capers of Wallingford, Felicia, Cass, Cecile, and Lily Mason were fan favorites. Richard explains, "We were told Wallingford could be on for one week and that was it and we just kept right on writing and he was like the heart of that group of characters. We had all these people who didn't have traditional families and they became a family. It always seemed to be the real spirit of the show that these people, who had no reason to be together and were completely different in every possible way, were best friends and watched each other's backs."

Carolyn explains her duties: "I make the characters stylistically consistent. When you have characters who are witty, it's a challenge to keep them always sounding like they're at the top of their form. It's not so much domestic chat. It has to have sophistication to it. I always say it's theatrical, the emotions are bigger."

Carolyn describes what defines the show: "There was always a very rigid class structure. There was always a very rich class, a middle class, and a blue collar. There were the Frames, the Matthews, and then Mac Cory. And Richard has said this—the good people could move through all three and be comfortable and the bad people were like Iris: they had to stay where they were. Ada could poke holes in the pretension."

In answer to what makes *Another World* unique in the soap opera lineup, Carolyn cites "the actor caliber"; Richard cites "the wit."

*I*t was a magazine article for *Cosmopolitan* called "Good Girls Who Like Bad Boys" that brought *Another World*'s current head writer, **Leah Laiman,** to write for daytime, originally for *General Hospital*. Laiman explains the soap opera genre, "The truth of the matter is, you are making up stories every minute of every day and you're getting to see it a very short time later—whether it's exactly what you wanted or not, it's done. Now try writing a movie and see what happens. You know if it gets on the screen at all, you're lucky, and if it's within five years you're really lucky.

"I've always felt—and it's obvious, it's nothing new—that it's love stories. It's romance and suspense, and not suspense in the sense of who killed so-and-so or who's going to be stalked next, although that can certainly heighten it. But it's emotional suspense. Every story, even a mystery story has to have an element of *when will they kiss?* Clearly in soap opera, family relationships are hugely important. But it has to be intertwined with the rest.

"Maybe what defines *Another World* is the fact that it is a more character-driven show. This show is about individual characters and how they interact with others who are equally appealing. The perfect example is Felicia and Cass. On another show, they would be related somehow. They would be brother and sister. But here they're not. They're just the deepest and closest and most loving of friends and I just find that true of a lot of characters, even when they are related. That's what the show's about. It's about character in a very specific and individual way."

*F*ollowing a long-standing *Another World* tradition co-head writer **Jean Passanante** came to daytime from the theater. "I work with Leah on everything," Passanante says. "We plan the week together and then one of us oversees the scripts. We tend to divide up. She's more in the outline front and I'm more on script front to some degree, although Carolyn (Culliton) certainly is the scriptmeister on our show, and a lot of what I do with Leah is working on story. It's been a very harmonious partnership. I

think we complement each other. She's a wonderful romantic storyteller and I tend to get dark and psychological. Everybody knows that people watch soap opera for romance and fantasy and escape. However, I think people watch soap opera because they develop a relationship with the characters over time. Although the show has its kind of out-there moments, it tends be realistic, in that people have real emotions and real experiences even though they are extreme and fanciful. Humor is a great thing. The days of turning on the soap to weep over your ironing board are long over. If we're going to buy the premise that we watch soaps to experience people's lives, we want to see characters in all situations and that includes humorous situations.

"*Another World* always had an extremely strong cast of very interesting people who were not cookie-cutter cutouts. It always had a dynamic, a supercharged quality. It didn't seem shy or domestic. Some of the families are now gone, but the central family is very strong with a strong female character in the middle. I still hear from people all the time who are so invested in Rachel's romantic life and her family and everything that she's been through. She's been a character that people strongly identify with and live through."

Inside the *Another World* Studio

Producer and show historian, **Scott Collishaw** and *Another World* go way back: "It was the very first  soap I ever watched. It's the only soap I've ever been hooked on. I started as a secretary, and have been here ever since! We have three line producers, and we split the producing schedule among the three of us. So the bottom line is you do two shows a week and then you have a week when you only do one." On the day of the shoot, I tell people, I have the best job in the world. I sit in the back of the room and I watch a TV and I get to say, 'That's good and that's bad.' I say,

Since its inception, *Another World* has taped its shows at the NBC studio rich in movie and televison lore in this quiet Brooklyn neighborhood known as Midwood. Mary Beth Scalia, manager of the NBC Brooklyn studios, says, "People always say, 'Oh, NBC has a studio in Brooklyn?' In an interview once I referred to us as what I call the firstborn child that moved out and went to Brooklyn to live on its own. We were built before Burbank—so before there was Burbank, there was Brooklyn! This building has so much history! Studio One was built in 1915 and Studio Two in 1953, when Midwood was a major film center. During the silent movie era, Warner Brothers owned Studio One and when the talkies came in, the Vidagraph Studios were built across the street. *Birth of a Nation* was shot in Studio One. The last film out of Vidagraph was *Baby Doll,* starring Carroll Baker. When television burst on the scene many popular and award-winning shows were produced from these studios: the fifties saw *The Hallmark Hall of Fame, The Bell Telephone Hour, The Perry Como Show* and Mary Martin's *Peter Pan,* and more recently, the first *Saturday Night Live.* Esther Williams taped specials here and her pool is underneath Studio One. From 1984 to 1987, the wildly popular *Cosby Show* occupied Studio Two."

'Fix the lighting. Their performance needs to be a little better there. Can she be angrier? Can she be happier? Can they make it sexier? I don't like that dress—can we change the costume?' Literally it runs the gamut, and I'm in charge. My feeling is that in good soap opera, each scene should have a point and something should happen in that scene that makes a step forward. My job as a producer is to understand what that point is, so when I'm watching the scene taped, I just want to make sure that's clear."

When he's not producing, Collishaw attends the weekly breakdown meetings. As show historian, Collishaw has "been sort of known for being the one in the breakdown meetings who says, 'You know, six years ago we kind of did something like this.' So I'm not always the most popular person in breakdown meetings."

At *Another World*, producer **Leslie Kwartin**'s area is writers, scripts, and character tracking. She feels that what makes *Another World* unique in the soap opera lineup is that it "seems to take more fantastic risks. I think its title, too, allows it to go somewhere else. Certainly in the nineties people are more willing to travel to that place of fantasy or the nonphysical. The culture's ready for us to do that."

As a line producer, **Carole Shure** says, "We are responsible for an episode from beginning to end. That means from pre-production through post-production. And we're the ones who approve that final show for the air. We're in on the edit, in on the scoring. If the script is long or short, we deal with that. If there are actors who have a problem with material, we deal with that. If a director has a problem for those one or two shows a week, ideally we follow that through."

A chance ticket to an Emmy luncheon led to **Michelle de Vito**'s present position as assistant to the executive producer. Michelle performs all administrative duties, not just for the executive producer, but for

the line producers as well, and that includes phones, expenses, supplies, appointments, distributing scripts, the daily pouch, fan mail, and much more. De Vito says, "My job is to make it as easy as possible for the executive producer. I feel like the mother. Everyone is close. I'm in charge of sending gifts for anything that comes up, any occasion. Whether it's a funeral, wedding, congratulations. I always put, 'With our love, your *Another World* family,' because it is."

Associate producer **Gina Taravella Ricci** interned at *Another World* when she was in college and has been there ever since. Gina is responsible for scheduling and there's a lot to keep straight: what sets go in what studio, what actors are on vacation or performing in a Broadway show, scheduling the babies on the show when they can be exposed to bright lights only briefly and need their naps! "As soon as I get the script, I read it and pick apart what sets are where and see what day they have to have it taped. We had a scene once, it might have been Jake and Vicky in Jake's old apartment. He was in a rage and he was supposed to throw things around. So he took these pillow cushions off the couch and started throwing them and all these script pages came flying out! The actors looked at the lines and shoved them under. You find scripts in the strangest places."

Production coordinator **Louisa Cross** says, "We're the hub of *Another World* on the production side of things." Her colleague **Jen Chambers** adds, "We get the control room and everyone ready for the following day of taping. We make sure the directors know everything, the producers know everything, the actors know everything. We get everyone to the studio. We get everyone home—which is an adventure." Creating a montage is a favorite assignment. Cross explains, "That's the most creative thing we do." Production coordinator **Daniel Griffin** does script continuity, which entails reading every script that comes into the building. And what kinds of things does he catch? "Just last week I noticed that Jake was in two places at once." He then passes that information on to script editor Carolyn Culliton. "Obviously the story lines are very intricate and they're all tangled up together," Griffin continues, "so it's my job to see through all the tangles and make sure that everyone is consistent. We have a medical adviser, whom I work with on a weekly basis. I'm responsible for making sure that any script that contains any sort of medical issues is accurate. If we're playing a series of scenes in a hospital room, obviously we're going to need the right medical equipment."

Casting director **Jimmy Bohr** says, "It's the casting

This is where production coordinators, Louisa Cross, Daniel Griffin, Jen Chambers, seen here with PA Kelsey Bay and Estabon Rolon, who mans the Xerox, hold down the fort.

Casting director Jimmy Bohr reviews resumes and headshots with his assistant casting director, Elizabeth Wilson.

director's job to understand the taste of the executive producers and the writers—to adjust your thinking, while retaining your own integrity taste. When we're casting a major contract role, I get a character description and hopefully an audition scene, and from there I generally put together my initial ideas of people who might be right for the part. I always put out a breakdown to all the agents, usually on both coasts, New York and Los Angeles. Then I start seeing people whom I don't know, or people whom I do know who might be right for the part. I can see hundreds of people if I have enough lead time. I try hard to bring a wide variety of personalities and talent to the table, anyone who might be remotely viable, because to bring all of the same type—what's the point?

What makes *Another World*'s characters unique? Bohr answers, "The characters have always been a little left of the mainstream. I always cast to a sense of humor, because I think if a character can have a sense of humor about themselves, it immediately adds a depth and a dimension. That's one thing that I think our show plays to. My associate **Elizabeth Wilson** does the extras and the under-fives [characters with under five lines] and she assists me in coming up with ideas for day players and contract players, so we work as a team."

Costume designer, **Shawn Dudley,** who works with designer **Rhonda Roper,** grew up watching *Another World*. "I've been on the show for three years and I basically feel like I've moved to Bay City. I'm the little dressmaker in Bay City—Mr. Shawn's Emporium!" How does he go about building a wardrobe for a new character? "In order to dress them I have to figure out who they are. I have to do a background on them. I create my own, basically, because where you're from, how you were raised, what you do, where you live, all that plays ultimately into the clothes that you wear. People mistake soaps as just something where you put pretty clothes on people. In some cases maybe that's true. In our case I want to create characters.

"I rarely take the actors shopping with me because it just takes so much time. I'm quick. In this business you have to shop, and I really hate shopping. So when I shop for these characters, I have to think, 'Okay, where would this person shop in real life?' and that's where I go. Remy is not going to shop in Saks. Felicia's not going to shop in The Gap. *Another World* has a reputation for being a well-dressed show, and we've got a whole handful of characters whom the audience demands a certain look from."

Liz Spagnola has been with the *Another World* costume design department for twenty years and has nothing but praise for the cast. Spagnola says, "When you come in that door, you're truly in another world."

Heavy is the head that wears the headpiece for the ball. Linda Dano studies her lines in full Lumina regalia.

Sean Rademaker (Kirkland Harrison) and Spencer Treat Clark (Steven Frame) are obviously enjoying the costumes they'll be wearing to their mother's annual Halloween party.

Hair stylist Stanley Hall gets Judi Evans Luciano (Paulina) ready for the set.

Head makeup artist Kevin Bennett works with makeup artists Maryanne Spano, Francesca Buccellato, and Eldo Estes. "Personally, I've been in *Another World* all my life," confesses Bennett. "I've watched it a long, long time. It's my baby and I handle it with tender loving care. I was starstruck the first day I walked in here and it was quite an interesting adventure. I had what I call a trial by fire on ice. My first day here was Jake's funeral, which was shot on 'location' outside the studio on 13th Street. It was 14 degrees that day. Here you have Judi Evans Luciano, the best crier on daytime, in tears for hours and hours. I mean they were freezing on her face! I remember I was standing out there, take after take, peeling tears off Judi."

Cindy Harrison shows off a Lumina costume.

Bennett says of his staff, "I'm totally blessed. The people who work with me in this department are the most unbeliev-

able makeup artists I have ever worked with. They are so professional and so talented and so able to meet any challenge and come through it. We sometimes speak almost in sign language, and we don't even need charts, even though you keep very concise charts for continuity. I feel strongly that the results you see onscreen just bring it forward because people just look really good on this show. They don't look made up."

Hair stylist **Stanley Hall** works with head hair stylist **Theresa Maria Siliceo** and stylist **Sasha Cummings.** A typical day is a long day, Hall says. "Normally there are three of us in the morning. We get here at seven o'clock on the dot. We set up rollers, blowers, anything that we need. Then around seven-thirty, everybody starts rolling in. They're supposed to come in with clean hair because we have to work pretty fast. Then we set them, if we're going to set them, and send them off to makeup with rollers in. Then they'll come back through here around a quarter after, and we'll take the rollers out and finish them off. They run down to wardrobe, get dressed, and then they're on the set. One of us will go down to the set and one will be up here. Somebody's always in the room because, depending on the time of the day, people are still coming through. Sometimes five women are up at once, and they all have to be ready at eight o'clock. The afternoon people come in around twelve-thirty, so it starts all over again."

Patrick Howe, art director for *Another World*, says, after the initial research, "It's pencil to paper and about working out a ground plan. That all gets drawn up and then goes to bid for a shop to actually construct all of that. While construction is going on, we focus more on the decor. We start to shop around for furniture and props that are going to go in it. We try to select props that suit the characters, providing the right mood for the kind of stories that they're involved in. The stage-hands actually hang the pictures and hang the drapes and lay the carpets and move the furniture around, but we tell them specifically where we want everything, down to every bush and leaf. They document it all through photographs and then they store it. Then there's the technical end of it, meeting with the directors and getting them in sync with the logistics of the space. It doesn't matter how good it looks when you're standing there in person seeing it, because the viewers at home have to see it on their television screen, and they're only going to see what the directors can shoot."

Music director **Ron Brawer** works with music director **Jim Kowal.** "Generally Jim does two shows a week and I do three shows a week." Brawer works with about a dozen composers or composers groups. Brawer describes how he scores a show: "The break-downs alert me to long-term music that I might need. Then I read the script and make notes where I think music is going to go. Then the show is shot and edited. I get a copy of the show, a dub. My copy has a time code window in it, and usually it has sound effects and dialogue. I watch the show from beginning to end without stopping so I get an overall picture of what the feel of the show, the rhythm of the show, is going to be, what the scenes feel like, if they're going to need music. For example, Carlino's or the Harbor Club normally would have source music (source music is music that the characters hear, as opposed to background of underscoring emotional music that the characters don't hear)—what characters are in those scenes will often dictate the kind of source music I'm going to play. If there's important dialogue, you have to be careful that the dialogue is heard."

Videotape editors **Matthew Griffin** and **Karen DeKime** work together on alternating days to prepare the show for broadcast. The editors work on something called pro tools, which is a new computerized method of editing that incorporates sound effects and music. DeKime says, "I don't think any other show does their audio or sound effects like we do it with pro tools. We just had to do a nightmare and it had to be creepy, so we had some whistling winds go through forest and we had some owls and wolves—whatever you can do to create a mood." Another main responsibility is to tighten a show when it's running long. Griffin concludes, "It's not just editing. Now you have to design and create, and think, 'How can we do it the fastest so it doesn't cost the show?'" Their mantra: "Get it down and get it out."

On the Set—Bay City Goes to the Ball: Episode # 8722

Tape: Thursday, October 1, 1998
Air: Friday, October 23, 1998

Production assistant **Alison McKiegan,** who alternates days in the booth with PA **Kelsey Bay,** says, "The booth is mainly timing. When the scripts come out we do an estimate on the show that requires you to read through the script and actually act out the scenes like you think the cast would do them. As you time the shows, you get better at predicting how actors will respond to different material and you can kind of figure out their speech patterns. You become a pretty good mimic! Of course, it's a guestimate, so you're never on the money. Then when you start production each day, when you're in the control room and you go to dry rehearsal, you get another run at it."

After taping, everything goes to edit, including the time codes for each scene. When they call up those time codes on the tapes, the scene should be there. Props are another big part of the job. McKiegan explains, "You create a prop sheet from the script

which lists every set and scene and every prop that's needed and the time of day. Then everybody out on the set for the day uses this as their guide for what they'll need for each scene. You try to track props for the writers from scene to scene. The writer might write 'someone rings the doorbell at Chris's apartment' and you know there is no doorbell, so you make it a door knock for a sound effect."

Stage manager **Dennis Cameron** describes his responsibilities: "I don't see a script until the day of production. In the rehearsal hall in the mornings, I work with the director to learn the blocking for the actors. That's also when I learn where the cues come in each scene. I learn which props are needed, any sort of special effects. I coordinate everything so I can then delegate when I get down to the floor and say, 'This is where an actor will start and this is where they carry their prop.' I'm also in charge of choreographing the background action in all the scenes, whether it is a restaurant or a hospital. The stage manager alone works with the extras and creates all the background atmosphere for any set, which is one of my favorite parts of the job. Part of the job is also readying the next set, warning people that they're going to be needed to come down to the floor so they can go to make-up and hair and wardrobe. These are called warnings. During taping I become the eyes of the director on the floor. The director is in the control room behind a wall and the only thing he can see is what a camera shows him. I obviously get to see everything. So once everyone has completed preparations for the taping of the scene or a dress rehearsal scene, I have to make sure that everybody's ready to then do it. I think of it as the director is the engineer and I'm the caboose. He actually drives the train, but I help steer it. Once you've determined that everyone's ready, meaning the actors and the props and the wardrobe, then you just sort of have to keep things in motion—one scene after the other, culminating in forty-two minutes of dramatic material to go on the air."

Before the actors go on set, director Michael Eilbaum takes them through their paces at dry rehearsal: "You come in the morning, do a dry rehearsal—where you're situated in a room some-where in the building far away from your sets, but you pretend that you're in the sets. You give the actors all their blocking and you discuss the various points of the scene that need to be hit while they walk through with scripts, taking their notes. That's the actor and director time. After dry rehearsal you'll do the entire show when we do camera blocking, which is for the technical crew. The actors will generally get a chance to run through their scenes, but we most likely won't deal with any problems with the actors unless it's a major problem—like someone physically can't get to point B because there's a wall in the way. You look at your shots. You see if it works, what doesn't work. You make changes. Audio tells you their problems. Lighting tells you their problems. And again, you find some middle ground. You figure out what you need to do. Then you do a dress rehearsal. Have a note session. Final touch-ups. Hair, makeup, wardrobe, and taping. Everything has to happen beforehand. You don't want surprises." During taping Eilbaum divides his time between the control room and the set. In the control room he studies the monitors—each monitor represents a different camera—and calls the shots.

235

Actress Sandra Ferguson (Amanda Cory) gets a touch-up on the set from makeup artist Eldo Estes.

Stage manager Jim Semmelman, dressed to the nines doing double duty as an extra and a stage manager, reviews the script. He says, "We're basically in charge; it's kind of a psychology game. You've got to learn your actors and how they work and the best way to cue them or to give them a line or a note. So in some ways you're a father/mother/baby-sitter/friend/confidant. You're the liaison between the directors and the producers and the actor." Veteran stage manager Leslye Fagin adds, "You need to be a cheerleader on the set and keep your sense of humor while you're mobilizing all those tired Lumina actors and extras."

Director Michael Eilbaum places his actors on the set.

Taylor Stanley (Remy Woods) gives her costume a whirl.

Rachel makes a grand entrance.

Vicky courts a string of ardent admirers.

True to its mantra, "We do not live in this world alone, but in a thousand different worlds," this show has been known to visit the world of the imagination more often than not.

Another World Presents

"The Case of the Stolen Heart" 2/12/92

It is 1992, a.k.a. 1942. Francesca (Frankie) is engaged to Dr. Dapper (John), who is in cahoots with a seductive nurse named Diana (Donna). Dr. Dapper and Diana are in the business of stealing hearts. As the mystery unfolds, it is clear that someone has stolen Francesca's heart and she won't marry Dapper until she finds it. Enter Cass A. Nova, P.I.

SCENE: RICK'S PLACE. NIGHT.

Dino screams on a sax as the elevator doors open and

Francesca and Cass A. Nova

Dr. Dapper and Diana

Francesca enters, carrying a small dog with a bow in its hair. As soon as Frankie steps into the restaurant, Rick, in a white dinner jacket, greets her.

RICK: Of all the gin joints in the world, you had to walk into mine, didn't ya, Francesca?

FRANCESCA: I always come back to what I like, Rick. (walks in) The place looks smaller.

RICK: Nope.

FRANCESCA: Maybe it's just my memories that are big.

RICK: Check your coat and Pookie for you?

FRANCESCA: (hands him dog) Sure . . . for old time's sake.

RICK: Whose old time's sake, honey?

FRANCESCA: . . . I'm here to meet Cass.

RICK: Cass A. Nova? You're not still chasin' after that low-life, ten-timing, debt-filching, no-account dreamer, are ya?

FRANCESCA: What do you think, Rick?

RICK: I think your corset's on too tight, that's what I think.

FRANCESCA: I haven't seen him in five years.

RICK: I remember that. You were here. . . . It was a dark and stormy night. . . . The room was filled with smoke and perfume. . . . I had more hair. . . .

FRANCESCA: Show him to my table when he gets here.

RICK: What are you going to say to him?

FRANCESCA: I can't tell you that, Rick.

RICK: Why not?

FRANCESCA: 'Cause then what would be left to talk about after the opening credits?

With Cass A. Nova's help, Frankie found her heart and they rekindled their affair.

The episode, a black-and-white takeoff on the film noir genre, won the Emmy for *Another World*'s directing team and the DGA award for director Susan Strickler.

Another World Presents

"The Vanishing Game" or
"Murder on the Honeymoon Express" 5/20/93

It was all aboard the Orient Express for the cast of *Another World*. After several failed attempts to reach the altar, Cass and Frankie were wed in a courtyard in Venice after being kidnapped and led there by their friends. They are honeymooning on the Orient "Honeymoon" Express.

SCENE: TRAIN COMPARTMENT. PRESENT. NIGHT. MOVING

We hear the train racing through the night and then

we open on Cass and Frankie's honeymoon compartment. Having made love, they are lying in each other's arms, sated.

CASS: Happy?

FRANKIE: Mmmm . . . perfectly. (She starts to laugh)

CASS: What's so funny?

FRANKIE: Nobody else showed up at the wedding, did you notice?

CASS: Huh?

FRANKIE: During the whole ceremony, I kept looking over my shoulder wondering which one of your exes was going to show up and stop this one, too!

CASS: (Settling in, he puts his head in her lap) Oh, c'mon, Frankie—it was just that one time with Kathleen. . . .

FRANKIE: (stroking his hair) Uh-huh . . . and what about Cecile, hmm? And Nicole—

CASS: (His eyes close, but he is smiling) Gone, Mary Frances. Vanished and banished from my memory, I promise. . . .

FRANKIE: (continues to stroke his hair as he dozes off) They better be, because in case you hadn't noticed, I can be a very jealous woman. . . .

CASS: . . . I know. . . .

FRANKIE: (She smiles more, touches his forehead, and then very softly) I love you, Cass, and will always be with you. In every lifetime, in every way. . . . Sweet dreams, my darling. . . .

Cass dozes off, and in a flashback set in the '20s, he imagines he's a rogue who has just enjoyed his last fling and is ready to tie the knot. Soon after he boards the Orient Express, Cass finds trouble and temptation as he is greeted by former lovers—Felicia, Cecile, Kathleen, and Nicole. Of course, in the end, true love wins out.

SCENE: DINING CAR. NIGHT. MOVING.

FRANKIE: (takes Cass's hand) Don't you understand, my love? This is how it's supposed to be . . . !

CASS: I know it now. . . . Heck, maybe I've known it all along. . . .

JAKE: (as lights dim) And yet another crime solved by you-know-who!

FELICIA: Okay—everybody back to their beds! It's almost time to wake up!

The lights are only on Cass and Frankie now.

CASS: How could I ever think of another woman when I'm so in love with you?

FRANKIE: I told you—the past is gone . . . we have wiped it away. . . .

CASS: You are everything to me, Frankie.

FRANKIE: And you are everything to me, Cass. . . .

They kiss and the train roars into a tunnel, as we . . .

CUT TO: ACT SIX C

TRAIN COMPARTMENT. PRESENT. NIGHT. MOVING.

Cass bolts upright in bed. Frankie is dressed in a negligee.

FRANKIE: (smiles) Weird dream?

CASS: The weirdest! (He hugs her) Rachel was a Countess and Dean was a . . . never mind. (He kisses her) Reality is a whole lot better, believe me.

FRANKIE: Just make sure the ladies stay vanished, okay?

CASS: (Stunned, he smiles) But . . . but how did you know?

FRANKIE: Because you are everything to me, Cass.

CASS: And you are everything to me, Frankie.

As they fall to the bed, Frankie's hand reaches up and wipes the window clean of Kathleen's, Cecile's, and Nicole's names.

A u d i t i o n   T a l e s

Anna Stuart (Donna Love)

"I auditioned for Felicia Gallant. I'd been out of work for a year after having done *Guiding Light* and I borrowed a 'Vanessa' outfit—a big white feather boa and a beautiful white pantsuit. I went first to collect my last unemployment check (they were not pleased to see me at unemployment looking like a million dollars). I had a few minutes before I was going to read and I had to kiss Cass [Stephen Schnetzer] in the audition. So I went to the ladies' room to gargle. I'm gargling Lavoris when the bathroom door flings open: 'Anna, we're ready for you!' And I coughed out the Lavoris all down my front! So there I am, trying to arrange this white feather boa to cover up the red that's all over the white pantsuit."

Alice Barrett (Frankie Frame Winthrop)

Frankie Frame was known for her New Age philosophy. The part wasn't originally conceived that way, but came about because of a piece of jewelry that the actress wore to the audition. Barrett remembers: "When Frankie first arrived in town, she was a caffeine-swilling woman, dressed a little bit like white trash, but always vivacious. She always had a lot of energy. Since I always wore my crystal, I wore it the day of my screen test, and the costume designer liked it, so she let me keep it on. A couple of months later, there was a scene which was actually Frankie and Cass's first kiss, even though it wasn't a purposeful kiss. We're spying on Lucas and we meet at a hot dog stand and Lucas comes walking by. So Cass grabs my face to kiss me, so that Lucas doesn't see me, because I was the one who was doing the investigating. I don't eat meat, so I went to the prop department, and I said, 'Could you guys get me a tofu burger or a chicken dog, because I can't do this scene. I can't eat the meat.' One of the line producers got a hold of that and decided that from that day on Frankie was a vegetarian. Then all of a sudden they noticed the crystal and boom! Frankie became New Age."

Joe Barbara (Joe Carlino)

"I'd come really close to some pretty big things the year I auditioned for *Another World*. So by the time this came around in November, I was sort of at the point where you stop getting your hopes up. If it was a year earlier, I would have been all excited. I read the description of the character and there were so many silly little things, but they all rang true to me. Number one: His name was Joe. It was Joe McConnell, by the way. There was a description that said he was a star quarterback of the St. Edward's something High School football team, which meant he went to a Catholic high school, right? Which I did. And then it said, 'And every day his mother would say a novena that her Joey would go to college.' It said 'her Joey,' which is what my mother said, and my mother says novenas for me all the time. And it was all these little tiny things in this description that totally rang true. I read this and I said, 'This is me!'"

Anne Heche (Vicky/Marley)

"When I screen-tested for Vicky, I was wearing my Levi's, and there were all these girls in their high heels and makeup. I thought, 'There's no way I'm right for this part.' So when I got it, I thought she must be like me. John Whitesell, our producer, called me into his office and said, 'Now, I don't want to change you, or anything you do offstage, but this girl has to be sexy: the strapless dresses, the hair and makeup. Oh, and by the way, you're playing twins.' That's when I found out I was going to be in a bathtub my first day, I was the bitch of the show, and playing twins. It was a real culture shock."

Linda Dano (Felicia Gallant)

"When I auditioned for Felicia, Stephen was the actor I auditioned with, thank God! The thing I remember most about the audition was what I had said to him during it. Paul Rauch was the producer at the time, and he came out and he asked me to do something different. And you know, you're always so terrified of these things. And I said to Stephen in an off-handed comment, 'God, I just don't think I can do this! I just don't know who this character is.' There was this great look on his face that I will never forget. And he said, 'What, are you crazy! You are this character!' And I suppose that that was true, or I wouldn't be here this long. From the second that we did that audition, our fate was sealed. He and I became friends."

Stephen Schnetzer (Cass Winthrop)

Schnetzer had been on *One Life to Live* playing the antithesis of his *Another World* persona, Cass. Says Schnetzer, "He was a conservative, blue-collar, Italian beer truck driver, Marcello Salta. And they asked me to re-sign, and I said I'd be interested in re-signing, but I'd like more story responsibility. I'd like more of a challenge. The executive producer at the time said, 'I can't promise you that. And the last thing I need is to promise you that and in six months have an angry actor on my hands.' And I remember saying, 'Well, thanks anyway, but I think I can do better,' and the day after my last day on *One Life*, I screen-tested for Cass. I listened to the universe and it was right, as always. I got the job and started in a month. It was great. It was home."

John Littlefield (Gary Sinclair)

"I originally screen-tested for the roll of Shane and I tested with Jensen [Buchanan] and it didn't really work. Then I was in upstate New York shooting a movie, and then I went to Africa and shot a movie. Then I tested for Cameron. And again I went away, and I think I was in Spain and I got this phone call: 'Well, you didn't get the role of Cameron.' I said, 'Oh, okay.' 'You got the role of Matt!' I said, 'Oh, okay, cool.' Then I was in Morocco and I got a phone call and they said, 'You didn't get the role of Matt. You got the role of Gary.' I said, 'Oh! Okay, but I read with Tim Gibbs and he plays Gary.' And they said, 'Yeah, he chose not to re-sign his contract.' I said, 'Oh, okay, cool. Right on.'"

And what was his first day on the set like? "Everybody was so grand." His first scenes were with Linda Dano. "I had thirty pages with Linda Dano. I took a shower my first day. And I had to cry. I had to scream. I had to laugh. I was in hell. Gary was in hell. He almost drank. And then I was with Linda. Then I broke that statue and I was screaming and crying and laughing. All in that day. But I couldn't think of a better day. It's so much better than just, you know, John Littlefield will now portray the character of Gary Sinclair: 'Hi, Josie. Bye, Josie.'"

first day on the set

Sandra Ferguson (Amanda Cory)

"It was twenty-three hours long—the debutante ball. Every character that was on the show was in this scene, so not only did I have to learn my immediate family and be acquainted with them, but I had to learn each person who I was walking up to. I had to learn their name, their character. It was like totally being thrown into the fire. It was horrifying. Absolutely horrifying. The most horrifying experience I think I've ever endured. I didn't even know who my relatives were at that point! I had never seen the show before and I never even watched the soaps. I just totally was not familiar with the whole thing. Yes, it was a horrifying experience. And the second day was twenty hours long. So it wasn't that much better."

Ellen Wheeler (Marley Love)

"My agent called me on a Friday at about six P.M. and said, 'Now, what soap did you audition for first?' I said, '*Ryan's Hope*.' And he said, 'Then what?' I said, '*Santa Barbara*.' 'And then what?' '*Days of Our Lives*.' 'Well, you were just cast on *Another World* and you start on Tuesday.' And I said, 'I can't be cast on *Another World*! I haven't even read for them.' And he said, 'No, there's a role that was supposed to start a week ago and they haven't been able to find anybody, but of course you have test tape floating around everywhere and they saw your test tape and they were desperate to have somebody. So even though they have never seen you, you have this job on A*nother World*.'"

Wheeler had never watched the show. "I had no clue! Before I even called my mom, I picked up the phone and called the restaurant where I was waitressing graveyard shift and said, 'I quit!' I packed my apartment and got on a plane on Monday, on the red-eye so that I got here in time to come to work on Tuesday morning. I got my scripts when I got to the hotel at four in the morning. I walked into rehearsal, and I was just totally, truly, completely baffled who these people were, and how I was supposed to fit in. What any of it meant. All of a sudden I had to have all of these scenes memorized. It was really quite a day for me!

"My first scenes were with Donna and Cecile. I had been at boarding school and I was coming back from Switzerland and it was because somebody was getting married and I think that it was my brother. I thought he was my brother, but he wasn't really my brother. But yes, he was getting married and I was coming back for the wedding. So then, my first day I'm in the midst of all that, trying to stay together.

"We finished taping and they said, 'Okay, we're moving to the set.' I come from a theater family, so I think, 'Oh, we're moving to the next set,' and I see everybody starting to move, so I go out and pick up cables to help them move down to the next set and somebody starts yelling at me. 'Put down those damn cables!' They come over and scream at me, 'You know, you can't touch those. That's union rules.' I start crying, 'I'm just trying to help!' Because, of course, I thought everybody would jump in. I had no idea. I was kind of a little moron, but you learn really quickly. And now I wouldn't touch a cable! I know better."

Wheeler left the role in 1986 and returned in 1998. "You really can pick up where you left off, and that's what it was like when I came back here. I was here my first day, and I was lying on a gurney with bandages all over my face, and I didn't have to speak. And they counted, 'Five, four, three, two, one,' and Anna Stuart took my hand. The second she took my hand and said 'Marley,' it was like no time had gone by. I was back, she was my mom. And I said, 'Know what? I'm back here with my family. I'm fine. I don't have to worry about a thing.' And I felt that total connection to Jensen, the second I was back. I didn't even know her, so that's really weird. We had been parts of the same person. We had helped create the same people. A part of what I did influences how Vicky is today and part of what she did influences how my Marley is today, so it's an odd thing to say, but it gave us a common ground immediately."

Mark Mortimer (Nick Hudson)

"I don't remember. I chose to forget. I was so nervous. My mouth was so dry, I couldn't even talk. I think Gary Donatelli was directing. He said,

'You're going to actually have to say the words, Mark.' I said, 'I will, I will say the words. I will say the words. I need some water. I can't. My mouth is sticky. I can't get the words out.' He said, 'Chill out. Don't worry. Everything's going to be fine.'"

Anecdotes from the Set...

Judi Evans Luciano (Paulina Cory Carlino)
"This is one of my favorite tales: the Tommy Tale. Tommy [Eplin, who plays Jake McKinnon] knocked me out! They were staging a fight between Jake and his half-brother, Kevin [Jamie Goodwin], and rehearsing it for the cameras. Here I was in really spiked heels with stretch spandex pants and this puffy jacket. Thank God I was wearing it! The director said, 'Move a little closer to Tommy.' He was about to take a swing at Kevin, and all of a sudden he goes whack and catches me right in the jaw! And in these little spiked heels I went tink-tink-tink boom! Out cold. Tommy was practically in tears over me. I mean, imagine being clopped in the face by a guy like Tommy, somebody who is so built. I never told him, but I couldn't eat solid food for two weeks, I was so sore."

Victoria Wyndham (Rachel Cory Hutchins)
"Paul [Rauch] ran this place like a benevolent dictator. There was so much horsing around, and he would allow it. We're called players for a reason. And so he allowed us to play, and there was such silliness. I mean, Nicky Coster and John Considine became such buddies, and so naughty. One day I was doing a scene in—I don't remember where . . .

in some office—and the music was playing, and it was some sort of bluesy, sexy, music. And all of a sudden I look off to the corner of the set, and there in my sight line Nicky and John are doing a striptease, right down to their boxer shorts. It was hilarious. Just to try and get me to laugh. There was so much horsing around and silliness, but the kind of thing that kept you going through a long day. And kept you inventing.

"Then there was another day that I was doing a very sad scene, a soliloquy on the phone. Rachel had to come into the Cory living room, and we had this large desk, but the kneehole part wasn't very large. So there I was in back of the sets trying to prepare for this, and I got the cue, went on, and sat down at the desk and wondered, should I make the call, shouldn't I make the call. And Rachel got more and more upset as she was thinking about it. And as I grabbed the phone, a hand grabbed my leg! Clearly one of my actor friends was underneath the desk! It turned out to be John Considine, who had gotten his six-foot-four lankiness—I don't know how he had done it—underneath that desk. And then, of course, he had to stay there for the whole scene. It was hilarious."

Tom Eplin (Jake McKinnon)
Tom Eplin is known as an actor who lives by the credo, "The show must go on." On the set saving Marley [actually her double] from a hospital fire, Eplin broke his ankle. "I had Marley in my arms, I kicked a door covered with fire down, and as I went through the door some of the grease that they put the fire out with was on the other side. I slipped on that and hit a wall. I had a stunt girl in my hands and she fell." How much time did he miss? Says Eplin, "Not one day. As a matter of fact, I taped scenes after that." It took "twenty stitches to fix, a plate, six screws, and a pin." Eplin also worked with walking pneumonia. "I checked myself out of the hospital and came back to work because I thought they were going to recast!"

Ellen Wheeler (Marley Love)

"It was just scary to me," Wheeler remembers feeling when she was first cast to play twins. "I'm a Mormon, I grew up in a family where nobody drank. I never wore a sleeveless shirt. I didn't wear shorts growing up as a teenage girl. It wasn't forbidden, it was just that my mom didn't do it, so we didn't. One of the things I did to get ready to play Vicky was read a romance novel. I'd never read one in my whole life! So there was just a lot for me to assimilate by watching other people and saying, 'Now, people who have lives like this, what are their lives like?' Because I didn't have anything in my own life to steady that background on. That was hard, as was keeping the twins distinct. The hardest thing is the feeling of being schizophrenic. I felt like there were three people in me. So there were things that were distinctly Marley, and things that were distinctly Vicky, but Ellen was both of those things together. So it felt really weird to go home at the end of the day, hating yourself because you had been jealous of yourself during the day. Or you were angry with yourself, or you were happy to see this other person, but it was yourself. And you always knew the emotions. You knew exactly what the other person felt, too. So while Marley might have been mad at Vicky or while Vicky might have been mad at Marley, she knew everything Marley felt because she wasn't a different person! But that was the challenge, to keep them separate when they were really coming from the same place. And then not let it make me totally insane at the same time."

How many times did she play the double characters during the day? Wheeler says, "Usually we tried to tape all of Marley's scenes together and all of Vicky's together. Sometimes that didn't work out. It didn't happen all the time, usually I changed twice in a day. Like I would do Marley, Vicky, and go back to Marley. But there were occasions when I would change back and forth five times in a day. It was hard on the makeup department and the hair department. It's kind of hard on everybody. I started doing my own makeup and hair and that was part of the reason, because when I got to be the person looking in the mirror applying the makeup, then it gave me that chance to change how I felt about myself. I needed to be able to change from one person to the other. I kind of needed that one-on-one time."

Actor Kale Browne, who played Michael Hudson, Marley's father, remembers, "One of the fun times I had was when Vicky dressed up like Marley and then talked to me, so that she could see what I really thought of Vicky. The way you could tell with Ellen Wheeler what character she was playing was by looking at her feet. She didn't know this, but when she played Vicky, her toes always pointed out. And when she was playing Marley, her toes pointed in."

Jensen Buchanan (Vicky McKinnon)

Buchanan remaraks on her strategy of playing twins, "The characters were somewhat defined before I played them, and I was always rummaging and struggling with this in my mind. My challenge when I took the parts on was not to make the characters as different as possible. It was to make them as close as possible, but still know that they were different people. I mean, wasn't that the ultimate challenge? Not to make the twins as, this is the kooky, crazy, funky-dressing, wild one and this is the reserved one. I wanted to see how close they could become and still be different."

Stephen Schnetzer (Cass Winthrop)

Schnetzer recalls the time he played femme fatale Krystal Lake: "I had my own personal dresser. His experience had been touring with Divine on Divine's European tour. Then Dustin Hoffman hired him on for *Tootsie* and he stayed with Dustin as an assistant after that. So while Dustin was playing *Death of a Salesman*, I was downstairs in the dressing room during a performance picking this dresser's brain, and he was giving me tips about lifts and the makeup. The most valuable thing he told me was about the walk. He said, 'When you walk, caress the inside of your thighs together and it will give you just the right sway.' And it did. Try it some-time!"

Joe Barbara (Joe Carlino)

When Joe Barbara was appearing in *Grease* he had some fun on the set with Tom Eplin: "We worked the word 'grease' into every scene. We only did it for a short period of time. You know, I'd be holding somebody back, and he'd say, 'Get your greasy hands off her.' We just threw it in there whenever we could."

When the character of Joe came on the show, he had a cat named Serpico. Barbara says, "I'm trying to think. What happened to Serpico? Bit the dust. Never knew what happened to him. Gone. You never actually saw him, we just talked about him. I'm aller-gic to cats. That's what was funny about it. I would just talk about him, you know, 'He's in the linen clos-et taking a nap,' or they'd have me literally opening cat food, throwing it down, yelling, 'Serpico, dinner!' And then start the scene."

Which leads Barbara to one of his all-time favorite scenes. "One time Pop is changing the wallpaper in my room and I come down all mad. I say, 'Pop what are you doing? The room's all upside down.' He says, 'Don't worry, Joey, I just changed the wallpaper. You're too old for cowboys anyway.' I say, 'They weren't bothering me, Pop! Does anybody ask me what I think? No! Of course not. So in the meantime, where are me and Serpico going to sleep tonight?' He says, 'You sleep in your sister's room.' I say, 'Oh, okay, you're not worried about me sleeping in a room with bunnies jumping rope over rainbows. But the cowboys were an emergency situation. We had to get rid of them this afternoon!' Love that. It was brilliant."

Kiss and Tell . . . .

Dennis Cameron (Stage Manager)

"Lovemaking scenes are very hard to direct, and as stage manager, I'm on set with the actors. And you have to coordinate with the wardrobe person the actual placement of sheets and towels and things like that, to make sure they don't show things that shouldn't be seen. I usually find myself having to stand in front of an actress who is half-naked, because there are certain members of the crew who might be interested in getting a little peek."

Judi Evans Luciano (Paulina Cory Carlino)

"The love scene I had with Mark [Pinter] was the hottest love scene I've ever done. I mean, it was directed great and it was just hot and nasty. In fact, I was embarrassed. I said, 'Dad, don't watch this today.' But I was really proud of those sex scenes."

Carmen Duncan (Iris Wheeler)

"I personally find love scenes difficult to do. I think you're worried about things like, is your dress going to fall off too much? And I also get the giggles a lot when I have to do love scenes. The slightest thing sets me off. I do get embarrassed by it!"

Stephen Schnetzer (Cass Winthrop)

"Love scenes make me nervous. I've had some doozies and I've been fortunate because the women I've been involved with have been really great. They made my job easier. They were good sports. I've been involved with some very interesting, attractive women. One of my most memorable love scenes was with Cecile when we were kind of mirroring *From Here to Eternity*, all over the beach, and she had drugged Cass with some kind of aphrodisiac (as if he needed it). I had such a bad sunburn and we had to tape it about half a dozen times, and the sand kept grinding into my skin. Ouch!"

a star is born in bay city

Another World is a show rich in theater tradition. Many of Broadway's brightest lights shone in Bay City. Tony Award winner Cleavon Little of *Purlie* fame played Captain Hancock. Charles Durning was Gil McGowan. Elizabeth Franz, Tony nominee for *Brighton Beach Memoirs,* was the evil Alma Rudder. Morgan Freeman played architect Roy Bingham, and Joe Morton (Dr. Able Marsh/Leo Mars) recently joined the cast of *Art.* Before she won a Tony for *Passion* and *The King and I,* Donna Murphy was DA Morgan Graves. And Daisy Egan of *Secret Garden* fame played a runaway living in a shelter. Fan favorite Cory patriarch Douglass Watson was discovered while acting in a Broadway play with the Andrews Sisters. Long-time cast members Brian Murray, Constance Ford, and Victoria Wyndham all brought distinguished Broadway credits to their roles. The list extends to directors Jack Hofsiss (*The Elephant Man*), Melvin Bernhardt (*Crimes of the Heart* and *Da*), John Tillinger (*Night Must Fall*), and Barnett Kellman, who went on to become a major sitcom director (*Mad About You* and *Murphy Brown*).

Actress **Susan Sullivan** remarks, "I must hand it to Paul Rauch and Pete Lemay—they used a lot of New York actors in the theater. They were both theater guys, and they'd go to the theater and see an interesting actor, and they would incorporate him into the show. So we had rich, interesting actors who became rich, interesting characters." Sullivan

Susan Sullivan

spent time in Bay City in the seventies as embattled heroine Lenore Curtin. Sullivan, who was a recast (not the role's original actor), says, "The other gal had been in prison. I came in after the murder. I remember a scene where I wrecked the place in a temper tantrum, which was of course such great fun to do—the scene with Val DuFour [Walter Curtin], in which I found out he had allowed Lenore to go through this horrible trial when he had been guilty. I confronted him with this and he started to cry—only when we were taping, never during rehearsal. It wasn't as the scene was written, and suddenly he was crying! And I wanted to kill him! I do think I ad-libbed a line about 'Oh, don't give me those crocodile tears' because it was just so infuriating!"

Sullivan remembers giving then executive producer Paul Rauch the idea for the legendary pairing of Rachel and Mac: "I just thought those two characters together would be great on the show—that sort of grasping, manipulative, needy, from-the-other-side-of-the-tracks female and this wealthy guy. Maybe it was synchronicity they came up with it at the same time, but I remember talking to Paul about it and saying, 'God! I think that would be a great idea.' And then there it was."

After several years in Bay City, Sullivan decided to try her luck in LA: "Connie Ford was the only person who gave me a name—an ex-husband of hers—when I left the show to come to California trailing this huge umbilical cord that I could go back if I didn't have any success. I was here for about three weeks and not very much was happening, and I called him up. He was on the Twentieth Century Fox lot, which is now the lot where I'm doing *Dharma and Greg.* He said, 'They're casting something right up the hill here.' It was for a *S.W.A.T.* 'The casting people don't know you but they'll take my word that you're good. Just go on up and read.'

"So I went up the hill and I walked in, and I was about 30 and the girls in the room were 18. No pores,

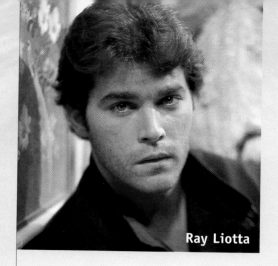

Ray Liotta

no nothing, you know, breasts, California Girls. The characters on soaps in the early days of the seventies weren't necessarily beautiful but they were all very good actors. So I thought, 'You know what, I'm probably better than anybody in this room.' And I went in and I read, and they were clearly impressed, because you have this facility from doing the soaps, you can pick up and read a script cold. Then they said to me, 'How are your legs? You'll have to be in a bathing suit.' And I thought, 'Oh God! You know what? I'm from New York. I'm not like the girls out here. They're a little jiggly.' I could see myself losing this part with that one little word, and I lifted up my skirt to show them my legs, and as I did I said, 'Help, Mother, I'm in California with my skirt up!' And they laughed and gave me the part. After that I was really blessed to pretty much continue working."

Her breakthrough part came in *Rich Man, Poor Man*. After that, *It's a Living* and, of course, Maggie on *Falcon Crest*. Today Sullivan plays the snooty mother of **Thomas Gibson** (ex-Sam Fowler) on the hit sitcom *Dharma and Greg*.

Many stars who went on to movie and television fame spent time in Bay City in the early stages of their careers. **Kelsey Grammer** appeared as Dr. Canard in 1984–85. **Billy Dee Williams** was an assistant DA in the sixties. From 1970 to 1971 **Rue McLanahan** played Caroline Johnson, a crazy housekeeper who worked for John and Pat Randolph. When she wasn't taking care of their twins or cleaning the house, Caroline kept busy by putting poison in Pat's soup because she was interested in her husband John. In 1977 **Eric Roberts,** older brother of Julia, played drugged-out rich kid Ted Bancroft.

Nancy Marchand of *Marty* fame was another consummate Broadway performer who made a brief appearance on *Another World*. Pete Lemay, who created her character, explains, "She was a friend of Iris's and she was dying of a heart condition. It lasted maybe six weeks . . . three months. She was an ex-show girl and she was singing 'Bye-Bye-Blackbird' on Iris's terrace when she died." Adds Lemay, "I got so many letters about that."

The seventies brought **Ray Liotta** of *Goodfellas* fame to Bay City in the role of good-guy Joey Perrini, part of the blue-collar Perrini clan. In his story line, Joey married Eileen, who died of a blood disease one day after they were married. Next he wed secret heiress Kit Farrell. *Another World* scribe Pete Lemay, who created the Perrini family, says of Liotta, "He was a brilliant actor and the camera loved him. The camera just went for him the way it did with the young Marlon Brando."

In a reverse move, the late **Howard E. Rollins Jr.** took a recurring role on *Another World* after he had received an Academy Award nomination for his portrayal of Coalhouse Walker Jr. in *Ragtime*. Rollins explains, "In Europe, actors take jobs no matter what the milieu and nothing is looked down upon. I have a lot of respect for soap opera actors." Rollins played angry Vietnam veteran Ed Harding, in what was scheduled to be a one-month stint, but he returned for an open-ended encore.

Appearing around the same time was **Jackee Harry**. Jackee brought singing, dancing, and stage credentials to her role as Lily Mason and went on to star as vampish Sondra

Howard E. Rollins Jr.

Clark on NBC's popular sitcom *227.* Harry took what was planned to be a one-day part as Thomasina Harding's streetwalking auntie and turned it into a major role that lasted almost two years.

Having been offered a grand total of five lines, Jackee had a fast consultation with her good friend Dorothy Lyman (Gwen Parrish Frame), who advised her to examine the other characters and find a space to fill. Harry realized that *Another World* had several nice-mannered middle-class black women, but what it didn't have was a "wild and crazy" one. Enter jive-talking, fresh-mouthed Lily Mason. A natural comedian, Harry became part of the famous "Three Musketeers" friendship of Felicia, Wallingford, and Cass.

Don Scardino, another man of the theater, played Chris Chapin, arch-enemy of the notorious Carl Hutchins and the love of Rachel's sister Nancy's life. A Broadway performer, most notably in *Godspell,* and a noted director (*Mass Appeal, Sister Mary Ignatius Explains It All for You*), Scardino spent several years as the director of Playwrights Horizons, one of New York's leading off-Broadway companies.

Both **Kyra Sedgwick** and **Faith Ford** played Julia Shearer when they were teenagers and then went on to fame and fortune elsewhere.

Sedgwick was barely seventeen and starting the eleventh grade when she landed the role of rebellious teenager Julia Shearer, a runaway teenage rock band's groupie. Said Kyra at the time, "My parents took my acting very seriously after they saw me in

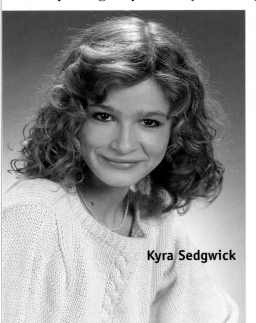

Kyra Sedgwick

my eighth-grade school play, but they told me a career in acting would involve a lot of hard work. To impress that upon me,

Faith Ford

they suggested I try going to a few auditions just to see what they were like, and that's how I ended up on *Another World.*

While Sedgwick played her, Julia experienced everything from mother problems, to same-age boy problems, to older-guy crush problems, to school and career problems. In her capable hands, Julia's glowing excitement with life was presented with the intense sincerity appropriate to her age.

Sedgwick left the part to go to college and went on to a career that would encompass films (*Born on the Fourth of July* and *Mr. and Mrs. Bridge*), television, the award-winning *Miss Rose White,* and recently, Lincoln Center's production of *Twelfth Night,* with Helen Hunt and **Brian Murray,** who played her father, Dr. Dan Shearer, on *Another World.*

Faith Ford followed Sedgwick in the role. While living in Louisiana, Faith participated in the National Forensic League's dramatic competitions and did extremely well. Her mother encouraged her to pursue an acting career after graduation. Ford described her character at the time: "Julia is very immature and very young." Ford also said she didn't plan to do soap operas forever: "I hope to get into film. I probably will be more marketable in nighttime television, though." That was in 1984. Ford, of course, went on to create the memorable Corky Sherwood, ex-beauty queen turned reporter, on *Murphy Brown,* and this year she got her own sitcom, *Maggie Winters.*

Another actor who made it big on nighttime television was **Christopher Knight.** Chris played Leigh Hobson on *Another World* in the early eighties after becoming part of the famous *Brady Bunch* as Peter

Brady in the hit show that defined television in the seventies.

Some other famous faces that appeared briefly in Bay City belonged to **Marla Maples**, who went on a date with Jason Frame; **Luke Perry**, who played Kenny, Josie's manager, and the young **Brad Pitt**, who played a high school student who befriended injured Vietnam vet John Hudson.

David Forsyth, who played John, remembers, "John was a basketball player and had been a champion in high school and he goes back and finds the high school and starts playing with cane in hand, and he looks up and his jersey is still up there. He had won the state championship and was kind of a hero in the high school, and this kid walks in and says, 'God, you're John Hudson, aren't' you?' 'Yeah, I am.' I had five scenes with this kid. I told the producer, 'This kid can act.' He was a really nice kid and I thought, 'This is an interesting relationship, this guy who's now crippled and this young kid who's got his whole life ahead of him.' Unfortunately for *Another World*, Brad Pitt was one who got away.

Anne Heche exploded onto the screen in 1987 in the role of Victoria Love, the spoiled, trouble-making granddaughter of villainous Reginald Love, a role that also encompassed her twin sister, Marley. *Another World* was Heche's dramatic television debut. Charles Keating (Carl Hutchins) said of his co-star, "What a natural talent that girl had. Dangerous, sexy, and alive. She was wonderful. She was very dynamic."

Anne's breakthrough film was *Donny Brasco* with

Anne Heche

Al Pacino, followed by *Wag the Dog* with Robert DeNiro and Dustin Hoffman. Then came *Six Days, Seven Nights* with mega star

Lindsay Lohan

Harrison Ford, followed by the remake of *Psycho*. And this is only the beginning of her film career.

Another recent *Another World* actress to make the trip from Bay City to Hollywood was **Lindsay Lohan**, who played Alli Fowler. This talented little redhead was a smash in 1998's holiday hit *The Parent Trap*, in which she aptly took on the part of twins.

Other recent graduates of the show, **Julian McMahon** (Ian Rain), appearing on NBC's cult hit *The Profiler*, and **Grayson McCouch** (Dr. Morgan Winthrop), appearing in the film *Armageddon* and UPN's new prime-time series *Legacy*, are making their way in the entertainment world.

While appearing on the show, talented singer/actress **Rhonda Ross Kendrick**, who plays Toni Burrell, found time to star in *The Temptations*, an NBC miniseries, which mirrored the lives of her mother, Diana Ross, and father, Berry Gordy Jr.

guest spots

As the first daytime drama to cast celebrities, *Another World* started a trend that became immensely popular. **Ann Sheridan**, otherwise known as the "Oomph Girl," was the first Hollywood star to appear on a daytime drama. She played Kathryn Corning from 1965 to 1966. Since then, other famous guests have dropped by Bay City to attend weddings, offer advice on everything from alcohol addiction to mayoral campaigns, and just plain entertain.

Internationally renowned actor and Academy

Award nominee for *The Defiant Ones,* **Theodore Bikel** made his daytime drama debut in 1982 on *Another World.* Known for his roles as Captain von Trapp in the Broadway production of *The Sound of Music* and Tevye in *Fiddler on the Roof,* Bikel had this to say about his character, Henry Davenport, one of the world's richest men: "Davenport is dapper, debonair, and sinister. There's something lurking there that is intriguing. He buys art and uses any subterfuge to drive down its price—particularly if it has been stolen—to get it cheaper." To sum it up, he was rich, crooked, stingy, and mean.

In 1983 distinguished Oscar-winning actor **José Ferrer** joined the cast of *Another World* to play flamboyant trial lawyer Reuben Marino in a limited guest appearance. Renowned and expensive, Marino was called in to represent multimillionaire Louis St. George, who was facing charges of international art theft, and his daughter, Cecile de Poulignac Cory, who was fighting to retain custody of her infant daughter, Maggie. Ferrer remembered, "The character of the trial lawyer has been with us in the theatrical world for many years, and it's a gratifying one to play. Many famous actors, including John Barrymore, Paul Muni, and Spencer Tracy, have been aided in their careers by playing trial lawyers. It's a healthy, surviving tradition." Ferrer also enjoyed his role because, he said, "I feel it will put me in touch on a daily basis with a vast audience I may not otherwise reach—and I have the fun of exploring one more avenue of the many streets of my profession."

On a legal note, actress and first lady of New York, Donna Hanover, played a judge during Grant Harrison's 1997 trial.

In 1988 **Betty White** came to Bay City as Brenda Barlow, an old para-

Joan Rivers

mour of Mac's from twenty-seven years before. Brenda wanted Mac to publish her memoirs. It was all part of "Where's Betty?" week, when Emmy-winner White made guest appearances on each of the NBC daytime dramas. By counting the number of her appearances on each program and submitting an entry, viewers were eligible for the grand prize of a week in Kauai, Hawaii.

Also in 1988, legendary talk-show host **Dick Cavett** made some special guest appearances on the show. As a teenager growing up in Lincoln, Nebraska, Cavett won local fame as a magician, and he put that talent to good use when he portrayed a nightclub magician on *Another World.* In the story line, Felicia Gallant interviewed Elizabeth Grayson, Miss America of 1982, on her morning program, *Breakfast with Felicia,* about the magical night of her crowning. Then Mitch, Cass, and Nicole visited a nightclub in Atlantic City and volunteered to take part in the magician's (Cavett's) show.

In 1989 the late **Virginia Graham,** always one to enjoy a good party, made an appearance at Cory Publishing's 25th anniversary celebration. Graham played Stella Stanton on the *Another World* spin-off *Texas.* On the show, Stella was the host of a game show aptly titled *Tall Texas Tales.*

In 1990 **Elizabeth Ashley,** playing Emma Frame Ordway, came to Bay City on the occasion of her daughter Sharlene's marriage to Dr. John Hudson.

That same year **Al Roker,** in his position as NBC reporter, interviewed Josie Watts, and in 1992 **Sally Jesse Raphael** stopped by Bay City to comfort Felicia after her lover Lucas's untimely death.

In 1997, with Grant Harrison's mayoral campaign in dire need of help, it was **Joan Rivers** as spin doctor Meredith Dunstan to the rescue. Said Rivers, "I try everything! I believe that if God gives you the chance and you don't go for it, you're just plain stupid! So when the NBC daytime soap *Another World* asked me to appear on the show as an unscrupulous businesswoman, I said, 'You bet!' They made me into a tough political publicist who had been hired to clean up the image of Bay City's mayoral candidate Grant Harrison. (This guy tried to murder his wife, blow up a truck, and spent time in jail for killing his brother—and they want my character to change his image!) I had so much fun! Look out Susan Lucci!"

Rivers remembers from her experience on *Another World,* "Here's something I discovered during my first hour of AW—soap actors are very professional. In one day, they learn more lines than Clint Eastwood says in six months. Last, but nowhere least, I even learned to cope with heartbreak, misery, tragedy. No, they didn't let me keep the clothes. But despite the nada on the Armani, I still want to thank *Another World.* They made me feel like a true soap star. So much so, I must now announce, I'm leaving to do prime time!"

let me entertain you

Music has always played a big part in the lives of Bay City residents. Roberta Flack, Ronnie Milsap, Gloria Loring, and members of Atlantic Starr are some of the artists who have sung at Bay City's nightspots and charity affairs.

Another World fan **Crystal Gayle** came on the show as herself to debut the song "You Take Me Away to Another World," which would become the show's theme song. Gayle performed the song with country singer/Broadway star Gary Morris, and it was included on an album they recorded together. Gayle was introduced on the show as a friend of Felicia Gallant, and as part of the story line she appeared on Felicia's talk show *Breakfast at Tops.* During her

Linda Dano and Crystal Gayle

stint on *Another World,* Gayle was almost attacked by the Sin Stalker, the serial killer who had been terrorizing Bay City, preying on women in love.

It was a show within a show in 1983, when *PM Magazine,* the nationally syndicated show, "covered" Bay City's charity benefit for Abel Marsh's (Joe Morton's) new eye clinic and then aired its own feature about *Another World* on its lineup of over a hundred stations. The affair was organized with the help of Marsh's famous brother, rock 'n' roll singer Leo Mars (also played by Morton), and took place at his club, the Warehouse. The evening featured live entertainment by superstar Grammy-award winner **Roberta Flack** and country/pop entertainer **Louise Mandrell.** Nearly everybody in Bay City came out to hear Roberta sing "Making Love" and "I'm the One," and Louise's rollicking "Runaway Heart" and "Romance."

It was the daytime debut for both performers. Mandrell, an *Another World* fan, said she was thrilled to finally get to meet the characters she'd watched for years. Said Flack at the time, "I'm the perfect one in the family to do this. My life is a soap opera." She added that she enjoyed doing *Another World* so much that she'd consider a running role on the

every day. I won't take phone calls when it's on, and I've even rearranged performances and interview schedules around the show. And I love Linda Dano! She's the Joan Collins of daytime television. When she asked me if I would be on the show—I said 'Yes, yes, YES!'"

The renowned pianist, who shared a love of flashy clothes with Felicia, returned to Bay City to perform at Felicia's wedding to rustic deep-sea adventurer Zane Lindquist. Dano's husband and mother attended the nuptials, as well. Dano explains, "My husband comes to all my soap opera weddings." One of the highlights of her work with Liberace was a piano duet—they played "Chopsticks" together.

Dancers from the **Dirty Dancers** concert tour and the film of the same name made a special guest appearance on *Another World* in 1988, along with New York radio personality Rich Stevens. Stevens introduced Bay City's newest singing sensation, Tiffany (B. J. Jefferson) at the popular Pelican jazz club. Tiffany wowed the audience with the hit song from the movie *Yes,* while the Dirty Dancers performed those sensual sixties numbers. Matt, Josie, Jamie, and Lisa joined the party.

When **Billy Porter** agreed to perform on *Another World* as Billy Rush, the talented singer found himself smack in the middle of a love story—Sofia and Matt's. The search for talent for their music company, C-Squared, brought Sofia and Matt to New York and a trendy nightclub called the Dive, where they discovered Billy Rush and signed him on the spot. Church-trained Broadway veteran Porter performed "Only One Road," which had its television debut on the show and became the love theme of these two young people with very complicated lives.

show, but as a "character," not as Roberta Flack.

Liberace in one of his several guest appearances on Another World.

Gloria Loring made a special guest appearance in 1987. It was New Year's Eve, and Bay City's residents were celebrating at Tops, Felicia's popular restaurant and nightclub. The highlight of the evening was Ms. Loring's rendition of "Somebody," a song that became the love theme for Cass and Nicole.

Liberace made several guest appearances on *Another World* in the mid-eighties. In the story, he met flashy romance novelist Felicia Gallant at an autograph session and invited her to a party. Later, Wallingford and Felicia paid him a visit in scenes taped at Liberace's opulent Trump Tower apartment, where he serenaded her with his signature song, "I'll Be Seeing You." Art imitated life in this story because Liberace was a great admirer of Felicia and Linda Dano. As he said at the time, "I've been a big fan of *Another World* forever. I watch it

home grown talent: dean frame

Bad-boy musician Dean Frame and wealthy Matt Cory teamed up to form their own music company, D&M Productions. Dean wanted to rock 'n' roll, and Matt wanted to prove himself away from the family business.

*A grand time was had by all when **Atlantic Starr** made a special guest appearance at Sassy's, a popular hangout for the "younger set."*

In the summer of 1991, *Another World* held a band search. Viewers were asked to call an 800 number on the bottom of the screen and vote for a backup band to appear with Dean on the show.

Excitement over the taping of Matt and Dean's music video, *Ladykiller,* had been building to a fevered pitch for weeks when Olivia Matthews, the video's lead dancer, was injured. Matt decided that the only person who could replace her was Jenna, a former convent school pupil and his current girlfriend. Jenna had doubts about the idea, but rose to the occasion to help Matt. However, whom she cared for—Matt or Dean—was still in question. Although she had been steadily seeing the all-American Matt, she was secretly harboring feelings for Dean, the rock 'n' roll rebel with a cause (named for James Dean). After their steamy *Ladykiller* duet, there was no question that her heart belonged to Dean, and the two embarked on a romance for the young at heart. Jenna became a partner in D&M, and when Dean left Bay City for his world tour, Jenna went with him.

And let's not forget our local talent still residing in Bay City. . . .

For KBAY's Fourth of July telethon, Joe Carlino did his Elvis interpretation and the crowd went wild! Actor Joe Barbara has also starred on Broadway in *Grease.*

On the occasion of the telethon, Bay City's favorite femme fatale, Krystal Lake, did her very special rendition of—what else?—"You Make Me Feel Like a Natural Woman."

Joe Carlino as Elvis

Bay City sensation
Dean Frame and the Rascals

Krystal Lake

s t a r s   f r o m   *a n o t h e r   w o r l d*

Themselves
Atlantic Starr
4/92

Reporter
Ann Baldwin
(Newscaster, WVIT-TV,
    W. Hartford, CT)
3/23/95

Henry Davenport
Theodore Bikel
8/82–1/83

Talk-Show Host
Bill Boggs
Early 1980s

Tracey Julian
Gabrielle Carteris
5/88–8/88

"Oliver Twist"
Dick Cavett
9/8 and 9/88

Tom Nelson
Steven Culp
1982

Reuben Marino
José Ferrer
1983

Herself
Roberta Flack
Early 1980s

Julia Shearer
Faith Ford
7/83–8/84

Herself
Crystal Gayle
3/23/87–3/27/87

Herself
Virginia Graham
5/89

Dr. Canard
Kelsey Grammer
Summer 1984

Judge Ellen
    Landregan
Donna Hanover
3/24 and 25/97,
    5/7–19/97

Lily Mason
Jackee Harry
3/83–6/25/86

Girl in Coney Island
    Shoot
Melissa Joan Hart
4/22/86

Madeline Thompson
Ilene Kristen
2/10/95 or 3/95,
    5/29/95

Renaldo
Julius LaRosa
1980

Himself
Liberace
5/16, 17, and 24/85,
    6/3/85, 2/17 and
    18/86

Liz Matthews
Audra Lindley
1964–69

Joey Perrini
Ray Liotta
Spring 1978–12/81

Captain Hancock
Cleavon Little
Early 1970s

Herself
Gloria Lorring
1/4/88

Griffin Sanders
Terrence Mann
10/89–2/90

Jason Frame's Date
Marla Maples
1988

Caroline Johnson
Rue McClanahan
1970–Autumn 1971

Himself
Ronnie Milsap
Autumn 1991

Himself
Gary Morris
3/27/87

Morgan Graves
Donna Murphy
2/89–3/91 (recurring)

Margaret Allen
Christopher Norris
10/16/98–present

Jimmy
Chris Noth
6/12/85–8/12/85

Limo Driver
Janet Peckinpaugh
(anchorwoman,
    WVIT-TV, W.
    Hartford, CT)
11/6/97

Kenny
Luke Perry
9/23/88–Autumn 1988

Chris
Brad Pitt
5/14 and 15/87

Billy Rush
Billy Porter
5/6/98, 8/28/98

Herself
Sally Jesse Raphael
1/26/93

Czaja Carnek
Ving Rhames
5/14/86–8/4 or 5/86

Meredith Dunston
Joan Rivers
7/9/97, 8/15/97

Construction Worker
Susan Roesgen
(anchorwoman,
    WDSU-TV, New
    Orleans)
11/5/97

Himself
Al Roker
1990

Michael Thayer
Gary Sandy
1969 (8 episodes)

Edward/Edouard
    Gerard
John Saxon
8/30/85–2/26/86

Raymond Gordon
Ted Schackelford
12/75–1/77

Reporter
David Schiffer
(News Director, WETM-
    TV, Elmira, NY)
11/10/97

Julia Shearer
Kyra Sedgwick
1982–83

Reporter
Dean Shepherd
(Anchorman, WNBC-
    TV, NY)
11/7/97

Kathryn Corning
Ann Sheridan
1966

Joyce
Rena Sofer
10/6/87–10/30/87

Cory Maid
Mimi Torchin
1/83

Patricia Kirkland
Janine Turner
12/86–3/87

Brenda Barlowe
Betty White
1/88

Assistant DA
Billy Dee Williams
1967

Officer Noonan
Jayson Williams (NBA
    star, NJ Nets)
7/13/98

Art Restorer
William B. Williams
    10/7/76

Dougie
Kevin Williamson
1990

They Speak to the Fans

*L*ynn Leahey, editor-in-chief of *Soap Opera Digest*, and Michael Logan, soap opera columnist for *TV Guide*, are highly respected journalists and chroniclers of the soap opera scene today. Both share a love of the medium, and when they speak, fans listen.

Lynn Leahey started at *Soap Opera Digest* fifteen years ago and has been editor-in-chief for the past seven. "I hadn't watched soap opera since I was a little girl with my mom. Like most soap fans, that's the way we tend to get started." On what makes *Another World* unique, Leahey says, "Every show has its signature characters that help to define its personality. While *Another World* isn't unique in having those characters, there wasn't another couple like Rachel and Mac. I think people loved following that story and the sacrifices that they made for each other.

"Also, I think people really could identify with a woman not trying to reform, but a woman's evolving from a vixen, the love of a good man turning her into something better. Here's this woman who comes from nothing and comes from a trashy background, and suddenly she's the lady of the house. That's fun to watch. There isn't another character like Rachel in daytime. No matter what happens around her, she's like the anchor.

"Taking over the couple's role are Vicky and Jake. They're unique. The actors are wonderful, but it's even more than that. Someone like Jake is so unpredictable, and so is Vicky, that you don't know what they're going to do, but you go for the ride with them.

Other show highlights, in Leahey's view, include the Cass-Kathleen-Frankie triangle. "You think it's going to be boring, cliché, a back-from-the-dead character, but they really made it interesting. You really believed it. I always love triangles when you don't know who to root for.

"Beverlee McKinsey, too, was incredible. You reacted to her. When you think of Iris on *Another World* it was one of a kind. Instead of a love triangle with two women the man's in love with, it was the woman he was in love with and his daughter, which was unusual. And it was different for a triangle to have the daughter causing all that trouble. Iris had a strength. To be able to have that kind of manipulative power was really interesting.

"Where other soaps have focused more on romance, so much of this is about family dynamics, about twins and their rivalry, and about Donna—it's these really strong, powerful family connections that make you do things you thought you never would. And that's life. Life isn't just about your boyfriend and your husband and adultery. It's about dysfunctional families and what they make you do, and you know they can make you turn in directions you never thought you'd go.

"It also helps to understand the motivations of characters when the family life is so well defined and well understood. No wonder Vicky's a mess—they shipped her out when she was born. *Another World* has a complexity to all its characters, which I think is valuable in a show, because you can turn them in all different directions and you never know how they're going to change. They could get better and they could get worse, and it all makes sense."

Leahey muses about the fans: "It's interesting to talk about the clichés, about how women who watch soaps are the ones that have time on their hands. It's actually the exact opposite. The women who watch soaps are so busy that they carve out this hour or two of time for themselves. It's really valuable to them. If I had to guess, I would say that if you looked at two women's schedules, and one watched soaps and one didn't, the one who watched

soaps is probably just as busy, if not busier, with children, with jobs, with volunteer work—she just makes the time for it. I really admire people who have this kind of passion for something and make the time for it, because it isn't easy.

"The fans are great. The connection they have with this show is just amazing. To be able to write a magazine for people who feel so deeply, I can't imagine a better job."

*M*ichael Logan started writing about soaps in the early eighties and has been with *TV Guide* for a decade. "Although I also write about many other areas of entertainment," Logan says, "I've always stayed involved in daytime drama because it's a fun world to be a part of and I very much respect the work that's done. That overwhelming concept of those people turning out five hours of television a week is just astounding. To me, the best acting in the world is on

these shows. As far as I'm concerned, Meryl Streep could sit down and watch Jensen Buchanan's tapes of *Another World* and learn.

Mark Mortimer (Nick Hudson) signs autographs for adoring fans outside the Another World studio in Brooklyn.

There's phenomenal work going on, and it's always been one of the appeals of *Another World* specifically."

Logan calls *Another World* "the Madonna of daytime drama. It's constantly had to reinvent itself. Look at its spin-offs. Look at that place in time where it went to an hour and a half. I don't think any show has had higher highs or lower lows than this one has, and it just keeps going."

Of the fans, Logan says, " I don't think there is any fan group that has been as ferociously loyal and rabidly devoted through such highs and lows. It's very easy to stay passionate about a show that has had much more linear success, but this has been so bizarre, so wild in its reinvention, that I think it's an ultimate tribute to the show and the fans that the audience has stayed so incredibly passionate.

"Some of the great moments of soap history are part of this show, like the great triangle of Alice, Steve, and Rachel that went on longer than just about any other triangle in soap history. I think one of the truly remarkable things is the Vicky/Marley character. Basically we look at that part as having been recast stunningly, brilliantly, three times, which is just another example of something that completely defies the laws of nature in soap opera.

"The show's been morphing since its very inception," Logan continues. "Irna oddly sort of created this with Bill Bell; Agnes Nixon brought success to it. It's almost like it was created by people whose expertise did not lie in what that show was, and so it was almost by necessity adopted by someone else. And when you get into the Harding LeMay, Paul Rauch era, then it becomes even more obvious—the new adoptive parents taking over yet again to keep this baby thriving.

"I think why people are so nuts for it still is that it's been through times of great testing. In troubled recent times, with Jake and Vicky, it refocused our attentions on romance in a way that really spoke to what we missed about this genre and how incandescent it can be. When Jake and Vicky were happening, it was intoxicating. There's nothing like being reminded how much we're in love with love. It's the dream that many people have of what the best kind of marriage is—that you're marrying your friend. That before it turns romantic you've established so much history and developed such a textured relationship that you're on a whole different foundation than if you're marrying in the kind of classic way most people in soaps marry, which is for the attraction."

Logan sums up his description of *Another World*: "It's this wild, wacky black-sheep child that's going to do it its own way."

Meet Mindi Schulman, *Another World's* Fan Club President

It all started when Mindi Schulman was in the seventh grade and she went home sick to her aunt's house. Schulman recalls, "My Aunt wanted to give me a little lunch, and I'm sitting in the kitchen and the TV's on in the living room and she hears a screech. She ran into the living room and I followed her. I'd never watched a soap opera. Right then and there I ended up bringing my sandwich in the living room fasinated by the show.

"Then *Another World* came on and she watched that as well. It was the early seventies, and it was Steven Frame and Alice, Pat Randolph and the twins, Michael and Marianne, Gwen Frame, and Donna and Michael. It was incredible. It just drew me right in, and ever since then I was hooked."

And how did she become fan club president? Schulman says, "*Another World* was playing a softball game against another show in Central Park. I'd watched the show for over twenty years, and then I met Tom [Eplin] and started talking to him."

First she took on Tom's fan club. "I didn't even know what a fan club was, so I had to learn quick," Schulman remarks. About five years later, the president of what was then known as the *Another World* Viewer Alliance stepped down and Schulman stepped

258

in. Says Schulman, "I'm lucky, because everybody from the production people to the Xerox people to the executive producers supports me and the fan club 150 percent. They treat me as part of the family. I couldn't ask for a better show to work with. They're a great group."

When Schulman took over the fan club, there were between 250 and 275 members. Last year over 800 members attended the annual fan club luncheon in New York.

Why is this fan club luncheon so popular? "First of all," Schulman answers, "the actors show up. If they don't do another appearance all year, that's the one that they do. When Connie Ford was alive, she came every year. She did nothing else, but she was at the fan club luncheon. They put together an incredible show that they write themselves. They take some real songs and change them to fit the characters."

Schulman says the actors love their fans. "That's the bottom line, and that is one day a year that they can show the fans how much they appreciate them." Schulman continues, "We start off with something that nobody else does. Each table has eleven chairs with only ten fans, and the eleventh chair is for the actor. They go table to table for about a half-hour of meeting and greeting with the fans."

The luncheon includes a raffle where prizes are clothes donated from wardrobe by costume designer Shawn Dudley and makeovers donated by makeup artist Kevin Bennett. Says Schulman, "People make their whole vacations and plan their lives around this event. They come from Germany, Australia, tons of people from Canada, California, Hawaii, South Carolina, Virginia, Connecticut, Rhode Island, West Virginia—from all the fifty states. It amazes me. "The fans are amazing. It's a great honor, and I'm lucky to work with the people that I do."

Fan Tales

The fans love their actors, but sometimes they get the actor confused with the character. The late Dou-

glass Watson, always a fan favorite, once said, "I've had people write and ask for jobs at Cory Publishing. They're very straight and send background material."

John Considine, who played the hated Reginald Love, encountered his share of angry fans. Recalled Considine, "The first thing that happened was someone walked by, did a double-take, came up to me, went 'Sssssss' in my face, and walked away."

She was topped by the woman who yelled out, "Hey, Reggie, you creep!" as Considine strolled through the stands at a Florida racetrack with one of his closest show business friends, Paul Newman (Newman was amused). The most bizarre incident was when someone strode up to John and angrily spit at his feet. "If it doesn't get any worse than that, it's kind of fun," said Considine. "But it is weird always doing scenes with people that hate you, because I think Reginald's fairly thick-skinned. I don't think he gives a damn what other people think—but I do."

During his seven-year tenure as *Another World's* head writer, Harding "Pete" Lemay had his fair share of encounters with the fans, which he chronicled in his book *Eight Years in Another World*. Some of the strongest reactions centered on Rachel's ever present threat to the romance of Alice and Steve. At one point in the story, Alice and Steve had been engaged three times, and one fan wanted to know when they were finally going to get married—because every time they'd been engaged, she'd bought a dress for their wedding. Another woman wrote that her mother would surely suffer a nervous breakdown if Rachel broke up Steve and Alice's wedding, and asked if Lemay could please keep the marriage intact, so she and her father could have "some peace and decent meals." The fan then added, "She's a nut, we know, but she loves the show more than anything else in the world."

The fans tend to get passionate about their favorite characters. During a four-month absence from the show, William Gray Espy, who played Mitch Blake, reported that the show received over 30,000 letters demanding his return.

And actors get a fair amount of rather odd requests. Says Timothy Gibbs, who played Gary Sinclair, "I had one fan who wrote that they loved the show, but their television wasn't working well and they wanted me to buy them a new TV." Linda Dano got that letter too.

The show has had its share of famous fans as well. Both Judy Garland and Tennessee Williams were avid watchers of *Another World*.

Linda Dano (Felicia Gallant) and Stephen Schnetzer (Cass Winthrop)

Linda: Do you remember when you wore a paper bag so no one would know you?

Stephen: I forgot about that!

And why was he wearing the paper bag?

Linda: Because he was the mystery guest!

Stephen: No, this is Paducah! We went to Paducah and we arrive—you know, demographically it was *Another World* country . . . maybe still is, please God—and we get to Paducah, we land, and the streets are lined.

Linda: Lined!!

Stephen: You know, it's like the coming of the Pope!

Linda: And then the morning that we were leaving, we're having breakfast in the hotel, and there's a line of strollers.

Stephen: "Touch my child. Heal me."

Linda: "Kiss my child."

Stephen: "Kiss my baby!"

Linda: We finish this breakfast, we meet all of these people. I'm talking about hundreds and hundreds of people lining up. We get into this limo, he turns—

Stephen: Waving like the Queen.

Linda: We're waving like the Queen. He turns to me and says—

Stephen: "They don't know that in a year I could be selling insurance!" She wet her pants!

Linda: I peed in my pants because it's true! A year from now, it's like—

Stephen: No perspective at all!

Elain Graham (Etta Mae Burrell)

"People love Etta Mae. Especially a lot of the African-American women and men. I get a lot of African-American men who stop me on the street and tell me how sexy I am, how glad they are that I'm on the show. And the women say, "My God, I'm so glad you're representing us and you're well-spoken." Not the same old stereotype. It really makes me feel good that Etta Mae is perceived that way by all races. I haven't received anything negative. You get some crazy fan mail, but, it's by strange people sometimes. Those that talk to me about my heritage, our heritage, the African-American letters that come in. . . . I cherish those a lot when they do come in."

Mark Pinter (Grant Harrison)

Pinter describes fan reaction to the manipulative Mayor Harrison as very positive. "Aside from hate mail, character-wise . . . and it's always couched in a compliment, 'I hate you, hate you, but I love you.' A lot of it is a how-could-you-do-that kind of reaction. I get a lot of 'how could you? I mean, don't you understand what a terrible person you are?!'"

Beverlee McKinsey (Iris Carrington Wheeler)

McKinsey, who played the equally manipulative Iris, says her fan reaction "was immense. It was huge. Iris was very, very popular and I didn't ever get hate mail. Never. They just loved to watch her do whatever she wanted to do. I never could understand that, but I figured they thought, "Well, you know, if I were that rich and powerful, I'd do some of that stuff, too." I don't know what the fans really thought, but the letters were all good. I mean, Alexandra Spaulding used to get terrible letters. Awful, awful letters. But not Iris."

Sandra Ferguson *(Amanda Cory)*

"Oh gosh. I have people that have named their children after the character, which is really amazing to me. 'Can you take a picture with my daughter Amanda?' and I look at them and they say, 'We named her after you.' Let's just say it's flattering. When I first started on the show, I did one of my first appearances. I had a woman get completely irate with me because I told her I didn't have the baby [Alli], that it was only on TV. She couldn't make the differentiation and she was furious.

Linda Dano *(Felicia Gallant)*

"Felicia once lost money on this show. And somebody sent me in the mail—no return address, just the first name—four hundred dollars. Four one-hundred-dollar bills. It said, 'I really want to thank you. I really hope this helps. Please buy yourself something nice.' I opened the envelope, counted my four hundred-dollar bills, and went right to the producer's office and said, 'I think I really like this story! I think we could hit gold with this!' And I never could return the money. Everybody here kidded me and said, 'Well, what are you going to do? You should give us a little party!' I said no! He said he wanted me to have a good time with it! Took me only a half hour to spend it!"

Joe Barbara *(Joe Carlino)*

"We're so lucky just to do this. There's so much that goes along with it. Fans you get to meet. People whose lives you get to touch. The good that you get to do. I've been to hospitals visiting little kids that are going to die, and raising money for them and touching people that way. Your letters and the way you conduct yourself in public has such an impact on people in a lot of ways. Then there are the professional things. I get to host the Emmys. I get to judge the Miss America Pageant. Overall, it's been amazing. And so many people came out to see *Grease*, which was great."

Judi Evans Luciano *(Paulina Carlino)*

"The whole weight story line—people really responded to that. I got so many letters from people who were anorexic, that it made them see what they were doing was wrong. People who were overweight. People who'd had babies. People who didn't have babies. People whose mothers had babies, whose sisters had babies. And, you know, it's okay to be who you are and not take the easy road out. That's going to hurt you and everybody else along the way.

"I just got a letter the other day that said, 'You saved my life. I'm twenty-three years old. I've been married for four years. I'm anorexic. I'm really trying not to be. I want to try and have a baby like you have, a beautiful son. And it doesn't matter if I'm skinny or fat. It matters who I am and it should matter to my husband and I think he feels that way. I'm going to make sure he feels that way. And make sure I feel that way.' It was just a beautiful letter."

Linda Dano *(Felicia Gallant)*

"There was this woman a few years ago. Her husband, who was a friend of my husband, Frank, whom he grew up with, sought him out, called him up, and casually mentioned (didn't say fan) that his wife watched me on TV. 'I'd love to get together with you again, Frank. It would be such fun . . . we should have dinner.' So I said, 'Yeah, sure, a friend of yours, great.' So they come to our home in Ridgefield, Connecticut, and the woman never stops grinning at me and she never calls me Linda, she only calls me Felicia. I ate my entire meal while her hand held mine—I never cut anything, I just ate with her hand on mine. Frank said something to me across the table and she literally turned on him— 'Don't you talk to my Felicia that way.' At three o'clock in the morning with all the gushing I couldn't see anymore. I was so tired, I got up and said, 'I've really got to go to bed'—and the woman started crying."

in loving memory...

Douglass Watson (Mac Cory)

The people who knew him, worked with him, and loved him remember Douglass Watson.

CHRISTOPHER GOUTMAN, EXECUTIVE PRODUCER

"Doug Watson was a consummate professional. An incredibly generous man. A modest man. And an emotional man. The whole joke about Doug was that he would cry before any woman in his scene would cry, but that was what was so dear about him. He was everyone's father, everyone's friend, mentor to many of the young cast members. Just a gentleman through and through, and a supremely gifted actor."

VICTORIA WYNDHAM (RACHEL)

"An actor of enormous charm, vitality, and character, a real southern gentleman adored by everyone he met. He had what all inspired actors have—a sense of play, or sheer enjoyment in the creative process."

BEVERLEE MCKINSEY (IRIS)

"He was the most extraordinary actor I've ever worked with. He was gorgeous in every way. He was beautiful to look at. He was beautiful to work with. Everything about him was wonderful. You had to know this man. Nobody could replace this man. Oh my, he was exciting to be around. Hard to describe so much charisma. It was really thrilling to be in his presence. I think about him a lot."

SANDRA FERGUSON (AMANDA)

[As Amanda Cory, Rachel and Mac's only child together, Ferguson knew Watson for a brief year and a half.] "I was very shy, and I regret that I didn't spend more time listening to him because I think I could have learned an awful lot from him."

MATT CRANE (MATTHEW CORY)

"It seemed that I worked with him longer, but it was only over a year. He was a really nice guy. He had an understated quality, too, in real life. He was just one of those people who have been on the show for a long time and he had a really good perspective about it. He came in and was fun to work with and set a good example as the head of the household. It was just a real pleasure to work with him."

SUSAN SULLIVAN (LENORE CURTIN)

"He was an exceptional actor—and I've worked over the years with a lot of actors. He had the capacity to listen. He was very gifted, and the best thing you can say about him, because it means a great deal to me, is that he was always a gentleman in the truest, roundest sense of that word. He was gentle, he was kind, and he had a very strong sense of himself and his own worth, and sometimes actors don't have that. And when you don't have that, the neediness sort of blinds you to other people and their needs."

CHARLES KEATING (CARL HUTCHINS)

"He was a true southern gent, Douglass, whose heart and passion were indeed in the theater and in poetry and romance. He was rooted in it and steeped in it and came from an ancient school. He had a kindness and a quietness about him. He added that kind of strength of character and purpose to the piece, that anchor, that made it possible for people like the villains to come in and play off of it. I think he enjoyed the scenes that we did together. We always had fun. We traveled backward and forward to

Connecticut together, so we always had a giggle. And I think Douglass enjoyed it from the standpoint—here I come out of a Shakespeare company and I was always spouting some bit of poetry or something, and he enjoyed all of that."

ANNA HOLBROOK (SHARLENE FRAME HUDSON)

"I'll never forget Doug Watson. I remember walking out the door with him one day. I was always concerned, I suppose, early on that I would not make it through the year and I said, 'You never have anything to worry about, do you?' I was reflecting on the fact that he was jumping into his car service to take him straight to Connecticut. And Doug took my hand and said, 'You never know anything.' Meaning you just never know when the jig is up—you just always appreciate what you have, and you never think you're the coolest thing to come along."

ALICE BARRETT (FRANKIE FRAME)

"Douglass died the week I joined the show. I had one conversation with him and he was utterly charming. I came on the month that the show was celebrating its 25th anniversary and I was in the middle of trying to figure out who killed Jason Frame, and the way the show was celebrating itself was that they were going to celebrate 25 years of Cory Publishing. Douglass, meanwhile, was going to go on vacation to a health spa and come back to do the 25th anniversary of Cory Publishing celebration, at which I was going to have a scene with him—we had the scripts already—I mean just a small, tiny sort of bump into him, 'Oh, hi, Mr. Cory.' Douglass, God bless his heart, said to me, 'So we're going to work together when I get back. I'm really looking forward to that.' And I thought, 'How dear! How totally dear!' He didn't have to do that at all. And he never made it back."

JIMMY HUTCHINSON (CREW CHIEF)

[Now retired, Jimmy Hutchinson spent twenty-three

Connie Ford

years behind the scenes at *Another World*.] "A gentleman, and friendly. He was good to the crew, interested in the crew. Bought dinner for the crew when we went late. Well liked by everyone—a terrific guy."

PAUL RAUCH (EXECUTIVE PRODUCER, 1972–83)

"I cast Douglass. He was just a phenomenally wonderful human being, a wonderful actor, friend, completely committed to what he did. It was a big loss."

MICHAEL LAIBSON (EXECUTIVE PRODUCER, 1988–93)

[Michael Laibson was the executive producer when the sad and devastating news of Douglass Watson's death reached the *Another World* studio.] "It was horrible. He was a beautiful, beautiful guy. He was such a gentleman and such an appreciator of what everybody did. He was so fair. He was very honest as an actor and as a person, and he was loved literally by everyone who worked with him. His death was a total shock. He was on vacation at a spa and just died.

"We were right in the midst of doing the 25th anniversary. It was really something because we had built it all around him and the anniversary of the company that he owned, and we knew we couldn't recast. There was just no way you could do that. So we had to have him disappear. We rewrote everything. A letter that he had written to congratulate everybody was read by Vicky Wyndham. She, of course, knew, and it was almost impossible for her to read this letter without responding to it knowing he was dead.

"We had to play the death eventually. It was really horrible. Everybody was crying, and when we did have to deal with the death of the character, we all went through the mourning again and the show went through a period of mourning. I remember Matt Crane just really fell apart when he heard, because the character was his father, but I think he was a father probably to many people in many ways. It was horribly devastating, but again the cast came through. The show must go on. . . ."

Connie Ford (Ada Hobson)

As Ada Hobson, Connie Ford played a no-nonsense woman. At her memorial on the show, her family described her as "tough, funny, full of love and loyalty" and a woman who always "said that one right truthful thing that made whatever problem you had manageable."

VICTORIA WYNDHAM (RACHEL)

"The reason they loved Connie Ford was because she was so real. She developed that character so beautifully. A bright, funny woman and every ounce an actress. That character was so grounded in reality, I think it was a real joy for her to play, to get out from under that Hollywood thing. She could play

felicia & cass remember mac ...

Linda Dano (Felicia Gallant) and Stephen Schnetzer (Cass Winthrop):

Linda: "A wonderful human being. The patriarch of the show."

Stephen: "He was the quintessential patriarch. I think of him all the time to this day. I go by his dressing room—mine was across from him while he was here—constantly thinking about conjuring up his spirit."

Linda: "The whole essence of *Another World* was Mac Cory, I think more than any other character that was ever here. He was so sweet. Nobody could play love like that—nobody. You give him love to play, God, he'd make you cry every time."

Stephen: "Grand opera."

Linda: "He made me crazy. He was a great role model. Great man."

Stephen: "Never negative."

Linda: "Never. You know that he used to go on trips—he traveled a lot all over the world. And he'd bring gifts back for everybody. Just tiny little things. My great story about Mac, about when I got the job—I started at the end of December and they had their Christmas party sometime in the early part of December, and I was invited to it even though I hadn't started yet. I met Doug Watson at the Christmas party and I met everyone else—Vicky Wyndham and everyone. When I started the next week, at the front desk there was a big bouquet of flowers from Mr. Watson and it said, 'You are the greatest thing they ever found. Welcome. Doug Watson.'"

scene:
Cory rose garden

ADA: I'm not ready to get old yet.

RACHEL: Once upon a time there was a woman who told me never to give in to my fears. The only time she would ever really be mad at me was if I gave up.

ADA: She had a big mouth.

RACHEL: I think she was pretty wise. She also told me that life was a great adventure and that death was just another beginning.

ADA: I didn't think you were listening.

those parts beautifully, but the Ada part was such a wonderful exercise for her in playing a part that she never got to play in life—she never got to be a mother and a wife. It was an extraordinary characterization when you knew Connie and knew what she was really like. It was the best of Connie. As far as I was concerned, when we had scenes together, she was my mother. It was so easy for the actress Vicky to believe Rachel existed because of Connie and Douglass and the ensemble that I had around me."

SANDRA FERGUSON (AMANDA)

"She was a great influence on me. She gave me a lot of insight into not only the business, but a lot of basic rules of life that I still, almost on a daily basis, reiterate. She lives on in my mind and in my thoughts. Amanda's relationship with her grandmother was a very affectionate one. Ada would be very, almost brutally honest—but then she'd make up for it in affection."

MATT CRANE (MATTHEW CORY)

"It was a pleasure to work with Connie. I'm glad I was there during that period when both of them [Connie Ford and Douglass Watson] were there. I look back on that with fond memories. It was nice because those people had been on the show for so long and they brought so much depth to it, and their history. And being the new person there and being accepted by them and participating in what they were doing and getting the encouragement and the support—it was really a special time."

Constance Ford was part of the Golden Years of *Another World* and the tradition of acting talent gleaned from the theater. In his book, *Eight Years in Another World,* Harding "Pete" Lemay writes that her talents were "as impressive as those of Maureen Stapleton, Kim Stanley, and Geraldine Page in the theater," and he delighted in writing for her.

MICHAEL LAIBSON (EXECUTIVE PRODUCER, 1988–93)

"I love Connie Ford. She scared people to death because she was definitely of the theater, and she was stormy, and she was just as passionate as a person. She knew this character inside out and she wasn't going to let anybody tell her anything that was contrary to what she believed this character would believe herself. I never was frightened of her. I was just kind of in awe of her energy. We hit it off really well. I remember telling her at some point, 'You know, if you have a problem with what's going on in the show, I want you to come in and tell me,' and she said, 'Oh, no, I can't do that. That's not my job. My job is to act. I may take it out on everybody else, but I'm not going to complain. That's just not done.'

"It was very hard to see her become ill. The audience clamored for her. They really wanted her, because she was such a formidable character on the show. She was working class and proud of it. Yet she could feel totally comfortable with the upper crust as well. But then she became ill and it became more and more difficult for her, her energy went away. I think it was cancer. She didn't tell anybody for a long time, but she was becoming weaker and weaker until she couldn't stand up, she couldn't memorize her lines anymore.

"We wanted to take care of her, but that meant that we couldn't use her as much as we wanted to or as the audience wanted to. But we also didn't want to say to the audience, 'The woman is sick,' because she didn't want everybody to know. She wanted to be treated like a professional until the last moment. She didn't want anybody fussing over her. She was great. She made that character, instead of it being the other way around. She really made that character."

Brent Collins *(Wallingford)*

Felicia, Wallingford, and Cass: They were the Three Musketeers, and their capers are among the highlights of *Another World*. He had been scheduled to appear for only four weeks, but irate fans pleaded for Wallingford's return, and three years later he was still there. Collins said at the time, "Who else would get into a gorilla cage and be trapped overnight for plot-line purposes?"

Linda Dano (Felicia Gallant) says, "I cry when I talk about Brent. I never have gotten over his loss. Isn't that funny that I've missed him so. He changed the perception of what little people are about. I've always believed that the world has based so much of their stupidity on fear. They don't understand something, so they're afraid of it, so they act badly about it. If you understand something, you don't make fun of it—embrace it and all the fear is gone.

"I used to say always about him and still do, that he changed the perception of all the millions of people who watch the show, that every one of those people, when they see a little person now, they are not afraid of them. They don't make fun of them. They remember their friend Wallingford. He would love to know that and I know he does know that, but what a wonderful tribute to leave for the world! What a great thing that is to have accomplished."

It was standing room only at St. Malachy's Church in New York City when Linda Dano and Stephen Schnetzer bid their friend good-bye.

Stephen Schnetzer: "The minute I met Brent Collins I liked him, and after working with him for about a day, I was crazy about the guy. I fell in love with him and his humor, compassion, generosity, integrity, tenacity, loyalty, friendship, innocence,

heart, and optimism. I'd like to be like Brent when I grow up. He was one of the most mature men I've ever known, with one of the most elevated spirits."

Linda Dano: "We really do have so much to celebrate. I look around at all your faces and at how many of you came today, and at all the beautiful flowers, and I think he would be thrilled, wouldn't he? He always loved a great show. I suppose that in a lifetime, you have many friends, many associates, people whom you care about, whom you love—but there are very few whom you planned to grow old with. And I suppose the part I hate is that he beat me to it, the little creep. I miss him. I not only miss him, but Felicia Gallant really feels the blow here. He did everything in life with gusto, with passion, with love. He made us all feel like we were his very best friends. We're very lucky. I will miss him all the rest of my life."

Another World is always proud to receive this prestigious honor. Winning an award voted on by your peers is certainly a career highlight, but anyone who's ever worked on a daytime drama can tell you it's a team effort to put on an hour show five days a week, fifty-two weeks a year—so hearty congratulations as well to all the nominees, the actors, the staff, and the crew, who make this phenomenon known as soap opera come alive on your television screens.

A w a r d Y e a r : 1 9 9 5 – 1 9 9 6

Outstanding Lead Actor in a Drama Series:
Charles Keating *(Carl Hutchins)*

Charles Keating remembers receiving the award: "It's delightful at the time. Absolutely delightful. But I accepted that very much as if I was the one who got to go up and collect it on behalf of all of us."

Outstanding Supporting Actress in a Drama Series:
Anna Holbrook (Sharlene Frame Hudson)

As Sharlene, Anna Holbrook struggled with a split personality that resulted in several identities, but the year she won the Emmy was the year her on-screen husband and soul mate John Hudson found comfort in the arms of Felicia Gallant. Holbrook recalls winning the Emmy: "At the time, it really was a most profound salute from my peers, and that's interesting because I'm very down-to-earth about awards, and the truth is, if you buy into good reviews, you have to accept the bad ones. So it's nice to have a group salute you and it meant a great deal to me, but the day-to-day opportunity to work and work and work, and more importantly, to be around the peer group who are working, is a real gift and it's a golden opportunity for people.

"Occasionally I'll pass the living room and I'll see the Emmy and it grounds me. I never knew it would do that for me. Something else I never knew I'd appreciate is the opportunity you have when you get up there to give a speech, the opportunity to say thank you to people who meant something to you. That's such a wonderful thing. It's a great podium. How often do you have an audience like that, where you can salute someone you love and adore! Or someone you have just appreciated because of how much they have backed you."

A w a r d Y e a r : 1 9 9 4 – 1 9 9 5

Outstanding Achievement in Music Direction and Composition for a Drama Series:

West Boatman, Composer
Ron Brawer, Music Director
Barry DeVorzon, Composer
Ed Dzubak, Composer
Richard Hazard, Composer
John Henry, Composer
Susan Beth Markowitz, Music Director/Supervisor
Rick Rhodes, Composer
Robert Sands, Composer

Carole Severson-Weiss, Music Director
Outstanding Original Song:
   "I Never Believed in Love"

Award Year: 1 9 9 4 - 1 9 9 5

Outstanding Achievement in Costume Design for a Drama Series:
   Margarita Delgado, Costume Designer
   Charles Schoonmaker, Costume Designer
Outstanding Achievement in Hairstyling for a Drama Series:
   Annette Bianco, Head Hairstylist
   Stanley Steven Hall, Hairstylist
   Joyce Sica, Hairstylist

Award Year: 1 9 9 2 - 1 9 9 3

Outstanding Lead Actress in a Drama Series:
Linda Dano (Felicia Gallant)

Linda Dano has been a fan favorite for years, playing the larger-than-life glamorous romance novelist Felicia Gallant. The year she won the Emmy, Felicia was struggling with the death of her beloved Lucas, a tragedy that threw her into the depths of despair, which led to a bout of alcoholism. Family and friends staged a painful intervention, and Felicia, always a survivor, struggled and overcame her addiction.

Dano remembers winning the Emmy: "Let me tell you, every time I've ever been nominated, it's been so overwhelming to me. It's so emotional for me. It's like I've come full circle somehow when I won that Emmy. I never dreamed in a million years that I would win it that night. I didn't listen to people who said, 'Oh, you're gonna win it. You're gonna win it.' I just didn't believe them. I just didn't think that would ever, ever happen.

"Obviously, I never prepared a speech. I just got up there and gushed away and forgot to thank John Aprea. Do you believe that? The whole crux of why I won that night was him and I never said his name. I said Stephen, I said Vicky, I just didn't say John—unforgivable. I've beaten myself up over that a hundred times.

"I'm always very tough on myself. I never think I'm very good. I hate watching myself. I always think, 'Oh, I should have done this. I should have done that.' I'm really, really critical of me. So to have people in my industry say, 'Bravo, you're a good actor,' was more than I could bear. So it was like the highlight of my career, and I'm very grateful for it. It really meant a lot to me. Still does.

"I took it to California because my parents still lived in California at the time. I was flying first class and I brought the Emmy, and everyone in the plane got to hold it. It went all the way through coach. Everyone held it so they could feel what an Emmy was like. I went out there to do an infomercial, and everyone in the audience got to hold it. Actually, my Emmy is a little frayed in the center—you know, the gold is kind of coming off it—because I did that. But yes, it was obviously a highlight of my career. And it always will be."

Outstanding Achievement in Hairstyling for a Drama Series:
   Angel DeAngelis, Head Hairstylist
   Annette Bianco, Hairstylist
   John Quaglia, Hairstylist
   Joyce Sica, Hairstylist

Award Year: 1 9 9 1 - 1 9 9 2

Outstanding Achievement in Hairstyling for a Drama Series:
   Angel DeAngelis, Head Hairstylist
   Annette Bianco, Hairstylist
   John Quaglia, Hairstylist
   Joyce Sica, Hairstylist
Outstanding Drama Series Directing Team:
   Susan Strickler

Casey Childs
Bob Schwartz
Michael Eilbaum

Award Year: 1990 – 1991

Outstanding Younger Actress in a Drama Series:
Anne Heche (Marley/Victoria Love)

Playing Bay City's resident saint/sinner was this talented teenager's first professional acting job and she made quite an impact. Actress Anna Stuart, who plays Vicky/Marley's mother, recalls one of the Emmy-submitted scenes: "When Annie was playing Marley and she finds out that Donna slept with Jake, we have this knock-down, drag-out, rip-roaring scene, and I remember we went straight to tape. I don't remember if we discussed it ahead of time. She may have said, 'If it's all right I may hit you back.' So we have this scene, and I will not really do those slaps. She says something and I 'slap' her, and she hauls off and hits me back! And I'm totally shocked. That was the scene they used for her Emmy reel."

Lifetime Achievement Award for Daytime Television: Procter & Gamble Productions

Award Year: 1989 – 1990

Outstanding Achievement in Costume Design for a Drama Series:
  Margarita Delgado, Costume Designer
  Charles Schoonmaker, Costume Designer
Outstanding Achievement in Hairstyling for a Drama Series:
  Angel DeAngelis, Head Hairstylist
  John Quaglia, Hairstylist
  Annette Bianco, Hairstylist
  Joyce Sica, Hairstylist

Award Year: 1988 – 1989

Outstanding Achievement in Costume Design for a Drama Series:
  Margarita Delgado, Costume Designer
  Charles Schoonmaker, Costume Designer

Award Year: 1985 – 1986

Outstanding Ingenue in a Drama Series:
Ellen Wheeler (Marley/Victoria Love)

Ellen Wheeler was cast as sweet Marley Love until then executive producer Steve Schenkel sensed that her range exceeded the part and created tough, streetwise Victoria Love, Marley's identical twin. Wheeler remembers winning the Emmy: "It would be silly to say it didn't mean a lot—it did. But I was so young, and it was the beginning of my career—it's like it didn't really compute. And it was only a couple of years ago, when I was sitting with my husband, and I think we were watching the Academy Awards, and I said to him, 'Wow, this is just so cool. I mean, I will never stop being in awe of this, of these people and what they've accomplished and what it must be like to be there and be part of those elite people who did something like that and had those kinds of accomplishments.' And he turned to me and said, 'You are one of those people.' It was the first time it really struck me. It did all of a sudden mean a lot more to me to say, 'I set out in my life to accomplish something'—and I haven't accomplished all my goals, I'm not saying, 'Oh, now I've finished and I can be done.' I'm just saying, I am part of something that as a little girl I watched and said, 'Someday, wouldn't it be neat to actually be there in that room.' Well, I've been there in that room! And they even called my name!"

When Wheeler won her second Emmy, for *All My Children*, she says, "I ran into my bathroom at home in my dress from the Emmys and cleaned my toilet, because I didn't want to get so wrapped up in the idea that I was now important. I wanted to come home and go, 'OK, you may have won, but you know what, you're still a real person who has to brush her teeth or you're going to get cavities, and who deals with her cellulite. All of those things are still happening to you.' So in my dress, I sprinkled Comet all over, scrubbed my toilet, then changed my clothes and went to the movies."

Special Classification of Outstanding Individual Achievement: Remote—Glen Cove

Another World traveled to Glen Cove for the double wedding of Rachel and Mac and Sandy and Blaine.

Award Year: 1980 – 1981

Outstanding Actor in a Daytime Drama Series: Douglass Watson (Mackenzie Cory)

In his book *Eight Years in Another World*, head writer Pete Lemay wrote about replacing the original Mackenzie Cory with actor Douglass Watson in the

unusual role of the older leading man: "Mac Cory was written out of the story for several months, and when he returned it was in the debonair person of Douglass Watson, whose infectious charm and inexhaustible acting range would lead us in any direction we chose." This beloved actor and two-time Emmy winner didn't prove them wrong.

Award Year: 1979 – 1980

Outstanding Actor in a Daytime Drama Series: Douglass Watson (Mackenzie Cory)

Award Year: 1978 – 1979

Outstanding Actress in a Daytime Drama Series: Irene Dailey (Liz Matthews)

She was the third Aunt Liz, and she too was cast by then executive producer Paul Rauch and head writer Pete Lemay. Liz had been established as a vain, controlling busybody. She had been written off the show, but the fans wanted her back. In his book *Eight Years in Another World*, Lemay wrote, "What she played went far beyond anything we expected and the Aunt Liz who had existed only as a vague blur in my mind sprang into vigorous form by the time she finished. . . . We had found our Aunt Liz, and her display of hard-learned, confidently conveyed acting technique was a preview of the richness and skill of the on-camera performances that followed it."

Award Year: 1977 – 1978

Outstanding Actress in a Daytime Drama Series: Laurie Heineman (Sharlene Frame Watts)

Award Year: 1975 – 1976

The collaboration of executive producer Paul Rauch and head writer Pete Lemay produced what were known as the Golden Years of *Another World*. Always an innovator, Rauch was the first to expand the show to the hour format. That was 1975, the year

Another World won the Emmy for Outstanding Daytime Drama Series.

Outstanding Daytime Drama Series:
Paul Rauch, Executive Producer
Joe Rothenberger, Producer
Mary S. Bonner, Producer

Award Year: 1974 - 1975

Outstanding Writing for a Daytime Drama Series:
Harding Lemay
Tom King
Charles Kozloff
Jan Merlin
Douglass Marland

Award Year: 1973 - 1974

Outstanding Art Direction or Scenic Design:
Otis Riggs Jr., Art Director

Award Year: 1996 - 1997

Nominees: Linda Dano, David Forsyth, Jensen Buchanan, Charles Keating, and Anna Holbrook
Jensen Buchanan remarked about her 1996–97 Emmy nomination, "It meant more to me than just about anything else in my career. It was such an exciting, thrilling time that not winning it just seemed like an addendum to the wonderful experience. It was great. I was very honored and very proud of my work that year."

Winners, Soapy Awards 1977

Favorite Villain: John Fitzpatrick (Willis Frame)
Favorite Villainess: Beverlee McKinsey (Iris Cory)
Actress Beverlee McKinsey recalls winning the award: "I won it the first two years they gave it as best villainess. It was very exciting! I was overjoyed! The first year we were on Merv Griffin's show, which was very exciting because you got an interview. The next year

we were on somebody's talk show that was on in the morning, and you got an interview there too. So I like it better than the ceremony today when you go up and get the award." Says McKinsey of her nine years as the scheming Iris, "That show was the highlight of my daytime career. There was never anything remotely like it afterward."

Winners, Soapy Awards 1978

Favorite Actress: Victoria Wyndham (Rachel Cory)
Rachel was created by the legendary Agnes Nixon, who said at the time, "The character has doom potential—she was destructive, but ultimately a greater threat to herself than to other people." When Victoria Wyndham took over the role, she gradually transformed Rachel from a misguided, insecure "heavy" into a more vulnerable, though still headstrong and fiercely independent, woman. It is a fascinating portrayal and remains so today.
Favorite Villain: Roberts Blossom (Sven Peterson)
Favorite Villainess: Beverlee McKinsey (Iris Cory)

Winner, Soap Opera Digest Awards, 1984

Outstanding Villainess: Nancy Frangione
 (Cecile de Poulignac)

Winner, Soap Opera Digest Awards, 1986

Outstanding Young Leading Actress:
Ellen Wheeler (Vicky/Marley Love)

Winner, Soap Opera Digest Awards, 1989

Outstanding Female Newcomer: Anne Heche
 (Vicky/Marley Love)
Outstanding Comic Actor: Stephen Schnetzer
 (Cass Winthrop)
It was "comedy tonight" with Cass and his cohorts Felicia (Linda Dano), Wallingford (Brent Collins), and Lily (Jackee Harry), not to mention Cass's turn as Krystal Lake and "her" entanglements with Tony "The Tuna."

Winner, Soap Opera Digest Awards, 1992

Outstanding Lead Actress: Anne Heche (Vicky/Marley Love)
Outstanding Male Newcomer: Paul Michael Valley (Ryan Harrison)
Outstanding Female Newcomer: Alla Korot (Jenna Norris)
Outstanding Younger Leading Actor:
 Ricky Paull Goldin (Dean Frame)

Winner, Soap Opera Digest Awards, 1993

Outstanding Younger Leading Actress:
 Alicia Coppola (Lorna Devon)

Winner, Soap Opera Digest Awards, 1995

Outstanding Lead Actor:
 Tom Eplin (Jake McKinnon)
Lynn Leahey of *Soap Opera Digest* says, "Jake's been a character that has always drawn a lot of fans.

Understandably so, because really from the minute Tom Eplin started, he just took charge of that character. He's a marvelous actor. He really is different. I think that there are actors like that—and every show has them—that you can't replace. They're just wonderful."

Winner, Soap Opera Digest Awards, 1996

**Outstanding Villain: Mark Pinter
(Grant Harrison)**

"This playing a villain and getting a *Soap Opera Digest* Award for best villain meant an awful lot," says Mark Pinter. "It really, really meant a lot. I'm glad I got it. I may never get another one, but that's OK because it's one of the true fan-voted awards."

Winner, Soap Opera Digest Awards, 1997

**Outstanding Male Showstopper:
Tom Eplin (Jake McKinnon)**

Winner, Soap Opera Digest Awards, 1998

**Outstanding Supporting Actress: Judi Evans Luciano
(Paulina Cory McKinnon Carlino)**

Luciano recalls winning the award: "It meant a lot because it's from the fans—that's the true award, that the people are actually entertained. Because a lot of times you don't know. You think, 'I'm not saving lives, I'm not doing anything, I go to work, go home.' You work in a studio, and you don't see people. But receiving an award shows you're doing something. You're affecting people! People are being touched and people are thinking differently or changing their lives. Or you're entertaining people. There's nothing wrong in that!"

Miscellaneous Awards

In July 1997, Victoria Wyndham celebrated her 25th year on *Another World* in the pivotal role of Rachel. At a gala celebration in New York, she was presented with a citation from Brooklyn Borough President Howard Golden. "I am an actor," said Wyndham, "and for an actor to have a twenty-five-year-long gig—it's just so wonderful." In honor of the show that has been taped in Brooklyn since its inception, Golden proclaimed July 22nd *Another World* Day.

Award Year: 1994

National Institute for Mental Illness DART (Depression Awareness Recognition and Treatment) Award

This award was given to Stephen Schnetzer for his portrayal of the manic-depressive Cass Winthrop. Schnetzer says, "It was a great opportunity to do something socially relevant. I think that's the first time daytime's ever touched on manic depression. The show was recognized for raising the consciousness and awareness of manic depression, and what was heartrending was meeting people on appearances during that time. They were coming out of the woodwork. I felt very paternal toward those people. People would come up to me and say, 'I'm manic depressive,' and I'd hug them and thank them for expressing their appreciation and their feeling that we supported them through the story."

Award Year: 1991

Directors Guild of America Award

This award went to the episode "The Case of the Stolen Heart," directed by Susan Strickler.

happy anniversary!

Another World premiered on May 4, 1964, in a very unusual way. William Matthews, the patriarch of the central Matthews family, had died. But that ending heralded a beginning, as viewers became acquainted with the lives and loves of the people of Bay City, in what came to be known as "the continuing story of *Another World*." That was thirty-five years ago.

In 1972 *Another World* was celebrating eight years on the air. Victoria Wyndham had taken over the role of Rachel, seen below seated next to her nemesis, Alice Matthews (Jacquie Courtney). These two women were in love with Steven Frame (George Reinholt, back row center), and neither was going to give him up without a fight.

Their tempestuous love story culminated in a special event, which marked the show's 10th anniversary. On May 4, 1974, Alice Matthews and Steven Frame were married on *Another World*'s (and daytime TV's) first hour-long show.

Off-screen, *Another World* celebrated its 20th anniversary at Windows on the World atop Manhattan's World Trade Center, where 350 people wined, dined, and danced. It was a memorable evening, made more so when Patricia Reed Scott, director of the Mayor's Office of Film, Theater, and Broadcasting, standing in for Mayor Ed Koch, delivered the following proclamation: "One of television's most popular and enduring daytime dramas, *Another World* celebrates its 20th anniversary today. Produced in our city during the past two decades, *Another World* continues to entertain millions of Americans, and its success is a source of pride to New York's television industry. Now, therefore, I, Edward I. Koch, Mayor of the City of New York, do hereby proclaim May 4, 1984, as *Another World* 20th Anniversary Day in New York City."

On air, Mac Cory said, "I can't tell you how happy Rachel and I are to be among the people we love the most. You know what I think? I think all of us ought to fix this particular moment in our memory forever. Happy Anniversary, *Another World*." Shortly before the cast reached its 25th anniversary in 1989, beloved actor Douglass Watson died unexpectedly.

Another World celebrated its 30th year on the air

1972

with a sixties bash—after all, that's when it all began. Many former residents returned to celebrate the 30th anniversary of Cory Publishing, including the redoubtable Aunt Liz.

The cast portrait was taken at a masquerade ball in 1995. To the shock of Bay City residents, Rachel had married Carl, Vicky was engaged to Ryan, Paulina was torn between Jake and Joe, and Michael Hudson was back in town.

On December 22, 1996, the cast and crew celebrated the taping of episode 8,000 of *Another World*! That's 8,000 episodes and still counting.

On the occasion of *Another World*'s 35th anniversary, the actors talk about what makes their show unique. . . .

Victoria Wyndham (Rachel Cory Hutchins)

"What made *Another World* great during those golden years was character-based writing that examined in minute detail the variations in those characters. Coupled with probably the finest acting ensemble on television—nighttime or daytime—taken from the theater. Our whole acting ensemble knew how to get maximum use out of words. Then we had a producer who was about quality and paid for it. And it was all up there on the screen. That's what we were about: the ensemble and quality being everything. But it started with the writing and the acting."

Stephen Schnetzer (Cass Winthrop)

"The most sweeping statement would be the really good people who have come through these doors. The talent of the acting company has always been held in considerable esteem industry-wide. And the sense of traditional values the show has always been strong in, which I think is exemplified in those memorial episodes, wedding episodes, party episodes, and special episodes."

Mark Pinter (Grant Harrison)

"I think it's the integrity of the characters and respect for the history of the show and where it's come from. All of the hundreds of actors who have

1987

1989

1992

1994

1995

isn't anybody I can point to in this cast who just wants to bring home a paycheck. Everybody really cares about the work. There are days when you're thinking, 'Listen, it's Friday, we just want to go home. No, we don't want to do this scene again.' But then everyone here is willing to look you in the eye and say, 'You know what, we can do it better. Let's go.' And that's rare. I've worked in daytime for twenty years, and that's the big difference I see here on this show, across the board from producers, to directors, to actors, to hair and makeup—everybody here cares."

Kale Browne (Michael Hudson)

"Brooklyn. I think there's something about working out of the mainstream, and working isolated out there in a way that doesn't really nurture stars, so to speak, because we're all in this lifeboat together. There's something very healthy about that. Consequently, we're all there together putting in a huge amount of hours and you get very close to the people who you're working with. It's like an involuntary family and it kind of has its ebb and flow. I had known people who were on the show in previous years and I always thought, boy, they hire good actors out there. I was honored to join the ranks."

Joe Barbara (Joe Carlino)

"It's a very real, very honest show. I get to play a character who tries to do the right thing in sometimes extraordinary, but other times very ordinary situations. And for the most part we deal with situations that the average person can absolutely relate to. They can see the choices that we make and whether we're right or wrong, they can see us struggle and try to do the right thing. And more often than not, they can learn from it."

Anna Holbrook (Sharlene Frame Hudson)

"I truly always thought of the opportunity to work as often as I did and to have a character as rich and marvelous as Sharlene was such a gift. And I've got friendships for life from being immersed like that. You don't have the opportunity to be as close to peo-

come and gone in the history of this show, and technicians, writers, directors, producers, and everybody who contributed to keeping the show on the air, but most importantly, Procter & Gamble, who have made the commitment to the show over the years. They have fought hard to keep the show on the air and there are many wonderful executives in charge of production, including Ed Trach, who went to the mat for the show. They care a lot about their shows. You've got to honor that and respect the contributions that these people have made over the years. That's who you celebrate. From Bill Bell to Irna Phillips, Agnes Nixon—all the greats have had something to do with this show. That's what's made it special."

Lisa Peluso (Lila Roberts Cory)

"I think we're real. And I think that's what sets us apart. We have moments when we're over the top, but for the most part, this show as a whole is not. Everyone here really strives to do their best. There

ple as when you're with actors and you have to be vulnerable and expose yourself. And you just hope that the people around you are going to let you take the risks and they'll love you for it, or go with you, support you. And so for the rest of their lives, for me, they're there. They're imprinted in my heart."

Ellen Wheeler (Marley Love)

"Really, almost nothing ever happens in a soap opera that hasn't happened to someone in real life. As outlandish as these things seem, and as off-the-wall as they are, these experiences happen to people—sisters show up who nobody knew existed and babies get switched. They don't happen to most of us, although almost all of us have had one or two major experiences in our life. In soaps, the experiences are no different, it's just that as a soap character, I'll have a lifetime's worth of experiences in one year. It gets compressed into a shorter amount of time and you're watching a whole bunch of people have them, so it gets heightened, because you're watching thirty people have experiences. But the social commentary is very real. When breast cancer is a big deal, then usually somebody deals with that on the show. When AIDS comes up, then someone deals with that on the show. When there's a war, one of the boys has to go off and fight the war. We deal with those things on the soap, because we're trying to deal with the same things people are dealing with in their real life. And I like being a part of that kind of history. We wear beautiful clothes, and we have fancy makeup and fancy hair, and we want what we do to be entertaining, but part of what we do is mirror society. Sometimes if you watch someone else go through it, then when you have to deal with something similar you are more prepared."

Kim Rhodes (Cindy Brooke Harrison)

"The acting. The people. The insulation. I think John Bolger once called us a dysfunctional little family and we really are. You know we can scream and bitch at each other, but so help me if anybody from the outside screams and bitches at anybody in here—I don't care who you are, you're wrong! The bond between the cast and the crew is incredibly close. Our crew is our group of cheerleaders: They clap, laugh, and feed us energy."

o r i g i n a l   c a s t

CHARACTER	ACTOR	YEARS
KEN BAXTER	WILLIAM PRINCE	1964–65
LAURA BAXTER	AUGUSTA DABNEY	1964–65
TOM BAXTER	NICHOLAS PRYOR	1964
ANN FULLER	OLGA BELLIN	1964
ALICE MATTHEWS	JACQUELINE COURTNEY	1964–75, 84–85, 89
BILL MATTHEWS	JOSEPH GALLISON	1964–68
GRANNY MATTHEWS	VERA ALLEN	1964
JANET MATTHEWS	LIZA CHAPMAN	1964–66
JIM MATTHEWS	JOHN BEAL	1964
LIZ MATTHEWS	SARAH CUNNINGHAM	1964
MARY MATTHEWS	VIRGINIA DWYER	1964–75
PAT MATTHEWS	SUSAN TRUSTMAN	1964–67
RUSS MATTHEWS	JOEY TRENT	1964–65
SUSAN MATTHEWS	FRAN SHARON	1964
MISSY PALMER	CAROL ROUX	1964–68, 69–70

c o m p r e h e n s i v e   c a s t   l i s t

CHARACTER	ACTOR	YEARS
OFFICER ADAMS	JOHN MATTEY	1995-PRESENT
WAYNE ADDISON	ROBERT MILLI	1969–70
	EDMUND HASHIM	1969
TOM ALBINI	PIERRINO MASCORINO	1979
	PETER BRANDON	1966, 79
ALISTAIR	ROBERTO GARI	1992–95
REX ALLINGHAM	STEPHEN SCHNETZER	1987
DINO AMATI	JOHN DEVRIES	1978
SHARON AMATI	KAUILANI LEE	1978
QUENTIN AMES	PETER RATRAY	1976–77
KEVIN ANDERSON	JAMES GOODWIN	1992–93
BLAIR BAKER	BRIDGET WHITE	1996
	KATHY TRAGESER	1995–96
HORACE BAKEWELL	THOMAS TONER	1983
BRIAN BANCROFT	PAUL STEVENS	1977–86
TED BANCROFT	LUKE REILLY	1983–84
	RICHARD BACKUS	1979
	ERIC A. ROBERTS	1977
ADAM BANKS	GEOFFREY EWING	1983–84
KYLE BARKLEY	ROGER FLOYD	1993–94
GREG BARNARD	NED SCHMIDTKE	1977–78
JOAN BARNARD	PATRICIA ESTRIN	1977–78
JOE BARRON	ANTHONY TERRELL	1991
BARROWS	PHILIP KRAUS	1983
ROY BARRY	ROBERT GIBSON	1979
SGT. BARTLETT	BENJAMIN HENDRICKSON	1983
EVAN BATES/FRAME	ERIC SCOTT WOODS	1994–95
	CHARLES GRANT	1988–1990
HOPE BAUER	ELISSA LEEDS	1966
MICHAEL BAUER	GARY PILLAR (aka Carpenter)	1966–67
DANNY BECK	STEVE BLANCHARD	1993
DARRYL BECKETT	ERIC LARAY HARVEY	1992–93
STRIKER BELLMAN	CLIFTON JAMES	1980
VICTORIA BELLMAN	ELIZABETH ALLEN	1980
DORIS BENNETT	LYNN MOWRY	1979
EMILY BENSON	ALEXANDRA NEIL	1984–85
DR. TAYLOR BENSON	CHRISTINE ANDREAS	1990–91
ROY BINGHAM	MORGAN FREEMAN	1982–84
MIRANDA BISHOP	JUDITH MCCONNELL	1980–81
BRIAN BLAKE	JERED HOLMES	1971–72
MITCH BLAKE	WILLIAM GRAY ESPY	1979–82, 86–90
CHRISTOPHE BOUDREAU	PETER RATRAY	1995
DR. EMILY BRADFORD	NANCY SNYDER	1994, 1997
DR. JOHN BRADFORD	JOHN CRAWFORD	1964–65
SCOTT BRADLEY	PAUL TULLEY	1978–80
	MICHAEL GOODWIN	1975–76
HUNTER BRADSHAW	ROBERT SEDGWICK	1984
GREG BRADY	ZACK GRENIER	1995
DR. BROGAN	PETER REARDON	1998
LEONARD BROOKS	JOHN TILLINGER	1978–80, 81–82
	JOHN HORTON	1977–78
	JOSEPH MAHER	1975–78
LEFTY BURNS	LAWRENCE KEITH	1967–68
ETTA MAE BURRELL	ELAIN R. GRAHAM	1996-PRESENT
JUDY BURRELL	KIM SYKES	1995–96
	SAUNDRA MCCLAIN	1993–95
	DARLENE LOVE	1993
TONI BURRELL	RHONDA ROSS KENDRICK	1997-PRESENT
CRAIG CALDWELL	MICHAEL STONE	1980
MARTIN CALLAHAN	CLEMENT FOWLER	1994
BEN CAMPBELL	DAVID BUTLER	1979
DAVID CAMPBELL	JIM MACLAREN	1991–92
JOYCE CAMPBELL	SARAH NALL	1984–85
DANTE MACKENZIE CARLINO		
	AUSTIN MICHAEL LUCIANO	1997-PRESENT
	BRANDON AND DILLON CASH	1996–97
EDDIE CARLINO	TONY MONTERO	1995
JOE CARLINO	JOSEPH BARBARA	1995-PRESENT
SOFIA CARLINO	DAHLIA SALEM	1995–98
TONY CARLINO	JASON CULP	1996
TONY CARLISLE	JOHN H. BRENNAN	1986–87
E. J. CARR	E. J. CARR	1995
ELIOT CARRINGTON	JAMES DOUGLAS	1972–74
	JOE HANNAHAM	1972
CHRISTY CARSON	PATTI D'ARBANVILLE	1992–93
DOUGLAS CARSON	PETER GALMAN	1992–93
DUSTIN CARTER	VINCE WILLIAMS	1996
RAFE CARTER	PHIL STERLING	1970
LUKE "LUCAS" CASTIGLIANO		
	JOHN APREA	1989–92, 93
FRANK CHADWICK	ROBERT KYA-HILL	1970
DR. CHRISTOPHER CHAPIN		
	DON SCARDINO	1985–86
MICHAUD CHRISTOPHE	SERGE DUPIRE	1985
BELLE CLARK	JANET WARD	1971–73
TED CLARK	STEPHEN BOLSTE	1971–73
SAMANTHA COERBELL	ANN KUTTRIDGE	1994

Character	Actor	Years
DR. EMILY COLE	JOANNA MERLIN	1970
ZACHARY COLTON	CURT DAWSON	1980–81
BRIDGET CONNELL	BARBARA BERJER	1985–98
PAUL CONNELLY	STEPHEN JOYCE	1979–80
RITA CONNELLY	CAMILLA CARR	1979
KEVIN COOK	LEE PATTERSON	1979–80
BILLY COOPER	EDDIE EARL HATCH	1993–95
	DAVID KING	1993
	REUBEN SANTIAGO HUDSON	1990–93
JESS COOPER	BILL MOOR	1981
ANGELA CORELLI	BRANDY BROWN	1994–95
CONNIE CORELLI	ANGELA PIETROPINTO	1994–95
ADAM CORY	ED FRY	1986–89
ALEXANDER MACKENZIE CORY		
	ADAM KISHPAUGH	1984–85
AMANDA CORY FOWLER HARRISON		
	SANDRA FERGUSON	1987–93, 98-PRESENT
	LAURA MOSS	1996–98
	CHRISTINE TUCCI	1993–95
	ANNE TORSIGLIERI (temp)	1993
	DANA KLABOE	1981–86
	NICOLE CATALANOTTO	1978–81
IRIS CORY WHEELER	CARMEN DUNCAN	1988–94
	CAROLE SHELLEY (temp)	1980
	BEVERLEE MCKINSEY	1972–80
JASMINE CORY	ALEXANDRA, SYNDNEY,	
	AND JACQUELINE LADEMAN	1998-PRESENT
MACKENZIE CORY	DOUGLASS WATSON	1974–89
	ROBERT EMHARDT	1973–74
MAGGIE CORY	LISA D. BRENNER	1995–96
	JULIE NATHANSON (temp)	1996
	JODI LYNN O'KEEFE	1995
	ROBYN GRIGGS	1993–95
	CAITLIN ROARK	1983–85
	NICOLE SCHRINK	1982–83
MATTHEW CORY	MATT CRANE	1988–97, 98-PRESENT
	JEFF PHILLIPS	1998
	BRIAN KRAUSE	1997–98
	DANIEL DALE	1986–87
	ALEXANDER PARKER	1982–86
	CHRISTIAN MAURICE	1982
	MATTHEW MAIENCZYK	1980–82
NEAL CORY	ROBERT LUPONE	1985–86
PAULINA CANTRELL CORY MCKINNON CARLINO		
	JUDI EVANS LUCIANO	1991-PRESENT
	CALI TIMMINS	1990–91
RACHEL DAVIS MATTHEWS FRAME CORY HUTCHINS		
	VICTORIA WYNDHAM	1972-PRESENT
	MARGARET IMPERT	1971
	ROBIN STRASSER	1967–71, 71–72
SANDY CORY	STEPHEN BOGARDUS	1993
	CHRISTOPHER RICH	1981–85
CULLEN	MICHAEL LAGUARDIA	1983
ANDY CUMMINGS	JIM SECREST	1969
WALLY CURTIN	DENNIS MCKIERNAN	1974–75
	JASON GLADSTONE	1972–74
	SCOTT FIRESTONE	1971–72
WALTER CURTIN	VAL DUFOUR	1967–72
DEREK DANE	KEVIN CARRIGAN	1989–90
GERALD DAVIS	WALTER MATHEWS	1970, 72–74
PAMMY DAVIS	PAMELA TOLL	1970
LILA DAWSON	MARY TERESA	1994
	KRISTEN WILSON	1994
LORETTA DELAHANTY	SLOANE SHELTON	1993–94, 97
	SUSAN MANSUR	1994–95
JASPER DELANEY	RALPH CLANTON	1970
DR. OLIVIA DELANEY	TINA SLOAN	1980–81
ROBERT DELANEY	NICOLAS COSTER	1970, 72–76, 80, 89
CAPTAIN SEAN DELANEY	ALAN NORTH	1984–89
BARRY DENTON	JOSEPH SIRANO	1994
CECILE DE POULIGNAC	NANCY FRANGIONE	1981–84, 86, 89, 93, 1995–96
	SUSAN KEITH	1979–81
ELENA DE POULIGNAC	MAEVE MCGUIRE	1981–83
	CHRISTINA PICKLES	1977–79
LORNA DEVON	ROBIN CHRISTOPHER	1994–97
	ALICIA COPPOLA	1991–94
MISS DEVON	EVALYN BARON	1983–84
TRACY DEWITT MATTHEWS		
	JANICE LYNDE	1979–81
	CAROLINE MCWILLIAMS	1976
DOOLEY	PAUL KATZ	1981
FRED DOUGLAS	CHARLES BAXTER	1965–71
ERNIE DOWNS	HARRY BELLAVER	1967–70
OFFICER DOYLE	ED HODSON	1994
LUCY DRAKE	BRITT SADE	1996
MITCHELL DRU	GEOFFREY LUMB	1964–71
AMY DUDLEY	DEBORAH HOBART	1980
JASON DUNLAP	WARREN BURTON	1980–82
DR. ROYAL DUNNING	MICHAEL MINOR	1983–84
BARRY DURRELL	DREW COBURN	1983
JUSTINE DUVALIER	VICTORIA WYNDHAM	1995, 97
BUNNY EBERHARDT	MARCIA MCCABE	1995
AL EDWARDS	ARTHUR FRENCH	1986–88
JULIE ANN EDWARDS	TARA WILSON	1986–89
ZACK EDWARDS	JAMES PICKENS, JR.	1986–90
SAM EGAN	DREW SNYDER	1982
RUDY ENRIGHT	JOEL SIMON	1979–80
DR. COURTNEY EVANS	STINA NIELSEN	1995–96
	BELLAMY YOUNG	1995 (recurring)
DEE EVANS	KATIE RICH	1985–86
BLAINE EWING CORY	JUDY DEWEY	1984–85
	LAURA MALONE	1978–84
CATLIN EWING	THOMAS IAN GRIFFITH	1984–87
CLARICE HOBSON EWING	GAIL BROWN	1975–86, 89, 93
CORY EWING	CARMINE RIZZO (aka Grey)	1976–85
FRED EWING	BARTON HEYMAN	1979
JEANNE EWING (baby)	MELISSA LUCIANO	1982–85
JEANNE EWING (baby)	BETTY MILLER	1983
LARRY EWING	RICK PORTER	1978–86, 89
CORNELIA EXETER	ANNE SEYMOUR	1978–79
DANNY FARGO	ANTONY PONZINI	1966–67
REGINALD FEARING	DILLON EVANS	1983
MR. FENEMAN	RONALD RAND	1995
GEORGE FENTON	WILLIAM ANDREWS	1983
GIL FENTON	TOM WIGGIN	1983–84
MARIE FENTON	LENKA PETERSON	1983
MAE FINKELSTEIN	SHEILA TOUSSEY	1994
VERA FINLEY	CAROL MAYO JENKINS	1977
ELLA FITZ	LOIS SMITH	1983
TRENT FORBES	TERRENCE MCCROSSAN	1994
ALEXANDRA "ALLI" FOWLER		
	ALICIA LEIGH WILLIS	1999-PRESENT
	LAUREN TOUB	1997
	LINDSAY LOHAN	1996–97
	HILLARY SCOTT	1993–95
	KERRI ANN DARLING	1988–93
LORETTA FOWLER	ROSEMARY MURPHY	1988

Character	Actor	Years
SAM FOWLER	BRIAN GREEN	1991–93
	DANNY MARKEL	1990–91
	THOMAS GIBSON (temp)	1990
	ROBERT KELKER-KELLY	1987–90
DEAN FRAME	RICKY PAULL GOLDIN	1990–93, 94–95, 98
DIANA FRAME SHEA	ANNE ROSE BROOKS	1981–82
EMMA FRAME ORDWAY	ELIZABETH ASHLEY	1990
	TRESA HUGHES	1975–76
	BEVERLEE MCKINSEY	1972
JAMIE FRAME	RUSSELL TODD	1990–93
	LAURENCE LAU	1986–90
	STEPHEN YATES	1983–85
	RICHARD BEKINS	1979–83
	TIM HOLCOMB	1978–79
	ROBERT DORAN	1973–78
	BRAD BEDFORD	1973
	TYLER MEAD	1973
	AIDEN MCNULTY	1972–73
	SETH HOLZLEIN	1970–72
JANICE FRAME CORY	CHRISTINE JONES	1978–80, 89
	VICTORIA THOMPSON	1972–74
JASON FRAME	CHRIS ROBINSON	1987–89
MARY FRANCES "FRANKIE" FRAME WINTHROP		
	ALICE BARRETT-MITCHELL	1989–96
MIMI HAINES FRAME	TRISH HAWKINS	1978–79
SALLY SPENCER FRAME EWING		
	TAYLOR MILLER	1985–86
	MARY PAGE KELLER	1983–85
	DAWN BENZ	1983
	JENNIFER RUNYON	1981–83
	JULIE PHILLIPS	1979–80
	CATHY GREENE	1975–78
SHARLENE FRAME WATTS MATTHEWS HUDSON		
	ANNA KATHRYN HOLBROOK	1988–91, 93–97
	LAURIE HEINEMANN	1975–77
STEVEN FRAME	SPENCER TREAT CLARK	1995–PRESENT
	JIMMY MCQUAID (temp)	1998
	MICHAEL ANGARANO (temp)	1998
	CHRISTOPHER CONROY	1994, 95
	JOHN NASH	1989–94
STEVE FRAME	GEORGE REINHOLT	1968–75, 89
	DAVID CANARY	1981–83
VINCE FRAME	JAY MORRAN	1978–79
WILLIS FRAME	LEON RUSSOM	1976–80
	JOHN FITZPATRICK	1975–76
MRS. FRANKLIN	KATE WILKINSON	1983
ILSA FREDERICKS	GWYDA DON HOWE	1981–82
ESTELLE FREMONT	JAN MAXWELL	1994
DANIEL GABRIEL	PETER LOCHRAN	1985
FELICIA GALLANT	LINDA DANO	1983–PRESENT
WILLIE GANNON	TIM DEHAY	1995
BRETT GARDNER	COLLEEN DION	1992–94
DR. RICHARD GAVIN	WILLIAM ROERICK	1974–75, 77
EDWARD/EDOUARD GERARD		
	JOHN SAXON	1985–86
DR. DAVE GILCHRIST	DAVID ACKROYD	1974–77
DR. ALAN GLASER	DAVID O'BRIEN	1987
LOUISE GODDARD BROOKS		
	ANNE MEACHAM	1972–80, 81–82
GOMEZ	STEPHANIE MARTINI	1986
	WANDA DEJESUS	1986
BEATRICE GORDON	JACQUELINE BROOKES	1975–76
OLIVE GORDON RANDOLPH		
	JENNIFER LEAK	1976–79
RAYMOND GORDON	GARY CARPENTER	1977–78
	TED SCHACKELFORD	1975–77
BILL GORMAN	DAVID COMBS	1983
VIVIEN GORROW	GRETCHEN OEHLER	1978–81, 83–84, 88–90
RICK GRAHAM	THOM ZIMERLE	1988–89
	RICK GIANESE/GIANASI	1988
LISA GRADY	JOANNA GOING	1987–89
GRAND DUCHESS	ABBY LEWIS	1995
EVAN GRANT	ALAN CAMPBELL	1983
MORGAN GRAVES, DA	DONNA MURPHY	1989–91
ALEX GREGORY	JAMES CONGDON	1965–66
DR. BERT GREGORY	HOUSE JAMESON	1965–66
CORA GREGORY	FLORENCE WILLIAMS	1965–66
DR. ERNEST GREGORY	MARK LENARD	1965
KAREN GREGORY	ELLEN WESTON	1965–66
DAPHNE GRIMALDI	LILIANA KOMOROWSKI	1985
JERRY GROVE	PAUL TINDER	1981
	KEVIN CONROY	1980–81
	MICHAEL GARFIELD	1979–80
MARGO GROVE	JUDY CASSMORE	1980–81
MRS. GUITTIEREZ	CARLA VALENTINE	1995
SCOTT GUTHRIE	BRONSON PICKETT	1998
KIT HALLOWAY PERRINI	BRADLEY BLISS	1979–81
RICK HALLOWAY	TONY CUMMINGS	1980–82
TAYLOR HALLOWAY	RON HARPER	1980
DEPUTY BOYD HANES	RON MATTHEWS	1998
ED HARDING	HOWARD E. ROLLINS, JR.	1982
QUINN HARDING	PETRONIA PALEY	1981–87
CATHY HARRIS	HARRIET HARRIS	1982–83
CINDY BROOKE HARRISON		
	KIM RHODES	1996–PRESENT
GRANT HARRISON	MARK PINTER	1991–99
	DACK RAMBO	1990–91
KELSEY HARRISON	KAITLIN HOPKINS	1992–94
KIRKLAND HARRISON	SEAN RADEMAKER	1996–PRESENT
	CONNOR RADEMAKER	1995–96
	RYAN AND KYLE PEPI	1995
	AUSTIN AND EVAN TENNENBAUM	1994–95
"FAUX" KIRKLAND HARRISON (Sean Patrick Miller)		
	WILLIAM AND EDWARD SILBER	1995
	BRIGITTE AND JOSEPH SYKES	1994–95
RUTH HARRISON	TANNY MCDONALD	1993
	CYNTHIA HARRIS	1992
RYAN HARRISON	PAUL MICHAEL VALLEY	1990–95, 96–97
SPENCER HARRISON	DAVID HEDISON	1991–95, 96
EMILY HASTINGS	MONA BRUNS	1966–67
VIC HASTINGS	JOHN CONSIDINE	1974–76
SERGEANT HAWKINS	GEORGE BAMFORD	EARLY 1980S
HAYWOOD	GORDON GOULD	1983
PHIL HIGLEY	MCLIN CROWELL	1979
HILDA	PAT SONES	1988–95
ZACK HILL	JOHN SEITZ	1983
ADA DAVIS HOBSON	CONSTANCE FORD	1967–92
	PEG MURRAY (temp)	1983
CHARLIE HOBSON	FRED J. SCOLLAY	1977–80
DENNY HOBSON	JAMES HORAN	1981–82
LEIGH HOBSON	CHRISTOPHER KNIGHT	1980–81
GREG HOUSTON	CHRISTOPHER COUSINS	1986–87
SAMANTHA HOUSTON	DEIDRE IMERSHEIN	1986
CLARA HUDSON	PEG SMALL	1995
	KATE WILKINSON	1987–88, 89
	SCOTTY BLOCH	1987
GREGORY HUDSON	CHRISTOPHER MARQUETTE	1996–97

	ALEX BOWEN	1996
	MORGAN HODGEN	1996
	BLAISE GARZA	1994–96
	CHRISTOPHER GAUTIERI	1993–94
	JOHNNY NELSON	1993
	JUDE SULLIVAN	1991–93
DR. JOHN HUDSON	DAVID FORSYTH	1987–97
MICHAEL HUDSON	KALE BROWNE	1986–93, 95–98
NICK HUDSON/NICK TERRY		
	MARK MORTIMER	1996-PRESENT
	KEVIN MCCLATCHY	1995–96
	JUSTIN W. CHAMBERS	1995
CARL HUTCHINS	CHARLES KEATING	1983–85, 91–98
CORY HUTCHINS	EDWARD AND JOSEPH STATEN	1997-PRESENT
ELIZABETH HUTCHINS	EDWARD AND JOSEPH STATEN	1997-PRESENT
PERRY HUTCHINS	DAVID OLIVER	1983–85
YOSHI ITO	KEVIN JOHN GEE	1992–94
ROGER JACKSON	GEOFFREY PIERSON	1992
JIMMY/DEAN WHITNEY	CHRIS NOTH	1985, 88
NEIL JOHANSSEN	JAMES HYDE	1997
CAROLINE JOHNSON	RUE MCCLANAHAN	1970–71
NEIL JOHNSON	JOHN GETZ	1974–76
GRANDMA JONES	JOSEPHINE NICHOLS	1985
KEN JORDAN	LEWIS ARLT	1990–91
KEVIN JULIAN	ERIC PAEPER	1988
ROB KAPLAN	MATTHEW ARKIN	1994
BERT KELLER	JOSH CLARK	1983
CLAUDE KELLY	ARTHUR E. JONES	1977
HANK KENT	STEVE FLETCHER	1992–94
RITA KENT	LINDA C. JONES	1983
SHERI KENT	LESLIE LYLES	1992–93
TOMMY KENT	CORY LEE ROGERS	1992–94
BESS KILLWORTH	CARMEN MATTHEWS	1983
SYLVIE KOSLOFF	LEORA DANA	1979–80
MR. KOYAMA	TOSHIRO YAMAMATO	1995
DANA KRAMER	PASEAN WILSON	1997–98
	KIMBERLY HAWTHORNE	1997
	CASSANDRA CREECH	1994
	MICHELLE HURD	1991–97
MARSHALL LINCOLN KRAMER, III		
	DEAN IRBY	1996
	ANDRE DESHIELDS	1995–1996
	RANDY BROOKS	1994–95
MEL LAFFERTY	ROD GIBBONS	1970
CAROL LAMONTE	JEANNE LANGE	1974–76
THERESE LAMONTE	NANCY MARCHAND	1976
DR. KURT LANDIS	DONALD MADDEN	1974
JIM LARUSSO	WALT WILLEY	1986
SCOTT LASALLE	HANK CHEYNE	1986–88
JUNE LAVERTY	GERALDINE COURT	1979
KIRK LAVERTY	CHARLES CIOFFI	1979
JESSE LAWRENCE	DONDRE WHITFIELD	1989–90
REUBEN LAWRENCE	CLAYTON PRINCE	1988–90
RONNIE LAWRENCE	B. J. JEFFERSON	1988–91
PEGGY LAZARUS	REBECCA HOLLEN	1986–87
CINDY LEE	DEE ANN SEXTON	1980
TOMMY LEE	LARRY ATLAS	1985
PHILIP LESSNER	ED BRYCE	1972–73
ALAN LEWIS	CRAIG SISLER	1983
HELGA LINDEMAN	HELEN STENBORG	1977–78
REGINE LINDEMAN	BARBARA EDA-YOUNG	1977–78
ZANE LINDQUIST	PATRICK TOVATT	1985–86
LINDSEY	LAURA BONARRIGO	1991
ROMALDA LITTON	MARCIA LEWIS	1994

ROSE LIVINGSTONE	ANN FLOOD	1986–87
DR. JERRY LOMBARDI	LOU LIBERATORE	1992
ELENA LOPEZ	JENNIFER MAKRIS	1995
DONNA LOVE HUDSON	ANNA STUART	1983–86, 89-PRESENT
	SOFIA LANDON GEIER (temp)	1990–91, 93
	PHILECE SAMPLER	1987–89
ELIZABETH LOVE (flashback)		
	ANNE HOWARD	1988
MARLEY LOVE HUDSON	ELLEN WHEELER	1984–86, 98-PRESENT
	JENSEN BUCHANAN	1991–94, 97, 98
	ANNE HECHE	1987, 88–89, 90–91
NICOLE LOVE	ANNE HOWARD	1987–89, 93
	LAURIE LANDRY	1986–87
	KIM MORGAN GREENE	1983–84
PETER LOVE	MARCUS SMYTHE	1985–87
	CHRISTOPHER HOLDEN	1985
	JOHN HUTTON	1982–84
REGINALD LOVE	JOHN CONSIDINE	1986–88
VICTORIA LOVE HUDSON MCKINNON		
	JENSEN BUCHANAN	1991-PRESENT
	CYNTHIA WATROS (temp)	1998
	ANNE HECHE	1987–91
	RHONDA LEWIN	1986
	ELLEN WHEELER	1985–86
SAM LUCAS	JORDAN CHARNEY	1967–70, 74
PHILIP LYONS	ROBERT GENTRY	1979–81
CHRIS MACALEER or MCALEAR		
	MARY LAYNE	1988
EMILY MADDUX	ALLISON MCDONNELL	1997
CHRIS MADISON	ERIC MORGAN STUART	1996-PRESENT
RICK MADISON	GERALD ANTHONY	1991–92
DR. RITA MADISON	FRANCHELLE STEWART DORN	1995–96
SALLY MADISON	KATHLEEN MAHONEY BENNETT	1991–92
DR. ABEL MARSH/LEO MARS		
	JOE MORTON	1983–84
DREW MARSTEN	DENNY ALBEE	1988
BUCK MASON	MARK JUPITER	1995
EMILY MASON	GAIL DIXON	1971
	IRENE BUNDE	1969–70
LILY MASON	JACKEE HARRY	1983–86
DR. ALICE MATTHEWS FRAME		
	JACQUELINE COURTNEY	1964–70, 71–75, 84–85, 89
	LINDA BORGESON	1981–82
	VANA TRIBBEY	1981
	WESLEY ANN PFENNING	1979
	SUSAN HARNEY	1975–79
BILL MATTHEWS	JOSEPH GALLISON	1964–68
CINDY CLARK MATTHEWS	LEONIE NORTON	1971–72
JIM MATTHEWS	HUGH MARLOWE	1969–82
	SHEPPERD STRUDWICK	1964–69
	LEON JANNEY	1964
	JOHN BEAL	1964
LIZ MATTHEWS	IRENE DAILEY	1974–86, 87–93, 94
	NANCY WICKWIRE	1969–71
	AUDRA LINDLEY	1964–69
	SARAH CUNNINGHAM	1964
OLIVIA MATTHEWS	ALLISON HOSSACK	1989–92
PAT MATTHEWS RANDOLPH		
	BEVERLY PENBERTHY	1967–82, 89
	SUSAN TRUSTMAN	1964–67
DR. RUSS MATTHEWS	DAVID BAILEY	1973–78, 79–81, 89, 92
	JERRY LANNING (temp)	1989
	ROBERT HOVER	1971–72

Character	Actor	Years
	SAM GROOM	1966–71
	JOEY TRENT	1964–65
DR. SUSAN MATTHEWS SHEARER		
	LYNN MILGRIM	1978–79, 82
	LISA CAMERON	1969–71
	RONI DENGEL	1964
	FRAN SHARON	1964
ED MCCLAIN	FRANK RUNYEON	1994
	STEVEN KEATS	1994
DR. PAULA MCCREA	BEVERLY OWEN	1971–72
DR. FRANCIS X. MCCURDY		
	ERNEST GRAVES	1968
BURT MCGOWAN	JOSEPH HINDY	1979
	WILLIAM RUSS	1977–78
GIL MCGOWAN	DOLPH SWEET	1972–77
	CHARLES DURNING	1972
NANCY MCGOWAN	JANE CAMERON	1984–87, 89, 93
	DANIELLE J. BURNS	1974–83
TIM MCGOWAN	CHRISTOPHER ALLPORT	1973–74
BEN MCKINNON	RICHARD STEEN	1984–85
CHERYL MCKINNON	KRISTEN MARIE	1986–88
JAKE MCKINNON	TOM EPLIN	1985–86, 88–95, 95–PRESENT
KATHLEEN MCKINNON WINTHROP		
	JULIE OSBURN	1984–86, 89, 91, 93
MARY MCKINNON	DENISE ALEXANDER	1986–89, 91
M. J. MCKINNON	SALLY SPENCER	1986–87, 91
	KATHLEEN LAYMAN	1984–86
VINCE MCKINNON	ROBERT HOGAN	1987–89, 91
	DUKE STROUD	1986
	JACK RYLAND	1984–85
GABE MCNAMARA	JOHN BOLGER	1995–97
JUDGE MERRILL	RALPH CAMARGO	1975
"APPLE ANNIE" MERRIMAN		
	LISA EICHHORN	1995
	PRUDENCE WRIGHT-HOLMES	1994
FIONA MERRIMAN	CHRIS LINDSAY ABAIRE	1995
GLORIA METCALF	ROSETTA LENOIRE	1972–74
LINDA METCALF	VERA MOORE	1972–81
LAURIE MICHAELS	KAILI VERNOFF	1995
ANDREW MILLER	MARK KEVIN LEWIS	1995–96
LAURIE MILLER	TESSA AUBERJONOIS	1995
MIKEY MILLER	BENJAMIN ALEXANDER	1990, 91
	JOHN ANDERSON	1988–89
PATRICK MILLER	GREG NAUGHTON	1994–95
SARA MONTAIGNE	MISSY HUGHES	1986–87
TYRONE MONTGOMERY	HENRY SIMMONS	1997–PRESENT
HANNAH MOORE	BLAKELY BRANIFF	1998
	JENNIFER LIEN	1991–92
HELEN MOORE	MURIAL WILLIAMS	1966–67, 69–75
LENORE MOORE DELANEY	SUSAN SULLIVAN	1971–75, 76
	JUDITH BARCROFT	1966–71
BOB MORGAN	ROBERT CHRISTIAN	1982
HENRIETTA MORGAN	MICHELLE SHAY	1982–84
MARY SUE MORGAN	TISHA FORD	1983
R. J. MORGAN	REGGIE ROCK BLYTHEWOOD	1982–83
DETECTIVE MORRIS	ROBERT GENTRY	1997, 98
KEITH MORRISON	FRED BEIR	1976
ADRIENNE MORROW	ROXANN CABALERO	1985
DR. MURRAY	JAMES CARROLL	1998
FLO MURRAY	MARCELLA MARTIN	1966–67
MADGE MURRAY	DORIS BELACK	1966–67
MELISSA NEEDHAM	TARO MEYER	1981–82
TOM NELSON	STEVEN CULP	1982
FAIRFAX NEWMAN	NICK GREGORY	1996
ALEXANDER NIKOS	JOHN APREA	1997–98
LIEUTENANT DICK NOLAN		
	LON SUTTON	1967
PEGGY HARRIS NOLAN	MICKI GRANT	1965–72
GLORIA NORRIS	JEAN DEBAEL	1990
JENNA NORRIS	ALLA KOROT	1990–93
ROCKY OLSEN	JOHN BRADEN	1975–77
BERT ORDWAY	ROBERTS BLOSSOM	1976–77
MOLLY ORDWAY RANDOLPH		
	ROLANDA MENDELS	1976–77
JANE OVERSTREET	FRANCES STERNHAGEN	1971–72
KEN PALMER	WILLIAM LYMAN	1976–77
	KELLY MONAHAN	1976
BUD PARKER	BERKELEY HARRIS	1979–80
HAZEL PARKER	PAMELA PAYTON-WRIGHT	1979–80
GWEN PARRISH FRAME	DOROTHY LYMAN	1976–80, 89
LEUEEN PARRISH	MARGARET BARKER	1978–79
ANGIE PERRINI FRAME	MAEVE KINKEAD	1977–79
	TONI KALEM	1975–77
JOEY PERRINI	RAY LIOTTA	1978–81
	PAUL PERRI	1978
ROSE PERRINI	KATHLEEN WIDDOES	1978–80
BRITTANY PETERSON LOVE		
	SHARON GABET	1985–87
REVEREND PETERSON	ROBERT STATEL	1994
SVEN PETERSEN	ROBERTS BLOSSOM	1977–78
DR. STUART PHILBIN	CHARLES SIEBERT	1971–72
BYRON PIERCE	MITCH LONGLEY	1991–92
CHRIS PIERSON	STEPHEN YATES	1975–76
ANDREW POLK	JOEL PECK	1994
DR. FRANK PRESCOTT	MASON ADAMS	1976–77
DR. PRESSMAN	JERRY PACIFIC	1997
STEFANIE PRESTON	SARAH MALIN	1991–93
PRINCE	MARK FRAZER	1983
SERGEI RADZINSKY	JONATHAN SHARP	1999–PRESENT
IAN RAIN	JULIAN MCMAHON	1993–95
COMMISSIONER RAINES	STEPHEN MENDILLO	1997
JOHN RANDOLPH	MICHAEL M. RYAN	1964–79
KAREN CAMPBELL RANDOLPH		
	LAURIE BARTRAM	1978–79
LEE RANDOLPH	BARBARA RODELL	1967–69
	GAYE HUSTON	1964–67
MARIANNE RANDOLPH HALLOWAY		
	BETH COLLINS	1980–82
	ADRIENNE WALLACE	1977–79
	ARIANE MUENKER	1975–77
	TIBERIA MITRI	1974
	JILL TURNBULL	1973–74
	LORIANN RUGER	1972–73
	TRACEY BROWN	1971
	LORA MCDONALD	1971
	JEANNE BEIRNE	1970
MICHAEL RANDOLPH	LIONEL JOHNSTON	1975–79
	CHRISTOPHER J. BROWN	1974
	GLEN ZACHAR	1974
	TOM SABOTA, JR.	1974
	TOM RUGER	1972–73
	TIM NISSEN	1972
	CHRISTOPHER CORWIN	1971
	JOHN SULLIVAN	1971
	DENNIS SULLIVAN	1970

Character	Actor	Years
JUDGE KATHRYN REEVES	ELAINE PRINCI	1997, 98
SERGEANT ZACK RICHARDS		
	TERRY ALEXANDER	1972–75
LUISA RIVERA	TERESA SOFIA RIVERA	1993–96, 97
TOMAS RIVERA	DIEGO SERRANO	1994–97
LILA ROBERTS CORY	LISA PELUSO	1997–PRESENT
SHANE ROBERTS/BOBBY RENO		
	ROBERT KELKER-KELLY	1996–98
BERNICE ROBINSON	JANIS YOUNG	1969–73
VICTOR RODRIQUEZ	CARLOS SANZ	1993–94
DR. DAVID ROGERS	WALTER MCGINN	1972
CHAD ROLLO	RICHARD BURGI	1986–88
DAWN ROLLO	BARBARA BUSH	1987–88
MISS ROSE	RANDY DANSON	1983
ROSS	ROBERT PHALEN	1984
ALMA RUDDER	ELIZABETH FRANZ	1982–83
CHARLIE RUSHINBERGER	RALPH OLIVER	1966–67
PILARA SANCHEZ	MARIE BARRIENTOS	1988–89
RAFAEL SANTIERO	LES BRANDT	1995–96
JORDAN SCOTT	J. KENNETH CAMPBELL	1980–81
RAYMOND SCOTT	JAMES PRESTON	1972–73
CORINNE SETON	PAMELA BROOKS	1976–77
HARRY SHEA	EDWARD POWER	1981–82
LORETTA SHEA	ANITA GILLETTE	1982
PETE SHEA	CHRISTOPHER MARCANTEL	1981–82
BARBARA SHEARER	CHRISTINE CAMERON	1971, 78
DR. DAN SHEARER	BRIAN MURRAY	1978–79
	JOHN CUNNINGHAM	1970–71
JULIA SHEARER	FAITH FORD	1983–84
	JANNA LEIGH	1983
	KYRA SEDGWICK	1982–83
MILO SIMONELLI	LOUIS ZORICH	1982
BILL SIMPSON	BEN HAMMER	1978–79
EILEEN SIMPSON PERRINI		
	VICKY DAWSON	1978–79
LORETTA SIMPSON	ELAINE KERR	1975–79
MORGAN SIMPSON	GARY TOMLIN	1979
CAMERON SINCLAIR	MICHAEL RODRICK	1998–PRESENT
GARY SINCLAIR	JOHN LITTLEFIELD	1998–PRESENT
	TIMOTHY GIBBS	1995–98
JANET SINGLETON	LISE HILBOLDT	1983
	ANNE KERRY	1983
MARK SINGLETON	ROBIN THOMAS	1983–85
MARIUS SLOAN	JESSE DORAN	1990
PAM SLOAN	KARIN WOLFE	1976
DR. ALTON SPADER	JOHN BOLGER	1994
DASHIEL ST. GEORGE	RALPH EDWIN MITCHELL	1997
LOUIS ST. GEORGE	JACK BETTS	1982–83
CAROLINE STAFFORD	JOY BELL	1988–91
STAN (Bartender at Sassy's)		
	CRAIG STRONG	1995
	JOHN O'CONNOR	1995
JORDAN STARK/DAVID HALLIDAY		
	DAVID ANDREW MACDONALD	1998–PRESENT
	JOSEPH BARBARA	1998
DARYLL STEVENS	RICHARD DUNNE	1976–77
JEFF STONE	DAN HAMILTON	1976–77, 79
QUINCY STONER	ALAN MANSON	1969–70
VIC STRANG	BEN MASTERS	1982
SIDNEY SUGARMAN	LARRY HAINES	1989
HARRIET SULLIVAN	JANE ALICE BRANDON	1972
KATHERINE SUTCLIFFE	HERSELF	1996
LINDA TAGGERT	JOYCE REEHLING	1983
CLIFF TANNER	TOM ROLFING	1977–78
TED	TOM LIGON	1990
TESS	KASI LEMMONS	1990
DAVID THATCHER	LEWIS ARLT	1983–84
JENNIFER THATCHER	SOFIA LANDON GEIER	1983
KEVIN THATCHER	TREVOR RICHARD	1983–86
MICHAEL THAYER	GARY SANDY	1969
BAILEY THOMPSON	TOM LIGON	1995
	STEVE BARTON	1994, 95
DR. DAVID THORNTON	COLGATE SALISBURY	1968–69
	JOSEPH PONAZECKI	1967
OFFICER BRIAN TIBBS	DAVID GIBBS	1995–97
TITO	TROY HALL	1998–PRESENT
	TONY TEMPLETON	1998
CARTER TODD	RUSSELL CURRY	1984–86
GRANT TODD	JOHN DEWEY-CARTER	1984–85
THOMASINA MASON TODD		
	PAMELA G. KAY	1984–86, 87
	SHEILA SPENCER	1982–83
GLENDA TOLAND	MAIA DANZIGER	1975–76
TONY "THE TUNA" JONES	GEORGE PENTECOST	1984–88, 94–95
JED TRACK	STEVE HURWITZ	1995
LILY TRAN	BOK YON CHON	1992
WALTER TRASK	REED BIRNEY	1994
DUSTIN TRENT	JAMES KIBERD	1989
TUGBOAT	NICK PLAKIAS	1997
LAWRENCE TUTTLE	JOHN DOMAN	1994
CHRIS TYLER	STEVE HARMON	1970
LAHOMA VANE LUCAS	ANN WEDGEWORTH	1967–70
ALISON VAN ROHAN	MARIN HENKEL	1995
MARK VENABLE	ANDREW JARKOWSKY	1972–73
VENA VENNUCCI	MALLORY JONES	EARLY 1980S
PHILIP WAINWRIGHT	JAMES LUISI	1975
COURTNEY WALKER	VALARIE PETTIFORD	1988–90
SLOAN WALLACE	ORLAGH CASSIDY	1992–93
WALLINGFORD	BRENT COLLINS	1984–88
MAISIE WATKINS	PATRICIA HODGES	1983–87
LUELLA WATSON	DOROTHY BLACKBURN	1970–71
JOSIE WATTS SINCLAIR	NADINE STENOVITCH	1998–PRESENT
	AMY CARLSON	1993–98
	ALEXANDRA WILSON	1988–91
BARBARA WEAVER	KATHRYN WALKER	1975–76
	ROBERTA MAXWELL	1974–75
EVAN WEBSTER	BARRY JENNER	1976–77
ALEX WHEELER	BERT KRAMER	1980
DENNIS CARRINGTON WHEELER		
	CHRIS BRUNO	1991–93
	JIM POYNER	1978–80, 89
	MIKE HAMMETT	1972–78
ANNE WHITELAW	MARY JOAN NEGRO	1981–82
ZAK WILDER	STEVE RICHARD HARRIS	1998–PRESENT
BUZZ WINSLOW	ERIC CONGER	1978–80, 82
CASS WINTHROP	STEPHEN SCHNETZER	1982–PRESENT
CHARLIE FRAME WINTHROP		
	LAUREN PRATT	1997–PRESENT
	KELLYANN MURPHY	1996–97
	LINDSAY FABES	1994–95
DR. MORGAN WINTHROP	GRAYSON MCCOUCH	1993–96
STACEY WINTHROP	HILARY EDSON	1989–91
	TERRY DAVIS	1982–84
REMY WOODS	TAYLOR STANLEY	1998–PRESENT
CHRISTINE WYLIE	TRACY BROOKS SWOPE	1982
PATRICIA WYLIE	BARBARA BAXLEY	1982
CAL ZIMMERMAN	JAY INGRAM	1977–78

another world show credits:1998-1999

Executive Producer
 Christopher Goutman
Directed By
 Lewis Arlt
 Gary Donatelli
 Michael Eilbaum
 Dan Hamilton
 Mary Madeiras
Written By
 Leah Laiman
 Jean Passanante
 Shelly Altman
 Richard Backus
 Peter Brash
 Chris Ceraso
 Richard Culliton
 Tom King
 Maura Penders
 Gordon Rayfield
 Carolyn Culliton
 Mimi Leahey
 Richard J. Allen
 Thomas Babe
 Sofia Landon Geier
 Edwin Klein
 Lynn Martin
 Mary Sue Price
 Courtney Simon
 Gillian Spencer
Producers
 R. Scott Collishaw
 Carole Shure
 Leslie Kwartin
Associate Producer
 Gina Taravella Ricci
Assistant to the Producers
 Kelsey Bay
 Leslie Oliva
Art Director
 Patrick Howe
Costume Designer
 Richard Shawn Dudley
Associate Costume Designer
 Rhonda Roper

Associate Directors
 Carol Sedwick
 Janet Andrews
 Dawn Kiernan
Finance Manager
 Skip Walker
Technical Director
 Vincent Bailey
Lighting Directors
 Howard Strawbridge
 Erich Mejia
Video
 Bill Vaccaro
Audio
 Tim Pankewicz
 John Miller
 Michael Duffy
Videotape Editors
 Karen Thomas DeKime
 Matthew Griffin
Stage Managers
 Dennis Cameron
 Leslye Fagin
 Jim Semmelman
Production Assistants
 Christopher Cullen
 Alison McKiegan
Casting Director
 Jimmy Bohr
Associate Casting Director
 Elizabeth Wilson
Cameras
 Thomas K. Hogan
 John Pinto
 Carl Eckett
 Rick Fox
 Eric Eisenstein
 Barbara Eastman
 Anthony Tarantino
 Jimmy Mott
 Steve Gonzalez
Electronic Maintenance
 Antonio J. Rivera
 Jerry Ryba
 Fred Syversten
 Norman Goldman

Scenic Designers
 Tim Goodmanson
 Brigitte Altenhaus
 Martin Fahrer
Scenic Artist
 Robert Franca
Wardrobe Supervisors
 Liz Spagnola
 Dan Hicks
Makeup Artists
 Kevin Bennett
 Maryann Spano
 Francesca Buccelatto
 Eldo Estes
 John Perkins
Hair Stylists
 Stanley Steven Hall
 Theresa Marra Siliceo
 Sasha Cummins
 Veronica Bakalenik
Assistant to the Executive Producer
 Michele DeVito
Production Coordinators
 Dan Griffin
 Louisa Cross
 Jennifer Chambers
Assistant to the Writers
 Amber M. Roberts
Music Producer/Director
 Ron Brawer
Music Director
 James Kowal
Theme By
 Dominic Messinger
Director of NBC Studio Operations
 Mary Beth Scalici
NBC Operations
 Larry Scotti
 Kristen Bradley
 Bob McKearnin
Medical Adviser
 Cora McCraw, R.N., B.S.N.
Production Managers
 Brian T. Cahill
 Louis J. Grieci
Executive in Charge of Production
 Mary Alice Dwyer-Dobbin

p h o t o   c r e d i t s

PAGE

Contents:	Courtesy of NBC/Al Levine
x:	Courtesy of P&G Prods. Inc./Newey
xi top:	Courtesy of P&G Prods. Inc./Jim Antonucci
xi bottom:	Courtesy of P&G Prods. Inc./Barry Morgenstein
xii top:	Robin Platzer
xii bottom:	Barry Morgenstein
xii-1,4:	Courtesy of P&G Archives
5:	© Globe Photos, Inc.
7:	© Globe Photos, Inc.
9:	© Globe Photos, Inc.
10:	Courtesy of P&G Archives
11:	© Globe Photos, Inc.
13:	© Globe Photos, Inc.
18:	© Globe Photos, Inc.
21:	© Globe Photos, Inc.
25:	Scott Walters
26:	Courtesy of NBC
27:	Courtesy of P&G Archives
29:	Courtesy of P&G Archives
30:	Courtesy of P&G Archives
31:	Courtesy of P&G Archives
33:	Courtesy of P&G Archives
34:	© Globe Photos, Inc.
35:	Courtesy of NBC
37:	© Globe Photos, Inc.
40:	© Globe Photos, Inc.
42:	Courtesy of *Soap Opera Digest*
43:	© Globe Photos, Inc.
45:	Courtesy of *Soap Opera Digest*
49:	E. J. Carr
50:	Courtesy of NBC
51:	© Globe Photos, Inc.
52:	Courtesy of NBC
55:	Courtesy of *Soap Opera Digest*
56:	Mike Fuller
60:	© Globe Photos, Inc.
61:	Lewis Brown
62:	© Globe Photos, Inc.
65:	© Globe Photos, Inc.
67:	Courtesy of NBC/Alan Singer
68:	Georg Lantosh
69:	© Globe Photos, Inc.
70:	© Globe Photos, Inc.
71:	Courtesy of NBC
72:	Courtesy of Linda Dano's Personal Collection
73:	Andrea Wagner
74 sidebar:	Brad Berman
74:	Courtesy of NBC
75:	Courtesy of NBC
76:	Kathy Blaivas
77:	Brad Berman
78:	Robin Platzer
80:	Scott Walters
81:	Craig Blankenhorn
82:	Cathy Blaivas
83:	Nora Feller
84:	Craig Blankenhorn
84 right:	Courtesy of NBC/Brad Berman
85:	Nora Feller
86:	Brad Berman
87:	Courtesy of NBC
88:	Courtesy of NBC
90:	E. J. Carr

91:	Robin Platzer
92:	E. J. Carr
93:	Ingo Kalk
94:	Victoria Arlak
95:	Robert Milazzo
96:	Barry Morgenstein
97 top:	Robert Milazzo
98:	E. J. Carr
99 top:	Barry Morgenstein
99 bottom:	E. J. Carr
100:	E. J. Carr
101:	Barry Morgenstein
102:	Barry Morgenstein
103:	Barry Morgenstein
104 top:	Barry Morgenstein
104 bottom:	Courtesy of P&G Prods.Inc./Barry Morgenstein
105:	Courtesy of P&G Prods. Inc./Barry Morgenstein
106 top:	Courtesy of P&G Prods. Inc./Jim Antonucci
106 bottom:	Jim Antonucci
107:	Courtesy of P&G Prods. Inc./Jim Antonucci
108:	Courtesy of P&G Prods. Inc./Jim Antonucci
109:	Courtesy of P&G Prods. Inc./Arthur Cohen
110:	Courtesy of P&G Prods. Inc./Jim Antonucci
111:	Courtesy of P&G Prods. Inc./Jim Antonucci
112:	Nora Feller
113:	© Globe Photos, Inc.
114-115, 116:	Scott Walters
114 top:	Craig Blankenhorn
115 top:	E. J. Carr
117:	Courtesy of NBC/Al Levine
118 top:	Scott Walters
118:	Nora Feller
119 top:	Cathy Blaivas
119 middle:	Courtesy of NBC/Scott Walters
119 bottom:	Scott Walters
122:	Robin Platzer
124:	Scott Walters
125 top:	© Globe Photos, Inc.
125 bottom:	© Globe Photos, Inc.
126 top left:	Courtesy of P&G Archives
126 top right:	Scott Walters
126 bottom:	© Globe Photos, Inc.
127 top:	Courtesy of NBC/Al Levine
127 bottom:	E. J. Carr
128:	© Globe Photos, Inc.
130 top:	Kathy Blaivas
130 bottom:	Scott Walters
132 top:	Courtesy of NBC/Alan Singer
132 bottom:	Barry Morgenstein
133 top:	Courtesy of NBC/Alan Singer
133 bottom:	Robin Platzer
134:	Courtesy of P&G Prods. Inc.
135:	Scott Walters
136:	E. J. Carr
136 inset:	© Globe Photos, Inc.
137:	Courtesy of NBC
138:	Georg Lantosh
139:	Barry Morgenstein
140:	Barry Morgenstein
142:	Robert Milazzo
145:	© Globe Photos, Inc.
146:	© Globe Photos, Inc.
147:	Courtesy of NBC
148 top:	Courtesy of P&G Prods. Inc./Barry Morgenstein
148 middle top:	E. J. Carr

148 mid. bottom:	Courtesy of P&G Prods. Inc./Barry Morgenstein
148 bottom:	Courtesy of P&G Prods. Inc./Barry Morgenstein
149:	Jonathan Exley
150:	E. J. Carr
152 top left:	© Globe Photos, Inc.
152 middle left:	Courtesy of Linda Dano's Private Collection/Al Levine
152 bottom left:	E. J. Carr
152 top right:	Cathy Blaivas
152 bottom right:	Robert Milazzo
153:	E. J. Carr
153 inset:	Cathy Blaivas
154:	Al Levine
155:	© Globe Photos, Inc.
156:	© Globe Photos, Inc.
157:	Courtesy of NBC/Al Levine
158:	Cathy Blaivas
159:	E. J. Carr
160-61:	© Globe Photos, Inc.
163:	© Globe Photos, Inc.
165:	Courtesy of NBC
166:	© Globe Photos, Inc.
168:	Georg Lantosh
169:	© Globe Photos, Inc.
170:	Robin Platzer
171:	E. J. Carr
172:	Courtesy of NBC
174:	© Globe Photos, Inc.
175:	© Globe Photos, Inc.
176:	Courtesy of NBC/Al Levine
177:	© Globe Photos, Inc.
178:	Nora Feller
179:	E. J. Carr
180:	Brad Berman
182:	E. J. Carr
183:	Barry Morgenstein
184:	Courtesy of P&G Prods. Inc./Barry Morgenstein
185:	Mike Fuller
186:	Nora Feller
187:	E. J. Carr
188:	Victoria Arlak
189:	Courtesy of NBC
190 top:	Barry Morgenstein
190 bottom:	E. J. Carr
191:	E. J. Carr
192:	Barry Morgenstein
193:	Barry Morgenstein
195:	E. J. Carr
196 top:	Courtesy of NBC
196 bottom:	Robin Platzer
197:	Barry Morgenstein
198:	© Globe Photos, Inc.
199 top:	Courtesy of NBC/Al Levine
199 bottom:	Danny Sanchez
200:	Courtesy of P&G Prods. Inc./Barry Morgenstein
201:	Barry Morgenstein
202:	Barry Morgenstein
203:	E. J. Carr
204:	Courtesy of P&G Prods. Inc.
205 top:	Courtesy of P&G Prods. Inc./Barry Morgenstein
205 bottom:	Courtesy of P&G Prods. Inc./Jim Antonucci
206:	Courtesy of P&G Prods. Inc./Arthur Cohen
207:	Robert Milazzo
208:	Barry Morgenstein
209:	E. J. Carr
209 inset:	© Globe Photos, Inc.
210 top:	© Globe Photos, Inc.

210 bottom:	E. J. Carr
211:	Barry Morgenstein
212:	E. J. Carr
213:	Courtesy of P&G Prods. Inc./Barry Morgenstein
213 inset:	Barry Morgenstein
214:	Courtesy of P&G Prods. Inc./Robert Milazzo
215 top:	E. J. Carr
215 bottom:	Barry Morgenstein
216:	Courtesy of P&G Archives
217:	© Globe Photos, Inc.
218:	Courtesy of NBC/Al Levine
220:	Courtesy of P&G Prods. Inc./E. J. Carr
221:	Courtesy of P&G Prods. Inc./E. J. Carr
222 top:	Courtesy of Procter & Gamble
222 middle:	Robert Milazzo
222 bottom:	Robert Milazzo
223:	Courtesy of P&G Prods. Inc./Barry Morgenstein
224 top:	Courtesy of P&G Prods. Inc./Jim Antonucci
224 bottom:	Greg Cherin
225:	Courtesy of P&G Prods. Inc./Barry Morgenstein
226:	Courtesy of Procter & Gamble
227:	Courtesy of Harding Lemay's Private Collection
228:	Courtesy of P&G Prods. Inc./Barry Morgenstein
229:	Courtesy of P&G Prods. Inc./Barry Morgenstein
230:	Courtesy of P&G Prods. Inc./Barry Morgenstein
231:	Courtesy of P&G Prods. Inc./Barry Morgenstein
232:	Courtesy of P&G Prods. Inc./Barry Morgenstein

233 top:	Courtesy of P&G Prods. Inc./Barry Morgenstein
233 bottom:	Courtesy of P&G Prods. Inc./Jim Antonucci
235:	Courtesy of P&G Prods. Inc./Barry Morgenstein
236:	Courtesy of P&G Prods. Inc./Barry Morgenstein
236 bottom two photographs:	Courtesy of P&G Prods. Inc./Jim Antonucci
237 top:	Craig Blankenhorn
237 bottom:	Robin Platzer
239:	© Globe Photos, Inc.
240:	Courtesy of P&G Prods. Inc./Robert Milazzo
241:	Courtesy of P&G Prods. Inc./Arthur Cohen
243:	Courtesy of P&G Prods. Inc./Arthur Cohen
246:	© Globe Photos, Inc.
247 top:	© Globe Photos, Inc.
247 bottom:	Courtesy of NBC
248:	© Globe Photos, Inc.
249 left:	Scott Walters
249 right:	Courtesy of P&G Prods. Inc./Barry Morgenstein
250 top:	Courtesy of P&G Prods. Inc./Barry Morgenstein
250 bottom:	Barry Morgenstein
251:	Courtesy of NBC/Al Levine
252:	Courtesy of NBC/Al Levine
253 top:	© Globe Photos, Inc.
253 bottom:	Barry Morgenstein
254:	Robin Platzer
255:	Barry Morgenstein
257:	Courtesy of P&G Prods. Inc./Barry Morgenstein